Holocaust Drama

The Holocaust – the systematic attempted destruction of European Jewry and other "threats" to the Third Reich from 1933 to 1945 – has been portrayed in fiction, film, memoirs, and poetry; however, there has been a lack of information about the theater of the Holocaust. The immediacy of theater affects us emotionally, subliminally, and intellectually in a direct way that few other art forms can duplicate. Theater of the Holocaust can pay homage to the victims, educate audiences, induce an empathetic response from the audience, raise moral and ethical questions for discussion/debate, and draw lessons from history. Including thorough critical analyses of more than thirty plays, this book explores the seminal twentieth-century Holocaust dramas from the United States, Europe, and Israel. Biographical information about the playwrights, production histories of the plays, and pertinent historical information are provided, placing the plays in their historical and cultural contexts.

Gene A. Plunka is Professor of English at the University of Memphis, where he teaches courses on modern and contemporary drama. His books on the modern theater include *Peter Shaffer: Roles, Rites, and Rituals in the Theater* (1988); *The Rites of Passage of Jean Genet: The Art and Aesthetics of Risk-Taking* (1992); *Antonin Artaud and the Modern Theater* (ed., 1994); *Jean-Claude van Itallie and the Off-Broadway Theater* (1999); *The Black Comedy of John Guare* (2002); and *The Plays of Beth Henley: A Critical Study* (2005).

CAMBRIDGE STUDIES IN MODERN THEATRE

Volumes for Cambridge Studies in Modern Theatre explore the political, social and cultural functions of theatre while also paying careful attention to detailed performance analysis. The focus of the series is on political approaches to the modern theatre with attention also being paid to theatres of earlier periods and their influence on contemporary drama. Topics in the series are chosen to investigate this relationship and include both playwrights (their aims and intentions set against the effects of their work) and process (with emphasis on rehearsal and production methods, the political structure within theatre companies and their choice of audiences or performance venues). Further topics will include devised theatre, agitprop, community theatre, para-theatre and performance art. In all cases the series will be alive to the special cultural and political factors operating in the theatres examined.

Holocaust Drama
The Theater of Atrocity

Gene A. Plunka

CAMBRIDGE
UNIVERSITY PRESS

CAMBRIDGE UNIVERSITY PRESS

Cambridge, New York, Melbourne, Madrid, Cape Town, Singapore,
São Paulo, Delhi, Dubai, Tokyo

Cambridge University Press
The Edinburgh Building, Cambridge CB2 8RU, UK

Published in the United States of America by Cambridge University Press,
New York

www.cambridge.org
Information on this title: www.cambridge.org/9780521494250

First published 2009
Reprinted 2010

Printed in the United Kingdom at the University Press, Cambridge

A catalogue record for this publication is available from the British Library

ISBN 978-0-521-49425-0 hardback

Cambridge University Press has no responsibility for the persistence or
accuracy of URLs for external or third-party internet websites referred to
in this publication, and does not guarantee that any content on such
websites is, or will remain, accurate or appropriate.

Contents

Acknowledgments

I would like to thank Dr. Stephen Tabachnick, chair of the Department of English at the University of Memphis, for granting me released time from teaching, which expedited my completion of the manuscript. I am indebted to Wayne Key of the University of Memphis Interlibrary Loan Office for his valuable assistance in ordering difficult-to-obtain journals and books. I want to acknowledge Jeremy McGraw, photograph librarian of the New York Library for the Performing Arts, for locating photos from the Billy Rose Theatre Collection for possible inclusion in my book. I am also grateful to photographer Carol Rosegg and press agent Jim Baldassare for permission to reproduce the photo of Robert Zukerman in the ArcLight Theater's production of *The Puppetmaster of Lodz*. Furthermore, I very much appreciate the diligent work of Dr. Victoria L. Cooper, senior commissioning editor of music and theatre at Cambridge University Press, for securing referees and moving the manuscript forward in the early stages of production.

Finally I want to express my gratitude to Dr. Naseeb Shaheen, Dr. Jackson R. Bryer, Mark Lapidus, Stanley Plunka and his wife Rhona, Harry R. Plunka, and Lillian Siegel for their encouragement and support. By constantly inquiring about the status of my research, my friends, relatives, and colleagues made the book much easier for me to complete.

1 Introduction

The Holocaust is typically known as the attempt by the Nazis to degrade, humiliate, and eventually destroy European Jewry from 1933 to 1945. The extermination of Jews began in June 1941 in the Soviet Union while deportation to the death camps proceeded from October of that year until 1944. Jews were systematically starved, beaten, and worked to death in 1,600 labor camps or ghettoes; 52 concentration camps and 1,202 satellite camps (*Aussenlager*) were created for the main purpose of instituting the Final Solution: making Europe *Judenrein* (free of Jews).[1] Other asocials that the Nazis deemed a threat to the Volk, including pacifists, people with mental health problems, Seventh Day Adventists, Gypsies (Sinti and Roma), criminals, political dissenters, and homosexuals, were also singled out for persecution. The original concentration camps found within Germany from 1933 to 1939 were designed to incarcerate political prisoners, religious opponents, and homosexuals. In 1939, Germany began its euthanasia program against people with mental health problems and physical disabilities, which soon led to their gassing. By 1942, the murder of Germans with disabilities led to the systematic gassing of Gypsies, Jews, and homosexuals in the extermination camps. The total death toll in the concentration and extermination camps was eleven million, approximately five to six million of whom were Jews; the total number of deaths of Gypsies and homosexuals is inconclusive, with the former ranging from 220,000 to 500,000 and the latter ranging from a low of 5,000 to a high of 220,000 (see chapter 10). Estimates of the total non-combatant deaths during the Nazi reign until the end of the Reich, including those murdered through starvation, disease, killing squads, massacres, bombings, and in *l'univers concentrationnaire*,[2] range as high as twenty million.[3]

Genocide, the intent to destroy a national, ethnical, racial, or religious group, has existed since antiquity. The Holocaust, however, differs substantially from previous or recent genocide in the way the Jews were systematically degraded, forced to suffer, and then murdered in assembly-line fashion with technological ingenuity and fanaticism, as, not merely "undesirables," but parasites, vermin, animals, or *Untermenschen* (subhumans).[4] Michael Burleigh and Wolfgang Wippermann argue that, above all, the Third Reich was intended to be a society based upon race rather than class, so World War II was fought primarily to create a new hierarchical racial order throughout Europe.[5] Anti-Semitic propaganda in Germany during the 1930s blamed the Jews as the internal enemy that caused the German defeat during World War I (the "stab in the back"), the humiliation of the Treaty of Versailles, and the moral decline during the Weimar Republic; Jews also became linked with world Bolshevism, whose successful revolution in 1917 was a visible reminder of the threat to National Socialism. Inculcated with the Hegelian notion of faith in the state and loyalty to the Volk, the Germans of the Reich were easily persuaded by the Nazi propaganda machine that the Jews were the enemies of the fascist state. Leni Yahil notes that the dissemination of *The Protocols of the Elders of Zion* in 1918, a fictional account of a Jewish attempt to rule the world, served as the source of inspiration for the notion that Jews interfered with the world economy.[6] Jews were thus associated with capitalism and communism, the two alleged threats to the Nazi utopia. Jews were not treated as individuals but instead were seen as satanic members of a race that could not accommodate to fascist society; the Jews were compared to various types of bacillus, parasites, or diseases, with genocide encouraged as the panacea. The Nuremberg laws outlawed Jewish citizenship and began a de facto legally allowable consensus that the Jews were socially unacceptable human beings and could thus be legitimately persecuted and then murdered.

The Nuremberg laws led to decrees that applied to Gypsies as well since the Nazis believed that such asocials (*Gesindel*, or "riffraff") carried alien blood and therefore could not marry with Aryans; the

2

Nazis also argued that tainted blood led to criminal activity, parasitical behavior, laziness, and promiscuity. During the Nazis' mass roundups of potential threats to national morale in 1938, many Gypsies, viewed as nuisances and plagues to Germany, were sent to concentration camps. In 1940, Adolf Eichmann linked Sinti and Roma to Jews when he deported Gypsies and Jews to the *Generalgouvernement* in Poland. When the Nazis invaded the Soviet Union in 1941, persecution of the Gypsies in Russia, Poland, and the Balkans turned to the policy of extermination. On 16 December 1942, Himmler signed a decree relegating Germany's Sinti and Roma to Auschwitz, thus linking Gypsies to the racial ideology that instituted the Final Solution; ultimately, more than 20,000 Gypsies perished in that extermination camp.

Although mass murder is not unique, the systematic and mechanistic efficiency of the Nazis distinguishes the Holocaust from other forms of genocide. Perhaps it was its sustained barbarity or the unimaginable enormity of the slaughter that has led historians and philosophers to describe the Holocaust as the seminal event of the twentieth century. While genocide obviously involves widespread killing, the Holocaust seems to be unique in the way that a race was degraded, forced to suffer, and dehumanized (in order for the murderer to be less burdened with guilt when exterminating "vermin"); thus, Jews were not allowed just to die, for they must also die in agony. Robert Skloot has aptly noted that the Holocaust has forced individuals to reassess their notions of humankind: "More than any other event of our time, the Holocaust has caused entire nations and peoples to revise understandings of themselves by provoking disquieting and continuous inquiries of the most moral kind."[7] Unlike any other historical experience, the Holocaust has altered our notions of human dignity, our conventional concepts of God and humanity, and the humanistic idea of civilization aspiring to the norms of cultural existence. As Elie Wiesel has inferred, "At Auschwitz, not only man died, but also the idea of man."[8] The annihilation, personal violation, and dehumanization of Jews preceded their deaths, which were now often carried out in mass graves without any of the ritualistic customs associated with mourning and the rites of dying. Alvin H. Rosenfeld observes that this rendering of a brutally imposed death made dying void of all personal characteristics,[9] further separating the Holocaust from other forms of genocide. Giorgio Agamben reiterates that it is indeed this "degradation of death" that constitutes the specific offense of the Holocaust.[10]

Although the Holocaust is a unique historical event, the term was previously used to designate generic, systematic murder of any ethnic group. In 1959, Ya'd Vashem, the Israeli Martyrs' and Remembrance Authority, began to use the Hebrew term *Shoah* as synonymous with the destruction of European Jewry. However, the term did not gain widespread acceptance until after Claude Lanzmann released his 1985 documentary with that title. In the late 1950s, Elie Wiesel was the first to coin the term "Holocaust" to represent the Jewish genocide of World War II and first used the word in print in a book review of Josef Bor's *The Terezin Requiem*, published in the *New York Times* on 27 October 1963.[11] The term caught on in the 1960s, particularly after the Eichmann trial, to the extent that, in 1968, the Library of Congress created a subject heading for the topic.

The term "Holocaust" is now widely accepted but may be inappropriate to represent the destruction of European Jewry during World War II. The "Holocaust" derives from *"holokaustos"* in the Septuagint, the ancient Greek translation of the Bible, which referred to the term as a burnt sacrificial offering to God in the Temple of Solomon. The Latin term *"holocaustum"* was transmitted from the Vulgate to the Latin Fathers to indicate the sacrifices of the Hebrews, as well as the martyrdom of Christians.[12] Milton used "holocaust" to describe chaos and destruction in his 1671 play *Samson Agonistes*. Wiesel's use of "holocaust" refers to the *Akedah*, the tale in Genesis in which God orders Abraham to sacrifice Isaac, who goes to the slaughter sans complaint or resistance. This archetypal vision of the Jews as God's "chosen ones" who must concomitantly suffer because of their burden most likely appealed to Wiesel; in other words, Isaac is forced to suffer because of circumstances beyond his control. This scenario has the Nazis in a quasi-priestly role as sacrificers to a God accepting the destruction of European Jewry as his sacrificial offering. The Jews, like Jesus, turn the other cheek and go silently to their deaths; the ultimate reward for their martyrdom, supposedly, is the creation of the state of Israel.

4

The previous discussion leads us to believe that the term "Holocaust" is inappropriate to describe the destruction of European Jewry during World War II. Most Holocaust scholars would challenge the notion of Nazis in the role of pious, god-fearing Abraham and would argue that the creation of the state of Israel as some sort of reward for the deaths of millions of innocent people is ludicrous. Moreover, Nazi crematoria cannot be equated with the burnt altar of Isaac's sacrifice; in short, it hardly appears that God and the Nazis make for good partners in the "sacrifice" of Jews. Zev Garber and Bruce Zuckerman add, "It is a fundamental disservice to those who died to transform them all into images of Isaac or Jesus. Their deaths should not be elevated to grand, even cosmic tragedy, but kept grounded on earth."[13] Finally, survivors would agree that martyrdom is not an appropriate term for the senseless murder of millions but instead serves as a means of falsifying their fates. The Hebrew term *shoah*, meaning "destruction" or "catastrophe," is a much more effective attempt to reflect the horror of *l'univers concentrationnaire* without referring to any type of ritual sacrifice. In this book, Shoah will be used interchangeably with "the Holocaust," and even though the former is more acceptable to religious scholars, the latter, through Wiesel's terminology and through the widely disseminated television miniseries *Holocaust*, has become a term culturally etched in our consciousness, for better or for worse.

Contrary to what one may think, the Nuremberg trials (there were a total of thirteen) did little to boost Holocaust studies. The Nuremberg Trial of Major German War Criminals began with much rhetoric on 20 November 1945 and ended on 1 October 1946 with the sentencing of twenty-two Nazi defendants accused of war crimes and crimes against humanity. However, the effect of the trial on German citizens was minimal because the tribunal was international, consisting of the United States, Britain, France, and the Soviet Union without much input from German authorities. Moreover, the only defendant to be condemned to death on charges of crimes against humanity was Julius Streicher, thus blunting any widespread focus on the Holocaust itself. After World War II, the West German administration of Konrad Adenauer, who was chancellor of the Federal Republic from 1949 to 1963, seemed to suffer from historical amnesia, focusing on the Cold

War and reinforcing the national myth that the German people never condoned National Socialism, knew very little about the actual genocide and certainly did not participate in it, and that it was controlled by only a few perpetrators; they tried to bury Germany's sordid recent past–a silence that was not broken until the student protests in 1968. In her study of postwar reactions to the Holocaust, Mary Fulbrook writes that in East Germany (the German Democratic Republic), a "state-sanctioned amnesia" downplayed the persecution of Jews and focused instead on the country's own exoneration of collective guilt through an attack on "the imperialist monopoly capitalist fascists" who caused the war.[14] Although West German courts continued to prosecute former Nazi war criminals during the 1940s and 1950s, the sentences were relatively lenient for even major offenses against Jews.[15] Postwar trials in Poland, Hungary, Yugoslavia, Greece, France, and Russia, while providing the requisite catharsis for each country, also localized the criminal offenses, which thus went relatively unnoticed in the international community.

In 1947, a Dutch edition of Anne Frank's diary, kept as her record of hiding from the Nazis in an Amsterdam annex from 12 June 1942 until 1 August 1944, was published, followed by French and West German versions printed three years later. In 1952, Doubleday published *Anne Frank: The Diary of a Young Girl*, marking the debut of recognizable Holocaust literature in the United States;[16] the book sold nearly twenty-six million copies and was subsequently translated into fifty-eight languages. On 5 October 1955, *The Diary of Anne Frank*, adapted for the stage by Frances Goodrich and Albert Hackett, opened at the Cort Theater on Broadway. The play turned out to be an enormous success with the public (more than one thousand performances) and with the critics, who honored it in 1956 with the Antoinette Perry (Tony) Award, the New York Drama Critics' Circle Award, and the Pulitzer Prize for Best Play. However, much of this success can be attributed to the fact that the play, on the one hand, is essentially a coming-of age-tale that appeals to adolescents, while, on the other, it simultaneously homogenizes the fight against evil through Anne's universally contagious youthful vigor and sanguine demeanor. The Goodrich and Hackett adaptation toned down both Anne's dark, foreboding vision and many of the Jewish references of her diary, optimistically stressing the fight against global oppression and evil rather than Nazi anti-Semitism. The play thus presented an acceptable sugar-coated view of the Holocaust for box-office appeal and mass consumption. With regard to the Broadway production, noted Holocaust scholar Lawrence L. Langer wrote, "An audience coming to this play in 1955, only a decade after the event, would find little to threaten their psychological or emotional security. No one dies, and the inhabitants of the annex endure minimal suffering."[17] Moreover, Anne's universal appeal for the goodness of humanity cheaply sentimentalizes the Holocaust as a ready-made tale of forgiveness, at times making her sound like a martyr who delivers a message of Christian love for all who suffer from oppression. The Americanization of Anne Frank was seen as the perfect iconography to represent a nation that had not fully associated World War II with the horrors of the Holocaust. Although *The Diary of Anne Frank* became required reading in many junior high schools and began to enter the American consciousness as part of the popular culture, including being made into a film in 1959, Holocaust survivors regarded the play as sentimental claptrap. Bruno Bettelheim seems to sum up their reservations about the adapted drama: "If all men are good at heart, there never really was an Auschwitz; nor is there any possibility that it may recur."[18]

Meanwhile, the Israelis during the late 1940s and 1950s were also attempting to understand the Holocaust that the East and West Germans were attempting to mold to their own respective interests and the Americans were trying to sugar-coat. Israel was striving to cope with the Diaspora, which now divided the country into two distinct groups. One segment of the population represented the Old-World European Jews who were displaced after World War II and whose mother tongue was typically Yiddish, Russian, or Polish; they came from a vastly different geographical region (unlike a Mediterranean climate) and did not easily fit into Israeli culture. The other group consisted of Jews native to Palestine, whose language was Hebrew and who were looking to the future of self-sufficient Israel rather than to the shame of the Holocaust as a model for behavior. The friction was palpable between the Diaspora Jews who represented the old culture, the world of the fathers, versus the new generation of sons, who were looking for positive role models while denying a passive Old World culture that seemed to go to the slaughter like sheep; the modern Israeli appeared to be the antithesis of the downtrodden Polish Jew, who was physically and psychically maimed. Haim Shoham characterizes this clash between the generations as a dialectic of action versus reflection, deeds instead of work, the world of the body as opposed to the spirit, and Israeli life contrasted with Jewish existence.[19] This friction played out in the Israeli courts during the 1950s, where Jews were put on trial for collaboration with the Nazis. The result was plays that reflected the tension between the Holocaust survivors and the Jews from Palestine, most notably represented in Nathan Shacham's *New Reckoning* (1954), Leah Goldberg's *Lady of the Castle* (1955), Aharon Megged's *Hanna Senesh* (1958), and Ben-Zion Tomer's *Children of the Shadows* (1962). Unfortunately, these plays were not translated until years later and thus had little widespread appeal outside Israel.

The single most important event to spawn the growth of Holocaust literature was undoubtedly the trial of Adolf Eichmann, who was captured by Israeli agents in Buenos Aires on 11 May 1960. The trial ran from 11 April to 15 December 1961 and became a national catharsis for Israel, which had not had the opportunity after the war to exert justice on Nazi perpetrators, as other countries were able to do. Unlike the Nuremberg trials, which focused primarily on crimes against peace and humanity, the Eichmann trial made the Holocaust specific to the annihilation of European Jewry, as dozens of witnesses testified about the devastation of the Shoah. Commenting on the Eichmann trial, Anat Feinberg perceptively reveals, "The Holocaust lost for a while its abstract quality, for here were creatures flesh and blood, no faceless mass of victims but individual human beings, who recounted and reenacted in their imagination all the horrors of Nazi atrocity."[20] For the first time, television was able to bring the Holocaust into myriad households, many North American viewers admitting that they had never before seen a Nazi. Hannah Arendt's account of the trial, initially serialized in the *New Yorker* and then published in 1963 as *Eichmann in Jerusalem*, raised diverse moral questions about how a seemingly typical, hard-working bourgeois citizen with strong family ties could be such a purveyor of evil. When Arendt coined Eichmann's role in the Final Solution as "the banality of evil," it seemed to hit a nerve that began to haunt the consciences of those who had previously ignored, or were unfamiliar with, the horrors of the Holocaust.[21] Coinciding with the Eichmann capture and trial was the appearance of important literary works about the Holocaust: Elie Wiesel's first novel *Night* (1960), Millard Lampell's adaptation of Hersey's *The Wall* for Broadway (1960), Primo Levi's *Survival in Auschwitz* (1961), Viktor Frankl's survivor testimony *Man's Search for Meaning* (1962), and the Berlin premiere of Rolf Hochhuth's controversial *Der Stellvertreter* (1963, *The Deputy*) under direction by Erwin Piscator. The Eichmann trial eventually spawned documentary drama, a genre largely based on witness reports, court records, and historical data, and became an art form unique to modern German theater; the most notable Holocaust documentary plays were Heinar Kipphardt's *Joel Brand* (1965), Peter Weiss's *Die Ermittlung* (1965, *The Investigation*), and later Kipphardt's *Bruder Eichmann* (1983, *Brother Eichmann*).

The Eichmann trial also precipitated a new West German interest in bringing Nazi war criminals to judgment, many of whom held important civil and political positions during the Adenauer administration. The most notorious of these court cases was the "Stafsache gegen Mulka und andere," better known as the Auschwitz trials, conducted in Frankfurt from 20 December 1963 until 19 August 1965. The Auschwitz trials of twenty-two defendants differed substantially from the Nuremberg trials, at least in the eyes of German citizens, because rather than being judged by an international tribunal, these former Nazis were now facing a German judicial system. Bernd Naumann's extensive coverage of the trial for the *Frankfurter Allgemeine Zeitung* made the court testimonies accessible to many German citizens. The results of the convictions of thirteen of the defendants (three were acquitted) invoked renewed interest in the Holocaust among a new generation of West German youths who were now questioning the roles of their fathers and grandfathers during the war. Attending the trial were two distinguished playwrights: Arthur Miller, who admitted to never having seen a Nazi before he had gone to Frankfurt, and Peter Weiss, exiled from his native Germany during World War II.

The results of their impressions of the trial were two of the most important Holocaust dramas written in the twentieth century: Miller's *Incident at Vichy* (1964) and Weiss's *The Investigation* (1965).

Two films broke new ground in Holocaust studies: *Judgment at Nuremberg* (1961) ran during the Eichmann trial while *The Pawnbroker* (1964) premiered at the height of the Auschwitz hearings. *Judgment at Nuremberg*, a docu-drama directed by Stanley Kramer, was based on the third Nuremberg trial (1948) of four Nazi judges standing accused before three American magistrates. The film was significant for its archival footage from Nazi concentration camps. With its international cast of well-known actors and actresses, including Spencer Tracy, Burt Lancaster, Maximilian Schell, Richard Widmark, Marlene Dietrich (Hitler's favorite actress), Montgomery Clift, and Judy Garland, *Judgment at Nuremberg*'s widespread viewing increased public consciousness about the Holocaust. Critics also lauded the film, which was nominated in 1961 for Academy Awards for Best Picture and Best Director but ultimately won for Abby Mann's adapted screenplay. *The Pawnbroker*, directed by Sidney Lumet, was notable as the first Holocaust film to portray the effects of the concentration camp experience on survivors rather than examining the Holocaust through its political or legalistic repercussions. Rod Steiger starred as Sol Nazerman, haunted in flashbacks of Auschwitz, where he lost his wife and family. The film shocked a public unaccustomed to grasping the personal implications of concentration camp internment on European Jews. The New York Film Critics Circle nominated Lumet for Best Director and Steiger for Best Actor in 1965, while the latter also received a nomination for an Academy Award.

On 16 April 1978, NBC premiered its four two-hour miniseries *Holocaust*, which portrayed the fictional lives of two families–one Jewish, one German–during the Shoah. Eventually, the miniseries was shown in more than fifty countries, including its airing in late January 1979 in West Germany and in March 1979 in Austria, the site of some of the filming (at the former concentration camp of Mauthausen). *Holocaust* was also widely released on videocassette; approximately fifty million people have seen the film.[22] When the miniseries aired in West Germany, it was widely excoriated by Elie Wiesel and West

German critics for its sentimental and contrived depiction of the suffering and for its tasteless blending of a serious subject with commercials for pantyhose; yet over twenty million viewers tuned in, making it an event of national significance.[23] The term "holocaust" now for the first time entered the West German vernacular, as schools, churches, government agencies, and the media tried to explain what was represented in the miniseries, including references to the Nuremberg laws, Kristallnacht, the various concentration and extermination camps that were depicted (Theresienstadt, Buchenwald, Sobibor, and Auschwitz), and the Warsaw ghetto uprising. Influenced by an unusually empathetic West German response to the Holocaust victims, the Bundestag revoked the statute of limitations for Nazi war criminals. Although other films followed, most notably Lanzmann's lengthy *Shoah* in 1985, Louis Malle's *Au revoir les enfants* in 1987, Steven Spielberg's *Schindler's List* in 1993, and Roberto Benigni's controversial *Life Is Beautiful* in 1997, none served to educate the masses more about the Holocaust than NBC's miniseries.

There is no obvious cause-and-effect relationship between the success of the television miniseries and the next generation of Holocaust plays; nevertheless, Holocaust drama seemed to flourish in its second renaissance from 1979 until 1990. In chronological order, the most salient of these plays are Martin Sherman's *Bent* (1979), Thomas Bernhard's *Vor dem Ruhestand* (1979, *Eve of Retirement*), Arthur Miller's *Playing for Time* (1980), C. P. Taylor's *Good* (1981), Christopher Hampton's *The Portage of San Cristobal of A. H.* (1982), Barbara Lebow's *A Shayna Maidel* (1984), Joshua Sobol's *Ghetto* (1984), Emily Mann's *Annulla: An Autobiography* (1985), Motti Lerner's *Kastner* (1985), Gilles Ségal's *Le Marionnettiste de Lodz* (1988, *The Puppetmaster of Lodz*), and Peter Flannery's *Singer* (1989). Apparently, a new generation seemed to avail itself of information about the Holocaust that was long kept dormant.

In 1949, although he was obviously aware of the Holocaust poetry of Nelly Sachs and Paul Celan, Theodor Adorno stated that to write a poem after Auschwitz was a barbaric act.[24] Adorno's statement about the inability of art and aesthetics to convey an appropriate humanistic perspective after the horrors of the Shoah created quite a stir among literary critics and theoreticians. Although Adorno later modified and clarified his interdiction to remind us of the importance of Holocaust remembrance,[25] in *Negative Dialectics* he was still insisting that "Auschwitz demonstrated irrefutably that culture has failed" and that "All-post Auschwitz culture, including its urgent critique, is garbage."[26] Irving Howe agreed with Adorno, arguing that the Holocaust leaves the artist intellectually disarmed: "To think about ways in which the literary imagination might 'use' the Holocaust is to entangle ourselves with a multitude of problems for which no aesthetic can prepare us."[27] As Michael Wyschogrod suggests, literature of the Holocaust necessarily imposes artificiality on mass suffering: "I firmly believe that art is not appropriate to the holocaust. Art takes the sting out of suffering ... Any attempt to transform the holocaust into art demeans the holocaust and must result in poor art."[28] The dilemma is whether Holocaust literature can ever truly represent the inhuman suffering experienced by the victims of the Shoah without doing injustice to their trauma.

Lawrence L. Langer has commented that Holocaust writing must be recognized as literature of atrocity.[29] Jean Améry, who speaks with authority as a survivor of Buchenwald, Bergen-Belsen, and Auschwitz, as well as a victim of Nazi torture at Fort Breendonk, agrees with Langer in his assessment of the Holocaust as a study of barbarism: "I must substantiate why, according to my firm conviction, torture was the essence of National Socialism—more accurately stated, why it was precisely in torture that the Third Reich materialized in all the density of its being."[30] Terrence Des Pres characterizes the atrocity specifically in terms of the victim's loss of job, class, tradition, family, and, in the concentration camps, a forfeiture of even their names and their hair. For Des Pres, this loss of culture can only be characterized as barbarism: "In the camps prisoners lost their possessions, their social identity, the whole of the cultural matrix which had previously sustained them."[31] Thus, Holocaust literature must be confronted with an order of reality that has no precedent in history; critics such as Adorno and Langer now wonder how art's imaginative vision can portray what the mind finds incomprehensible and devoid of a suitable context for conveying the information. Certainly, the ultimate reality of *l'univers concentrationnaire* is, as Langer suggests, not the fact of death, but the victims' state of eternal fear of constant death, reducing humanity to primitive terrors of such magnitude that there is no suitable historical objective correlative.[32] Since the Holocaust has no point of historical or even mythical comparison, it would seem to transcend the metaphoric expression of literature; in short, literature's imaginative realm must inevitably fail in converting the Holocaust into universally understood terms. Sidra DeKoven Ezrahi reiterates the notion that literature of the Holocaust cannot adequately generate familiar paradigms of human experience through an imaginative vision. Ezrahi argues that culture, portrayed through literature, is incapable of representing the Holocaust:

> The implementation of the Final Solution–not an eruption of the chaotic forces of violence but a systematized, mechanized, and socially organized program– was a mockery of the very idea of culture that had survived into the twentieth century. No symbolic universe grounded in humanistic beliefs could confront the Holocaust without the risk of being shaken to its foundations.[33]

Ezrahi questions whether literature can be commensurately degenerate to represent Auschwitz in its unprecedented brutality–hell on Earth, a catastrophe beyond human comprehension. Michael Taub astutely assesses the dilemma of the incongruity between art and the Shoah: "We agree that art can only create an illusion of reality, so how can it depict an event as overwhelming as this?"[34] The Holocaust forces us to reconsider the previous humanistic concerns of faith, dignity, religion, heroism, the righteousness of the human spirit, and the respect for death and mourning. Holocaust writing is therefore now asked to conjure up images of a world in which a reality too atrocious to imagine exceeds the imaginative vision. As Holocaust survivor Giorgio Agamben writes, "After Auschwitz, it is not possible to use a tragic paradigm in ethics."[35]

If the literature of atrocity must face the fact that the Holocaust has no historical precedent and is thus beyond the metaphoric spirit of imagination, language also must be insufficient to convey its spirit.

George Steiner explains the disparity between language and the Holocaust experience: "The world of Auschwitz lies outside speech as it lies outside reason. To speak of the *unspeakable* is to risk the survivance of language as creator and bearer of humane, rational truth. Words that are saturated with lies or atrocity do not easily resume life."[36] With this seemingly unbreachable chasm between the imaginative vision and the atrocity of the Holocaust, and with language being insufficient to bridge the divide, Elie Wiesel has concluded, "By its uniqueness, the holocaust defies literature."[37] Moreover, the artistic representation of the Holocaust can degenerate into its trivialization by eliciting pleasure from an audience titillated by the sadism of torture, violence, and degradation of innocent sufferers–at times, even the titillation of naked bodily pain could well represent the historical record. Furthermore, the artistic representation of the Holocaust is much more dubious for the playwright, who must consider the effects of the play on a live audience, which witnesses the unfolding of an event they will never really know or understand without having directly experienced the extremities of *l'univers concentrationnaire*. Lawrence L. Langer explains how Holocaust literature cannot depict annihilation, an experience that is not typically part of our humane cultural tradition: "We lack the psychological, emotional, and even intellectual powers to participate in a ritual that celebrates *such* a demise. We feel alien, not akin. The drama of fate reminds us that Man, should he so choose, can die for something; the drama of doom, the history of the Holocaust, reveals that whether they chose or not, men died for nothing."[38] Elie Wiesel goes as far as stating that, rather than approaching the Holocaust by way of poetry, novels, theater, television, or film, interested individuals should read the diaries of victims such as Emanuel Ringelblum or Chaim Kaplan, study the historical accounts by Raul Hilberg, Lucy Davidowicz, Martin Gilbert, or Michael Marrus, or view documentaries, such as Alain Resnais's *Night and Fog* or Claude Lanzmann's *Shoah*.[39]

Adorno and Wiesel have posited a literature of silence about the Holocaust to avoid its trivialization and its frequent lack of respect for the dead. Writers have not complied with their wishes but instead have insisted that the most significant way to pay homage to the dead is through an obligation to bear witness. One of the major aspirations of those who survived the extermination camps was a desperate need to tell the story in order to honor those who were degraded as vermin, suffered unmercifully, and then were slaughtered without due process of the rites of death. Bettelheim challenges Adorno and Wiesel: "But if we remain silent, then we perform exactly as the Nazis wanted: behave as if it never did happen."[40] Indeed, at the beginning of *The Drowned and the Saved*, Primo Levi recalls that the Nazis boasted of a psychological victory over the prisoners of the concentration camps by threatening to destroy the evidence and by acknowledging that the crimes committed against them were too monstrous for any audience to believe: "However this war may end, we have won the war against you; none of you will be left to bear witness, but even if someone were to survive, the world will not believe him."[41] Alvin H. Rosenfeld also disagrees with Wiesel and Adorno, stating that silence about the Holocaust grants the Nazis one more posthumous victory: "If it is a blasphemy, then, to attempt to write about the Holocaust, and an injustice against the victims, how much greater the injustice and more terrible the blasphemy to remain silent."[42] Although it is true that the Holocaust has no recognizable historical antecedent and is thus a unique event, the Shoah is not so incomprehensible or unfathomable as to relegate it to the realm of mysticism; if this were true, Holocaust literature would be virtually nonexistent instead of flourishing. Even the literature of atrocity, replete with acts of violence that seem incomprehensible to the civilized mind, can be perceived as an explicable event; in short, a logical person can make sense of an illogical phenomenon. Wiesel and Adorno, however, do serve an important purpose in Holocaust studies, for they are the watchdogs for writers who may go to extremes in their callous or trivial treatment of a sacred historical event. Most importantly, the literature of the Holocaust educates audiences who may be unfamiliar or naive about what has been described as the most significant historical event of the twentieth century. The Holocaust forces us to confront some of the most challenging moral and ethical issues of modernity, including the philosophical debate of good versus evil, the existential notion of individual and collective responsibility in a Judeo-Christian society, the value of art in times of extreme situations, the role of God in the modern wasteland, and the need to understand survivor guilt and our own as well.

Drama seems to be an ideal medium to represent these eternal conflicts and dilemmas. Theater affects us emotionally, subliminally, or intellectually (sometimes simultaneously) in a direct way that poetry and fiction cannot. The theater also possesses a powerful immediacy effect between actor and audience that no other art form can match. The audience can serve as a community participating in a palpable rite of mourning for the Holocaust victims. In the introduction to her collected plays about the Holocaust, Elinor Fuchs astutely observes, "That rite cannot take place without the participation of the community of spectators as living witness. In the very act of representing the annihilation of the human community, then, the theatre itself offers a certain fragile potentiality for re-creation."[43] Thus, despite the objections from Wiesel and Adorno, drama has proven to be an effective medium for representing the Holocaust. Robert Skloot has suggested five potential objectives for playwrights confronting the Holocaust: pay homage to the victims, educate audiences, induce an empathetic response from the audience, raise moral and ethical questions for discussion and debate, and draw lessons from history.[44]

With Skloot's criteria in mind, one realizes that the form of the play the playwright chooses makes all the difference in whether the Holocaust will be sanctified or treated sacrilegiously on stage. Wiesel confirms that the form of the play must be carefully considered: "In order not to betray the dead and humiliate the living, this particular subject demands a special sensibility, a different approach, a rigor strengthened by respect and reverence and, above all, faithfulness in memory."[45] On the one hand, the Holocaust is a historical event that would seem to benefit from an objective realistic staging. However, as Michael Taub has pointed out, realism is problematic to represent the Shoah: "The question of realism is particularly critical in the theater; for, if authors/directors choose to show history as 'real' as possible, they expose themselves to criticism from survivors and experts who will invariably find fault with this or that aspect of the production."[46] In truth, the abject degradation of the Holocaust is virtually impossible to imitate on stage through any sort of attempt at mimesis. Realism appears to be inappropriate to represent an event that is so horrifying, "unnatural," nightmarish, unimaginable, and irrational that logic and scientific inquiry–the nineteenth-century origins of realism and naturalism–seem to be undermined. In *The Holocaust and the Literary Imagination*, Lawrence L. Langer noted the inadequacy of realism to represent the Holocaust: "To establish an order of reality in which the unimaginable becomes imaginately acceptable exceeds the capacities of an art devoted entirely to verisimilitude; some quality of the fantastic, whether stylistic or descriptive, becomes an essential ingredient of *l'univers concentrationnaire.*"[47] Since the Holocaust is essentially concerned with the divorce between humanity and God and an acknowledgement of the emptiness of an imposed Absence, or as the French might deem it, a deeply rooted *angoisse*, one might think that these metaphysical issues would lend themselves perfectly to theater of the absurd. However, dramatists seem to have recognized that the danger of representing the Holocaust as theater of the absurd becomes a risky gamble of distorting historical reality, turning the Shoah into an event that precludes its sanctity and uniqueness. Moreover, the causality of the Shoah can be traced to anti-Semitic antecedents in Germany, whereas theater of the absurd rebukes such rational and logical connections. Armand Gatti's *La Deuxième Existence du camp de Tatenberg* (*The Second Existence of the Tatenberg Camp*) is the only Holocaust drama of the twentieth century that comes close to theater of the absurd, but Richard N. Coe makes a convincing argument that even a loosely applied definition of the term sets Gatti's notion of "absurdity" clearly apart from the pataphysics of Ionesco's plays or the "realm of infinitudes and paradoxes" of Beckett's theater.[48] Thus, playwrights are caught in a bind: realism cannot match the historical veracity of the catastrophic events of the Holocaust and theater of the absurd betrays their inviolability. Nevertheless, playwrights have experimented with different forms to represent the Holocaust, including realism (Arthur Miller's *Incident at Vichy*), epic theater (Tony Kushner's *A Bright Room Called Day*), surrealism (George Tabori's *The Cannibals*), black comedy (Peter Barnes's *Laughter!*), verse drama (Nelly Sachs's *Eli*), melodrama (Frances Goodrich and Albert Hackett's *The Diary of Anne Frank*), classical tragedy (Rolf Hochhuth's *The Deputy*), and documentary theater (Peter Weiss's *The Investigation*).[49]

Edward R. Isser estimates that in excess of 150 Holocaust dramas have been produced in the United States, Europe, and Israel, while Alvin Goldfarb lists 257 Holocaust plays written through to 1997;[50] obviously, the scope of my study must be defined before I delve into an analysis of the plays. My definition of Holocaust drama includes those plays written about Nazi genocide conducted between 1933 and 1945; this international canon also covers the dramas concerned with the aftereffects of such genocide, which typically includes survivor testimonies or the portrayals of the psychological ramifications on survivors. Although the Holocaust involves Nazi oppression of threats to the Reich other than Jews, there are no major Holocaust plays about the persecution of Gypsies, people with mental health problems, those with physical disabilities, or other "asocials;" the one major play about the Nazi treatment of homosexuals, *Bent*, will be discussed in chapter 10. Obviously, this study cannot do justice to 257 plays, so parameters must be set. I will not discuss plays that are unpublished or unproduced; performance pieces, such as Jerzy Grotowski's *Akropolis* or Josef Szajina's *Replika*, are also beyond the scope of this study. For the most part, I will examine the most salient plays of the last half of the twentieth century; minor dramas, particularly those that repeat the same motifs of the major plays, must be omitted to avoid repetition and for the sake of some semblance of brevity.

I believe it is helpful to clarify the types of theater that I do *not* consider to be representative of Holocaust drama. First, plays that treat World War II generically without focusing specifically on the Shoah are not Holocaust theater; these include myriad dramas, many of them dealing with historical figures such as Hitler (David Hare's *Licking Hitler* or Joan Schenkar's *The Last of Hitler*), Hermann Göring (Romulus Linney's 2), Dr. Josef Mengele (Charlie Schulman's *Angel of Death*), or Rudolf Hess (Howard Brenton's *H. I. D.* [*Hess Is Dead*]) . Other plays that concentrate on the aftereffects of the war, such as Wolfgang Borchert's *Draussen vor der Tür* (*The Outsider*), are also outside the scope of this study, even when the aftereffects tangentially involve guilt about one's actions toward Jews during the war (e.g., Jean-Paul Sartre's *Les Séquestrés d'Altona* [*The Condemned of Altona*]). Many of the absurdist plays could be interpreted as a plunge into the Void after the breach between humanity and God directly resulting from World War II; such visions of the apocalypse, as presented in absurdist dramas such as Beckett's *Fin de partie* (*Endgame*) or Ionesco's *Les Chaises* (*The Chairs*), are not Holocaust plays. Although it is often difficult to separate National Socialism from the Holocaust, the dramas of anti-fascism (e.g., Lillian Hellman's *Watch on the Rhine*), those that focus on the threat of fascism (e.g., Robert Sherwood's *There Shall Be No Night*), or plays that are parables of fascism (e.g., Bertolt Brecht's *Der Aufhaltsame Aufstieg des Arturo Ui* [*The Resistible Rise of Arturo Ui*] or Stanley Eveling's *The Strange Case of Martin Richter*), although they may be tinged with elements alluding to racism, cannot be considered to be Holocaust theater *per se*. Finally, plays that primarily deal with anti-Semitism (e.g., Franz Werfel's *Jacobowsky und der Oberst* [*Jacobowsky and the Colonel*]) or that are overtly anti-Semitic (e.g., Rainer Werner Fassbinder's *Der Müll, die Stadt und der Tod* [*Garbage, the City and Death*]) cannot claim to be theater of the Holocaust because the emphasis is not on the Nazi genocide as it directly relates to such anti-Semitism.

I am approaching Holocaust drama from two distinct points of view. First, my intention is to critique the plays in such a way as to ensure their accuracy and faithfulness to the Shoah, alerting the reader when the playwright deviates from the historical record or manipulates the Holocaust for artistic purposes. The Holocaust, obviously, is multi-faceted, and thus playwrights have a wide latitude in the way the Holocaust is represented on stage unless the event is trivialized or the dead are not respected. The other "hat" that I wear is as a drama critic who must examine the form, content, and stage techniques to make sure that they mesh effectively. In short, an effective piece of Holocaust literature may or may not be a play that works on the boards; this study will thus take into account each play's particular production history as well.

2 Staging the Banality of Evil

Hannah Arendt's *Eichmann in Jerusalem* was an ennobling treatise that changed the way Nazis were depicted on stage. This chapter explores the Nazi mentality through Arendt's concept of the "banality of evil" as depicted in Donald Freed's *The White Crow: Eichmann in Jerusalem*, Cecil Taylor's *Good*, Peter Barnes's *Laughter!*, and Thomas Bernhard's *Vor dem Ruhestand*.

Adolf Eichmann was a mediocre student and subsequently a salesman for an electric company before joining the National Socialist Party and then entering the SS in 1932. He was an ambitious young man who married in 1935 and soon began to realize that the Nazi Party provided him with the means to move up in the ranks and thus to develop enough security to take care of his family fairly well. Arendt explains Eichmann's motivations in the early part of his career: "From a humdrum life without significance and consequence the wind had blown him into History, as he understood it, namely, into a Movement that always kept moving and in which somebody like him–already a failure in the eyes of his social class, of his family, and hence in his own eyes as well–could start from scratch and still make a career."[1] Eichmann quickly became an expert on Jewish affairs and then advanced in the Party to become the Nazis' leading authority on emigration; as such, Eichmann worked closely with Jewish leaders to achieve their mutual goal of emigrating Jews to Palestine during the 1930s. Conditions altered drastically for Eichmann after the adoption of the Final Solution at the Wannsee Conference, for his relatively safe job dealing with emigration now changed to making each country in western and central Europe Judenrein, which caused logistical nightmares for him. Eichmann, a mid-level bureaucrat who rose through the ranks of the Nazi hierarchy because of the significance placed on genocide of the Jews, eventually became *Obersturmbannführer* (equivalent to lieutenant colonel) reporting to Heinrich Müller whose boss was Ernst Kaltenbrunner (replacing the assassinated Reinhard Heydrich), Himmler's subordinate.

At his trial in Jerusalem in 1962, Eichmann pleaded "not guilty in the sense of the indictment," which meant that although he found himself guilty in the eyes of God, he was not guilty according to German law. He showed no guilt and took no responsibility for his crimes. Although Eichmann argued that he worked closely with Jews to help them with their desired emigration and felt no personal animosity toward them, the judges refused to believe that a typically "normal" bourgeois citizen of the Reich could be incapable of distinguishing right from wrong. Eichmann, however, had been consistent in his steadfast pursuance of his duties according to German law, which was especially important during the war years when disobedience meant treason. Eichmann argued that Hitler, who rose from colonel to Führer, represented the will of the German people, a man whose vision created prosperity during the worst period of unemployment in German history. Even when the Final Solution became apparent, Eichmann realized that civil servants (represented, for example, at Wannsee), as well as the high-ranking military officers that he so emulated, all agreed that the goals of the genocide were noble and just; Eichmann's conscience was thus in tune with the voice of "respectable society." In short, Eichmann was not only obeying the laws of the land, he was also doing what was lawful and righteous for himself and for his family.

The Nazis adopted code words and euphemisms for Jewish genocide. German war documents refrained from using terms such as "murder," "extermination," or "liquidation;" instead, they embraced innocuous phrases such as "Final Solution," "resettlement" (*Umsiedlung*), "labor in the East" (*Arbeitseinsatz im Osten*), "evacuation" (*Aussiedlung*), "labor camp" (*Arbeitslager*) or "transit camp" (*Durchgangslager*) rather than extermination camp, "special installations" (*Spezialeinrichtungen*) instead of gas chambers, "special treatment" (*Sonderbehandlung*): the code word for the killing operation, and "prompt-employment unit" (*Einsatzkommando*), the elite squad assigned to kill Jews in Russia. Even Jews in the ghettoes gradually learned to understand what "deportation" latently connoted. However, what was most amazing about Eichmann's trial was how he acted as a functionary or automaton, a mere cog in the administrative bureaucracy of the Nazis. As a sort of dehumanized robot, Eichmann became a role player rather than a thinking, empathetic human being capable of making responsible decisions. In other words, Eichmann certainly understood the Nazi euphemisms for Jewish genocide, but he behaved as a good bureaucrat turning the other cheek rather than as a moral person who might challenge authority when basic humanistic values were abused. Official bureaucratic jargon became Eichmann's vernacular because he was incapable of thinking for himself; even at the trial, he spoke in clichés. Arendt asserts, "The longer one listened to him, the more obvious it became that his inability to speak was closely connected with an inability to *think*, namely, to think from the standpoint of somebody else."[2] Eichmann simply had done what he had been ordered to do–ship millions of people to their deaths. What was terrifying about the trial, and what was to become an emblematic image in the minds of several playwrights, was that Eichmann did not seem to be a monster but instead appeared to be a typical bureaucrat, like countless other Germans, conscientiously and effectively doing a job. Arendt sums up the prototypical image of the Nazi persona, the "banality of evil," that seems to have stuck with many scholars and artists who have written about the Holocaust: "The trouble with Eichmann was precisely that so many were like him, and that the many were neither perverted nor sadistic, that they were, and still are, terribly and terrifyingly normal."[3]

Although there are several plays about Eichmann, the most literal dramatic representation of Arendt's *Eichmann in Jerusalem* is American playwright Donald Freed's *The White Crow: Eichmann in Jerusalem*, which was staged from 27 July to 29 September 1984, under direction by Charles Marowitz at the Los Angeles Actors' Theatre. The two-act play occurs in Jerusalem in 1960, where Eichmann, recently kidnapped from Argentina, is undergoing pre-trial examination by social psychologist Dr. Lillian Baum. Although Baum is a fictional character, Eichmann is drawn substantially from Arendt's portrayal of him.[4] Luckily, in 1939, Dr. Baum left Germany, where she had been raised, eventually emigrating to Palestine via England; the rest of her family perished at the hands of the Nazis, including her husband, who was a victim of Mengele's scientific experiments. Thus, Baum had a personal vendetta against Eichmann and was curious to discover what makes such a mass murderer tick; however, the emphasis of the play is clearly on Eichmann, not Baum.

As Eichmann recounts his personal history for Dr. Baum, the audience learns that he is a prototypical German citizen, not a sadist or masochist intrinsically perverted to do evil. His father was very religious and raised his son to believe in God and the tenets of the Evangelical Church. Adolf has been a good son, a "perfect" father to his own offspring, a lover of music who plays the violin well, and a pillar of the community. He admits that he did not volunteer to join the Nazi Party but was instead recruited by Kaltenbrunner. As Arendt noted in her book, Freed reiterates that Eichmann fraternized with the leading Zionists, agreeing with their position on emigration while cherishing Theodore Herzl's *The Jewish State* as nothing less than "a classic." Eichmann even boasts about plans he had to set up a Jewish state in Poland or Madagascar and then laments that his altruistic intentions were stifled by the war in Russia and eventually by Hitler's edict to exterminate the Jews. The association of the Jews with worldwide Bolshevism had been internalized by Eichmann consistently enough for him to conclude, "In wartime you destroy your enemy."[5]

Dr. Baum's goal is to cross-examine Eichmann to extract from him an admission of his own guilt and responsibility for his role in the Final Solution; in the original production at the Actors' Theatre, the audience, seated in simulated "jury boxes" outside the acting space, virtually became part of Eichmann's interrogation.[6] Eichmann argues that he was merely obeying German laws and thus acting legally, doing justice to the legacy of Hegel's insistence on adherence to the law and to the Jews who wanted to emigrate. He describes himself as a benign bureaucrat: "Like any good functionary, I threw myself into my job" (14), idealistically working with "total dedication" (32).

Instead of assuming legal responsibility, he insists on being "legally innocent" (16). Eichmann explains how his vision of genocide conformed to the will of the typical civil servants who participated in the Wannsee Conference, where Heydrich introduced the concept of the Final Solution:

> Not one official there–and I was the low man, taking notes,
> only–not one man raised one objection. Not one. And these
> were civil servants from the old Reich, not the SS, not the Party.
> These were bourgeois "gentlemen" who had never deigned to
> give my type the time of day. And here they were tripping over
> each other to tell us how to make 10.3 million Jews "disappear" ...
> I drank my fine wine and thought, "Today I am Pontius Pilate.
> I have no guilt. Who am I to judge? These are the powers that be
> and they have smiled on the entire affair." (30)

Eichmann assumes the role of undistinguished functionary, a cog in the wheel, Mr. anono-mass hiding behind the righteousness of the well-oiled Nazi bureaucratic machinery. Robert Skloot discusses Eichmann's mentality: "As a good bureaucrat, he is all *absence*. Within the moral topsy-turvy of the play there is more than a suggestion that Eichmann has a legitimate claim to 'the anonymity of victimage.'"[7] As a bureaucrat, Eichmann hid behind the euphemisms the Nazis adopted for their policies on genocide. Eichmann admits to conforming to the Party language in which code words, such as "Final Solution," "evacuation," "special handling," "resettlement," and "labor in the East" (31), could be deciphered by any Nazi bureaucrat. Baum tries to penetrate this vast network of Nazi bureaucracy: "Your bureau, sir, was Roman Numeral IV-B-4. 'Roman IV' stands for Gestapo; '4' for religion; and 'B' for Jews!"; Eichmann responds by defending his individuality: "I am flesh and blood, not Roman numerals" (26).

Eichmann wants to be considered an anonymous bureaucrat as well as an individual who takes responsibility for his actions by doing what is best for the state and for his family. As a former salesman, Eichmann is proud to follow a man who rose from corporal and through the power of his rhetorical skills "became Fuhrer of a people of eighty million!" (33). Under Hitler's guidance and direction, a nebbish (an ineffectual, timid person), a "pieter Schlemiel" (an unlucky person) such as Eichmann, could progress through the ranks and impress family and friends. Baum tries to expose Eichmann, the ambitious individual, hungry to be someone of worth: "You knew who you were: Slow boys at school, sly boys at home. You grew up to be nonentities, corporals, salesmen on a draw, lumpenproletariat scum looking for a parade–" (37).

Baum's dilemma, then, is to coerce Eichmann into assuming responsibility for his individual actions rather than hiding behind the anonymity of bureaucratic behavior conditioned by clichés and automatic responses. She pleads with him: "Hear me: how do you want to be remembered by History? (*Indicates tape recorder.*) A voice in the mob–or as a human being who–" (39). She exhorts Eichmann to be one of the White Crows–Hitler's dissenters who stood up against unjust racial policies. Dr. Baum's quest is quixotic, for Eichmann retreats into his defense that he was merely a cog in the wheel, and anyone in his position, including Dr. Baum, would have done the same: evil is ubiquitous, which makes it reasonable. Eichmann was merely following orders, the same as Baum, who has certain directives from Ben-Gurion. In the denouement, Eichmann, when given the opportunity to take responsibility for his crimes, regresses to a conditioned lackey: "You will not order me? ... You will not help me?" (44). Even when Baum turns off the tape recorder and puts the gun aside, Eichmann accuses her of following orders according to a proscribed plan. Baum the interrogator is equated with Eichmann the bureaucrat. Moreover, Freed seems to imply that we, the jury, would have acted no differently as ordinary citizens caught up in the inexorable demands of citizenship and statesmanship. Freed, in placing the jury onstage, confronts us with the dialectic of whether moral responsibility succumbs to or can subvert the typical human desire of adherence to a legal, yet corrupt, bureaucracy, which ultimately leads to personal and professional rewards.

Eichmann is also the prototype for Johnnie Halder, the protagonist of Scottish playwright Cecil Philip Taylor's *Good*, which debuted in London on 2 September 1981 at the Royal Shakespeare Company's small Warehouse theater under direction by Howard

Davies. On 22 April 1982, the production transferred to the larger Aldwych Theatre in London, where it ran until 29 May. After its commercially successful run in London, partly attributed to Alan Howard's masterful portrayal of Halder, *Good* opened on Broadway at the Booth Theatre on 13 October 1982; the New York reviews were mixed, and the production closed on 30 January 1983.[8]

Taylor, who, as a Jew feared being relegated to a concentration camp in England or Scotland had Germany won the war and whose father had fled the anti-Semitic regime of czarist Russia, seeks to explore the notion of how a typically "normal" or "good" person in a totalitarian society can be misguided to do evil. In his Author's Note to the play, Taylor writes, "It still seems that there are lessons to be learned if we can examine the atrocities of the Third Reich as the result of the infinite complexity of contemporary human society, and not a simple conspiracy of criminals and psychopaths."[9] Arendt's depiction of the complex phenomenon of the pervasiveness of Eichmann's banality of evil as emblematic of the German mentality forms the basis of Halder's persona, rather than the simplistic notion that identification with the tenets of National Socialism resulted from aberrations of sadists or perverted psychopaths.

Halder earns an honest living as a professor of literature specializing in Goethe. He also seems to be a prototypical bourgeois family man trying to survive life's hardships. *Good*, originally a three-act play but later edited to two acts by director Howard Davies, traces Halder's escapades in Hamburg, Frankfurt, Berlin, and Auschwitz from 1933 until 1942. Halder is saddled with an incontinent mother whose dementia has already put her in a coma and whose need for twenty-four-hour care has made her suicidal. Although his wife is reasonably attractive, she is inept at domestic duties, including cooking and cleaning. Halder's three children keep him honest at home,[10] but he cheats on his wife with his mistress Anne, one of his doting students.[11] In short, Halder has immense personal responsibilities exacerbated by the heavy toll that the Depression has taken on families in Germany.

Halder did not volunteer to join the Nazi Party; instead, he was chosen as a suitable comrade because of a treatise he had written on euthanasia. Just as Kaltenbrunner recruited Eichmann into the SS,

Halder, who had written his pro-euthanasia novel as a result of his mother's physically deteriorating condition, drew the admiring attention of Goebbels. Halder's wife Helen had warned him that he could lose his lectureship at the university unless he joined the party. Halder, who admits to fantasizing while talking to himself, realizes that the risk of not joining the Nazis might endanger his family: "I don't like failing ... Failing throws me into a panic state ... It's not good" (8).[12] Thus, Halder, the humanist, becomes a Nazi. Susan Friesner astutely observes, "Expertise on the subject of Goethe's *Faust* has not in fact taught Halder anything about the real nature of bargains made with the devil."[13] Thus, Halder's "good" intentions about writing a book on mercy killing to end compassionately the lives of those incurably suffering from dementia, and his noble aspirations of supporting his family at all costs, are circumvented by the Nazis who view euthanasia as a sanitized, civilized medical procedure for mass murder.

Halder lives in a type of fantasy world that precludes the evil endemic to Nazi Germany. Edward R. Isser notes that Halder "justifies and rationalizes his behavior as he moves from a state of relative moral innocence to one of complete degeneracy."[14] Halder fondly recalls that the marble hall and fancy chandeliers of the Nazi Party headquarters reminded him of the fantasy world of *The Student Prince*: "It was a wonderful feeling–joining. You have no idea, the emotional heights it lifted me to" (29). Enlisting in the Nazi Party gave the relatively alienated Halder a feeling of common brotherhood (29). Moreover, as Robert Skloot notes, Halder convinces himself in his fantasy world that having a Jewish friend such as Maurice Gluckstein precludes any inclination of possible anti-Semitism on his part.[15] Throughout the play, Halder, a great music lover, hears dance bands playing songs that distract him from his descent into evil. Skloot suggests that when the music is upbeat, sentimental, and romantic, Halder is diverted from his moral decline.[16] Halder organizes the book-burning ceremony at the university where he teaches, is active during Kristallnacht, lectures his students about the dangers of the highly self-centered philosophy of Judaism, aids the Nazis in their plans for euthanasia, and winds up as an adjutant in Auschwitz. His working relationship with Eichmann is described as "excellent" (55) since the two of them seem to be mirror images of the decent, ambitious family man doing whatever it takes to survive. Although his professional life prospers, Halder abandons his wife, children, and his best friend Maurice. Even the mercy killing of his mother now has Nazi overtones of the gassing of undesirables in the extermination camps, as Halder perhaps subliminally hints to the doctor supervising the euthanasia, "But it needs to be much more ordinary and reassuring ... Could it be made to look like a bathroom, perhaps ... So that the patients are reassured and believe they are being taken for a bath" (45).

Halder's fantasies are reinforced by his only friend, foul-mouthed psychiatrist Maurice, whose own anti-Semitism spurs Halder to embrace Nazi ideology. When Maurice argues that the Nazis cannot afford to ignore the wealth of Jewish intelligence in Germany, Halder confirms his friend's assessment of the dire situation: "You're right ... All that anti-Jewish rubbish ... You're right ... Just balloons they throw up in the air to distract the masses" (6). When he confirms the value of Jewish intelligentsia to Anne, we realize that Halder lives in a fantasy world: "Their ideal might be a Germany without Jews ... But the *reality* is Jews are part of Germany ... It's not real, a Germany without Jewish doctors, scientists, chemists ... and *capitalists* for Christ's sake" (26). Halder even convinces himself that by joining the Nazi Party he can push them more toward a humanistic perspective. Halder, the humanist who teaches literature at Frankfurt University, can even rationalize the book-burning ceremony as a means of moving from knowledge of books to learning from experience: "If you looked at it from the philosophical standpoint, that the burning is symbolic of a new healthy approach to university learning ... Man does not live by books alone" (39). Hitler is viewed by Halder as merely "a mystic idealist" (48) whose *Mein Kampf* is reduced to "metaphysical racialist rubbish" (48) sustaining an ideology that is nothing more than "a temporary aberration" (48). Kristallnacht was one such aberration, rationalized by Halder as "Excesses are bound to happen" (57), merely a "basically humane action" to shock the Jews into the reality of their situation (57).

When Eichmann supervised the emigration of Jews from Germany, he was quite comfortable with his duties and worked closely with the Jewish community to achieve Nazi goals. However, when the deportations were ordered, Eichmann then was out of his element; this frustration interfered with his personal goals. Halder also grows increasingly angry with Maurice because of the Jewish issue that affects his personal life. With regard to Maurice, Halder muses, "I love him. But I am not going to prison for him. I couldn't stand going to a Nazi prison. (*To Maurice:*) I'm looking at this meal we're sitting down to" (33). Realizing the horrors of the Depression, Halder refuses to lose his meal ticket because of his Jewish friend. Although he recognizes an element of cowardice in his decision to abandon Maurice, Halder reminds himself that he is the family breadwinner: "All these people depending on me. (*To Maurice:*) If it was just myself. But I have two wives, two children and a blind mother, Maurice" (46). Halder sets priorities for himself, and his personal problems far outweigh Maurice's persecution as a Jew:

> Me ... If I *died*. That would worry me ... The idea of being
> snuffed out ... If I got *cancer*. That would worry me. Or if they
> stuck me in one of those concentration camps and one of
> Himmler's perverts got at me ... That worries me ... If Anne
> stopped loving me and ran off with another man ... that would
> worry me. I've got a whole scale of things that could worry me ...
> The Jews and their problems ... Yes, they are on it ... but very far
> down, for Christ's sake. (58)

Halder eventually blames the Jews for disrupting the complacency of his life as he begins to see Maurice not as a friend, but as an omnipresent reminder of his own ambivalence between his humanism and his ambitious drive to prosper in Nazi society. Halder claims that Maurice's paranoia is merely an anxiety disorder. Halder, like Eichmann, is forced to obey orders in order to rise through the ranks; therefore, inevitably, the obstacle to prosperity must be the Jews rather than the Nazis. Halder extends his anger to the victims: "I was looking for a peaceful day in the garden. I wish they'd get these bloody Jews out of their system. Why didn't they all get to hell out of here years ago, while they still had a chance" (59). Halder ultimately begins to abandon himself to fantasy, ignoring the reality of Nazi brutality toward the

Jews: "It's the Jews' fault ... They are responsible for pushing Germany into this Jewish, moralistic, humanistic, Marxist total fuck up" (65). Maurice wonders how Halder could be so confused as to blame Jews for their own persecution and challenges his friend to stop fantasizing. Halder explains that there is no objective moral truth, so Maurice should accept the world as it is. Halder makes it explicit to Maurice that the only reality is his self-centered personal comfort: "You know what I could do with? A good thick slice of ham ... two eggs ... black bread and butter ... hot mug of coffee ... and seeing Anne ... could do with my arms round Anne more than anything else just now" (67).

As Susan Friesner reminds us, the main point of Taylor's play is that the aberration of Nazi Germany could recur since so many ordinary citizens, like Eichmann, became Nazis so quickly and embraced the National Socialist philosophy so passionately.[17] Halder is not a monster or a psychopath, and his humanistic values indicate that he is no worse, and possibly even better, than most of us; despite that awareness, we see how ordinary individuals can turn into moral monsters sucked into an insidious society. Perhaps a glaring weakness of the play is, as Bernard F. Dukore has argued, that Taylor's use of amiably sentimental music associated with Halder portrays him as all too human–warm and lovable, at worst, misled–to audiences; even Halder's abandonment of Helen in favor of younger Anne is serenaded by "My Blue Heaven," thereby associating Halder's elopement with bliss rather than infidelity.[18] The point is well taken because Taylor wants us to understand that, like Eichmann's banality of evil, Halder is swept up in circumstances that were morally wrong but legalistically valid. Harriet Margolis writes, "*Good* uses the Nazi era in Germany as an emblem for evil incarnate and to stage an artistic discussion on individual responsibility faced by such evil."[19] However, critics have disagreed with Margolis, arguing that such discussion of individual responsibility is nonexistent, and Taylor's refusal to take a stand "plays into the hands of *in*human totalitarianism,"[20] or that a benign verdict of innocence by virtue of being human muddles the play.[21]

Until Halder arrives in Auschwitz, he is perennially immersed in his own fantasy world. Before leaving for Auschwitz, he confirms his illusions to Anne: "Yes ... We probably are ... *good* ... Yes ... Whatever that means" (68). However, when he arrives at Auschwitz, Halder experiences an epiphany; while listening to the band play a Schubert march, he realizes, "The important thing was ... The significant thing: the band was *real. Up band ... Halder watching them ... The band was real!*" (69). Gone are the sweet illusory arias, such as "I'm Always Chasing Melodies," "You Are My Heart's Delight," the pastorals of the Berlin Philharmonic, Bach's fugues, and Mendelssohn's violin concertos, all of which served to nourish Halder's fantasies. Auschwitz is the reality for Halder; his life in Germany was merely fantasy. In paying homage to Taylor's career after he suddenly passed away in 1981, Benedict Nightingale wrote, "His plays are full of people who think themselves enlightened, progressive, or simply 'good,' not realising the extent to which they're deceiving themselves."[22] The reality for Halder is that Auschwitz is the type of place for which his best friend Maurice is destined. Ultimately, the play is less concerned with Halder's moral flaccidity than it is with the delusions of the common person in doing what seems legally acceptable in a barbaric society. *Good* does not ask us to sympathize with Halder; instead, we pity him for being indifferent, like so many of us.

British playwright Peter Barnes's *Laughter!* consists of two one-act plays, *Tsar* and *Auschwitz*, that were initially presented at the Royal Court Theatre in London on 25 January 1978. Although Barnes is a rather prolific playwright whose best work is generally regarded to be *The Ruling Class*, for which he won the John Whiting Award, he has had difficulty getting his plays produced and, despite his mordant comedy in the tradition of Ben Jonson, his verbose anti-Establishment dramas appear to be a bit esoteric for the general public; *Laughter!*, for example, in a production directed by Charles Marowitz, closed on 11 February 1978, after less than a three-week run at the Royal Court Theatre in London. Barnes spent two years researching and writing *Laughter!*, working daily on the play from 9:30 a.m. to 5 p.m. at the British Museum. Most of this research related to the statistics on Auschwitz spewed out by Gottleb at the end of the second part of the twin bill.[23]

Auschwitz provides the quintessential example of how ordinary citizens can get immersed in what Arendt describes as the banality of evil. For the play to be effective, Barnes must get the audience to identify with the Nazi bureaucrats onstage who unwittingly codify Auschwitz's smooth functioning as an extermination camp. As we shall see, Barnes lulls the audience into passivity through the numbing bureaucratic language, allows us to identify with the three Nazi bureaucrats, and then lures us into laughter about genocide, all of which serves to make us complicit in a carefully crafted web of evil that Barnes traps us into accepting as normal activity.

Auschwitz occurs in an administrative office in Berlin in 1942, where three Nazi functionaries perform typical clerical duties. The three Nazis seem to represent a microcosm of German society, for they appear to epitomize different generations: Else Jost, the secretary, is the youngest; Viktor Cranach appears to be middle-aged; Heinz Stroop is close to retiring. During the first half of the play, the audience is lulled into a passive state by the highly bureaucratic language that is virtually impenetrable; Barnes, true to his reputation, appears to be all words and little action. The audience virtually tunes the play out as the language becomes nothing more than jargon and gobbledygook. For example, Cranach's first words as he dictates a memo set the tone for the first half of the play: "WVHA Amt Ci (Building) to WVHA Amt Di/i. Your reference ADS/MNO our reference EZ/14/102/01. Copies WVHA Amt D IV/2, Amt D IV/4: RSHA OMIII: Reich Ministry PRV 24/6D. Component CP3 (m) described in regulation E(5) serving as Class I or Class II appliances and so constructed as to comply with relevant requirements of regulations L2(4) and (6), L8(4) and 7."[24] The audience is inundated with the minutiae of office bureaucracy that is particularly germane only to these Nazis. Cranach's comments to Else, such as, "Paper size A4 not A3 and the margins should be nine elite character spaces, seven pica on the left and six elite, five pica on the right" (108), lull the audience into a stupor. John Lahr has stated that Barnes has dehumanized language, producing a "psychic numbing" effect among the spectators.[25] The three bureaucrats work for a ministry that supplies concrete and cyanide for the death camps such as Auschwitz; as a passive audience, we become bored witnesses to the atrocities. Like millions of other Germans during World War II, we also become complicit with the banality of evil.

The audience begins to understand that these three likable bureaucrats have much in common with many of us. Cranach must work because he has just taken out a second mortgage. Many of Else's relatives have been killed during the war, but she cannot be jaded because she still has bills to pay, particularly since her mother has bought a new set of furniture. Besides, Else, whose Roman Catholic beliefs preclude any form of dissent, explains, "Obedience is regarded as a principle of righteous conduct. So I look on National Socialism as Catholicism with the Christianity left out" (113). Stroop, who is on the verge of retirement, realizes that dissent can mean unemployment, so he admits to doing his job to the best of his ability: "You can't please everyone, so I find it best to keep pleasing my superiors" (111). Even black marketeer Wochner, who delivers contraband to the bureaucrats, views National Socialism as an economic opportunity: "Nothing'll stop us then, we'll be the paymasters of Europe. It'll be easy. No more uncertainties, we'll be able to judge a man's worth at a glance by his credit rating, know right from wrong, success from failure, by the amount of money in our pockets" (122). Like the seemingly benign Eichmanns of the world who do their jobs to get promoted, thereby supporting their families, these functionaries can become immune to the concepts of guilt and responsibility. Thus, the Nazi foundation, like any totalitarian society, is built upon the idea that a multitude of bureaucrats must perform their jobs without dissent for the system to function properly. Cranach admits that Hitler's authority is derived directly from ordinary German citizens: "You see, despite what our enemies say, he can only govern with the consent of the German people" (110). Barnes depicts how the Nazi mentality can be implicit in our bureaucratic culture of the quotidian.

When Gottleb, the die-hard fanatical Nazi enters, the tone of the play shifts; the audience now becomes less mesmerized by the bureaucratic diction and more interested in the interaction among Gottleb and the functionaries. As Gottleb goads the bureaucrats into telling anti-Nazi jokes, which he tape-records, the audience begins to see him as a dangerous spy. The result is that when Cranach asks, "what do you call someone who sticks his finger up the Führer's arse?!" and responds with, "A brain surgeon!" Gottleb informs him that the penalty for such an infraction is death (131). Gottleb's method of entrapment suggests Gestapolike tactics, which Barnes's audience will obviously despise. Furthermore, Gottleb tries to coerce Else and Stroop into admitting that it is Cranach's voice they hear making the damaging comments on the tape. Bernard F. Dukore has commented that Gottleb's Nazi fanaticism is so ruthless that he becomes estranged from audiences, forcing us to identify further with Cranach, Else, and Stroop.[26] Audiences can relate to such bureaucrats who tell jokes to ease tensions at work, but the spectators are simultaneously appalled by Gottleb's merciless dogmatism.

Vivian M. Patraka points out that Cranach, Else, and Stroop deny the literalness of what they do through an abstract distancing of writing, numbering, and jesting.[27] Gottleb, however, removes the abstract from their work when he states that the bureaucratic jargon for CP3 (m) described in regulation E(5) refers to the new concrete flue for the crematoria at Auschwitz. Moreover, the Roman numerals followed by consecutive Arabic numbers that the functionaries banter about so freely actually refer to the masses of people cremated in the extermination camp. Eric Sterling has noted, "The numbers become abstract and thus do not represent actual people, so in the minds of the civil servants, they bear no relationship with death."[28] To code murder through mass-produced numbers makes genocide less threatening and more palatable. Gottleb disdains the abstract in his vivid description of the horrors of Auschwitz, including the selections, the mistreatment of babies as footballs, the debasement of prisoners, the horrendous living conditions for the slave workers, death by starvation, injections of chloral hydrate and phenol to kill quickly, methods of torture, and mass gassings that leave victims to die in their own urine and feces. As Gottleb continues his litany of horror, the filing cabinets that hold the abstract euphemisms for murder now spring open to reveal dummies that visibly represent the dead bodies covered in filth. A stylized *sonderkommando* squad then enters with hooks, knives, and pincers to separate the gold teeth from the corpses before they are cremated. After Gottleb's litany of genocide, Cranach, Else, and Stroop try to mitigate the horrors of Auschwitz behind the safety of their bureaucratic language. However, the implication is clear: in hiding behind the guise of bureaucratic jargon, the civil servants have tried to disassociate themselves from Nazi genocide. After all, Eichmann, the bureaucrat, testified at his trial that he never killed a Jew nor did he order their deaths; he, like Cranach, Else, and Stroop, merely had ambitious personal reasons for their motives and never had any reason to murder Jews. More frightening is the fact that the civil servants follow the dictum that Nazi regulations are law and therefore must be obeyed; they do not think about the consequences of acting blindly without assuming responsibility for their actions. Cranach, in particular, does not assume responsibility for his actions because the state makes decisions for him. In an interview with Clive Barker, Barnes explained, "People want security at any price. They don't want to choose. They don't want to be given the chance to choose how to conduct their lives. Most people prefer the security of being told."[29]

Cranach, Else, and Stroop prefer the idyllic world they were accustomed to before Gottleb described the realities of Auschwitz. When Halder, who retreated to his imaginative visions and musical interludes, was confronted with Auschwitz, he exclaimed that the band there "was real." Barnes uses the same language when Gottleb challenges the three civil servants to open their eyes to the truth of Auschwitz: "You can't shut it out, not word play, dream play, I've been there! It's *real*!" (141). The bureaucrats have the answer to their dilemma: they throw Gottleb out of the office and close those nasty filing cabinets; in short, if you do not like the message, get rid of the messenger, or "root it out"—the play's refrain.[30] Cranach insists that future generations will see that administrators at Auschwitz were nothing more than "ordinary people, people who liked people, people like them, you, me, us" (143). Cranach, Else, and Stroop then sing to the audience, urging them to join in: "This is a brotherhood of man. A benevolent brotherhood of man. A noble tie that binds, all human hearts and minds. Into a brotherhood of man" (143). By implication, we, the audience, are complicit as well in this "brotherhood" since we have ignored the horrors of the Nazi genocide while laughing at the bureaucrats' jokes and empathizing with them in their hostility toward Gottleb, the truth teller.

The epilogue to *Auschwitz* is the most bizarre scene in Holocaust drama. Similar to *Good*, Barnes situates the denouement of his play in Auschwitz. Abe Bimko and Hymie Bieberstein, also known as the Boffo Boys of Birkenau, decked out in striped threadbare prisoners' tunics, wooden clogs, and undertakers' hats, do a song-and-dance routine to the tune of "On the Sunny Side of the Street." They tell jokes that derive from the music hall or from vaudeville but are now in a much different context since death soon appears imminent for both men: "The way to beat hydrocyanide gas is by holding your breath for five minutes. It's just a question of mind over matter. They don't mind and we don't matter" (145). As the music fades, we hear the hissing sound of the impending gas chambers. In vaudeville, a corny act that was dead on its feet was yanked by a hook from the wings; this act is literally going to be dead. An act that did not "slay us" in the music hall would be hissed by the audience; the Boffo Boys of Birkenau will be slain by the Nazis, who now do the hissing in the form of administering the gas.

The epilogue is confusing for audiences, who typically do not know how to react. The title, *Laughter!*, suggests that Barnes's play is a comedy, and Cranach, Else, and Stroop have already told us jokes that the audience has laughed at appropriately. The truth is that the corny vaudeville jokes told by Bimko and Bieberstein are no less humorous than the anti-Nazi jokes we heard from the three civil servants. Until we reach the segment on Auschwitz, the play served to function as comedy; W. B. Worthen concurs: "The Nazis' pratfalls, their Hitler jokes, their mania for 'heiling,' and so forth, become a kind of schtick."[31] However, in the epilogue, the audience is now confronted with black comedy–laughter elicited through the pain and agony of human suffering.[32]

Barnes's attitude toward black comedy's insistence on making the audience feel uncomfortable can best be understood if we examine the first half of the twin bill, *Tsar*. In a prologue to the play, the Author, presumably speaking for Barnes, states, "Comedy itself is the enemy. Laughter only confuses and corrupts everything we try to say. It cures nothing except our consciences and so ends by making the nightmare worse. A sense of humor's no remedy for evil."[33] As a Brechtian-type narrator who eliminates suspense by informing the audience of what lies ahead, the Author ties together Ivan the Terrible, the protagonist of *Tsar*, and Auschwitz: "Laughter's the ally of tyrants. It softens our hatred. An excuse to change nothing, for nothing needs changing when it's all a joke" (343). The Author urges us to "root out comedy" (343), a desire that seems strange coming from Barnes, who was weaned on the amusement park entertainment of the seaside resort town of Clacton-on-Sea, grew up admiring the music hall (he attended until the halls were demolished in the late 1950s), and makes no apology for his affinity to the plays of Ben Jonson.[34] Barnes, however, actually does agree with the Author: "I've always queried the adage that if you can laugh at a subject, that somehow alleviates the injustice or the cruelty or the oppression. I postulate that sometimes, indeed very often, laughter, far from alleviating it, actually encourages oppression and cruelty."[35] As the Author in the prologue to *Tsar* makes his plea for rooting out laughter, a feeble response to immoral injustice, he receives a pie in the face, allows his bow tie to pinwheel, squirts water from his buttonhole, and then drops his pants. When the audience inevitably laughs at these vaudevillian gimmicks, Barnes's point about laughter diverting us from serious moral issues that should command our attention is made.

In *Laughter!*, Barnes confronts and indicts the audience for laughing in the face of slaughter. Christopher Innes's conflation of laughter and slaughter is insightful: "The pun implicit in the contrast between the title of *Laughter* and its subject of slaughter, two words identical but for a single letter, is typical. Barnes works through the fusion of opposites, both within and (in his characteristic pairing of one-act double bills) between plays."[36] *Tsar*, which occurs in despotic Moscow in 1573, focuses on the brutalities of Ivan the Terrible. The audience is complicit in laughing at what the Author in the prologue has already determined for us to be a comedy–the plight of Prince Nikita Odoevsky, impaled on the stake, covered in congealed blood, and reduced to screaming from the torture inflicted upon him. After Ivan spears Vaska Shibanov's foot, we laugh when Ivan asks him why he remains standing there, and the latter responds, "'Cause my foot's pinned t' the floor, Sire" (350). Thus, laughter is a shield against the reality of human suffering, much as it was for Bimko and Bieberstein. Moreover, as Ivan the Terrible recounts the genocide he committed in medieval Russia, the audience, attuned to the sight gags of the play and conditioned by the Author's slapstick routine in the prologue, cannot help but find opportunities to laugh.

At the end of *Tsar*, Samael tells Ivan, "You made death too personal, arbitrary, a matter of chance: too much like life. In the coming years they'll institutionalize it, take the passion out of killing, turn men into numbers and the slaughter'll be so vast no one mind'll grasp it, no heart'll break 'cause of it" (365). As the play closes and Ivan strains to listen to "Deutschland Über Alles," Samael's comments clearly form the segue to *Auschwitz*. The personalized brutalities of Ivan the Terrible lead directly to the impersonal genocide of the Nazi regime. The slaughter, based on whim during feudal times, is now institutionalized by the Nazis.

In *Laughter!*, Barnes incriminates the audience that laughs in the face of totalitarian regimes. In the prologue, the Author poses the question that dominates both of the one-act plays: "So, in the face of Attila the Hun, Ivan the Terrible, a Passendale or Auschwitz, what good is laughter?!" (343). Laughter becomes the means to engage in denial rather than to confront the seriousness of genocide. In Brian Woolland's analysis of the play, he noted, "If an audience laughs it becomes complicit in the horrors of the drama."[37] Barnes implicates the audience, accusing the spectators of the same complicity shared by Cranach, Else, and Stroop, who laugh at atrocity. Moreover, we can now understand the relevance of the epilogue. Bimko and Bieberstein make jokes about their imminent death; the comedy suggests their complacency and inability to act. Joking about the problem is futile, an excuse to avoid confronting the brutal reality of their fates. Eric Sterling sums up Barnes's use of comedy as an irresponsible reaction on the part of the audience: "Barnes forces audience members to examine the horrors of the Holocaust and their own indifference to the suffering of the victims."[38] Barnes has commented on the implications of the play's message about the need to assume responsibility, rather than laugh at the banality of evil:

> When we did *Laughter* at the Royal Court, I used to go into performances, and I felt waves of hate coming out of the audience. They actively loathed it. Actively. It came out like

steam. The actors used to say: "God we could feel it up on the stage." The British want a theater of reassurance, one of affirmation. They do not want a theater of disturbance.[39]

By succumbing to the monotony of the bureaucratic jargon of the civil servants, by identifying with Cranach, Else, and Stroop, by endearing ourselves to the comedy of personalized and institutionalized despotism, and by laughing at the painful suffering of Bimko and Bieberstein, the audience is forced to assume its share of the guilt. Barnes urges audiences to think for themselves rather than act as if they were "little Eichmanns" using laughter, clichés, and euphemisms to disguise the reality of genocide.

Austrian playwright Thomas Bernhard's *Vor dem Ruhestand* opened in Stuttgart at the Staatstheater on 29 June 1979 under direction by Claus Peymann; in 1986, the play was produced for the first time in East Germany at Berlin's Deutsches Theater. Translated as *Eve of Retirement*, the three-act play was staged in the United States at the Guthrie Theater in Minneapolis on 24 September 1981, in a production directed by Liviu Ciulei, and then in London at the Gate Theatre during the 1997–1998 season. Bernhard has won the Austrian National Prize, the Bremen Literature Prize, the Grillparzer Prize, and the Georg Büchner Prize, primarily for his fiction. As a playwright, Bernhard is well known in Austria and Germany, but, although his eighteen dramas have been translated into more than twenty languages, he has yet to establish an international reputation in theater circles. *Eve of Retirement*, like most of his plays, has never enjoyed widespread popularity.

Bernhard himself is known primarily as a "difficult" and frequently controversial playwright. His plays are nihilistic, focusing on disease, misanthropy, perversity, degeneration, madness, depravity, and death.[40] Stephen D. Dowden notes, "Even in Austria, a country famous for curmudgeonly intellectuals, Thomas Bernhard stands out as a grand master of contempt and malediction."[41] Such "contempt and malediction" may have been sown early in his life due to the incompetence of medical authorities who placed him in various hospitals and convalescent homes where Bernhard contracted tuberculosis that plagued him throughout his life, or due to his exile to a home for maladjusted children in which his bed wetting became a source of ridicule, or due to brutal, pedantic teachers who forced the adolescent to practise his violin in a shoe closet and also demanded that even crippled students raise their crooked arms to salute Hitler. Bernhard, born in 1931, was old enough to remember Austria's Nazi heritage, and his constant evocation of his country's dismal historical record and its concomitant pathological denial of the Holocaust is perhaps the main reason why his plays are so controversial.

Bernhard's deeply rooted misanthropy that focuses on life's dark side has prompted critics to compare him to Jonathan Swift, Thomas Mann, Franz Kafka, Samuel Beckett, and August Strindberg.[42] Martin Esslin has made the comparison between Bernhard and Beckett explicit in their use of monologic voices to convey characters caught up in the prison house of their own consciousness, their compulsive solipsistic talkers, and their tragicomic visions laced with savage black humor spat out with venom and derision to depict a bleak universe.[43] Moreover, Bernhard's plotless plays, static situations, and cardboard characters[44] who communicate as if they are disembodied voices, all serve to conflate Beckett and Bernhard. The comparison between Bernhard and Strindberg is also noteworthy, for Bernhard's playwriting appears to be similar to the drama Strindberg wrote after his "inferno" period ended in 1896, particularly with regard to the ubiquitous evil that Strindberg portrays in plays such as *The Ghost Sonata*. However, *Eve of Retirement*'s unrhymed free verse without punctuation, indicative of Bernhard's musical background, creates a rhythmic structure unlike the dramas of Beckett or Strindberg; although the content of Bernhard's play may resemble those of Beckett or Strindberg, Bernhard's musical refrain replete with varied repetitions is more closely akin to Maurice Maeterlinck's symbolist dramas that are laced with stichomythia.

Eve of Retirement is an assault on the legacy of National Socialism in which Arendt's concept of Eichmann's banality of evil is fully brandished on Bernhard's bourgeois audiences. Writing in 1988, Rüdiger Görner phrased the relationship between Bernhard and the Holocaust succinctly: "Bernhard's resentment centres on what he sees as an unreflected, opportunistic glorification of a defunct past which gave rise to one of the most despicable collective aberrations of this century."[45] Whereas Beckett typically sets his plays in timeless space in a nondescript setting that could be universally understood, Bernhard's play is set in Germany or Austria in 1979. The specific incident that spurned *Eve of Retirement* was the Hans Karl Filbinger affair.[46] In 1966, Filbinger, in an overwhelmingly lopsided vote, was elected governor of Baden-Würtemberg, whose capital is Stuttgart, the site of the premiere of the play. Filbinger's platform was based on a law-and-order program of censorship and surveillance to combat the encroaching threats of the intellectuals in the left-wing segment of government who protested against the silence of German citizens toward the Holocaust. Filbinger even tried to oust Bernhard's director and longtime friend Claus Peymann from his post at the Württemberg State Theater. German youths were protesting against former Nazis who held important government positions and were now receiving substantial pensions. Filbinger was one such Nazi who was formerly Hitler's naval judge. After the war, he sentenced a German sailor to death for deserting the Reich; he also handed out death sentences for minor offenses. Filbinger's response to the left-wing dissenters was to continue attacking the liberal press while trivializing and evading the charges leveled against him. Eventually, Filbinger resigned but was awarded a medal of honor for distinguished service and became honorary chairman of the right-wing Christian Democratic Union. In *Eve of Retirement*, Rudolf Hoeller is one such former Nazi, who now, as a chief justice, will retire with an enormous pension. When Vera comments, "Then again we do have a President now/ who was a National Socialist,"[47] the German–Austrian audience in 1979 would have intuitively understood the reference to Filbinger.

In *Eve of Retirement*, Chief Justice Hoeller, formerly an SS officer and concentration camp commandant, gets together on 7 October with his sisters Vera and Clara for their annual celebration of Himmler's birthday. The play is a recurrent symbolic event of mockery and derision, as Bernhard forces his German–Austrian audience to sit through a diatribe that glorifies the moral depravity of a society corroded by its Nazi past. Bernhard sarcastically reinforces the agony through the repetition of a ritualistic event. William E. Gruber perceptively argues, "Bernhard's characters have little new to say to each other; on the contrary, we get the clear impression that what is being said and done has been said and done many times before."[48] Himmler's birthday becomes the focal point for the reification of Nazism for modern German society. Hitler's birthday would have been a more logical choice for celebration, but the Führer was still widely idolized as the savior who brought Germany out of the Depression, reducing unemployment while concomitantly increasing national pride. The choice to glorify Himmler more closely associates contemporary German society with the brutality and depravity of the Gestapo and the concentration camps. As Jeanette R. Malkin reminds us, *Eve of Retirement* portrays Himmler as an archetype who ritualizes history through private memory of a German–Austrian public.[49] Ritual typically provides legitimacy to cultural constructs; in this instance, as Joseph A. Federico has suggested, the ritual is codified as "the tenets of the National Socialist universe are reified into unquestionable dogmas."[50]

Eve of Retirement is structured as a preplanned ritual whose events have been played out annually for decades as the most important day of the year. The pre-ritual enactments occur during the afternoon of 11 October, while Hoeller remains at work. During the previous year, Clara was forced to shave her head and pose as a concentration camp inmate. This year, however, that indiscretion is dispensed with, but all of the other Nazi accoutrements are brought out for the occasion, including Hoeller's SS officer's uniform. As Vera carefully and systematically irons the uniform, hangs the jacket on the window, polishes the boots, and pins the Iron Cross on for visual effect, the audience is consistently, and for a prolonged period of time, beginning to associate the objects with the fetishizing of Nazi iconography. When Rudolf enters, his body becomes the object of fetishization, as Vera massages the former Nazi and then undresses him. Under the careful scrutiny of Himmler's omnipresent persona expressed through his prominently displayed photograph now highlighted in a new silver picture frame, the Hoellers eat the festive meal. Three bottles of Von Metternich champagne, the vintage that was served in the concentration camp, are consumed. After perusing the photo album and drinking the second bottle, Vera and Rudolf go to bed together–in short, incest caps off the successful evening celebration.

The ritualistic celebration becomes a glorification of the "golden years" of the past–a nostalgia for the illustrious time of Nazi reign. The past is mythologized as a golden age personified by Himmler's archetypal presence. Himmler only met Rudolf once, but the lunch he shared with him in the concentration camp was never to be forgotten. Moreover, Himmler is directly responsible for the Hoellers's well being because forty years ago he intervened against the construction of a poison plant (to exterminate insects) adjacent to their home. The Hoeller household lives in the past, personified by their refusal to change the curtains, update the furniture, paint the rooms, or fix the cracks in the ceiling. Rudolf remembers his concentration camp personnel as a model unit with the highest discipline, always ready for inspection. He recalls, "We were executing a mission/ for the welfare of the German people" (190). As Rudolf peruses the photo album, we are given a nostalgic tour through the history of the Third Reich from 1939, when Rudolph enlisted in the army, until 1945, when the Allies bombed Germany. The concentration camp where Rudolf was substitute commander is remembered as having "pretty" trees located in "a lovely countryside" (188). Rudolf is gleeful when he sees the photo of his drunken spree in Poland, where he learned of the French surrender to the Nazis. Rudolf also has fond memories of his labor as *Obersturmbannführer* (Eichmann's exact title), in which he selected Jews to either die or toil in the labor camp. He is particularly proud of shooting Ukrainians, whom he dismisses as "nothing but traitors" (197). Rudolf muses that he was glad not to be in Auschwitz, but then casually dismisses the carnage there: "During the war you can't have any feelings/ and you actually don't have them" (202). Furthermore, Rudolf does not have a bad conscience about his war-time activities; he states, "I only did my duty/ and I paid my dues" (161), referring to the ten years after the war in which he was forced to hide in a cellar. Meanwhile, during the trip down memory lane, the horrors of the Third Reich are juxtaposed with remembrances of idyllic vacations in which Rudolf communed with nature, all of which is made all the more palatable by the serenade of Beethoven's "Fifth Symphony" in the background. Bernhard realizes that his German–Austrian audience will see through this sarcastic incongruity of German history and, through their long-term memory, will separate the idyllic from the realities of the concentration camps and the Russian front, implicating them through their own knowledge of history.

Coinciding with the Hoellers's glorification of their Nazi past is the notion that National Socialism is morally righteous through its veneration of the great German cultural tradition. Vera claims, "My love for the theatre comes from father/ my love for music from mother" (142). Their father read Schopenhauer and Nietzsche to the children. Vera plays the piano and Rudolf the violin, acknowledging, "Without music it's so empty here" (168). Vera is duped into believing, "The arts are a means/ of saving oneself" (143), and Rudolf reiterates this idea as well: "A civilized nation can make its own music" (192).[51] Vera assures her brother that retirement will be culturally enriched: "We'll make our music again/ you'll play the violin/ I'll play the piano/ Beethoven Mozart Chopin/ And we'll go to the opera" (195). The family is even planning a retirement vacation, a cultural excursion/ back to antiquity" (176). Moreover, Rudolf pairs cultural enrichment with the war when he states that the great tragedy occurred when the Americans bombed Germany: "The Americans destroyed our culture/ not only did they destroy all our cities/ they also destroyed our entire culture" (191). Bernhard's play is essentially a comedy, and any audience inevitably must laugh at Rudolf's hyperbolic notion that the Americans, rather than the Nazis, were to blame for Germany's cultural deterioration.

Not only does the past reflect an idyllic time of nostalgia, but the future also looks bright because of the influence of National Socialism in Germany and Austria. Rudolf is the prime example of the prospering of Nazism, since he has been a successful Chief Justice and a pillar of the community who is about ready to retire and enjoy a large pension. Forty years after Himmler argued against the poison gas factory on their land, Rudolf has successfully disputed in court the construction of another toxic gas plant on virtually the same ground; Himmler's spirit thus lives on in the good judge Rudolf Hoeller. The tenets of National Socialism have been ingrained to such an extent that they are celebrated as rituals. The resurgence of Nazism is inevitable according to the Hoellers, and Rudolf represents the chosen hero leading the way. Vera says, "The majority thinks like us and must do so secretly/ Even if they insist on the contrary/ they still are National Socialists all of them" (204). Rudolf gloats in the fact that the leading politicians are former Nazis, directly implicating the audience in the Filbinger affair. Joseph A. Federico sums up Bernhard's position about the link between Germany's moribund past and its future: "Through the reification of National Socialist roles and institutions, the pervasiveness of this obsession is made dramatically apparent: National Socialism appears natural, normal, and inevitable."[52] Bernhard's play touches a nerve with regard to the secret obsession of National Socialism still lurking in German consciousness–an ideology that, as Jeanette R. Malkin reminds us, "is cyclical and refutes change."[53]

Rudolf and Vera acknowledge the present-day corruption in Germany, largely due to the Americans and their notion of democracy that has infiltrated the country after the war. Clara became a paraplegic when the Americans bombed her kindergarten class during the war. Vera admits, "Today's children grow up like savages/ This descent into barbarity comes from America" (156). Rudolf understands that the spirit of American capitalism is ruining the country, turning it into a moral wasteland: "The profit mongers get their hands on everything/ The world has never been so brutal/ profit guides and governs everything" (158). If the Nazis had won the war, Germany would be prospering; instead, its moral values have declined. Rudolf asserts, "Americanism has poisoned us/ Those who glorify democracy/ are in fact its murderers" (163). As a judge, Rudolf has seen the disastrous effects that a liberal democracy has on the judicial system. He bemoans the fact that criminals are given life sentences and then are on the loose after serving only fifteen years. The audience will certainly have an uncomfortable laugh at Rudolf's assertion that today's criminals are cynical and indifferent toward their victims, whereas during the reign of the Reich, such murderers, he says, "didn't exist in our days/ such elements simply didn't exist" (176).

Rudolph and Vera agree that Germany is in a state of chaos because of the Jews, who they claim were rightfully put in their places during the Third Reich. Bernhard forces his spectators to come to grips with their own consciences as Rudolf engages in a vitriolic attack on Jews. Through platitudes and clichés passed on from generation to generation, the audience recognizes its own Nazi mentality for blaming the Jews for all of Germany's woes. Vera tells Clara, "Your father was a Jew hater/ like ninety-eight percent of the population" (138). Vera imprints the reality of anti-Semitism on the contemporary German–Austrian audience that must hear this litany of anti-Jewish diatribe without chance of egress:

> but the Germans hate the Jews
> even as they claim just the opposite
> that's the German nature
> you can't get around it
> because you can't get around nature
> in a thousand years the Jews will still be hated in Germany
> in a million years. (138)

Like Eichmann, who worked intimately with many Jews and mutually agreed with their goals of emigration, Rudolf says he "met hundreds and thousands" (163) who were decent. Rudolf, however, associates the typical Jews with the despicable Americans who bombed Germany and then introduced the corrupting influence of democracy: "it's the ruthless Jew I'm talking about/ who under the guise of democracy/ exploits nature and wrecks the earth" (163). Jews become associated with the moral depravity endemic to modern Germany: "The good German detests what's going on in this country/ Depravity hypocrisy general stupefaction/ The Jewish element has taken root everywhere" (172). *Ipso facto*, the gassing of Jews is treated as an innocuous way of solving Germany's problems. Like Eichmann, Rudolf was merely obeying orders in exterminating Jews, acting as a role player who legally followed German law in a struggle of good versus evil. Bernhard implies that the Nazi attitude toward the Jews has become ingrained as a natural part of the German vernacular. Gitta Honegger remarks, "The most frightening, absurd aspect of Bernhard's play is that even anti-Semitism has been reduced to a cliché and as such has become even more hideously dangerous, because it is deeply ingrained in our unreflected use of language which carries the equivalent unreflected emotional response."[54]

Vera and Rudolf appear to be good citizens, albeit Nazis. They appreciate art and music, share a love of nature, are well respected in the community, take care of their handicapped sister, and successfully fight against a poison gas factory being built in their neighborhood. The audience, however, intuitively perceives that the family seems to be warped. Gitta Honegger writes, "If the aging Höller children appear to be the nice people next door, they have terrible secrets."[55] Vera and Clara praise their maid for being a deaf mute, for she cannot hear their secrets nor can she tell them to others. Rudolf, with all of his success, never married; as a matter of fact, there seems to be something inherently suspect about three aged siblings who are unwed and thus have no children. Incest becomes the morally depraved means for Vera and Rudolf to propagate the tenets of National Socialism, for they seem to be wedded to Nazism. Although they abhor the fact that Himmler committed suicide, their mother also did so. The Hoellers seem to be cursed with secrets that they refuse to share with outsiders. Vera admits, "We haven't had a visitor in years/ because that's how Rudolf wants it" (130). Rudolf acknowledges that the family has "cut off all social contacts" (172) as if there is a dark underside to their lives. In the past, visitors were invited to celebrate Himmler's birthday with the Hoellers. Now, the celebration has turned into a clandestine affair. Before the festive dinner, Rudolf checks to make sure all the doors and windows are locked securely (183). Vivian M. Patraka compares the festivities to a gothic narrative, a ghastly atmosphere in which there are paranoid references to their horrible house, the family's insanity and fanaticism, and their hidden taboos, all suggesting that something "happened" to them.[56] In this sense, the play can be compared to Sam Shepard's *Buried Child*, an allegorical saga of a family, ruled by an aging patriarch, mired in a tragic, mythic curse. Just as Shepard's play concerned an American society whose vital spirit was now lost in a stifling, noncaring, repressive environment, *Eve of Retirement* becomes an archetypal portrait of the cursed spirit of National Socialism. This time the aging patriarch of the desolate wasteland winds up drunk and waving a pistol in what is supposed to be perceived by the audience as a holy day of the year. Moreover, as Donna L. Hoffmeister has indicated, the monologic speeches of Vera and Rudolph before and during the celebratory ritual suggest that the "interminable flow of words demonstrates the isolation between characters."[57] In short, not only are there family secrets that preclude outsiders from entering into the ritual, but the truth is verboten for the insiders as well. The audience thus gets the impression that Eichmann's "banality of evil," a vision of typical bourgeois mentality, is frighteningly grotesque.

Clara, the left-wing socialist, seems to represent a dissenting view to National Socialism. She writes letters to the editor about politics, tormenting Rudolf and Vera who view her as a dangerously insane fanatic. Rudolph compares his sister to vermin: "She turned into a beast/ in her wheelchair/ a filthy rotten beast" (180). The Nazi mentality is to destroy enemies of the state, including one's own siblings. Vera mentions institutionalizing her in a prison (128), a sanitarium (124), or perhaps drowning her (120). Rudolf suggests leaving the paraplegic on her own, which would mean an agonizing death (180). He explains to Clara, "in our time we simply put the likes of you/ under gas" (180). To Rudolf, Clara is expendable: "Let me tell you Clara/ I wish you'd drop dead/ and leave us alone" (181). Clara's role in the ritual is safe when she shaves her head and performs as a concentration camp inmate; her handicap is also perceived as a blessing, for it would be a profanation of the Nazi spirit for her to stand when Vera and Rudolf make their annual toast to Himmler. In truth, Clara says very little in defense of her opposition to National Socialism. Rüdiger Görner believes that Clara's silence throughout the play is a means of revenge, a method of extinguishing her brother.[58] This reading, however, is difficult to defend. Instead, Clara's silences and her paralysis infer her inability to find a viable alternative to the fascist ideology imposed on her by Vera and Rudolf. When Vera confronts Clara with the words that end the play, the audience is explicitly implicated as well: "you and your silence/ you and your endless silence" (207).

When Rudolf suffers a heart attack in the denouement, the play becomes a parody of the ritual that has been enacted on stage. While realizing that Rudolf's fate now depends on a Jew, Dr. Fromm, Vera tries to remove all Nazi paraphernalia from the scene, including

Himmler's picture. Vera meticulously ironed Rudolf's clothes and polished his boots in the pre-ceremonial ritual; now she strips her brother of his SS uniform rather unceremoniously. Jeanette R. Malkin writes, "Now, those same clothes are not only torn off his body, they are shorn of their symbolic value as the fetishized objects become a collection of theatrical props. Juxtaposing the figure of the eternal Nazi to the final image of the clown whose pants are pulled off on stage, Bernhard gives us grotesque pantomime."[59] The stage essentially becomes de-Nazified of its ceremonial accoutrements–a reversal of the ritual we have just witnessed. Since this deconstruction is essentially accomplished for the sake of a Jewish doctor, nothing more than vermin according to the tenets of National Socialism, we realize the hypocrisy of a family now fully revealed to be ashamed of their activities. Rudolf's dying body leaves us with the final image of the collapse of a worn-out ideology.

Eve of Retirement forces audiences to confront what Arendt described as typical Nazi mentality expressed by Eichmann's banality of evil. Bernhard demands that spectators understand how the tenets of National Socialism remain indigenous to Germany and Austria.[60] He exposes the moral depravity of a complacent bourgeois society, seemingly innocuous, familiar, and benign on the surface yet exposed as replete with its own innate prejudices and biases. His satiric comedy challenges audiences to confront their latent dark sides that could produce the Eichmanns of the world, rather than sitting paralyzed, in silence, like the hapless Claras.

3   Culture and the Holocaust

On 29 September 1933, the Nazis created the Reich Chamber of Culture, which forbade Jews from participating in all cultural activities, including theater, motion pictures, journalism, art, and literature. Jews were thus dismissed from all positions that they held in cultural spheres. Nevertheless, despite the Nuremberg laws that deprived Jews of German citizenship, Martin Buber in 1936 encouraged Jews to assume a renewed interest in their own cultural activities. Jews formed the Kulturbund, which provided employment for thousands of actors and musicians disallowed from performing on German stages. In writing about the Kulturbund, Holocaust historian Lucy S. Dawidowicz states, "In the first years of its existence, about 8,500 presentations were offered–operas, plays, concerts (orchestra, chamber music, choir, and soloists), lectures, recitations, cabaret performances, ballets, film showings, and art exhibits."[1]

When the Nazis herded Jews into the ghettoes of eastern Europe, culture became paramount. Although Jews were forbidden to perform works by Aryan composers and writers, they compensated in other ways. Art became an important medium for the release of the imagination, as well as a means of defying the Nazis. Hundreds of songs were written, many from Yiddish folklore, to boost morale. Sidra DeKoven Ezrahi reports that underground organizations produced numerous literary manuscripts and performed skits that adapted biblical themes to the suffering of the Jews under Nazi rule.[2] As conditions worsened in the ghettoes, the demand for literature increased in order to relieve the daily tension, maintain a discipline of the mind, retain a vestige of civilized life, and cultivate self-esteem; especially popular were detective, war, and adventure stories, as well as devotional literature. Literary works were smuggled into the ghettoes, where small libraries soon were established. Diaries were written to bear witness to the Nazi genocide, to assuage the daily misery and persecution, and to nourish one's own sense of humanity. Amateur and professional entertainers performed comedy acts, song-and-dance routines, and satires on ghetto bureaucracy in such venues as cafes and public kitchens. Yehuda Bauer reports that a few ghettoes, such as those in Vilna and Warsaw, had their own orchestras,[3] while others enjoyed string quartets or adult and children's choral groups. Theater, in particular, was an important social institution that enhanced one's self-esteem, reinforced a sense of group solidarity, and maintained social cohesion. The Warsaw ghetto had five theaters while Vilna and Lodz each had two.

Obviously, in the concentration and extermination camps, cultural activities were vastly limited. However, opportunities to smuggle in books to the *lager*, play in the camp orchestra, or recall passages from great literary works increased morale and often provided prisoners with the will to endure. For example, in *Survival in Auschwitz*, Primo Levi remembers how reciting verses from Dante's *Divine Comedy* encouraged Pikolo, the messenger-clerk of the Chemical Kommando, to rediscover his humanity.[4] Fania Fenelon, the survivor of Auschwitz who becomes the focal point of Arthur Miller's *Playing for Time*, surely was able to endure the Holocaust because of her role as an artist. Through her prior training with the eminent French theater director, Louis Jouvet, Auschwitz survivor Charlotte Delbo recalls how she often took the inmates to the theater by reciting the lines of Giraudoux and even performing scenes from the plays of Molière. Delbo attests to the power of art to recapture the purity of childhood amidst the omnipresent terror and to rekindle dormant imaginations: "It was magnificent because, for the space of two hours, while the smokestacks never stopped belching their smoke of human flesh, for two whole hours we believed in what we were doing."[5] Art helped people survive the concentration camps because it uplifted their spirits and served to heal their badly damaged souls. Rosette C. Lamont is succinct about the role of art in *l'univers concentrationnaire:* "Hope cannot cure malnutrition, but for a young, basically strong person the desire to live was often stirred by memory, that of one's personal past, and that of the collective past we find in works of art."[6] This chapter will examine plays that explore the role of culture in the ghetto (*Ghetto*), in the concentration camp (*Playing for Time*), and in a situation where death is imminent (*Mister Fugue or Earth Sick*).

Israeli playwright Joshua Sobol's *Ghetto* premiered at the Haifa Municipal Theater in April 1984, where it won the Israeli David's Harp award for best play; the following year, the play was met with enthusiasm and protest when it was staged at the Freie Volksbühne in Berlin.[7] The American premiere occurred at the Mark Taper Forum in Los Angeles in October 1986. From 1984 until 1989, the play was staged in more than a dozen countries, including France, Sweden, the Netherlands, Norway, Denmark, Austria, and Belgium, as well as in the United States (Washington, DC and Chicago). In April 1989, the play ran simultaneously in London (staged at the Royal National Theatre by Nicholas Hytner), where it won the Evening Standard and London Critics Award for best play of the year, and in New York (at Circle in the Square). Elie Wiesel criticized the Circle in the Square production (which was staged by Gedalia Besser who also had directed the play in Haifa), claiming that the drama was nauseating in its images of collective degradation, depravity, exhibitionism, and mockery of Jews who allowed themselves to be seduced by the Nazis.[8] The play closed after only twenty-five performances. In the 1990s, *Ghetto* was still being performed worldwide (Sobol himself directed the play in Essen during 1992), including productions on college campuses (e.g., Ball State University during October 1991 and Southern Illinois University in January 1992) and in repertory theaters (e.g., Performing Arts Project in Kobe, Japan, during June 1995).[9]

Sobol did three years of extensive research on the Vilna ghetto in Lithuania before completing the play, including traveling to Poland, Russia, and Germany, talking with survivors, reading Vilna librarian Hermann Kruk's diary and other memoirs, and interviewing the artistic director of the theater. Vilna was a hub of Jewish culture in the first half of the twentieth century, a city replete with Jewish publishing firms, newspapers, printing presses, several chorales, a classical and modern dance school, two jazz ensembles, and an avant-garde Yiddish theater (they even performed O'Neill and Pirandello) that earned the city the moniker of "the Jerusalem of Lithuania." In 1939, the Jewish population totalled more than fifty-seven thousand. On 24 June 1941, the Nazis occupied the city and soon created a *Judenrat* (Jewish council). In various *Aktionen (Special Campaigns)*, Jews were systematically murdered at Ponar, around seven miles from Vilna; others were starved in the ghetto or sent to concentration camps in Estonia. After the ghetto's liquidation on 24 September 1943, approximately twenty-five hundred Jews remained alive.

Ghetto focuses on the theater that was established in Vilna by Israel Segal under the auspices of ghetto police chief Jakob Gens on 18 January 1942. In his diary entry written the day before the first performance, Kruk wrote, "In a cemetery there can be no theatre." The public, however, disagreed and found that their spirits were uplifted by the performances. In his postscript to the play, Sobol writes, "Driven by his conviction that normalization and productivization of the ghetto were the key to saving as many people as possible, Gens regarded the theatre not only as a source of livelihood and employment for the actors but also as an invaluable emotional outlet which would boost morale and help to normalize ghetto life."[10] In the first year of production, the theater staged 111 shows, with performances typically sold out weeks in advance. By the time the ghetto was liquidated, seventy thousand tickets had been sold.[11] Alfred Cismaru discussed the vital importance of culture in the lives of the Vilna ghetto community: "In the many diaries confiscated by the Germans and discovered by Sobol, there was repeated mention of how each play replaced a meal not had; how a piece of classical music made one forget, or bear, a physical injury; how an aria of an opera or an operetta, lingering in one's head, made sleep, even restful sleep, possible."[12] In an interview with the *New York Times*, a month and half before Wiesel criticized the Broadway production, Sobol described *Ghetto* as an affirmation of life, a Jewish victory over the Nazis.[13] The heightened sense of living that the theater provided gave the ghetto dwellers a spiritual and moral affirmation of their lives, which for Sobol was just as important as the armed resistance in which others were engaged. Sobol reiterated the importance of such cultural vitality in the lives of the Jews in Vilna: "Without it, there is

no accounting for the ability of the defenseless survivors to cling daunt-
lessly to life, to retain their joy of life in the face of armed tormentors
and murderers."[14]

Ghetto, consisting of three acts, occurs in the 1984 Tel Aviv
apartment of Srulik, the chief puppeteer of the Meidim Theatre in the
Vilna ghetto.[15] The play is similar to a Pirandellian play-within-the-
play, as the one-armed Srulik recalls events that occurred in Vilna
between 1941 and 1943. As his apartment walls collapse, the stage is
inundated with the clothing of the dead collected in the ghetto and at
Ponar; this garb serves a practical purpose, for it becomes the costumes
for the theater's actors and actresses.[16] The clothes serve as a visible
reminder of the ominous shroud of death that the ghetto is faced with
daily but also, as the threads that keep the theater in costume, they
function spiritually as well. Srulik is awed by the fact that people who
were to be deported the next day came to the theater the night before,
obviously for spiritual comfort. Ghetto includes nine songs, many of
which contain lyrics that were uplifting to Vilna residents, particularly those displaced from the rural areas and forced into the ghetto.
For example, Chaja provides a catharsis for the suffering Lithuanians
in exile from their homes as she sings, "I long to see my home once
more/ Is it the way it was before?"[17] The songs become a vital spiritual
force that is shared collectively by an otherwise beaten and humiliated
community who are inspired when they hear Chaja lament, "I long to
know them once again/ The things I took for granted then./ The songs
I sang, the dreams I dreamed/ Are more enduring than they seemed"
(167). The theater even promotes the idea of liberation, as when Chaja
on May Day sanguinely sings of an imminent Russian victory: "Never
say you can't go on, your day is done/ Yes, a thick and smoky mist
enshrouds the sun;/ But the sound of marching feet is drawing near/
And they're beating out the message: We are here!" (205). Gens agrees
that the theater provides needed self-esteem: "That's what I want:
show them they have a culture–a language, a powerful inheritance: an
inner life" (168). Understanding that the Nazis are trying to destroy the
souls of the Jews, Gens sees the theater as the antithesis to the spirit of
genocide. Even Kittel, the Nazi overseer of the ghetto who loves classical music, admires the raw energy inspired by the Jewish cultural

activity (175). Moreover, Weiskopf, the tailor whose practicality leads him to suggest that Jews could be saved through meaningful employment patching war-torn Nazi uniforms, is overwhelmed by the stacks of clothing in the theater; in other words, even for the culturally deficient, the theater provides! Finally, Kruk, the naysayer who objected to performing in a cemetery, ultimately understands that theater represents salvation of the soul: "Every form of cultural activity is essential here in the ghetto ... The fascists can kill us at will–it's not even a challenge for them. But they can't achieve their real aim: They can't obliterate our humanity–not as long as we cling to a spiritual life, not as long as we reach for the good and the beautiful ... Theatre is essential" (208). Sobol supports this vision, noting that the main point of the play revolves around the will to live, a heightened sense of surviving, which the theater provided in defiance of choosing death as the easy way out of misery.[18]

Srulik's ventriloquism is yet another example of the efficacy of performance in evading the harsh realities of the Holocaust. Sobol has described performance, which he refers to as "the carnival," as a means of eluding one's social situation, an artistic resource that can liberate one from all laws, taboos, and restrictions.[19] Through his dummy, Srulik can vent his pent-up frustrations even at Kittel, for Kittel, an affirmed lover of culture and one with a modicum of a sense of humor, can acknowledge the novelty of the schtick. Srulik realizes he could never talk directly to Kittel as the dummy does, for example, insulting the SS officer about his stupidity (197). The dummy provides Srulik with a type of refuge from reprisals, a means of evoking hostile sarcasm without assuming direct responsibility for the indiscretion. Through the dummy, Srulik tells Kittel, "Stick your head in the water three times and pull it out twice" (97). Under the guise of praising the Nazis for their generous character, the dummy is able to mock their recent war losses: "Germans always give back, it's in their character. You took Krakov–you gave it back. You took Stalingrad, you gave it back" (198). In short, Vivian M. Patraka reminds us of the brief respite that culture provided the Vilna ghetto residents: "The life-sized dummy in this play, attached to the character Srulik, is a comic convention for expressing a wisecracking, bitter hostility that the actual inhabitants of the ghetto must repress."[20] The Nazis may destroy bodies, but they cannot destroy the cultural voice of the Jews, for even Kittel's massacre of the theater troupe leaves Srulik, now one-armed because the dummy has been shot off his hand, to tell the story. In his "Playwright's Note" preceding the text of the play, Sobol equates the survivor's tale with the power of Jewish cultural achievement: "History should be a constant and permanently-living presence, the fruits of creative and imaginative memory" (154). Srulik, the puppeteer and singer, creative in his imaginative vision yet with his amputated arm serving as a visible reminder of the terror, becomes the ideal person to reimagine the past. Sobol thus views the cultural heritage of the Vilna ghetto as spiritually inspiring to future generations who want to learn about the Holocaust: "So this is a victory–the Nazis didn't leave any legacy which uplifts you, but these Jews in the Vilna ghetto did leave a legacy which for me is very uplifting and which gives me a lot of hope."[21]

Kruk questions the efficacy of theater in a cemetery. As a librarian, Kruk understands the power of books to transmit the historical record to future generations. Moreover, as a cultured person, he acknowledges, "One should always try to live in the presence of art–if possible" (170). Kruk views the theater as merely a means of placating Nazi sentiment toward the arts, telling Gens that he supports the workers' union boycott of the performances. As a Bundist,[22] Kruk believes that the wandering Jew of the Diaspora is lost without a cultural heritage and traditions. Kruk is not speaking of Talmudic traditions, for he is not religious. Instead he laments the loss of art among the Jews of the ghetto: "Without culture, they lose their identity" (192). Kruk can mistakenly appear as if he were a withdrawn individual who simply prefers the isolation of diary writing to the public exposure of a shared theatrical experience. Instead, he represents Wiesel's opinion that the best way to learn about the Holocaust is by reading the primary literature, such as diaries, memoirs, and historical accounts, rather than through other artistic means of expression.

With regard to his Vilna triptych, Sobol declared, "I think the plays tell a story about resistance, and about the many ways that human beings have at their disposal to resist projects of destruction, annihilation, and dehumanization."[23] Gens, whose goal is to save as many bodies as possible, also understands that preserving the spirituality of the Jews is equivalent to resisting the Nazis' dehumanization policies.[24] Gens states, "They're after our souls. They're trying to get inside–reach down our throats, to the essence that's inside. Our souls. And that must never happen" (184). Realizing that the Red Army will eventually liberate the ghetto, Gens valorized saving the souls of Jews rather than working with a meager underground movement, which surely would have led to martyrdom.[25] Understanding Weiskopf's philosophy that Jewish productivity would have the Nazis believe in Jewish indispensability, Gens views the theater as a means of providing employment, as well as offering spiritual comfort. Gens, like Srulik–Sobol, thus embraces the rejuvenating power of the theater (he is also somewhat akin to Kruk, whose notion of saving souls comes from gathering books for a library). The play begins and ends with Srulik's recollection of the Vilna theater troupe; in essence, Srulik, the only living member of the troupe, provides us with survivor testimony about the Vilna ghetto through documentary drama. Freddie Rokem perspicaciously realizes, "The realist document has been confined to the memory of the individual, and the work of art can thus liberate and communicate it."[26] Without Srulik's testimony, the transcendent spiritual power of the Vilna ghetto would not exist. Thus, Gens, understanding the salvific power of the theater, ultimately plays a key role in preserving the memory of Jewish culture during the Holocaust, much like Sobol himself does by writing the play.

In 1976, Fania Fenelon published with Marcelle Routier *Sursis pour L'Orchestre*, which was translated in 1977 into English as *Playing for Time*, an account of her survival as a member of the orchestra in Auschwitz-Birkenau. Arthur Miller adapted the novel for his television screenplay, filmed in November 1979 and shown without commercial interruption by CBS on 30 September 1980. The broadcast starred the controversial Vanessa Redgrave, whose public support for the Palestine Liberation Organization spawned charges of desecration of the memories of Holocaust victims. In 1985, Miller revised the screenplay as a two-act realist drama; however, *Playing for Time* has yet to receive a major production in England or the United States, with the only performance at the time of this writing having been at the 1986 Edinburgh International Festival.

Fania Fenelon (née Goldstein) and her younger brother joined the French Resistance in 1940. As a chanteuse, Fania performed for the German soldiers during the Nazi occupation of France. After an informer alerted the secret police of Fania's work as a courier for the Resistance, she was arrested by the Gestapo and sent in 1943 to Drancy, a detention center. In spring 1944, she was deported to Auschwitz, where, as an internationally recognized cabaret singer, she joined the forty-seven-member, all-female orchestra, the only one of its kind in *l'univers concentrationnaire*. Before Auschwitz was liberated in January 1945, Fania was sent to Bergen-Belsen, where she remained until the arrival of British troops on 15 April 1945; she barely survived the Holocaust, weighing only fifty-six pounds and close to dying of typhus upon liberation of the camp.

Playing for Time traces Fania Fenelon's degradation and dehumanization in Auschwitz through to her resurrection like a phoenix from the ashes by way of the salvific power of art. Primo Levi and Bruno Bettelheim have agreed that survival in the concentration/ extermination camps was largely a matter of chance, especially with regard to the selections for gassings.[27] However, Terrence Des Pres has demonstrated the importance of solidarity and camaraderie among the *Häftlinge* (camp prisoners), maintaining that individualists almost always perished, while those who aided the fallen had a much better chance of survival.[28] Although the need to bear witness was a strong incentive for surviving, it was often insufficient by itself. Bettelheim claims that a major trauma of the concentration camp experience was the destruction of one's social support system, including one's network of friends, family, and business associates.[29] Individuals losing their network of support consequently lost self-respect and self-esteem, despite the innate will to live. The only counter solution to the dilemma was to develop strong group morale that would rekindle the instinct for survival. Fenelon's story was attractive to Miller because it demonstrated how free will could prevail even in a concentration camp, where typically all moral judgments had to be suspended. In *Playing for Time*, Miller shows us how culture, in this instance music, provides Fania with a privileged position, boosts group morale, and replenishes the soul in the midst of unimaginable deprivation.

As a member of the orchestra, Fania assumed a privileged role in the camp. She had access to showers, heat, and toilets, and while the other inmates toiled in the muddy fields all day, which had debilitating effects on their bodies, Fania and the other orchestra members practised their art, which took a less strenuous toll on their lives. Orchestra members were allowed to partake more freely in goods smuggled in from Canada, the section of the camp responsible for sorting the belongings of the deportees. Moreover, as Christopher Bigsby implies, their status as orchestra members ennobled their souls: "They might be forced to play their instruments but those instruments, and the music they played, constituted a resource. Even as they were forced to entertain those who imprisoned them, they could find within the music an alternative world, even a source of beauty."[30]

The quandary that Miller explores in *Playing for Time* is how culture can be so ennobling for various individuals yet have no humanistic effect on those who strive to do evil. On the one hand, the Nazis use the orchestra's music as a means to assuage their consciences and console their spirits for the dehumanizing work that they perform. On the other, the music, played to accompany work details and while prisoners are being led to the gas, is nothing more than a Nazi tactic to belittle, mock, and deride the prisoners. At one point, Fania is spat on by a fellow inmate during the morning serenade after Alma Rosé, the orchestra director who was actually Gustav Mahler's niece, mistakenly assumes, "we play them off to work keep their spirits up."[31] The concert arranged for the sick and mentally ill is such a contradiction, for the ostensible purpose is for Dr. Mengele to observe the effects of music on the insane. Yet the reality is nothing but a mockery, as several of the mentally ill cling to each other like monkeys while others dance in ecstasy before being wheeled out to the gas chamber. In essence, as Jay L. Halio asserts, *Playing for Time* probes the incongruity of the coexistence of human evil and human beauty.[32]

Before Fania is elevated through the transcendent power of art, she is systematically degraded by the Nazis. Cramped in a boxcar like cattle, with no water and an overflowing bucket as a makeshift toilet,

Fania arrives at Auschwitz dazed and bedraggled. She has already suffered from a beating at the hands of the Nazis while in detention at Drancy. Upon arrival, she is relieved of all of her personal possessions and stripped of all vestiges of humanity. In the Nazi attempt to remove the deportees of their individuality, Fania's head is shaved, and then she is given a tattooed number as a sign of her identity.

Fania, however, is not merely a number, for her art has given her international status and with that, a sense of importance in life. Fania tells the younger Marianne, "I've always had to have an aim in life ... something I wanted to do next. That's what we need now if we're ever to get out of here alive" (16). Even before joining the orchestra, Fania communicates a sense of *joie de vivre* through artistic expression, narrating to Marianne a tale about princes and princesses, much like Charlotte Delbo, whose recreations of classical French drama enlivened the spirits of the women in Auschwitz. During Fania's first audition with the orchestra, her piano rendition of *Madame Butterfly*'s inspiring melodies provide her with spiritual comfort despite her physical deterioration: "*In Fania's face and voice, now more confident and warm, are the ironic longings for the music's life-giving loveliness*" (20–21). Frau Mandel, chief of the women's section and a music lover, gives Fania a pair of warm boots. Fania soon realizes that being an artist literally sustains her, for Mengele, another music aficionado whose job it is to exterminate even half-Jews like Fania, keeps the orchestra members alive only to serve his cultural palate. She is literally "playing for time."[33] Realizing that she could be executed anytime at Mengele's whim, Fania further immerses herself in cultural endeavor by maintaining a diary–a means of remembering through art. Moreover, Fania's personal memoir winds up as a repudiation of the Nazi spirit that tried to eradicate individuality. Christopher Bigsby explains, "A memoir is what it says. It is the invocation of a resistant memory to deny such reductivism."[34] Furthermore, because of the tensions among the Jews and the Poles, Fania vows to murder a Polish woman if she survives. She was absolved from committing such an atrocity by the redemptive power of art–the act of writing a memoir that emphasized the importance of collective solidarity among Jews and Poles.

Fania's music becomes the inspiration for the collective will to live. As Fania plays the piano before her comrades, the stage directions indicate, *"The music brings up their lust to live and a certain joy"* (31). Art induces humanism, which for Fania, becomes the focal point of maintaining a sense of dignity to inspire the group to endure. Fania understands that she cannot be selfish, for it is the orchestra that must prosper in order for the individual to survive. Thus, Fania is committed to the well-being of her comrades, urging others like Marianne to share their food with the group (43, 55). When individuals in the orchestra fail to play up to par or when parts of the orchestra are removed for personal use by the Nazis, which occurs when the piano is usurped, Fania panics because the power of art to enliven is diminished. Linda Yellen, the producer of the television film for CBS, states that Miller's message is that the survival of one person depends on the survival of all, and Fania recognizes that, as musicians, "we all better be in harmony a lot more than we are."[35]

Fania's artistic ability is the motivating force behind her humanity that inspires the other orchestra members. Her insistence that she will not join the orchestra without Marianne literally saves her young acolyte's life. Although hungry herself, Fania consistently shares her food with others, providing them with nurturing sustenance. Fania even adopts a maternalistic attitude toward Marianne, offering advice about her self-destructive behavior. Fania elevates the spirits of the other orchestra members by singing songs and enlightening them with tales of the latest cultural trends and fashions in Paris. Kimberly K. Cook acknowledges that Fania's motivations are essentially humanitarian, not self-serving: "Fania spends most of her time on the train and in the camp forming attachments to other prisoners; her consistent goal is not physical survival, it is connection."[36] Of course, playing in the orchestra is much less strenuous than the daily grind of manual labor indigenous to Auschwitz, but, as Susan C. W. Abbotson has observed, art also provides Fania with spiritual strength that maintains her humanity amidst the chaos.[37] Art allows Fania to preserve her dignity despite the fact that she shares no other ideology with her colleagues. Although Fania is half-Jewish, she refuses to be defined by her religion or any other ideology. Instead, she views herself as a humanist: "I am sick of the Zionists-and-the-Marxists, the Jews-and-the-Gentiles, the Easterners-and-the-Westerners, the Germans-and-the-non-Germans, the French-and-the-non-French. I am sick of it, sick of it, sick of it! I am a woman, not a tribe!" (53). When Fania's yellow star deteriorates, she resews it, not to embrace her half-Jewishness, but, as Christopher Bigsby so aptly observes, as a sign of solidarity with her Jewish colleagues in the orchestra.[38]

Unfortunately, several of the musicians in the orchestra espouse ideologies that do not lead to the humanism that culture can nourish. Hélène hopes the communists will replace the fascists once the war is over. Esther's Jewish pride colors her dream of living in Palestine after the Holocaust. Susan C. W. Abbotson recognizes that Hélène and Esther dream of the future but have no sustaining humanism to maintain any sense of hope in the present.[39] In the denouement, Hélène and Esther fade out of the play, their dreams seemingly unimportant in Miller's humanistic world view. Even Alma Rosé learns little from her art, which she views as pure aesthetics; instead, she is conceited, boasting that her father was first violin in the Vienna Philharmonic and bemoans her fate as conductor for such a ragtag group. Her brand of humanism consists of beating the women who miss their notes, claiming that Furtwängler disciplined the same way. Alma's art is designed to placate the Nazis rather than to inspire collegiality that will help the group members to endure. Her transfer to play for the troops is rationalized as performing for a different brand of Nazi: "I will be playing for honorable men, not these murderers here! Soldiers risk their lives!" (72). Alma's snobbish attitude comes back to haunt her as Frau Schmidt, jealous of any Jew having a chance at freedom, poisons her before she can leave the *lager*. Even Mala's rebel ideology fails as a sustaining presence for the orchestra members. Although Mala's attempt to escape is momentarily laudatory for the prisoners, her death suggests useless martyrdom and nothing more.

In contrast to Fania's humanism is Marianne's spiritual resignation. Marianne has always been dependent on her family and has never ventured beyond school or home until her deportation. Fania bonds with Marianne to nurture the neophyte, both of whom share French nationality and are not overly religious. Unlike Fania, who looks out for the spiritual wellbeing of the group, Marianne is selfish. Whereas Fania shares food rather than turn into an animal, Marianne steals rations from her colleagues. Moreover, Marianne prostitutes herself to the kapos, who, well aware of her vulnerability, are more than glad to exchange food for sexual favors. Marianne justifies her promiscuity by throwing the guilt back on Fania: "You know what they think of us out there? We're no better than prostitutes to be entertaining these murderers" (37). Fania regrets Marianne's descent into animality in much the same vein as the SS guards overseeing the camp. Rejecting Fania's humanistic spirit obtained through the inspiring power of their art, Marianne becomes like an animal whose only gratification is food and sex. Marianne even is bitter toward Fania, the only person trying to mentor her and the one individual who kept her alive by insisting that she be brought into the orchestra. Fania tries to teach Marianne the importance of attending to the soul rather than the body, but Marianne's neglect for the emotional and spiritual becomes self-destructive. Near the end of the play, Marianne, ever self-centered, is jealous that Fania comforts Etalina, who has just witnessed the gassing of her parents and sisters. Later, when she is temporarily designated as a kapo, Marianne beats Fania to the ground. Marianne's fate is fitting: she dies of cancer a few years after the war, perhaps Miller's indication that her early death is the result of a ravaged body.

Fania vacillates between a humanistic concern for her colleagues through the saving graces of her art and a potential prostitution of that art by the Nazis for the purpose of doing evil. Fania realizes that her singing is a spiritual inspiration, yet one that is also used to feed the spirit of the Nazis to enable them to continue murdering. The art that fuels Fania's desire to form caring, nurturing relationships with the orchestra members is compromised by her implicit participation in the Nazi genocide. Fania admits she is conflicted about the role of the orchestra in the *lager*: "We can't ... we can't really and truly wish to please them" (48). As twelve thousand people are being gassed daily, Fania wonders whether her art elevates the soul or is primarily a tool for collaboration.

Shmuel, the Jewish electrician of the men's camp, is the voice of conscience who tips the scales for Fania during her crises of indecision.

Edward R. Isser argues that Shmuel is a prophetic, mystical figure with antecedents in Hasidic literature.[40] In a microcosm seemingly devoid of God's presence, Shmuel urges Fania to be God's witness and maintain the humanism necessary to sustain meaningful survival. His first pronouncement to Fania, "Live!" (33), comes directly after Fania is spat upon and thus develops doubts about her complicity with the Nazis. Upon their next encounter, Fania asks Shmuel why he has chosen her as the conduit, and he replies, "Oh, I always know who to pick! Someone has to see this. Someone has to remember. And it is you" (39). This comment is reminiscent of what Elzvieta later says about Fania's humanistic perspective on life: "You are someone to trust, Fania ... maybe it's that you have no ideology. You're satisfied just to be a person. One senses so much feeling in you" (64). Susan C. W. Abbotson comments that Shmuel's job as an electrician is to fix wires and shed light, that is, make connections; as such, he connects with Fania and makes certain that she stays focused in trying to make her humanistic vision contagious.[41] Shmuel implies that Fania plays a pivotal role in bearing witness as a survivor and should not agonize over whether she is prostituting her art in collaborating with the Nazis in order to survive.

The artistic culture that coincides with Fania's humanism allows her to consider the Nazis as human rather than as evil monsters. For example, Frau Mandel views Alma and Fania as talented musicians yet subhuman according to Nazi standards. Esther reproaches Fania for not recognizing Mandel as an anti-Semitic murderer, to which Fania responds, "Don't try to make her ugly, Esther. She's beautiful and human. What disgusts me is that a woman so beautiful can do what she is doing" (42). Fania begins to understand the crux of her dilemma, which becomes Miller's seminal focus of the play: culture is purposeful for those who value its humanistic perspective. As an existentialist, Miller adopts Sartre's viewpoint that the choices one makes may be based upon *mauvaise foi*, or flaws in human nature. Fania, like Miller, is uncomfortable with the simplistic notion that the Nazis are not human because their actions are inhumane. All humans share the capacity for good or evil, depending upon the choices they make in life. Even Fania has the potential for being one of the collaborators through her acquiescence. However, Fania learns that art, when used to promulgate humanism, is a means to transcendence and moral absolution. Fania's humanistic spirit transmitted to her colleagues actually saves her life, for when she is semi-conscious and ill with typhus, her friends carry her to safety upon liberation. Fania's ultimate vindication is her memoir, which subsequently resulted in Miller's play, demonstrating the humanistic power of art to release the imaginative ability to bear witness and thus codify the chaos of the Holocaust.

French dramatist Liliane Atlan's *Monsieur Fugue ou le mal de terre* (*Mister Fugue or Earth Sick*), a one-act play written in eight days, was first performed under Roland Monod's direction in 1967 at the Comédie de Saint-Étienne and then was staged in the fall of that year at the Théâtre National Populaire in Paris. In 1972, *Monsieur Fugue*, which ran five months at the Habimah Theatre in Tel Aviv, won the Prix du Théâtre Habimah and the Prix Morderaï Anielowicz. The play has been produced in Poland, in the United States (New York University), and by L'Union des Etudiants Juifs de France (27 October 2004).

In 1932, Atlan, née Cohen, was born to Jewish parents who had left Salonika, Macedonia, to settle in France. As non-natives of France, the family was subject to deportation after the German occupation. Liliane and her younger sister Rachel were sent into hiding in Auvergne and then Lyon. Since Rachel had Jewish features, the two sisters were confined to home for fear of being discovered. Only twelve years old, Liliane began improvising performances: "We had to entertain ourselves. My sister would dress up, would disguise herself. She was the audience. I was the stage: the actors, the author."[12] All of Liliane's grandmother's family had perished in the Holocaust. Her brother was deported to Auschwitz but miraculously escaped. After he returned and told Liliane (then reunited with her parents in Montpellier) about the horrors of the extermination camp, she felt guilty about surviving in relative safety while her brother suffered; Liliane, then sixteen, became anorexic. While studying to be a French teacher, she was trying to come to grips with the philosophical ramifications of the Holocaust and thus turned to Hebrew texts, such as the Talmud, the Midrash, and the Kabbala, which serve as the foundations for several of her plays.

Mister Fugue demonstrates the power of the creative imagination to assuage the imposing terror of the Shoah. Four children–Yossele, Raissa, Iona, and Abracha–climb out of a sewer in an unspecified ghetto that has been in flames for eight days. They carry a doll to recall their four-year-old friend Tamar, who has since died at the hands of the vanquishers. The children are war-ravaged, bedraggled, in rags, and seem to be savages. Like animals, the children are loaded onto a barbed wire cage on the back of a truck heading for the fictional Rotburg, the Valley of Bones, where they are to be murdered, then cremated. The journey is to take one hour in the fog and mist, which is approximately the time span of the play. Grol, the slow-witted sergeant who has been baiting children to their immediate deaths, feels guilty about his past transgressions and has a change of heart, volunteering to accompany the children to Rotburg.[43] The adolescents thus refer to Grol as Mister Fugue, a reference to what they believe must be his disturbed state of consciousness in fleeing from his proscribed duties.

Mister Fugue has its antecedents in the work of Gatti and Antonin Artaud, two playwrights Atlan has revealed as influences on her writing.[44] Much of *Mister Fugue* is modeled upon the way Gatti mixes scenic time–interspersing past, present, and future–to violate the realistic conventions of the theater. The dialogue Atlan employs is often similar to the surrealists' random juxtaposition of images, as represented in a play such as Artaud's *Jet du Sang*. Bettina Knapp writes that Atlan's visceral theater, designed to shock the spectator, is distinctly Artaudian.[45] Atlan's predisposition toward the irrational in violation of the principles of a Cartesian universe suggests the influence of the surrealists, or possibly the pataphysics of Alfred Jarry or Eugène Ionesco. Atlan's cynical tone and her preoccupation with the absurdity of existence also reminds one of Beckett's theater. Moreover, the archetypal journey from within the souls of the children to Rotburg, literally a place to die at the hands of a nebulous enemy during an unnamed time, intimates the mythical aspect of theater of the absurd. On the other hand, Jewish children suffering at the hands of an army destroying their homes and then exterminating them represents the verisimilitude of Holocaust theater.

The children, wise beyond their chronological years and very street-smart, abandon all vestiges of their religious world to rely solely on culture, transmitted through their story telling. With religion having failed them, Iona is mocked for praying "to a shit god."[46] The children wonder how God could allow such atrocities to go unchecked, the prayer machine now broken when, for example, Abracha's grandfather was sent to his death. Abracha states, "Or when they split my sister's kidneys with a hatchet, it gushed over everything, he's red all over, our merciful God, and I piss on him" (64). Raissa recalls a dancer who was gunned down by the soldiers while reciting psalms reserved for the Day of Atonement. With regard to her own imminent death, Raissa laments, "I don't understand why God does dirt to children" (103). Yossele questions the efficacy of an absent deity, concluding, "He's sick, our good God" (66). Abracha suggests the irony of even asking for God's attention: "If you don't call him, then God, he can't guess that you need him. He's an old schmuck" (72). The children laugh at the absurdity of the sordidness of a god-forsaken world—a brutal, hollow, mirthless laugh that Peter Barnes would indeed find offensive as an extraneous gesture. Even before Christopher, the commanding officer, shoots Iona and then has the children bury him, Iona recites a prayer for the dead—cynical yet comically sarcastic: "Blessed art Thou, Lord of the Worlds, who did not give them time to grow rotten from being too old" (92). The children invoke the spirit of the Golem, an automaton-like figure in Hebrew folklore without a soul. Judith Morganroth Schneider perceptively notes, "Because the sewer children have been violently degraded, especially in the Jewish part of their identity, they identify with the soulless, destructive Golem and irreverently parody sacred texts."[47] What little these children have seen of life has made them "earth-sick." In her introduction to the English version of the play, Elinor Fuchs writes about Atlan's cynicism: "Religion, hope, aspiration, the value of achievement, a belief in order, in human goodness—the entire realm of the 'ideal' is despoiled" (xv). *Mister Fugue* is acerbic and abrasive in Atlan's challenge to the fundamental philosophical principles of Western society. One cannot but wonder if such nihilism was derived from Artaud's Gnosticism.

The children occupy themselves with tales of the imagination that serve to negate the traumatic effects of the Holocaust. Vivian M. Patraka comments, "In opposition to the social that has been annihilated in material terms, they [the children] depict the creation of imagined socialities of 'Jewishness' in resistance to a fascist discourse that erases and defiles."[48] Atlan presents a situation that is much more dire than that represented in the Vilna ghetto by Sobol, or even in Auschwitz in *Playing for Time*, for in *Mister Fugue*, the children are going directly to their deaths without chance of egress, unlike the former two plays where death may have been imminent but was still unassured. In the most brutal scenario possible, the children play charades of events occurring in better times. As the children move from one tale to another and become various characters in different times and places, the effect resembles the transformational techniques Joseph Chaikin introduced in his Open Theater workshops of the early 1960s. The effect is to defy the linearity of realistic theater, moving into the interchangeable realm of time and space that Gatti preferred. The omnipresent reality of the seemingly long ride to death is thus obliterated by past and future tales that make the present a silent absence.

Mister Fugue personifies the importance of cultural transmission in a genocide designed to eradicate all traces of Jewish culture. Through the imaginative visions of a culture transmitted to them by their parents, the children maintain their humanity in the worst possible circumstances. Tamar functions like Srulik's dummy, allowing the "ventriloquist" a catharsis, this time in the form of an admission of fear with regard to the effects of the devastation in an unspeakably bleak wasteland. For example, Iona hums a lullaby to Tamar: "Don't tremble, don't tremble, it's not really cold. Here, the cart won't take you away" (61); the children soothe Tamar–a self-reflective imaginative act. They fantasize about school (a much happier idyllic time), sing raucous songs, laugh at their plight, mime the selection process familiar to all engaged in ghetto roundups, fantasize about being wealthy and living in palaces, gorge their emaciated bodies on visions of sumptuous meals, and Raissa dreams of her future marriage to Yossele. Amidst the urban blight, the children turn to exquisite visions of nature, particularly the sea and sky. Grol is depicted as a type of Messiah, taking the children to the Promised Land. Even at the end of the journey to Rotburg, when they disembark to face death, Abracha and Raissa are preparing for the opera. Raissa's last words before the cremation suggest the efficacy of art's metaphoric power as diversion from the inevitability of death: "It's good, going away" (104). Atlan admits that she was trying to recreate the capacity to marvel that she saw in the Jews of Theresienstadt, who never stopped writing poetry, performing plays, or composing music until their deaths.[49] By the end of the journey, the children age dramatically as if to suggest that all of life has been played out performing their fantasies en route to Rotburg; as Fuchs suggests, "life has been performed ... and exhausted" (xv).

Grol's tales, devoid of the imaginative spirit of his captive audience, are too literal for the children. At first, he recounts sentimental stories about ghetto life and his role as exterminator. Gradually, Grol's vision becomes more tinged with the morbid reality the children intuitively understand, eventually expressed metaphorically: "Death, she's an old woman, she has a pinched nose, yellow lips, her skin is brown, creviced, as though she'd already become earth" (88). His noble sacrifice becomes all the more significant as he makes the children feel at ease by playing roles in their fantasies and asking them questions about Jewish lore and biblical traditions.

With its slow destruction of innocent children, *Mister Fugue* is a harrowing drama, one that is difficult to watch. Although the term "Nazi" is not referred to anywhere in the play, thus universalizing the genocide, Atlan's drama is endemic to the Holocaust experience. Edward R. Isser argues that Atlan's decision to represent the sadistic behavior of the Germans throws the play out of balance.[50] Christopher hits Raissa with a stick, shoots Grol in the leg, murders Iona and makes the children bury him, and throws the Tamar doll under the truck. His gripe against the children is their use of culture, not as a panacea for the Holocaust, but as a temporary distraction from the reality of death. He tells Grobbe, "You don't understand. They're resisting us, from the inside" (84). The play begins with the ghetto in flames and ends with the fire of the crematoria; instead of Atlan toning down the genocide, as Isser would suggest, she reinforces it to remind us of the ubiquitous terror. In between the two fires, we are presented with what Robert Skloot has described as images of "childhood defiled in the Nazi land of fog and flame."[51] In short, Atlan presents culture (the fugue), in the form of a polyphonic cacophony of tales, temporarily mitigating the genocide (earth-sick) that she reminds us is always omnipresent.

4   The Holocaust as Literature of the Body

Hitler left school in 1905 without completing his final examinations and thus without receiving a diploma. He was adept at freehand drawing but excelled only in gymnastics. Hitler's focus on the body rather than the intellect or the arts would become a key issue in the Nazi agenda. In his first major public address, on 13 August 1920 in Munich, Hitler extolled the virtues of economic reform and claimed that the Jews degraded and exploited labor.[1] This was the first association of National Socialism with labor and the disassociation of Jews with hard work, which was to become one of the major tenets of *Mein Kampf* and later of the Nazi party. During the Weimar Republic, Jews were over-represented in trade, finance, commerce, the arts, and the sciences yet under-represented in agriculture and industry, the occupations associated with manual labor. The Jews were thus branded as shirking physical labor and incapable of doing honest work, nothing more than a liability to the prosperity of the state. During the latter stages of the Depression, Hitler stressed the need for manual labor, excluding the Jews as subalterns with regard to his future for Germany; the Jews were put in the same category as people with mental health problems, homosexuals, and those with physical disabilities, all of whom were seen as biologically crippling to the Reich. For example, the Hitler Youth movement had as its guiding principle the idea that the body of each child belongs to the nation, and thus each boy or girl was responsible for maintaining a healthy body. Hitler stressed twice daily compulsory physical education for youths, with particular emphasis on boxing for boys–a sport that he believed developed aggressive tendencies and improved agility and dexterity.[2] Moreover, the Reich

Physician actually published several hygienic duties to be followed by each child, including such mandates as exercising, eating plenty of fruits and vegetables, drinking fruit juices while avoiding coffee, shunning alcohol and nicotine, getting at least nine hours of sleep nightly, practicing first aid, and maintaining healthy teeth.[3]

During the 1930s, the Nazis were becoming increasingly anti-intellectual while focusing their priorities on the body. The SS, considered first and foremost to be an elite fighting force of warriors, glorified in living by the body's crude claims, not by cultural compulsions. Goebbels himself adopted the credo, "when I hear the word 'culture,' I reach for my gun."[4] Hitler mocked the Boy Scouts as effeminate, claiming that the Hitler Youth movement stressed discipline and physical activity. Meanwhile, the Nazis staged book-burning rallies, raided art galleries, and as they purged Jews of all academic and professional positions, destroyed the intellectual integrity of the majority of German institutions.

After the passage of the Nuremberg laws, Jews were viewed as impure bodies threatening the health of the Volk. Sexual contact with Jews was strictly forbidden. In the late 1930s, the Jewish body became the object of physical attacks, particularly bearded Jews who were subject to beatings and shavings, the latter a form of emasculation of their manhood. To reinforce the concept of the Jews' aversion to work, the Nazis forced the Jews into labor on the Sabbath and on Rosh Hashonah and Yom Kippur, the Jewish holy days. Although Jews were herded into approximately 1,600 labor camps and ghettoes, very little productive work was done by Jews there.[5] In the occupied territories in eastern Europe, the Nazis forced Jews into meaningless labor, such as having them clean streets with toothbrushes, merely because they believed that Jews doing any type of hard labor went against their natural constitution. Daniel Jonah Goldhagen writes, "In the Germans' minds, to compel Jews to do manual work, or indeed any honest work, was to make them suffer, because it was antithetical to their natures."[6] The labor camps were designed ultimately to enslave Jews so cruelly and recklessly that work became secondary to the goal of systematically forcing Jews to suffer before their deaths; in short, the labor camps were merely a slave system for the purpose of genocide.

The concentration camps were designed to work Jews and other *Häftlinge* to death. The greeting sign in many of the camps, most notably Auschwitz, "Arbeit Macht Frei," was a sarcastic joke for the Nazis, for most of the work accomplished included menial tasks of no significance, such as moving a pile of rocks from one location to another and then back again. The concentration camp experience became an assault on the body. During the deportations, prisoners often were forced to wait in hot or cold weather for hours before the trains were loaded. Then they were herded like cattle into freight cars and suffered during the journey without water or proper sanitation facilities. Charlotte Delbo mentions that many traveled for as much as eighteen days in boxcars, entering the *lager* having "lost their minds."[7] Upon arrival, the Jews had all their possessions removed, including their shoes and clothing; even their names were lost, replaced by a tattooed number. In short, the Nazis deprived Jews of their family, friends, homes, fortunes, and occupations, thereby eradicating the cultural matrix that previously sustained them while leaving the body to suffer. Jews had their hair shorn so that any trace of individuality was erased. Often, their native language, which distinguished a sense of national pride, was lost as well. When they showered for de-licing, the inmates realized that they were left only with their naked bodies. By robbing the prisoners of the respect individuals demand, the Nazis made it easier to treat them brutally.

Concentration and extermination camp life consisted of an unmerciful attack on the body. Intellectuals were treated with contempt by the SS and the kapos, who favored Jews that were laborers by profession. Thus, Jews who did manual labor were more likely to survive camp brutalities–culture even became a liability. As Jean Améry contends, "So it was that in Auschwitz everything intellectual gradually took on a doubly new form: on the one hand, psychologically, it became something completely unreal, and on the other hand, to the extent that one defines it in social terms, a kind of forbidden luxury."[8] Prisoners were subject to constant hunger, thirst, fatigue, and harassment.[9] Giorgio Agambem claims that malnutrition in the camps began with weight loss, muscular asthenia, and dissipation of energy, progressing to the indifferent mechanical gaze of the walking dead.[10]

Typhus, dysentery, and diarrhea continually eroded these bodies. Lice were ubiquitous, serving to spread disease, particularly typhus; most inmates were also covered with fleas and scratched themselves shamelessly. Delbo recalls the effects of disease on the body: "One can turn a human being into a skeleton gurgling with diarrhea, without time or energy to think."[11] Lacking proper medical care, Jews in the extermination camps saw their bodies deteriorate, which made it easier for the carefully groomed, expertly tailored, healthy SS to accept the notion that they were subhuman. This idea is reiterated by Holocaust historian Robert S. Wistrich: "The camps were designed to create a debilitating sense of impotence in their victims, to literally reduce them to *Untermenschen* and thereby remake them in the image of Nazi propaganda."[12] Inmates also were forced to stand outside without outer garments during roll calls that typically lasted for hours, exposing them to brutally cold temperatures, snow, or rain during work details that endured for as much as seventeen hours a day, seven days per week. As punishment, the *Häftlinge* were often forced to remain outside in frigid weather all night without shelter, an experience that taught that in extreme conditions, one's life depended on a strong body.[13]

In the concentration and extermination camps, the body was gradually reduced to excrement. Constantly in a nervous state of mind due to the Nazi administration of excessive brutality and the ever-present threat of "selection" for gassing, Jews were never at ease. Primo Levi mentions that this nervous energy combined with consumption of salty soup forced each inmate to urinate every two or three hours nightly.[14] There was only one bucket for each blockhouse, so by morning, after each prisoner relieved himself, the floor was covered in urine and feces. Allowed to use the latrine only twice a day, inmates had to ask permission if the urgent need arose; there was never any toilet paper. Most of the time, they were forced to relieve themselves in the fields in which they labored, or even in their soup bowls. Prisoners were always inundated with mud, grease, blood, and excrement. Terrence Des Pres admits, "The fact is that prisoners were *systematically* subjected to filth. They were the deliberate target of excremental assault. Defilement was a constant threat, a condition of life from day to day, and at any moment it was liable to take abruptly vicious and sometimes fatal forms."[15] The stench of excrement coupled with the smoke of burning bodies from the crematoria was also unbearable. Many never had a chance to wash except when near muddy water, and those that did not partake of washing soon lost their dignity and died. This relentless excremental assault deprived individuals of their humanity while reducing the body to an object of disgust and self-loathing. As the body erodes, the spirit soon is befouled as well, making survival insurmountable. Des Pres concludes, "When cleanliness becomes impossible and human beings are forced to live in their own excretions, their pain becomes intense to the point of agony. The shock of physical defilement causes spiritual concussion and, simply to judge from the reports of those who have suffered it, subjection to filth seems often to cause greater anguish than hunger or fear of death."[16]

Bodily pain and suffering were typical in the *lager*. For no apparent reason except to inflict suffering, inmates would occasionally be forced to run through a gauntlet of SS armed with striking canes, whips, clubs, straps, belts, or walking sticks. Selective beatings occurred to make examples of prisoners who violated any of the camp rules or who performed subpar work. With the daily toil taking its toll and sleep almost always deprived because of stressful conditions, prisoners were constantly fatigued. Falling prey to fatigue meant being assigned to "sick" blockhouses, where selections were always made for the gas chambers; falling unconscious due to fatigue at roll call was particularly dangerous, for the dogs were trained to sink their fangs into fallen bodies. Life evolved into survival of the body, free from the hindrances of intellect or culture. Torture was always reserved for those who failed to conform to camp decorum. Jean Améry describes the effects of torture on the psyche: "Frail in the face of violence, yelling out in pain, awaiting no help, capable of no resistance, the tortured person is only a body, and nothing else beside that."[17]

Intellect, particularly if divorced from political or religious tenets, was useless in the *lager*, where everything centered around the body. Primo Levi acknowledges that in the camps, thinking was futile because of the predominance of chance dictating life; moreover, thought was deleterious because it kept "alive a sensitivity which is a source of pain."[18] The intellect's imaginative and spiritual powers were slowly eradicated until nothing remained but the body. As Charlotte Delbo realized, "People did not dream in Auschwitz, they were in a state of delirium."[19] Terrence Des Pres agrees with Delbo, arguing that survival was more of a biological imperative than a cultural one.[20] The need to maintain one's dignity and to expect assistance in return in order to survive was a type of behavior that was practical rather than based on reason or intellect. As Des Pres acknowledges, dignity was thus reduced to the only element of life left untouched by the Nazis: "Stripped of everything, prisoners maintained moral identity by holding some inward space of self untouchable, and they did it by the way in which the body itself was carried and cared for."[21]

French playwright Charlotte Delbo's 1966 *Qui rapportera ces paroles?* (*Who Will Carry the Word?*) is a powerful dramatic representation of the abused body in *l'univers concentrationnaire*. The premiere of the play occurred on 14 March 1974 at the Cyrano Théâtre in a production directed by François Darbon. Delbo had joined the Young Communists in 1932, where she met Georges Dudach, whom she married two years later. While studying philosophy at the Sorbonne, she interviewed director Louis Jouvet for Dudach's literary journal, *Cahiers de la jeunesse*. Impressed with the way she captured his dry wit and sense of irony in the published article, Jouvet hired her in 1937 as his administrative assistant. In May 1941, Delbo accompanied Jouvet's theater troupe on a tour of South America. On 15 November 1941, despite Jouvet's strong objections, Delbo returned to France to work with her husband in the Resistance. Charlotte and Georges were arrested by the French police on 2 March 1942 when they were caught printing anti-Nazi leaflets. Both were sent to La Santé prison in Paris. Georges rejected the offer to work for the Nazis in a German labor camp, which would have spared his life, and so was shot on 23 May 1942 at the age of twenty-eight. Delbo was transferred to Romainville prison on 24 August and from there was sent to Auschwitz-Birkenau on 24 January 1943, in a convoy of 230 mostly non-Jewish political prisoners. Delbo remained in Birkenau and then Raisko, a satellite camp two kilometers from Auschwitz, until her transfer to Ravensbrück in January 1944. There she was liberated by the Swedish Red Cross on

23 April 1945 and returned to France two months later.[22] The first volume of her Holocaust trilogy, *Aucun de nous ne reviendra* (*None of Us Will Return*), was written in 1946 when she was still convalescing in a clinic, but Delbo refused publication of the memoir until it had stood the test of time, which, for Delbo, was not until 1965 (Delbo actually promised her Auschwitz compatriots to write about their suffering). The second volume, *Une connaissance inutile* (*Useless Knowledge*), was completed in 1947 and printed in 1970. *Who Will Carry the Word?* is a dramatization of Delbo's remembrances of Auschwitz depicted in these first two novellas. The last book, *Mesure de nos jours* (*The Measure of Our Days*, 1971), rounds out the triptych that was published by Editions de Minuit in 1971 as *Auschwitz et après*.[23]

Delbo's main dilemma in *Who Will Carry the Word?* revolves around the problem of accurate representation of the extermination camp on stage without sensationalizing or trivializing the Holocaust. Delbo's experience under Jouvet's tutelage and her knowledge of Artaud's *mise en scène* provide her with the theatrical skills to stylize the Shoah and still be faithful to the event. Auschwitz is evoked through the use of Artaudian lighting effects and various movements, always slow, to indicate mood. In his introduction to the play, Robert Skloot observes, "Spotlights, sirens, and the gestures of the actors complete the stage effects which impress on the audience the barren and brutal environment of the concentration camp."[24] There are twenty-three women between the ages of twenty-five and thirty in the cast, yet, although Françoise represents Delbo herself, their names, costumes, and faces are irrelevant, for this is a play about the collective spirit of these women to survive.[25] The setting is a desolate landscape, a place beyond the imagination. The structure of the play consists of a prologue and epilogue that bracket twenty-four short scenes in three acts that are performed without intermission.

As the title suggests, *Who Will Carry the Word?* concerns the need to bear witness in a debilitating universe that is eroding the body. As Karein K. Goertz has observed, "The most striking gender marker in Delbo's writing is her attention to the female body as the original site of violation, the repository of memory, and the medium through which the dead speak. The body is the privileged site of remembrance, authenticity, and agency."[26] Most of the women in the play are political dissidents or Resistance fighters who have a rebellious, determined desire to defy the Nazis but are deterred by the demands on the body. Although they each have names, the Nazis have shorn their hair, tattooed them with numbers, and clothed them identically in order to reduce their humanity and turn their bodies into anonymous objects to be eventually discarded. In act one, scene one, Françoise is debating whether to commit suicide or suffer through bodily misery. She clearly indicates that her once-defiant spirit of resistance has now fallen prey to the demands of her body: "I have a choice, between becoming a cadaver which will have suffered for only eight days, which will still be clean enough to look at, and one which will have suffered fifteen days, which will be horrible to look at."[27] Claire reminds Françoise that she is a role model for the younger women who may imitate her suicidal path. Claire admonishes her friend, stating that there must be at least one person to return to bear witness. Yvonne, however, states the case for the deteriorating body replete with dysentery overwhelming the instinct for survival: "You can no longer look at yourself when you gradually dissolve, turning into dirty water, when diarrhea is dripping from you night and day without being able to do anything to stop it, to hide yourself, to wash. I am turning into dirty water" (280). Lawrence L. Langer observed that in Delbo's representation of the Holocaust, living is "merely physical exertion, while dying is the literal defeat of the body."[28] The scene ends with the only saving grace in the play–the ability of the women to help each other to maintain their sense of dignity and drag their bodies through the misery so that at least one of their members can bear witness.

Throughout the play, the women's bodies are constantly being ravaged, with virtually each scene representing a specific type of bodily torture. Jennifer L. Geddes points out that Delbo's main achievement is not passing on knowledge of the camps, but instead helping us see what extreme suffering is like rather than how we might imagine it to be.[29] For example, the cold takes its toll, especially during roll calls, where the women must huddle together and exchange outside places in groups of five to avoid the weather's harshness. Françoise laments, "Here, blades, needles of cold pierce you straight through. Jaws of cold crush you. Cold contracts the fibers of your flesh, even those on the tongue, even those of the heart" (283). In *None of Us Will Return*, Delbo reiterates the effects of cold weather on the prisoners: "The cold bruised our temples, our jaws, making us feel that our bones were about to break, our craniums to burst."[30] Through gestures and movements of the actresses, the audience experiences how the physical pain of cold leads to a private universe of torture and suffering. Vivian M. Patraka explains: "Delbo's evocation of cold in this play amounts to a 'poetics of atrocity'–one that renders through metaphor, works through, tries to measure, however incompletely, the shift in a fundamental understanding of the body, that is, what cold means in the 'other universe' of the concentration camp."[31] Moreover, the physical toll has made the women emotionless, walking over dead bodies like automatons: their spirits have succumbed to bodily pain.

Delbo stresses the dehumanization process of weakening the body until unbearable suffering leads to death. A kapo beats Sylvie for breaking ranks, and when Claire intervenes, her skull is smashed. Elisabeth's legs are swollen, a sign that she has perhaps three days to live. Dédée worked in the cold snow for days, contracting pneumonia and a three-day fever that led to her death. Yvonne says her spirit is broken because her dysentery is draining, and without a chance to wash, she abandons hope: "I look at my body disappearing and I don't care. I only wish it didn't take so long" (300). Aurore dies of thirst, a condition of bodily torture that Delbo so vividly describes in her own memoir, *Auschwitz and After*: "I'd been thirsty for days and days, thirsty to the point of losing my mind, to the point of being unable to eat since there was no saliva in my mouth, so thirsty I couldn't speak, because you're unable to speak when there's no saliva in your mouth. My parched lips were splitting, my gums swollen, my tongue a piece of wood."[32] Other anonymous women are beaten as they run through a row of kapos armed with sticks, whips, and canes; those who stumbled, fell, or did not run fast enough were sent to the notorious Block 25, where they were selected for gassing. Still others are bitten to death when they collapse during roll call, as the dogs are trained to sink their fangs into the necks of the fallen. When typhus attacks the body, the end is near, but Denise admits, "That's the best death here. You're delirious almost immediately and soon fall into a coma" (313). Bodily decay is thus another part of the genocide process specifically designed as one more form of mass execution.

Delbo's play demonstrates how these women lose their sexual identity through bodily decimation. Nazi policy was designed to rid the human body of all visible signs of beauty and pride, turning humans into vermin that begged to be destroyed as threats to a healthy Volk. Delbo, as a student of Jouvet, knew how to make the body malleable enough to express human emotions on stage and thus designed her play as a dirge of the body representing a loss of femininity, which meant diminished sexuality as well. Nicole Thatcher notes that the loss of femininity is concomitant with the prisoners' descent into animality, "penned in sheds, tattooed, beaten, shouted at."[33] Atrocity has desensitized their feminine sense of compassion, making these women lose their vitality and spirit. Their natural sense of nurturing is negated when the women must watch in frustration as their loved ones are sent to their deaths without any possibility of being able to offer comfort or support. Nicole Thatcher remarks, "The appearance of the body plays an important role in women's cultural framework; the numerous descriptions of women's physical state or clothes indicate Delbo's feminine awareness."[34] The women become sexless, a shell of their former fondly remembered femininity. Françoise realizes that her shorn hair and decrepit body have made her sexless, and Yvonne, in response, muses, "If the men who loved us could see what has become of us" (275). The loss of a woman's hair was particularly demeaning as a deprivation of femininity. These women can only dream of their idyllic past when they had control of their own bodies and therefore could maintain their sexual identities.

After seventy days, only three women remain alive of the two hundred deported: Denise, Françoise, and Gina. Through sheer attrition of bodies, the audience realizes that this play reflects a literature of the body, now personified by the absent body. Gina is forced to join the White Kerchief Kommando, a unit that undresses children, sprinkles them with gasoline, and then burns them to death in a ditch. Instead, Gina decides to commit suicide by running for the electrified barbed wire, knowing that she will be shot en route. Gina's suicide is a means to preserve dignity in a wasteland–the only meaningful death in a moral microcosm that otherwise slowly destroys the body.

Françoise, alias Delbo, poses the quintessential question concerning the body's survival: "What defense do we have against cold, against contagion, against lice, against filth, against thirst, against hunger, against fatigue, that overwhelming fatigue?" (290). Gina also views the dilemma as essentially corporeal: "We must not permit them to triumph over our corpses" (290). Terrence Des Pres argued that survival in the *lager* depended on forms of social bonding to maintain the dignity necessary to negate the assault on the body.[35] Although the Nazis tried to erase individuality in the camps, Delbo, whose emphasis is on group survival, nevertheless refuses to see these women as an anony-mass, making sure that they are referred to by name. Each woman has her own distinct past and her own sense of beauty. Although all of these women have been members of the Resistance, they survive not through individual heroism, which would be a futile gesture, but through solidarity expressed physically by means of bodily support. Vivian M. Patraka relates this sense of bonding to the title of the play: "The trope of carrying extends to visual figuration since the women carry, support each other psychically, morally, and physically as in the roll call scenes where whoever falls is killed."[36] Using a choral structure of voices to represent group solidarity, Delbo emphasizes the importance of human connections so that at least one person will survive. The women offer varied forms of physical contact as a means of bonding and sharing. During the roll call, *"They all rub their arms, rub each other's backs, huddle close to one another, etc."* (283). After the roll call, *"They walk painfully, giving each other assistance, often two by two"* (288). Françoise describes the "hands-on" camaraderie of the women as a saving grace:

> I mean those who practically carried me in their arms when I
> couldn't walk, those who gave me their tea when I was choking
> from thirst when my tongue was like a piece of rough wood in
> my mouth, those who touched my hand and managed to form
> a smile on their chapped lips when I was desperate, those who
> picked me up when I fell in the mud when they were so weak

themselves, those who took my feet in their hands at night
when we were going to sleep, and who blew on them when I felt
they had begun to freeze. (317)

Rosette C. Lamont agrees that the prisoners fight the deterioration
of the body with bodily solidarity: "Their own may be doomed to
extinction by the master plan of the 'heroes' of the new order, but it
is against that order that the women form a living chain, each link a
body."[37] The women often speak of their misery in the collective "we;"
despite the fact that each woman was a hero of the Resistance, their
plight is shared as a collective body.

In the last scene of the play, Denise and Françoise, the only two
women left alive, announce their return from living hell. They realize that language is incapable of conveying such bodily pain and torture. Moreover, their actual presence indicates that the impossibility
of survival must be questioned by any disbelievers. Françoise understands that the audience will be hesitant to accept ghosts who returned
without the linguistic ability to explain the Holocaust. Nevertheless,
despite Adorno's admonition that language is inadequate to convey
the terror of the Shoah, Delbo's play is life-affirming: Denise and
Françoise have kept their promise to bear witness for those who cannot. Moreover, Delbo's play becomes the fulfilled promise to her own
colleagues who died at Auschwitz.

Who Will Carry the Word? is a major theatrical achievement.
Despite the fact that the concentrationary camp experience is impossible to replicate in the theater, Delbo manages to succeed without
depicting a Nazi on stage or dramatizing visible death. As in Greek
theater, all of the violence remains off stage. She avoids literal representation of the camp through the use of lighting and movement of the
characters. Kerchiefs solve the problem of shaved heads. The play is
somber, grotesque, poignant, yet somehow nightmarish and unreal–
all conveyed through stylized lighting effects, gray or muted colors,
and orchestrated movements that defy realism or melodrama. The
dialogue is ascetic yet poetic, as if to convey a sustained, somber rhythmic monologue of the body. Although there are twenty-four scenes,
they flow as one austere unit. In short, Delbo studied with Jouvet, one

of the great theater directors of the twentieth century, so she knew what would work on the boards and was thus most qualified to "carry the word" to theater audiences.

French playwright Michel Vinaver's *Par-dessus bord* (*Overboard*), which ostensibly does not appear to be a Holocaust drama, is implicitly concerned with the Nazi association of the Jewish body with excrement. Vinaver, née Grinberg, whose parents were Russian Jews who emigrated to France, fled with his family to the Free Zone during the German occupation. In April 1941, Vinaver, the teenager, sailed with his family to New York to avoid Nazi persecution. By the time Vinaver had completed *Par-dessus bord* in 1969 after two years of work on the play, he had already been an employee for sixteen years with Gillette, was married, and was raising four children. Vinaver began his tenure with Gillette as an administrator supervising four people in Annecy, became managing director of Gillette Belgium in 1960, managing director of Gillette France in 1966, and was influential in Gillette's acquisition of S. T. Dupont, which finally occurred in 1970; he then became managing director of Dupont until his resignation in 1978. Vinaver's business background and his concomitant growth as a playwright during the 1960s is significant because it serves as the foundation for Passemar's conflict of interest in *Overboard*.

Par-dessus bord, 250 pages upon completion, was rejected for publication by Jacques Lemarchand, Gallimard's drama editor. The play was published by L'Arche in 1972, but its production was problematic. *Par-dessus bord* contained twenty-nine different locales, several music and dance interludes, and fifty characters; the play's running time was eight to nine hours. Director Roger Planchon, who decided to stage the play in the manner of a 1940s American musical, persuaded Vinaver to prepare a shorter version.[38] Being an astute businessman and marketing analyst, Vinaver, despite his reservations, drastically cut the play to three hours, although he added several music and dance routines. Planchon mounted the play at the Théâtre National Populaire in Villeurbanne in March 1973 and then at the Théâtre National de l'Odéon in Paris during May 1974. The full-length version was staged by Charles Joris at the Théâtre Populaire Romand in La Chaux-de-Fonds, Switzerland, premiering on 3 June 1983. In a production directed by

Sam Walters, *Overboard* was given its first British performance at the Orange Tree Theatre in Richmond on 2 October 1997.

Overboard reflects Vinaver's search for new forms of theater, discarding, or "throwing overboard" the conventions of drama. Eschewing plot, character, and direct discourse, *Overboard* instead has a polyphonic structure in which scenes and diction overlap to produce a rhythm similar to a musical score. Vinaver discards every form of punctuation in the play except the question mark, thus providing actors with the chance to construct their own rhythms from the stream-of-consciousness dialogue. Vinaver has stated that he uses words like a painter employs line and color, or a musician composes notes.[39] In *Les Travaux et les jours*, Vinaver admitted that his penchant for form and rhythm gave him a closer likeness to painters and composers rather than to writers.[40] Like a symphony that produces a multitude of sounds, *Overboard* juxtaposes various images of low and high culture, from the mythical to the banal, thus offering varied interpretations of events rather than the traditional single meaning. Vinaver remarks that *Overboard*'s structure of six "movements," rather than acts or scenes, was borrowed from the comedies of Aristophanes and took the form of "transgressions, combat, agon, counter-transgression, feast, and marriage."[41] However, although the Aristophanic structure would seem to lead to linearity, Vinaver favors a choral effect in which strands are interwoven, thus making a single interpretation problematic. Instead, this polyvalent form, which borrows the Brechtian notion of distancing through interruptions that negate Aristotelian unities, allows motifs to merge, overlap, and penetrate each other. This merging and overlapping of themes is important since the Holocaust is not the dominant motif of the play. However, an awareness of Vinaver's technique leads us to understand how images of the Shoah are embedded in the play's contrapuntal structure.

Vinaver claims that his starting point is always banality within disorder, a style designated as theater of the quotidian.[42] Vinaver recalls that as a child, he was astonished when permitted to do simple things, such as open a door, run, or stop running, and feared that these basic rights might be withdrawn.[43] David Bradby comments about the quotidian as Vinaver's starting point for writing: "Almost obsessively, he insists upon the banality, the ordinariness, the absolute flatness of the material from which he begins."[44] Vinaver deems magma, the tediousness and banality of everyday life, as the essence of existence. He states, "The landscapes which help us recognize ourselves, to position ourselves in the world, are obliterated by the 'magma' of everyday life."[45] Vinaver uses the quotidian as a means to decipher life's intricacies because he believes that history emerges from day-to-day magma. Gideon Lester, who translated *Par-dessus bord* into English, notes, "Although his themes are inherently political–unemployment, the growth of capitalism, the demise of the nuclear family–Vinaver is no ideologue, rather an observer and compulsive classifier of the minutiae of daily existence."[46] *Overboard* inundates the audience with the magma of everyday life as the professional world of big business conflates with the personal lives of the characters, allowing us to establish connections between the two seemingly disparate microcosms.

Nothing is more quotidian than excrement and anality. *Overboard* describes the competitive corporate challenges facing Ravoire et Dehaze, a French company manufacturing toilet paper. Passemar, a Shakespearean, buffoonlike narrator, provides a running commentary of the French firm's capitalistic ventures.[47] The six movements of the play take us through the various stages of the toilet paper company's development. Passemar learns that Ravoire et Dehaze's sales have been dropping while the family-based corporation is feeling the pressure from its chief competitor, United Paper Company, an American firm manufacturing "softies." Ravoire et Dehaze tries to meet the challenge by repackaging the toilet paper in red, white, and blue wrappers, to appeal to the spirit of French nationalism. When this policy fails miserably, the bank agrees to bail them out if changes in management are forthcoming. Ravoire et Dehaze makes staff changes, treating human beings as disposables along the way. Executives and sales personnel who have been with the company for years are now seen as expendable (thrown overboard), providing Vinaver with the opportunity to conflate capitalistic enterprise with excrement. Eventually, all of the marketing and personnel changes are moot, as the American company decides to buy Ravoire et Dehaze as its own profitable subsidiary.

Overboard presents a literature of the body in the way Vinaver both describes how Jews were treated as excrement by the Nazis and then uses this motif to embed the idea of anality as an excremental assault on the audience. Moreover, as Anne Ubersfeld has realized, Vinaver's play equates money with defecation, since Ravoire et Dehaze's profits from their toilet paper sales depend upon an understanding of bodily excretion.[48] Excrement neither functions as symbol nor allegory but rather as a quotidian, literal representation of how its production is directly related to corporate profits, thus also equating the pleasure of defecating with the joy of profitability. Furthermore, Vinaver extends the imagination to 1968, the time of the writing as well as the time of the play's action, which Rosette C. Lamont reminds us was a pivotal year in French politics; thus, Vinaver implies that the student revolution, pinpointed by a psychologist in the play, was nothing more than "collective defecation."[49]

In a perceptive essay, Michael David Fox argues that *Overboard* stages the Holocaust by producing an excremental assault on the audience. Fox qualifies the comparison: "This excremental assault does not, of course, begin to compare with what was done to the Jews in the Holocaust. It does, however, create for the spectator a sense of forced immersion in the excremental."[50] Vinaver contrasts two Jewish characters in the play: the elderly Cohen, who rose through the ranks to become the company's chief accountant, and Alex Klein, an Auschwitz survivor. Throughout the play, Cohen tells stories about his Jewish heritage and is referred to only by his distinctly Jewish last name; as a matter of fact, we never find out his first name. Cohen has prospered in the business world through assimilation, loyalty, and by following orders. Fox infers that by living by his wits, Cohen is reminiscent of the Old World European Jew surviving in the ghetto as a marginalized individual.[51] On the other hand, the much less religious Alex is referred to only by his first name, almost as if his last name, and concomitantly his heritage, has been obliterated. As a toddler, Alex accompanied his parents to Auschwitz. His mother, a noted concert pianist, was placed in the Auschwitz brothel and was spared the gas chamber because the commandant, an ardent music lover, summoned her from the brothel twice each week to play Mozart sonatas for him.

Alex discusses the death of his father in Auschwitz: "They shot my father with several others while they were shitting in the latrines they reckoned that it was taking too long my father was a distinguished Latin scholar specialising in early Roman history in his youth he was also a famous football player."[52] Alex is now a jazz musician who runs his own Montmartre nightclub that caters to an immigrant clientele of blacks and Arabs. Unlike Cohen, Alex is glib and nihilistic, yet adaptable to change. When the nightclub falters as free jazz becomes unfashionable, Alex transforms the business to center on his girlfriend Jiji's "happenings" as the primary means of entertainment. Moreover, as Kevin Elstob has realized, Alex, in his music that appeals to marginalized individuals, and through the unconventional artistry of his "happenings," will fit into a company such as Ravoire et Dehaze, which now must throw "overboard" their traditional means of doing business if they want to survive.[53]

Ravoire et Dehaze becomes acquainted with Alex through Jiji, the beatnik daughter of sales representative Lubin. Ravoire et Dehaze begins to view Alex as an icon of the perfect manager who can adapt to an environment of constant change, which earmarks the business landscape. Moreover, Alex's cynicism and intellectualism (he is also a brilliant mathematician) make him the ideal management type, somewhat of a carbon copy of Vinaver himself. Alex's jazz, which includes intervals of saxophone, flute, and drum renditions, is much like Vinaver's own symphonic compositional style of playwriting. However, the underlying reason for bringing Alex into middle management of Ravoire et Dehaze is his survival in Auschwitz, where he was treated as excrement, even watching his father perish in the feces of a latrine. Since there was no toilet paper in Auschwitz, which Alex describes as his "childhood playground" (89), he obviously lived in excrement. Reszanyi, a psycho-sociologist hired by Ravoire et Dehaze to conduct a motivational study, says, "At an early age children pass through a phase in which the libido is concentrated in the anal region the child experiences poo-poo as its own child or creation" (91). Apparently, Alex, the product of excremental assault in Auschwitz (as Des Pres would have it), has never been able to abandon this anal stage. Moreover, Reszanyi concludes, "money is nothing but fecal matter expressed in a form which need not be repressed because it has been deodorised dehydrated and polished to a shine" (91). Thus, the executives at Ravoire et Dehaze view Alex as the personification of the motivated piece of excrement needed to explicate the intricacies of the toilet paper industry. Although Alex's excrement is associated with pain and suffering, the managers at Ravoire et Dehaze tend to ignore that aspect and focus on its association with business and profit mongering. When Alex accepts the position, his speech stresses excrement linked with misery and death: "My father died falling backwards into a pool of shit pushed by an SS officer and now I'm" (136). The audience instead refuses to listen, urging Alex to speak louder while drowning him out with their mundane conversations.

Alex's girlfriend Jiji participates in "happenings," a type of performance art created by Clas Oldenburg in the 1960s.[54] Jill describes one such "happening": "Two people are holding my head and the third unfolds and sharpens a cutthroat razor he shaves me my hair falls in the pool together with all sorts of other things from the other actions which slowly fill the pool up" (54). For Alex, the image of shaved heads recalls Auschwitz, particularly his own mother's bald skull (55), and the operative word "action" reminds him of the Nazi *Aktion* in the Ukrainian city of Lvov. The improvised "happenings" performed by Jiji transform for Alex into the "unconnected episodes" (55) of the Nazi *Aktionen*; there is much resemblance here, for the *Aktionen* seemed to be spontaneous and without cause, and thus were typically initiated to keep Jews off balance and confused. With "happening" now equated with *"Aktion"* in Alex's mind, he describes the brutality of Nazi genocide in Lvov.[55] After his graphic description of the *Aktionen*, the banker Ausange comments on lending Ravoire et Dehaze money: "You asked me for two or three million we feel you need six million" (57). The reference to the six million Jews murdered during the Holocaust follows Alex's discourse on genocide in Lvov. With the excrement associated with the Shoah equated with capital, and with the traditional stereotype of the Jew as capitalist, it is clear that Alex is the ideal person to market toilet paper for Ravoire et Dehaze.

Much of the play concerns the association of excrement and capital, which becomes subliminally related to Alex's managerial capability. The toilet paper manufactured by Ravoire et Dehaze is insufficient, thus hurting the company's sales. Mme. Alvarez tells Passemar that even the expensive Excelsior toilet paper "disintegrates and everything's left in your hands" (9). Ravoire et Dehaze hire an American marketing firm to help them reassess the precise function of their sales product. Jack Donohue and Jenny Frankfurter try to make business manager Benoît Dehaze realize that understanding excrement is tantamount to improving sales. Jenny tells Benoît that the company's notion of its toilet paper is too abstract and remote; instead, the company must sell some emotion, "Beginning with the act of shitting" (62). Jenny encourages Benoît to view defecation as a pleasurable act, which would help market their product: "The feeling you get when you take a shit Ben if you'd make the effort and concentrate on the feeling of the stuff passing through the anus ultimately becoming detached" (78–79). Jack convinces Benoît "That shitting is a pleasure" (79), and although toilet paper is merely an aid to the joy of defecation, Jack claims, "It's our job to infuse this aid with all the symbols of a pleasure made even more desirable by being forbidden" (79). Jack and Jenny even engage Ravoire et Dehaze executives in a spontaneously arranged guided tour of the anus, posing questions about its function, its location, its description, and its product, which Jenny assures the managers is "An ore from which you'll extract enormous wealth" (75). Meanwhile, as Michael David Fox suggests, the Holocaust connection with excrement becomes explicitly denotative through Jenny's persona: "The shaved head of Alex's mother is counterpointed not only with Jiji's shaved head, but also with the shaved head of American marketing consultant, Jenny Frankfurter."[56] Ravoire et Dehaze also unleash market researchers who ask their customers about lavatory facilities, bowel movements, diarrhoea, constipation, stool odor, and activities engaged in while on the toilet (64).

Ravoire et Dehaze decide that part of their marketing strategy will be to come to terms with excrement in an attempt to demystify it for their customers. Psycho-sociologist Reszanyi tries to make the bathroom a familiar place through common linguistic identification: "The lexical distribution of names attributed to the place of evacuation is striking the loo the lavatory the john the smallest room the toilet the w.c. the little boys' room where can I wash my hands" (93). The marketing strategists plan to disassociate guilt from potty training and then convince the customers that Ravoire et Dehaze's product is akin to anal eroticism. After brainstorming about dozens of names for a new brand of toilet paper, the executives arrive at "Moss and Heather." David Bradby observes that the name "is the one finally chosen for its ability to encapsulate the myth of cleanliness and release associated with nature."[57] The idea is to sell more toilet paper by associating excrement with natural bodily functions.

Throughout the play, the audience is subliminally reinforced with the Rabelaisian notion that the theater of excrement is a literature of the body.[58] Writing about Planchon's production at the Odéon, John Burgess remarked that the set consisted of "huge toilet rolls in deep glowing purple,"[59] reinforcing our immersion in excrement. Even when the focus is not explicitly on toilet paper, many of the references are scatological. For example, Cohen tells Fernand Dehaze, "for the last two months there's been a considerable outflow and very little coming in" (29). Ravoire et Dehaze's management is vividly portrayed by their employees: "They're arseholes" (15). Benoît's wife Margery describes her husband's adjustment to the company's new management style: "You bug the shit out of me with your in the swing and go with the flow" (23). Passemar depicts the dance of the choreography of Professor Onde's tale about the death of Baldr and the struggle between the Ases and the Vanes as "scatological" and full of "all the crap to come" (73). Product manager Peyre, upon listening to marketing analysts Donohue and Frankfurter extol the virtues of defecation, remarks, "I'm sorry but to watch yourself dropping a turd in the bowl isn't exactly a transcendental moment" (76). Jenny then reprimands Peyre for feeling guilty about "having fiddled around with your shit with no end of pleasure" (77). Peyre then asks Jenny, "Have you finished?" and she retorts, "Did you hear that? 'Have you finished?' Those are the words his mother used when he wouldn't get off the potty" (77). Benoît interjects with, "I don't see any deep intuition in all this crap" (77). Jack, the American, is even more blunt about the need for Ravoire et Dehaze to appeal to the consumer's susceptibility to the pleasures of defecation:

> the consumer is basically a great mouth and a great arse stuff has to go in and it's got to come out and where it comes out is what interests us Saint Augustine said *"inter urinas et faeces nascimur"* we are born between urine and faeces everything is concentrated in a couple of square inches suffering love ecstasy and filth we come out from there and it comes out of us and then we wipe man is an animal that wipes after shitting you find me one other animal that wipes. (102)

Even a benign character such as Father Motte keeps the emphasis on the scatological: when talking about birth control, he states, "Filth and dereliction the pill is the excrement of our civilisation" (23), and then comments that the pope's encyclical "Is an attempt at stopping this diarrhoea" (24). Finally, if the audience somehow overlooks these constant subliminal reinforcements, the spectators will certainly get the message when they open up their gift packages that include real moss and heather, as well as a roll of toilet paper packaged with a picture of an idyllic wild forest (115).

The association of Alex's degradation in excrement as an Auschwitz survivor is also subliminally embedded in the play. "Action" (read *"Aktion"*) is the code word that reinforces the image of Alex's defilement in filth and excrement. Benoît asks Jack about the company's potential "course of action" (63). Passemar, writing the play about the demystification of excrement, decides to eliminate the interludes that "interrupt the flow of the action" (65). Peyre describes the marketing of toilet paper as "Action in the offing" (80). Jack, speaking to the executives of Ravoire et Dehaze, explicitly associates the salesmanship of toilet paper with Jewish business sense, thereby linking excrement with Alex:

> JENNY: In the end marketing is everything
> JACK: Which means nothing shit you kids have a hard time shaking up the bugs in your brains unleashing yourselves now stand by here come the Tablets of the Law according to Donohue

and Frankfurter there are seven laws just as there are seven
branches on the candlestick of Moses they're written down on
the sheets which Jenny is handing out now listen. (81)

Alex is to be Ravoire et Dehaze's savior, the new marketing genius
viewed distinctly as the result of the excremental assault on the body.
As if the implicitness of this association is not evident, Vinaver stages
a mock recreation of Auschwitz at Alex's nightclub, interchanged with
a conversation between Benoît and Ausange about corporate takeovers.
Jiji, seated on a swing, shoots a pistol at four of the customers in The
Clinic. Their association with Jews is clear by the stage direction calling them "the four chosen people" (125) involved in *various actions*
(125) in which they are violated by Jiji, who throws objects at them. Jiji
makes the reference to the Holocaust more poignant: "and you cry out
you cry but the world doesn't hear you" (125). This is reminiscent of
Alex's speech about Auschwitz, which goes unheard when he is introduced to the executives at the wedding banquet. After Jiji's "happening" concludes, Alex envisions turning the basement into a stage for
further "happenings." Alex, however, cannot refrain from associating the "happening" with the Nazi *Aktionen*, which means genocide:
"We're going to get up this basement as a gas chamber it's not much of
a job all we need is a few pipes" (128). Meanwhile, Benoît's language
also reflects business as genocide as he discusses the encroachment
of American capitalism on Ravoire et Dehaze: "If we slow down the
Americans will have time to catch their breath and crush us" (128).
Thus, the audience is intuitively and explicitly continually reminded
that Alex, the Holocaust survivor who understands business as becoming one with bodily excrement, will be the ideal manager at Ravoire et
Dehaze.

    Overboard, like Delbo's *Who Will Carry the Word?*, is an
important dramatic achievement relating literature of the body to
the Holocaust. Vinaver's play goes one step further than Delbo's
in the way it relates excremental assault on the body to the modern
corporate body. Michael David Fox's comment is insightful: "As
dramaturgical strategy, much of the play's force comes from the juxtaposition and intersection of the everyday and the banal with the

horrors of the Holocaust.[60] Vinaver focuses on the quotidian in the world of big business to characterize the present plight of modern capitalism. Meanwhile, in the past, the Nazis' reduction of the Jew to excrement, and the concomitant *Aktionen* that initiated Jews to their bodily degradation, is depicted as its own type of banality. Vinaver's play thus allows the audience to witness Alex's smooth transition from the world of past banality to the present state of quotidian free enterprise, as each microcosm is represented as the terrible plight of bodies corrupted by their own waste.

5 Transcending the Holocaust

Most Holocaust playwrights have readily tied the Shoah to political, social, or economic conditions prevailing in Germany during the 1920s and 1930s. Two Holocaust dramas, *Eli* and *The Diary of Anne Frank*, transcend the Holocaust by universalizing the experience, leaving the audience with the philosophical notion that the Shoah was essentially a quasi-moral or religious battleground, a momentary phase of history in which evil temporarily triumphed over good.

German poet and playwright Nelly Sachs emigrated to Stockholm, Sweden, in May 1940 after receiving Nazi orders to report to a forced labor camp. She wrote the verse drama *Eli, Ein Mysterienspiel vom Leiden Israels* (*Eli: A Mystery Play of the Sufferings of Israel*) in 1943 before the culmination of the Final Solution, making it the first Holocaust drama ever written. *Eli* was initially broadcast in Germany as a radio play in 1958 and then premiered on stage in Dortmund in 1961. Courted by the Gesellschaften für Christlich–Jüdische Zusammenarbeit (Societies for Christian-Jewish Cooperation), an organization that tried to maintain a Christian-Jewish dialogue in postwar West Germany, Sachs soon saw her play highly praised by German theater reviewers for its spirit of conciliation.[1] *Eli* has since been staged in Sweden, Great Britain, and the United States, where it premiered in 1981 at the Guthrie Theater in Minneapolis. On 10 December 1966, Sachs and Hebrew writer Samuel Joseph Agnon shared the Nobel Prize in Literature, thus giving Sachs, previously virtually unknown outside of Germany, international recognition as a Holocaust writer who mediated postwar tensions.[2]

Adhering to the Brechtian *gestus* and German expressionist tradition of structuring plays in the form of *stationen, Eli* is composed of seventeen often-isolated episodes. In the expressionist style of Ernst Toller, Georg Kaiser, Walter Hasenclever, Oskar Kokoschka, and Reinhard Sorge, Sachs adopts a musical, dreamlike, rather than a realistic, form for the play. As a poet attuned to linguistic rhythms, Sachs is more concerned with intensified language than with plot or action, and the characters in the play often engage in long verse monologues more suited for poetry than for theater. Moreover, Sachs's emphasis on language and rhythm conveying the harmony of a symphony was obviously more important to her than the impracticality of staging a drama in which wombs dissolve in smoke, bleeding mouths appear, and Eli's tooth gnaws at a murderer–all of which Sachs obviously sensed figuratively as if she were writing a poem. The language tends to be "expressive" rather than literal or descriptive, again reflecting Sachs's orientation toward expressionistic drama, which was typically written by poets. Moreover, the use of a protagonist (Michael) on a quest to determine meaning in a nihilistic, apocalyptic universe is also a reflection of the type of German expressionism that Sachs was familiar with before her exile. Finally, Sachs's subordination of minor characters to nameless "types," considered to be akin to automations, or what Sidra DeKoven Ezrahi refers to in *Eli* as "nonspecific archetypes of social roles," is endemic to expressionist drama.[3] David Bronsen infers that Sachs's play derives from German expressionism:

> As in Expressionist drama, the majority of the characters in *Eli*
> are identified generically: "a washer-woman," "a woman," "a
> man," "A knife-sharpener," "a deformed man," "a blind girl,"
> "a beggar," "a rabbi," etc. Expressionism, like Nelly Sachs'
> dramas, is not interested in individual psychology but in the
> fate of humanity, so that each character stands for all of its
> kind.[4]

Like the expressionistic characters who reflect the identityless puppets or marionettes depicted as victims of modern industrialized society, Sachs populates *Eli* with disembodied voices of the post-Holocaust era.

While writing *Eli* in sheltered exile over a few nights during 1943, Sachs had already heard about the atrocities against the Jews of her native Germany. She therefore tried to establish contact with her Jewish roots in a renewal of faith. Through Martin Buber's influence, she read the Old Testament, particularly the Psalms, and was introduced to Hasidic tales and texts from the Kabbala, many of which stem from the Zohar, a book of Jewish mysticism. Sachs's study of the Zohar was also enriched during this time when a friend gave her a copy of Gershom Scholem's *Jewish Mysticism*.[5] Hasidism was formed in eighteenth-century Poland as a combination of myth and tradition promulgated by its founder Israel ben Eliezer, known as the Baal Shem, who provided his followers with renewed faith.[6] The place of Hasidism's germination (Poland) became the inspiration for Sachs, who now found in Hasidism timely parallels with the German atrocities against the Jews of Poland, who desperately longed for a renewal of faith. In short, Sachs, in exile, apparently felt guilty about surviving the Holocaust and wrote *Eli* as a means of assuaging the guilt by recording the suffering as a cyclical historical event that universalizes misery. By doing so, Sachs becomes a seer, a Jewish mystic akin to the Baal Shem. Thus, as Ruth Dinesen suggests, Sachs regains her identity as a German Jew by accepting the renewed faith of Hasidism as her calling: "She embraces the biblical myth, the history of the Diaspora, and considers herself, in Buber's sense, a part of the dispersed and persecuted Jewish people, who are entrusted with a special God-given task."[7]

In *Major Trends in Jewish Mysticism*, Gershom G. Scholem discusses the tenets of Hasidism: "'Oh taste and see that the Lord is good.' It is this tasting and seeing, however spiritualized it may become, that the genuine mystic desires."[8] The Jewish mystic assures herself of the good, wise, and just God of Creation, Revelation, and Redemption. The role of the mystic is to act as seer interpreting the hidden and symbolic meanings of the Torah. Scholem writes, "On the whole, the philosophers of Judaism treat the existence of evil as something meaningless in itself."[9] Sachs agrees, and regards evil as fundamentally nonexistent if one believes in God. Sachs refuses to dwell on the question of evil during the Holocaust by focusing instead on transcendence and the meaning of death. God, the Jewish mystic believes, may momentarily turn his back on humanity but will return with benevolence once prayer is renewed. In a postscript to the play, Sachs described *Eli* as providing this transcendental renewal of faith: "The play is designed to raise the unutterable to a transcendental level, so as to make it bearable, and in this night of nights, to give a hint of the holy darkness in which both quiver and arrow are hidden."[10] In this context, the suffering of the Holocaust is seen as recurrent archetypal activity, what Sidra Ezrahi refers to as "a series of reenactments of the pageant of death."[11] In *Eli*, Sachs essentially transforms historical time into mythical time, the latter repeating itself endlessly. Dinah Dodds comments, "For her [Sachs], the years 1939–1945 were not linear history but rather constituted one revolution of a repeating cycle."[12] Setting the play in the nebulous time of "After martyrdom" (2) focuses on the cyclical nature of Jewish suffering rather than on the specific atrocities associated with the Third Reich.

Eli recounts the tale of Michael, a cobbler, who seeks to find the murderer of eight-year-old Eli, who was killed when his parents were being dragged away to their deaths by an unknown enemy. In anguish and despair, Eli, calling on the heavens to save his parents, blew his shepherd's pipe; the guard, believing that the boy was sending out a secret signal, struck him dead with a blow from his rifle butt.

On the surface, *Eli* contains realistic elements to suggest that the Holocaust is the subject of the play. Despite the fact that the time element is nebulous, the setting is specific and intimates the aftermath of the Holocaust: *"The marketplace of a small Polish town in which a number of survivors of the Jewish people have come together"* (3). The Washerwoman recalls how Eli's parents were torn from their sleep in what appears to be a type of *Sonderaktion* (Special Campaign). A bricklayer remembers how Gad "slaved himself to death in the quarry" (9), an obvious reference to Nazi work camps. An Old Man recalls his escape from what presumably had been a mass burial after the slaughtering of a *shtetl* vibrant with life, only to be miraculously saved by a soldier who was not intoxicated during the purge (32–34). As if a seer writing in 1943 before the extent of the devastation is known, Sachs, in scene eleven, has visions of the extermination camps. As the voice of the Camp Commandant, the Chimney mocks the Creature, represented as Hirsch the Jewish tailor, who is forced to stoke the fires of the crematoria: "whimpering of little children in smoke,/ mothers' cradle songs in smoke,–/ Israel's way of freedom in smoke" (36). Related images depict girls being separated from their mothers (18), lovers from lovers (18), sons from mothers (21), and children being thrown onto flames (30).

Although these images ostensibly directly related to the Holocaust, Sachs's play transcends the Shoah by universalizing it as a recurrent act of suffering undertaken by the chosen people. Vivian M. Patraka attempts to characterize *Eli* specifically as a typical Holocaust drama: "Many of their lamentation monologues focus on what happened in the Polish village before or as people were being taken away. Thus the play seizes this history as it was at its moment of disappearance."[13] Although Jewish genocide is referenced, there is no mention of Germans, Nazis, or the Third Reich. Instead, the genocide against Jews is considered to be part of a universalized ubiquitous evil that removes Germans from guilt or responsibility. As Susan E. Cernyak-Spatz indicates, Sachs was not interested in dramatizing a specific historical event but was more concerned with the philosophical implications of the universality of good, evil, and divine justice, and as such, was acting as a faith healer or spiritual seer.[14] To Sachs, Jewish history is a cyclical tale of suffering that, as Ezrahi notes, takes place "not in a civilization but in a barren landscape of screams."[15] Sachs transcends the mystery of the Holocaust by positing it to be inscrutable, a time of the broken covenant.

Eli begins with the image of the rebuilding of the fountain, the centerpiece of the marketplace, marking the return to renewal for a Polish community that is in ruins. Dodds suggests that the rebuilding of the fountain can be viewed as a chronicle of the Jewish people, for each time wandering Jews have been displaced, they dug new wells to persevere.[16] The time is Rosh Hashanah, the Jewish New Year, which indicates the chance to start anew. The rebuilding and the concomitant coming of the New Year invigorate the spiritual sense of the community. As the shofar is sounded, the First Worshipper remarks, "The air is new–/ gone is the smell of burning,/ gone is the smell of blood,/ gone is the smell of smoke–/ the air is new!" (24). The time appears ripe for the community to reingratiate itself with the unity recently lost with God, thus renewing the broken covenant.

Ehrhard Bahr notes that Eli's Hebrew name indicates that he is a god-child, which would explain why he pointed his flute toward the heavens when pleading for help before the deaths of his parents.[17] Thus, a spiritual leader such as Michael, the saint-mystic of the Baal Shem, one of the Thirty-Six Pious or Just Men (*Zaddikim*) in every generation who, according to the Talmud, are servants of God restoring the balance between destructive and healing powers, must find Eli's murderer. Michael is a cobbler, one who, the Washerwoman notes, "stitches sole to uppers" (7). Bahr writes that shoemaking was considered to be a mystic trade; moreover, Jakob Böhme, the German mystic who strongly influenced Sachs with his training in the Kabbala, was also a shoemaker.[18] Stitching the upper leather to the sole relates to references in the Zohar, where "lower" and "upper" correspond to the union between humanity and God. Michael, as God's representative, takes on the burden of the quest to find Eli's murderer, thus affording the Polish village the time to rebuild.

In Sachs's play, the atrocities of the Holocaust remain unmentioned; instead, the focus is on a generic sense of renewal through continuous periods of suffering. In scene two, the Bricklayer and his apprentice Jossele rebuild houses amidst the rubble, as if this were the normal cycle of events. Michael begins his quest to find Eli's murderer, framing the search archetypally: "I seek the dust/ which since Cain has mingled/ with every murderer's dust and waited" (14). Dodds astutely remarks, "By creating on multiple levels, Nelly Sachs effects a suspension of historical time and replaces it with mythic time where past, present and future are indistinguishable."[19] *Eli* thus becomes a drama of transcendence in which Jewish genocide is subordinated to a more universalized view of human suffering. Elinor Fuchs aptly delineates Sachs's purpose in writing the play: "Still, at the deepest level *Eli* is an attempt to transcend historical suffering and to summon as a source of strength the millennial tradition of Jewish messianic hope in the face of adversity."[20]

Michael, armed with a shepherd's pipe, a magic flute reminiscent of Eli's musical instrument, finds renewal during his quest for

Eli's murderer. The marketplace, whose inhabitants cannot forget the recent deaths and sufferings, winds up in festive dancing (20). Spirits are renewed at the time of the New Year. The Beggar acknowledges, "A door is a knife/ and parts the world in two halves" (27). The reference is to the idea that when one door closes, another opens–especially apropos for the New Year. Sachs is known primarily as a writer whose poetry consistently explored the mysteries of death, the eternal closing of doors; in contrast, *Eli* occurs "after martyrdom" but is essentially concerned with how renewal negates the cyclical nature of death.

During scenes fifteen and sixteen, Eli's murderer disallows his own son the opportunity to blow on Eli's pipe, in effect, denying him the opportunity to commune with God. Eli's murderer, generically referred to as the Man, is then told in the next scene that his child is dead. Bahr writes, "The child dies, not because of the sins of his father but because of the denial of his yearning for God."[21] In the final scene of the play, Michael, in contrast to the godless Man he confronts as Eli's murderer, represents the guardian angel of the Baal Shem. Michael is faced with an embryo in its mother's womb, as the guilty Man's hands slowly crumble away before he fades into death. Michael, however, does not kill Eli's murderer; instead, divine will crumbles him to dust. The embryo suggests a rebirth–as one dies, another is born. This cyclical sign is a means to universalize God's presence, intimating that there is life "after martyrdom." Anders Österling sums up Sachs's point in scene seventeen: "The ending denotes a divine justice which has nothing to do with earthly retribution."[22] Michael has served his purpose as the earthly redeemer in whose soul God works; the burnt-out village can now begin to rebuild. A Voice calls for such regeneration: "Footprints of Israel/ gather yourselves together!" (51). Sachs, searching for meaning in exile in Sweden while her fellow Jews suffered during the Holocaust, essentially wrote *Eli* as a positive statement about life. The vision that she creates has little to do with the historical reality of the Shoah; instead, Sachs transcends the Holocaust by envisioning life as a series of recurrent trials and tribulations of the chosen people. Humanity is degraded momentarily but will now rebuild. Hate and revenge do not provide the answers; rather, rebuilding derives from a renewal of faith. Sachs employs Hasidic motifs to expand the Holocaust from its historical basis to a universal, mythic component, thereby converting deeply rooted *angoisse* into a positive force.

No single work of literature has been a metonym for the Holocaust more than the diary of Anne Frank. The diary is without question the most widely read piece of Holocaust literature. Translated into more than fifty languages, Anne's Frank's diary, composed when she began the entries at age thirteen and ending with her last entry at age fifteen, has reached millions of readers and spawned documentaries, television specials, films, teaching guides, videos, children's books, and various theatrical adaptations. The publication of the diary marked the beginning for many Europeans and Americans of their first awareness of the Shoah, particularly among young people who were unfamiliar with the specific horrors of the genocide and often had no idea of its dimensions. The sentimental portrayal of Anne Frank as an innocent victim of fascists was so endearing to the worldwide public viewing the play that her story became the hallmark for how Jews fared during the Third Reich. While the *Diary of Anne Frank* served to educate the general public about the Holocaust, it also transcended the now-accepted vision of the Shoah because of American Cold War politics and a need to sugar-coat the play for mass appeal among Broadway audiences. In order to explain how this distorted vision of Anne's diary evolved, we must delve into the history of the play.

Anne's father, Otto Frank, was the lone family survivor of the war and returned to his Amsterdam home on 3 June 1945, after his internment in Auschwitz. In August, the Franks' devoted friend Miep Gies gave Otto a copy of Anne's diary, composed while her family was hiding in the annex between 12 June 1942 and 1 August 1944. After editing out several of Anne's comments on sexuality, puberty, and any anecdotes that might adversely affect the living, as well as any harsh critical comments about her parents, Otto turned the text over to Contact, a Dutch publishing company; in 1947, fifteen hundred copies of the diary were published as *Het Achterhuis* (*The House Behind*), Anne's original title. In 1950, American novelist and playwright Meyer Levin read the French translation of the diary and contacted Otto about his willingness to find an American publisher and adapt the diary for the stage. Levin was working as a war correspondent attached to the Fourth Armored Division at the time and was present when the Americans liberated Dachau and Buchenwald and after the British liberated Bergen-Belsen, where Anne died after being detained at Westerbork and then transported to Auschwitz. Levin immediately felt that he was the ideal person to adapt the diary for the stage. He shared a Jewish heritage with Anne, felt close to her as a fellow writer, and could not forget the images of the skeletons buried in mass graves at Bergen-Belsen, one of which, he imagined, might have been Anne's own body. Levin also assisted Jews in their emigration to Palestine, produced two films about the subject, and, in his 1950 memoir, *The Search*, documented the effects that the emotional impact of the Shoah had on him. On 9 April 1951, after several American publishers had rejected the manuscript, Otto signed a contract with Doubleday for the publication of Anne's diary in the United States. Levin, in reviewing *Anne Frank: The Diary of a Young Girl* in the *New York Times Book Review* (15 June 1952), essentially launched the book's publication. Doubleday immediately had doubts about Levin's capability to write a suitable adaptation for Broadway because Levin, primarily regarded as a novelist rather than a dramatist, had virtually no connections among Broadway insiders. Doubleday turned the project over to producer Cheryl Crawford in summer 1952, who soon decided to solicit Lillian Hellman's help to secure a distinguished playwright;[23] Levin, however, kept his hopes alive by sending Otto a radio script, arguing that he was the ideal person to adapt the diary for the stage. After Crawford became incensed over Levin's behind-the-scenes intervention, Otto turned to Kermit Bloomgarden to produce the play.

Bloomgarden and Hellman conspired to turn the diary into a play that would serve their own agendas. By the mid-1930s, Hellman was a committed Stalinist who defended the Hitler-Stalin pact of 1939 and wrote plays supporting the communist agenda. She was a nominal Jew with no religious training or background, was anti-Zionist, and even opposed the immigration of Jews to the United States during the war. After the war, she viewed Stalin's purges against Jews to be merely a means to maintain Party orthodoxy.[24] In 1952, Hellman appeared before the House Un-American Activities Committee (HUAC), defending her stance in the witch hunt to purge the arts of communist influence and stigmatize artists who maintained Party loyalties.[25] After the hearings, during the early years of the Cold War, Hellman obviously became more aware of how closely the federal government tied Jews with communism, so she, like many Broadway producers and Hollywood writers, made a conscious effort to portray Jews in a positive manner and make them appear "less ethnic." However, Hellman's primary goal was to use theater as socialist propaganda against fascism. She had the endorsement of Bloomgarden, who had produced Hellman's plays and was not just a casual supporter, but also her lover.[26] Otto gave his consent to turn the rights to the play over to Bloomgarden.[27]

Hellman commissioned Frances Goodrich and Albert Hackett, a gentile husband-and-wife Hollywood writing team to adapt the diary for the stage. The Hacketts were well known in Hollywood writing circles, having penned thirty-two screenplays, mostly musicals and light comedies. They had received Oscar nominations for adapting *The Thin Man* (1934), *After the Thin Man* (1936), *Father of the Bride* (1950), and *Seven Brides for Seven Brothers* (1954); they also had won Writers' Guild Awards for *Easter Parade* (1948) and *Father's Little Dividend* (1954).[28] Goodrich and Hackett even had a hand in the screenplay for the ultimate "feel-good" Christmas film, *It's a Wonderful Life.*[29] They were particularly known for their debonair dialogue and scripts that had box-office appeal. Thus, Bloomgarden was reassured that Goodrich and Hackett could deliver a play that would have mass appeal to theatergoers. Contributing financially to organizations being investigated for their communist leanings, Goodrich and Hackett, although never formally subpoenaed before Congress, were questioned by HUAC and were thus political colleagues of Hellman in their mutual animosity toward the witch hunt enforced against their show business friends. Ralph Melnick writes, "In a word, the Hacketts were safe. They could be depended upon by Hellman to deliver a script with the proper ideological focus, properly deethnicized, and with the Holocaust itself lightened with touches of sweet comedy to mask the particularism of the horror out of which the *Diary* had emerged."[30]

Goodrich and Hackett began by doing research on Amsterdam, Jewish culture, and teenagers. A rabbi was consulted so that Goodrich and Hackett could write the Hanukkah scene. Later, director Garson Kanin intervened, arguing that the Hanukkah scene needed to stress celebration and gift giving; the songs, he argued, could not be sung in the original Hebrew, which would only serve to "alienate the audience."[31] After Hellman and Bloomgarden approved the sixth draft of the play, Kanin was assigned to direct the production, and Otto made final alterations to the script. Subsequent to a trip to Amsterdam to visit the annex, the Hacketts completed drafts seven and eight. Kanin and Bloomgarden were primarily interested in guaranteeing that the play's comedy would work well on Broadway; this was assured during the tryout in Philadelphia, where Bloomgarden lauded the success of the play by stating, "It was just wonderful. We got every laugh."[32] To assure its Broadway success, more comedy was added in the eighth draft while references to the Holocaust were eliminated or deemphasized.

On 5 October 1955, *The Diary of Anne Frank* premiered at the Cort Theatre on Broadway, where it ran for 717 performances.[33] The play received very positive reviews and garnered all of the major awards for best play in 1956: the Pulitzer Prize, the Antoinette Perry (Tony) Award, and the New York Drama Critics' Circle Award. The play went on a national tour of major North American cities while a bus tour played to smaller venues. On 1 October 1956, *Das Tagebuch der Anne Frank* was simultaneously staged in Düsseldorf, Berlin, Karlsruhe, Hamburg, Konstanz, Aachen, and Dresden. Within months, the play had been successfully performed more than 2,200 times in fifty-eight German cities and ninety-five theaters, where more than a million Germans were emotionally affected by their country's grave transgressions during the war.[34] In 1959, the film version, directed by George Stevens with a screenplay by Goodrich and Hackett, although not a box office bonanza, was an international success. In the film, dark-haired model Millie Perkins, whose image reminded the public of a young Elizabeth Taylor, played the role of Anne, essentially turning the film into a Jewish version of *National Velvet*. Alvin H. Rosenfeld perceptively notes, "Given the power of American popular culture in the postwar period and the influence it has exerted in countries around the world, the American version of Anne Frank quickly took hold elsewhere."[35] To promote the film worldwide, the president of Twentieth Century Fox even boasted to the press, "This isn't a Jewish picture, this is a picture for the world."[36] In 1978, the play was successfully revived in New York. More recently, in 1997, Wendy Kesselman adapted the Goodrich and Hackett play for Broadway. Kesselman and director James Lapine set out to portray the unexpurgated Anne by restoring passages of the diary that Otto had excised, focusing more of the attention on Anne's ethnicity, and making the play darker by closing it with a description of Anne's condition upon death in Bergen-Belsen. Nevertheless, Natalie Portman played Anne as a joyous adolescent experiencing her budding sexuality for the first time. Molly Magid Hoagland's review of the 1997 Broadway production summed up much of the critical reaction: "Despite the changes, this is still the same sentimental play about a luminous, flirtatious, idealistic Anne Frank that made the critics swoon 40 years ago."[37]

The reality of the fate of the Frank family and their friends from 6 July 1942, when eight Jews went into hiding in the annex, until their arrests on 4 August 1944–a period of over two years–is nothing but grim, as expressed by Anne in her diary. They were forced to spend nearly ten hours of the day in silence, shared rations, never went outdoors, never drew water or flushed the commode during daylight, and lived constantly in fear and anxiety. In her diary entry of 9 October 1942, Anne laments the fate of the Jews who are rounded up by the Gestapo and transported in cattle cars to Westerbork, where "the people get almost nothing to eat, much less to drink, as water is available only one hour a day, and there's only one toilet and sink for several thousand people."[38] Anne puts the blame squarely on the Germans for their brutality toward the Jews: "Fine specimens of humanity, those Germans, and to think I'm actually one of them!" (55). From her window, she views the nightly roundups of Jews. Anne describes the parade in her entry of 19 November 1942:

> It's like the slave hunts of the olden days. I don't mean to make light of this; it's much too tragic for that. In the evenings when it's dark, I often see long lines of good, innocent people, accompanied by crying children, walking on and on, ordered about by a handful

of men who bully and beat them until they nearly drop. No one is spared. The sick, the elderly, children, babies and pregnant women–all are marched to their death. (72–73)

The conclusion that Anne draws about humanity is not that people are good at heart, but that because evil exists, humanity's fate is precarious at best. In her diary entry of 3 May 1944, Anne writes, "There's a destructive urge in people, the urge to rage, murder and kill. And until all of humanity, without exception, undergoes a metamorphosis, wars will continue to be waged, and everything that has been carefully built up, cultivated and grown will be cut down and destroyed, only to start all over again!" (280–81). Anne's life in the annex was largely torture for her. On 30 January 1943, she revealed, "I'd like to scream at Mother, Margot, the van Daans, Dussel and Father too: 'Leave me alone, let me have at least one night when I don't cry myself to sleep with my eyes burning and my head pounding. Let me get away, away from everything, away from this world'" (84). After nearly two years in the annex, Anne sounded defeated: "I've asked myself again and again whether it wouldn't have been better if we hadn't gone into hiding, if we were dead now and didn't have to go through this misery, especially so that the others could be spared the burden" (307). In short, as Cynthia Ozick so aptly characterizes it, "All in all, the diary is a chronicle of trepidation, turmoil, alarm."[39] Anne's fate does not suggest that she was ever an icon of faith and idealism. After her confinement at Auschwitz, she was transported with Margot to Bergen-Belsen. There she slept in overcrowded tents camped on mud, unable to wash, while being systematically starved to death. Hannah Elisabeth Pick-Goslar, who saw Anne at Bergen-Belsen, recalls a broken girl, depressed by the apparent deaths of her parents.[40] Another eyewitness recalled Anne's last days: "She was in rags. I saw her emaciated, sunken face in the darkness. Her eyes were very large."[41] Margot died first, and then, a day or two later, sometime in March 1945, Anne, lice-ridden, perished from typhus.

Lawrence L. Langer reminds us that the tragic fate of Anne Frank was exclusively due to the fact that she, like millions of others, suffered and eventually died because she was Jewish–and for no other reason.[42] Bloomgarden, Kanin, and the Hacketts took this basic tenet of the Holocaust and subverted it for political and commercial purposes. Although the Hacketts admittedly undertook the task of converting a diary, essentially private writing, for public consumption, which is the essence of theatrical presentation, they did not do justice to the Holocaust experience Anne documented when they embellished Anne's words, sugar-coated the information, or added material of their own. Goodrich and Hackett, attempting to create an uplifting, less harrowing depiction of the Holocaust, made Anne into a sentimental heroine; in short, as Alvin H. Rosenfeld suggests, Anne's story transcended the ugliness and brutal reality of the Holocaust.[43]

Although the play obviously occurs in Amsterdam during the years of World War II and immediately afterwards, and although Anne is referred to as being Jewish, her persecution as related to anti-Semitism is muted. Nazis are referred to in the play but are never seen on stage (even when the Franks are arrested, we do not see the actual event); instead of the fear that the Gestapo evokes in contemporary audiences, Goodrich and Hackett prefer to envision the menacing force as the innocuous Green Police. No one in the play dies or is tortured, and intense Jewish suffering is minimized. Admittedly, Anne does refuse to throw away her Star of David,[44] the threat of Mauthausen is mentioned (66), and Mrs. Van Daan refers to being possibly dragged off to a concentration camp (103), but aside from these sentiments, the Jewish element is suppressed. Edward R. Isser astutely recognizes, "The cultural identity of the family is neutered and muted. The bitterness of Anne toward an indifferent Christian world, the strident Zionism and outspokenness of her sister, and the deep religious faith of her mother are ignored."[45] Even the Hanukkah scene that ends act one is reduced to a generic festive (read non-Jewish) celebration extolling a "Lord our God, Ruler of the universe," who has given the Frank family "life and sustenance and brought us to this happy season" (84). What so angered Levin was that Anne's diary was distinctly a Jewish story that was muted by the Hacketts. In her diary entry of 11 April 1944, Anne laments her plight as being a result of anti-Semitism:

> We've been strongly reminded of the fact that we're Jews in chains, chained to one spot, without any rights, but with a thousand obligations ... Who has inflicted this on us? Who has set us apart from all the rest? Who has put us through such

suffering? It's God who has made us the way we are, but it's also God who will lift us up again. In the eyes of the world, we're doomed, but if, after all this suffering, there are still Jews left, the Jewish people will be held up as an example ... God has never deserted our people. Through the ages Jews have had to suffer, but through the ages they've gone on living, and the centuries of suffering have only made them stronger. (261–62)

Goodrich and Hackett not only delete this from the play, but also change Anne's words to turn anti-Semitism into a benign statement about universal suffering: "We're not the only people that've had to suffer. There've always been people that've had to ... sometimes one race ... sometimes another ... and yet ... " (168). The deaths of six million Jews is reduced to a historical anomaly that "sometimes one race" and "sometimes another" is forced to endure.

In limiting the sectarian nature of the play, Goodrich and Hackett attempted to universalize the plight of the eight sequestered Jews, intimating to audiences that these people could be any refugees suffering during war. In an interview with the *New York Times*, Kanin stated, "This play makes use of elements having mainly to do with human courage, faith, hope, brotherhood, love, and self-sacrifice. We discovered as we went deeper and deeper that it was a play about what Shaw called 'the life force.'"[46] Anne becomes the mouthpiece for life's injustices, the dignity of the human spirit, and the triumph of good versus evil. Indeed, when Peter's faith is waning, Anne chimes in with, "I still believe, in spite of everything, that people are really good at heart" (168). Moreover, in a voice-over that ends the play (but which does not have such a climactic role in her diary), thus cementing and reinforcing Anne's humanism for the audience leaving the theater, Anne reiterates what has become her epitaph: "In spite of everything, I still believe that people are really good at heart" (174). In truth, Anne often comforted herself with a positive attitude in order to counterbalance the misery and death that daily inundated her family. David Jortner suggests that these lines, presenting a universal message of Christian love and understanding, alter the play from the Jewish experience during the Holocaust to a more universalist narrative of "man's inhumanity to man."[47] In transforming the grim details of Anne's actual diary into a play that parlays the hope of a triumphant spirit to mitigate despair, Goodrich and Hackett have minimized Jewish suffering by universalizing the experience.[48] Moreover, Anne's euphony to Peter that Jews are not the only people who have suffered transforms her from a victim into a universalized type of Christian martyr, idealized through her acts of forgiveness, love, and understanding. Furthermore, as Bruno Bettelheim has argued, Anne's final statement about the goodness of all human beings ignores the serious implications of the Holocaust: "If all men are good at heart, there never really was an Auschwitz; nor is there any possibility that it may recur."[49]

Goodrich, Hackett, and Hellman certainly politicized the play for their own purposes as a statement against fascism rather than as a drama depicting the fate of the Jews during the Holocaust. In their Marxist approach to the play, Hellman and the Hacketts held the Stalinist view that humanity is benevolent, and evil results from the class structure or how economic power is misdistributed. Goodrich and Hackett shift the focus of the play to the misery caused by war, with the underlying assumption that fascism inevitably leads to war. Bloomgarden, when instructing the Hacketts on what to emphasize as they were drafting the play, reminded them, "The diary is a symbol of ... the war and all its misery and pain and wasted hope."[50] Goodrich, Hackett, and Hellman essentially played upon American fears of fascism abrogating democratic rights to life, liberty, and pursuit of happiness. These fears assuaged any guilt America had had of entering World War II after Hitler's declaration of war on the United States on 11 December 1941, and, during *The Diary of Anne Frank's* initial staging in 1955, shortly after the loss of life during the Korean War, the play was, as Albert Wertheim suggests, a salve to Americans.[51] Anne herself views life as cyclical, stating that good will prevail: the underlying assumption is again that once fascism is destroyed in favor of a more enlightened political system, the world will be changed for the better. Moreover, the witch hunt of the McCarthy era, culminating in the HUAC hearings, certainly reinforced the connection between communists and Jews, and with the Marxist subtext of the play, the emphasis on cleansing Anne Frank of her ethnicity must have been palpable. Finally, the horrible fate of those hiding in the annex was determined by a thief, an informer who revealed the hiding place to the Nazis. To Hellman, Goodrich, and Hackett, well acquainted with the backstabbing associated with the HUAC hearings, fascism meant Gestapo-like tactics of using informers to turn friends against each other. Judith E. Doneson explains the implications for audiences: "A system which breeds informers can lead to tragic results, especially when the victims are innocent, as was the case with Anne, as well as those who found themselves blacklisted."[52] In essence, Goodrich and Hackett changed the focus of this Holocaust play to prey upon audiences of the 1950s, who feared the extent to which informers could damage one's life and family.

Through the commercial influence of Bloomgarden, and later in the writing process, Kanin, Goodrich and Hackett transcended the Holocaust tale by turning it into a coming-of-age story of idealistic adolescence. Instead of Anne Frank as the emaciated, lice-covered, malnourished victim of Nazi persecution, her legacy has become a popular culture fantasy of an average teenager seeking attention and love in an estranged, adult world that fails to understand her. In one of their letters to Bloomgarden, Goodrich and Hackett describe Anne as

> A young girl like other young girls who wriggled, giggled and chattered ... A captivating, bright spirit whose self discoveries of the joys, sorrows, terrors of adolescence was always leavened with wit and humor ... A young girl with the same hopes and dreams and foolish romantic ideas, the same moments of seriousness and yearnings and bewilderment that all boys and girls have. She might have been your neighbor's teen-aged daughter–or your own.[53]

Kanin, to whom the published play is dedicated, compared Anne to Peter Pan and the smile of the Mona Lisa: a radiant, youthful presence whose spirit endures forever as a shining star.[54] Natalie Portman, who played Anne on Broadway during the 1997 revival, read the play as a tale of spirited adolescence: "it's funny, it's hopeful, and she's a happy person."[55] At a crucial point in the play, immediately before Anne acknowledges that she believes people are really good at heart, she states, "I think the world may be going through a phase, the way I was with mother" (168). Anne's conflation of the growing pains of adolescence with fascism is exactly the desired effect sought by the politicized Hacketts and the commercial hawkers, Bloomgarden and Kanin. The implication is that humanity will outgrow fascism, as surely as teenagers will pass through puberty. Wertheim frames the absurd comparison fairly eloquently: "The Golgotha of World War II is contracted, diminished, and domesticated into some global teenage mood swing, 'a phase.'"[56]

The Holocaust story is transcended and even undermined by the emphasis on Anne's adolescence. For example, Norbert Muhlen explained the appeal of the play in West Germany soon after the war:

> Many young Germans identify with Anne Frank, see in her the prototype of all youth–helpless, imprisoned, at the mercy of elders, defiant of the outside world and terrified within. And the persecution and murder of Jews seems to them to be merely a peculiar external circumstance–secondary in importance to the personal tragedy of the heroine.[57]

The Diary of Anne Frank degenerates into a domestic drama that, in some ways, could occur in virtually any Western environment in the twentieth century. Anne even describes the environment as typical and nonthreatening: "You know the way I'm going to think of it here? I'm going to think of it as a boarding house" (24). Anne is depicted as a normal teenager who wants "some fun ... someone to laugh and clown with" (33), who loves to dance (33), and aspires "to ride a bike again ... to have new clothes from the skin out ... to have a hot tub filled to overflowing and wallow in it for hours ... to be back in school with my friends" (83). Like most adolescents, Anne argues with her parents (53), complains about the constant criticism she receives (72), and feels misunderstood: "I feel utterly confused. I am longing ... so longing ... for everything ... for friends ... for someone to talk to ... someone who understands ... someone young, who feels as I do." (132). Her adolescent attraction to Peter, whom she kisses twice, represents the Bloomgarden–Kanin emphasis on romance that they insisted Goodrich and Hackett infuse into the text strictly for commercial gain. In short, the play became a popular culture genre for teenagers worldwide, or as Alan Mintz states, Anne's life represents "the stuff of adolescent exuberance and turmoil everywhere and always: the need for love, the confusions of puberty, the budding interest in boys, the ambitions for the future, the skirmishes with parents, the misunderstandings and self-dramatizations."[58]

Not only do Goodrich and Hackett portray the Anne Frank story as a coming-of-age adolescent tale, but they idealize it as well. Edward R. Isser characterizes the domestic drama as "a Jewish version of the Swiss Family Robinson: danger exists outside the shelter, but inside it is safe, warm, and full of love."[59] If the play emphasizes traditional family bonding, Anne, almost saint like and unsullied, is certainly the family unit's ultimate peacemaker and care giver. As a humble soul, she chastises herself for "the things I did ... that were wrong" (82), comforts an ill Mr. Van Daan (152), offers to give her rations to the hungrier members of the annex (155), and courageously provides confidence to her family once they are discovered by the Gestapo (170). Anne's spirit represents a beacon of hope while simultaneously suggesting an adolescent vision that views the world as awry but the idealistic young as pure. Anne exclaims, "We're trying to hold onto some kind of ideals ... when everything ... ideals, hopes ... everything, are being destroyed! It isn't our fault that the world is in such a mess! We weren't around when all this started!" (127). Anne is the ultimate positive role model who tries to find the silver lining in the worst of situations. Mr. Frank even has the gall to say, "But Anne was happy in the camp in Holland where they first took us" (172). The play ends with Anne's famous line affirming the goodness of humanity, while Otto chimes in with "She puts me to shame" (174). In short, the affirming message of the play is closer to an idealistic *It's a Wonderful Life* than to the reality of the Holocaust. Lawrence L. Langer, however, questions whether this celebration of the human spirit through such a lively imagination can ever remain untainted by the enormity of the crime that the Holocaust represents.[60]

A committed Holocaust poet-playwright such as Nelly Sachs transcended the Shoah through the Hasidic spirit of conciliation and renewal of faith. To Sachs, the Holocaust was a cyclical historical event–another period of Jewish suffering that would eventually pass while God's benevolence was temporarily on hold. Although their means to the end were completely different for Sachs and the Hacketts, the *result* for Goodrich and Hackett was quite similar to Sachs's vision. Anne Frank, an idealistic teenager, viewed the Holocaust as merely a "phase," a brief historical glitch in which evil triumphed over good. Unlike Sachs, however, Goodrich and Hackett transcended the Holocaust by focusing on the evils of fascism and the commercial viability of Anne's postwar popular culture mentality.

6   Marxism and the Holocaust

Although *The Diary of Anne Frank* was written by Goodrich and Hackett as an anti-fascist response to the Holocaust, its explicit commercialization for Broadway consumption masked the tacit Marxism. Two artists who make their Marxist message of primary importance in responding to the Holocaust are Swedish playwright Peter Weiss and American dramatist Tony Kushner. Both are strict disciples of Bertolt Brecht, the most influential Marxist playwright/theoretician of the twentieth century, and they modeled their Holocaust dramas, *The Investigation* and *A Bright Room Called Day*, respectively, upon Brecht's Marxist vision.

Peter Weiss's father was a Slovak Jew who converted to Protestantism when he married a German Christian. Peter grew up in Nowawes (Potsdam today), Bremen, and Berlin, but because his father was originally from Czechoslovakia and was not a German citizen, he was not allowed to salute Hitler in school. Although Weiss was baptized and, according to Jewish custom, would not be considered Jewish because his mother was Protestant (Jewishness defined as matrilineal), Nazi law designated him as non-Aryan. Weiss admitted, "I never particularly thought of myself as a Jew. I was simply a Berliner and a German."[1] To avoid Nazi persecution, the family emigrated to England in 1935, moved to the Czech town of Warnsdorf in 1936 (where Weiss learned for the first time that his father was Jewish), and after a brief sojourn in Switzerland, Peter rejoined his family in Sweden in January 1939. In exile from Germany, Weiss became a Swedish citizen, began writing in Swedish, and tried to establish himself as a painter, exhibiting his works in Stockholm. In his book on Weiss, Robert

Cohen discusses Weiss's alienation in exile: "Sweden, spared from war because of its strong anticommunism and its tolerant attitude toward Nazi Germany, showed little sympathy for emigrants, especially Jewish emigrants."[2] During his exile in Sweden, Weiss's intimate friend from his years in Czechoslovakia, Lucie Weisberger, perished in Theresienstadt after Weiss's attempt at rescue by offering to marry her failed. Weiss, the seemingly eternal emigrant and wandering Jew who had escaped death while others died in the concentration camps, began to question his own identity.

In March 1964, Weiss attended the Auschwitz war crimes trial held in Frankfurt am Main from 20 December 1963 to 20 August 1965, in which twenty-two defendants responsible for the operation of the extermination camp were being tried. During the court proceedings, Weiss read Bernd Naumann's reports on the trial published in the *Frankfurter Allgemeine Zeitung*. In the June 1965 issue of *Kursbuch*, Weiss published "Frankfurter Auszüge" ("Frankfurt Excerpts"), a transcribed fragment written as an account of the trial. On 13 December 1964, Weiss visited Auschwitz and wrote about the experience in an essay titled "Meine Ortschaft" ("My Place"). Weiss, feeling guilty about his inability to save Weisberger from death,[3] wanted to examine the conditions that others like her had to endure at the hands of the Nazis. Moreover, as Jürgen E. Schlunk astutely observes, Weiss's "special attraction of Auschwitz lies in the notion that there he might find an answer to his own identity."[4] After touring Auschwitz, Weiss wrote, "It is a place for which I was destined but which I managed to avoid. I have no relation to it, except that my name was on the lists of the people who were supposed to be sent there for ever."[5] The Auschwitz trials were somewhat impersonal to Weiss; by visiting the extermination camp, Weiss attempted to identify more closely with the victims— one of which could have been him. After viewing first-hand the extent and capability of human barbarism, Weiss became intrigued by "an investigation" of why such atrocity could occur. Robert Holub sums up Weiss's motives to turn what he learned upon visiting Auschwitz into a play: "He left with a debt to those who perished to understand their deaths and to make their sufferings known to a broad public."[6] Weiss returned to Frankfurt in early 1965 to attend the trial again and then, after a year of studying court transcripts, records, speeches, and interviews, attempted to present the facts of the trial as "documentary theater."

Weiss's *Die Ermittlung: Oratorium in 11 Gesängen* (*The Investigation: Oratorio in 11 Cantos*), originally titled *Anus Mundi* in draft form, premiered in East and West Berlin and several other German cities on 19 October 1965. Seventeen major German theaters staged *Die Ermittlung* in 1965; the play was soon mounted in over thirty European cities.[7] Erwin Piscator directed the West Berlin production at the Freie Volksbühne, which featured the witnesses rising from an audience that was made to feel as if they were part of the courtroom proceedings; Piscator's desired effect was to bring documentary theater directly to the masses.[8] Several of the theaters, such as those in Cologne and Munich, considered the play to be unwieldy and chose to recite it–albeit unsuccessfully. A week after the premieres, a few German radio stations broadcast the play without realizing that its theatrical effectiveness would be lost on the radio airwaves. Early notable productions of the play included Peter Brooks's staging at the Aldwych Theatre in London after a public midnight reading by the Royal Shakespeare Company in late 1965; Peter Palitsch's 1965 Stuttgart version, the only West German variation that did not delete Weiss's references to the then-present capitalist government that followed the Adenauer administration, yet was controversial because of its use of actors cast interchangeably in the roles of the accused and the witnesses; and Ingmar Bergman's eerie direction at Stockholm's Royal Dramatic Theater in February 1966 in which the audience, sitting in glaringly bright spotlights, was made to feel that it, too, was on trial. A film version of the play was directed by Peter Schulze-Rohr in 1965 as well. The most controversial rendition of the play was Thomas Schulte-Michaels's 1980 West Berlin production; the setting was a sleazy nightclub where those on "trial" were cross-examined as if they were part of a television quiz show in which Jews, Nazis, and West Germans were equally vilified. *The Investigation* has been consistently popular worldwide during the last thirty-five years of the twentieth century, with productions in New York, Moscow, Buenos Aires, Montevido, and Tel Aviv.

During the Auschwitz trial in 1965, Weiss published two essays about Dante and the *Divina Commedia*: "Vorübung zum dreiteiligen Drama *divina commedia*" and "Gespräch über Dante." In his notebooks, Weiss consistently compared himself to Dante: both were Jewish, driven into exile from their native homelands, persecuted as victims, ill most of their lives, and emotionally attached to a dead woman (Beatrice for Dante and Weisberger for Weiss).[9] In the warped world of Auschwitz, Weiss inverts Dante's structure of the *Divina Commedia*. The Inferno of Dante's world, strangely enough for Weiss, now becomes the managed world of capitalism and technology of postwar Germany, where war criminals are rewarded, rather than punished, for their crimes. Paradiso is deserted, empty–the world of the victims, the surviving "dead" of Auschwitz who await their liberation, living in eternity with the disaster through which they previously suffered. Purgatorio is the region of doubt, wavering, and eternal conflict with regard to which side to be on, thus offering the possibility of change.[10] The structure of the play is consistent with the Marxist dialectic of thesis, antithesis, and synthesis; in other words, after the Inferno and Paradiso, in which the victims struggle with their executioners, the synthesis (Purgatorio) lies in the Marxist concept of change that is possible only through a socialist regime.[11]

Dante's *Divine Comedy* is structured into thirty-three cantos that form the Inferno, Purgatory, and Paradise, thus bringing the text to 100 songs.[12] Weiss followed Dante's model in *The Investigation*, which consists of eleven songs or cantos that correspond to eleven stations on a route of horror that follows the deportees on the ramp to their deaths in the crematoria; each song is divided into three parts, matching one-third of Dante's overall structural output and corresponding to one section of the *Commedia*. Dante's trek through the nine circles of hell eventually led to the ice that froze Lucifer; Weiss's trek through the hell of Auschwitz leads to fire rather than ice. The tripartite structure employed by Dante is fundamental to Weiss's use of the number three. Weiss condensed testimony of 409 witnesses and twenty-three defendants at Frankfurt into a five-hour play whose components were divisible by three: three members of the court, nine witnesses, and eighteen accused.[13] Moreover, the subtitle of Weiss's play, "an oratorio," corresponds to his designation of Dante's *Divine Comedy* as an "oratorium."[14] The title, *The Investigation*, represents the content of the play simultaneously depicted in the form of the Auschwitz trial and the search for the causes of how executioners exploit victims; the subtitle refers to a choral work consisting of recitatives, arias, and choruses–the structure of the play represented by judges, witnesses, and accused–in short, a work of art that contrasts with the juridical notion of the main title. Erika Salloch writes, "Thus, Weiss's choice of the bureaucratic, unemotional sound of the main title, *Die Ermittlung*, designates the content, and with the elevated tone of the subtitle he refers to the form. They are to be understood as the thesis and antithesis of the play, its dialectic consisting of the relationship between content and form."[15] In short, Weiss essentially employed Dante to provide the form for the play in contrast to the Auschwitz trials, which provided the content, thereby solidifying the Marxist dialectic.

Attempting to achieve literal authenticity, Weiss chose documentary theater as the form for *The Investigation*. In the "Note" that precedes the published text of the play, Weiss stated, "This condensation [of the trial] should contain nothing but facts. Personal experience and confrontations must be steeped in anonymity. Inasmuch as the witnesses in the play lose their names, they become mere speaking tubes."[16] According to Weiss, documentary theater is reportage, a means of adopting authentic material and presenting it on stage without any invention by the playwright. Weiss was uninterested in ascribing guilt to individuals since his goal was to indict the system that exploits them. In an interview conducted in 1968, Weiss stated that documentary theater flattens human character because "the point is not to depict individual conflicts, but patterns of socio-economic behavior."[17] Therefore, the nine witnesses are assigned mere numbers to represent the hundreds who testified during the trial, whereas the eighteen accused retain individuality because they were named in the proceedings. Weiss focused on the original courtroom testimony, which he, at times, reproduced verbatim but also condensed and reconfigured without adding material of his own, although he did alter the sequence of court speeches. Rather than simulating closure, which was obviously achieved during the Frankfurt trial, Weiss's play leaves us instead with only documented facts, for he wants the audience to think about the political system that is under indictment rather than about the guilt of individuals. Although the testimony in Frankfurt was often quite emotional, Weiss insists on the facts being sanitized of empathy so the audience can concentrate on thinking about the dialectic rather than being affected by feelings or sentiments. Obviously, individuals make history, yet Weiss prefers to view history as a continuum of political and economic movements. Weiss infers, "My plays do not have conventional lead roles. The lead roles are played by history and ideas."[18] By writing documentary drama, Weiss, then, fashions himself to be a scientist objectively reporting events as they occurred during the Auschwitz trial. However, critics such as Hedy Ehrlich tend to view Weiss's intentions as less than scientific: "He thus pretends to be merely a reporter of facts, a kind of impersonal mouthpiece, while in reality he distorts these facts by taking them out of context, by rearranging the testimony in an order that suits his thesis, and by stripping the trial of its emotional impact."[19]

To counterbalance the strictly objective, scientific nature of documentary theater, Weiss set the play in free verse, providing an aesthetic poetic element. The irregular free-verse lines of three or four unrhymed and unmetered beats seem foreign to the everyday rhythm of five-beat idiom and instead create a staccatolike, laconic effect that inhibits emotional expression. Often, performances of the play were delivered by actors who functioned as automatons speaking the lines in monotone. Weiss eliminates any punctuation that might reduce the staccato effect and any italics that would provide emotional emphasis during dialogic exchanges. Weiss's dialogue is essentially slow and flat, with a natural pause at the end of each line, thus inducing the audience to reflect on why Auschwitz occurred. By reducing the sometimes emotional speeches of the original Auschwitz defendants to the level of raw data, Weiss deemphasizes individual suffering and pathos to focus on his political ideology. The virtually toneless language thus is highly impersonal yet factual and objective; Weiss's goal is to depersonalize the witnesses in order to indict the fascist system behind the individuals.

Weiss, baptized and raised as a Christian, considered himself to be nominally Jewish to the extent that his Jewishness merely linked him with the oppressed who were victimized by colonialistic and imperialistic governments. Weiss, however, was a fully committed Marxist whose writings consistently conflated fascism with capitalism. Weiss first began reading Marx in summer 1965 but had come into contact with Marxism earlier through his reading of Brecht's plays in grade school in Berlin during the early 1930s. When interviewed shortly after the premiere of *The Investigation*, Weiss admitted to Walter Wager that Brecht greatly impressed him and was a major influence on his work.[20] Gunilla Palmstierna-Weiss, Weiss's third wife who shared his life for nearly thirty years, stated that her husband particularly admired Brecht's precise language, his music, his use of alienation effects, and his political frankness: "Peter knew all of Brecht's work–also Brecht's political writings, his poems, and of course his songs."[21] In fall 1966, approximately one year after the debut of *The Investigation* in German theaters, Weiss admitted, "Brecht is the one who has helped me most, because he never wrote anything just for the sake of the dramatic event but rather to show how the world is and find out how to change it."[22] Weiss's commitment to Brechtian Marxism was codified in "10 Arbeitspunkte eines Autors in der geteilten Welt" ("An Author's Ten Working Points in the Divided World"), an essay he wrote a few weeks before the premiere of *The Investigation*. In that article, Weiss blames the fascist state and the capitalist system for Auschwitz, renounces his bourgeois origins, and claims socialism provides the ultimate truth. Weiss, like Brecht, believed that art is ineffective if it does not attempt to change life. In an interview for *Encore* in 1965, Weiss stated, "I think it's absolutely necessary to write with the point of trying to influence or to change society."[23] A year later, in an interview for the *New York Times*, Weiss explained the fundamental tenet of his playwriting: "Every single word I put down and present to the public is political–i.e., aimed at achieving a specific effect."[24] Weiss promulgated his desire for revolution to eradicate capitalism and replace it with socialism, inferring that the universal evil of modern society is predicated upon economic conditions that inevitably exploit individuals. Weiss was explicit about his affinity toward socialist regimes: "But I know exactly, as Brecht knew, that this society, the Western bourgeois and capitalistic society, is not a society I like to live in."[25]

Weiss adopted Brecht's concept of alienation effects to create a scientific theater in the format of a debate that would encourage the audience to think about the dialectic, rather than react to characters and plot emotionally. Weiss stated, "I wanted a scientific investigation of the reality of Auschwitz, to show the audience, in the greatest detail, exactly what happened."[26] Weiss's documentary theater ignores plot and character in favor of the presentation of facticity. Weiss inundates the audience with statistics and precise dimensions–data that are based upon what could be measured and counted at Auschwitz. Weiss's main purpose in the meticulous documentation of statistics is to equate the impersonalization of the fascist extermination machinery–a carefully calculated factory of efficiency–to capitalistic bureaucracy. Weiss told Walter Wager in May 1966, "But the extermination of the Jews during the German Nazi regime was so enormous and so well organized that it had a very special aspect, almost in the way of a factory."[27] The Auschwitz trials work well for Weiss's ultimate purpose because individuals in the extermination camps were described as being treated as objects or mere pawns in a vast fascist machinery; indeed, individual pain and suffering become more anonymous as the statistics increase. Moreover, the constant barrage of data, minutiae, and statistics during the play's five-hour span makes *The Investigation* unbearable, thus disallowing the worn-out audience to sustain any consistent emotional identification with the victims since the focus inevitably is on factual information.[28] Erika Salloch astutely realizes that Weiss's factual language eschews metaphor since everything is literal, while nothing is "transferred": "Weiss, by contrast, contracts everything, chisels it to the degree that the listener cannot let his imagination roam but is forced to an exact viewing of the concentrated model."[29] After hours of testimony about shootings, deaths by injections, starvation, gassings, beatings, and tortures, the audience is numbed, totally drained of emotion, inured, and desensitized–pliable automatons for Weiss's *lehrstück*. Moreover, Weiss ignores the verdict of the Auschwitz trials, offering the audience no chance for a catharsis in order for the spectators, sanitized of all possible purging of their emotions, to focus on an objective assessment of the reasons individuals exploit others.

Weiss, following Brecht's intentions, reduced the audience's emotional empathy for characters to have them concentrate instead on rational thought. Although the deeds of individuals at Auschwitz were obviously on trial in Frankfurt, Weiss instead chose to universalize the atrocities as phases in a historical continuum. Thus, although *The Investigation* is obviously based on the Auschwitz trials and the names of the defendants were adjutants of Auschwitz and no other extermination camp, the setting of the atrocities is not mentioned. Moreover, although we recognize that the majority of those murdered in the extermination camp were Jews, the word "Jew" is not mentioned in the play; the executioners were Nazis, but the word "German" also goes unmentioned. The implications are that an Auschwitz could occur anytime during history, any fascist system could produce such executioners, and any similar socioeconomic system could exploit any race of people, whether they are Jews or not.[30] In universalizing the play, Weiss eliminated the sometimes highly emotional testimony given in Frankfurt and reduced the witnesses to anonymous and virtually identityless "speaking tubes." Weiss's treatment is based on objective courtroom testimony in which the statements of witnesses, the interrogations by the court, and the responses by the defendants are factual opinions that do not arouse our emotions. The danger inherent in the play, then, is, as Robert Skloot notes, the idea of subordinating Jewish suffering to a more universal statement about political ideology: "Weiss's indictment of the capitalist system of the West for having produced Auschwitz, besides being dubious in the extreme, has produced a stage play of remarkably callous proportions, perhaps an ironic monument to the Marxist system he prefers."[31] Furthermore, as Sidra DeKoven Ezrahi infers, if Weiss had restored specific names to the witnesses, the effect would have been to give personality to them as well, thus creating audience empathy and therefore tainting his plea for scientific detachment.[32]

Weiss uses Brecht's concept of distancing to prevent the audience from emotionally identifying with the victims of Auschwitz. In the "Note" that precedes the play, Weiss laments the impossibility of staging Auschwitz (ix), or, as he stated to Paul Gray, "having people 'act' the concentration camp."[33] Instead, the Brechtian concept of having events narrated[34] allows Weiss the opportunity to distance the audience from the horrible reality of Auschwitz and focus instead on how *l'univers concentrationnaire* could possibly ferment. Weiss was talented enough as a playwright to represent Auschwitz on stage; the idea of not being able to depict the extermination camps realistically provides Weiss with an excuse to set the play in a courtroom where events are narrated, thus creating the distance that precludes emotional identification with the characters on stage. Since there is no set by means of props or decoration, we therefore never see Auschwitz and thus concomitantly are removed from the actual place of horror. Robert Cohen's comment on the play is insightful: "*The Investigation* is not a historical drama about Auschwitz, but rather a play about the Frankfurt trial."[35] By distancing the audience from Auschwitz and by numbing the spectators with hours of narrated statistics about the horrors of the camp, Weiss focuses on the incomprehensibility of the Holocaust and forces us to "investigate" rationally whether the event could occur again in capitalistic postwar German society.

The Investigation is virtually devoid of stage directions, as well as emotional reactions from witnesses and defendants. The one stage direction and the sole emotion that is consistently portrayed on stage is laughter from the defendants. In essence, the laughter serves as the antithesis to the thesis of the accused (criminal defense), thus forcing the audience to make its own conclusions (synthesis) about the dialectic. The laughter of the defendants can only lead the audience to the idea that the system that produces such callousness is corrupt. Moreover, laughter is carefully choreographed to correspond to Weiss's experiment with the form of the play. Hatja Garloff notes that Weiss's emphasis on laughter as the only emotion represented in the play "recalls the musical form of an oratorio (which is in the subtitle of *Die Ermittlung*), functioning as the chorus, while the individual, whiny vindications correspond to the arias."[36]

Weiss equates victims with executioners, thus removing individual responsibility from demonic activity in Auschwitz while concomitantly blaming the fascist system for the Holocaust. During his early years in the Gymnasium, Weiss was forbidden to give the Nazi salute because his family members were Czech citizens; his classmates went on to become Nazis. As a Jew, Weiss could never be a Nazi, a perpetrator; instead, he could easily have been a victim destined for Auschwitz. Since Weiss did not know of his Jewish heritage until his exile, he later understood that his will had nothing to do with his actions; he simply could not have joined the National Socialist Party as his colleagues did. If his father had not been Jewish, Weiss, like his classmates who relished the attraction of Nazi power, may well have been one of the executioners. In his interview for the *New York Times*, Weiss admitted, "All my friends were ordinary, good Germans, and most of them were killed or wounded in the war. Some may even have obeyed orders at Auschwitz. Might I not, too?"[37] Although Weiss's fiction and his outspoken views expressed in interviews suggest that he identifies with the oppressed, including Jews, South African blacks, the Vietnamese, and other victims of colonialism, racism, and imperialism, his notion of the interchangeability of victims and executioners downplays individual responsibility and puts the onus on the fascist and capitalistic systems that inherently seek to exploit the weak and disenfranchised. Witness 3 echoes Weiss's own sentiments: "Many of those who were destined/ to play the part of prisoners/ had grown up with the same ideas/ the same way of looking at things/ as those/ who found themselves acting as guards" (107); to phrase it more bluntly, Witness 3 adds, "And if they had not been designated/ prisoners/ they could equally well have been guards" (107–8). Since Witness 3 is the most perceptive person in the play and one whose views were not part of the original Auschwitz trials testimony, these words, conspicuously added by Weiss, obviously convey not only the notion that individuals had no control over their actions, but also that the accused are no more guilty than the victims. The fact that no indictment is made at the end of the play suggests that the individuals on trial cannot be guilty of crimes committed by a socio-economic system.

The Song of the Death of Lili Tofler and the Song of SS Corporal Stark are the only cantos in *The Investigation* dramatizing the plight of individuals—one a victim and the other an executioner. Their positions in the play as cantos five and six, respectively, out of the total eleven, suggest not only their centrality but also intimate the significance of the conflation of victim and executioner in Weiss's mind. Lili Tofler was a young typist who smuggled a letter to one of her fellow prisoners. Although Boger pressed a pistol to her head during a four-day torture period, she refused to reveal the name of the prisoner receiving the letter. Olaf Berwald argues that in the Lili Tofler episode, "The story of the courage and death of an individual Shoah victim emerges."[38] On the contrary, Lili Tofler's death is a *fait accompli* that removes individual choice as an option. Tofler violated the rules of the *lager*, which meant automatic death; the fact that she refused to name her friend and was thus tortured by Boger changed nothing, for she was shot anyway. SS Corporal Stark, only twenty years old, is, in contrast to victim Lili Tofler, the classic executioner. Stark is enamored with the poetry of Goethe, proud that he passed his exams at the Gymnasium in 1942, studied law, and became an instructor in an agricultural school after the war. His humanistic education plays no role whatsoever in preventing him from committing atrocities in Auschwitz. Instead of being able to think and act for himself, Stark's individuality is subordinated to fascist ideology. Stark abrogates any notion of individual responsibility for his crimes, characterizing the executions thus, "But it was an order/ It was my duty as a soldier" (152). Weiss indicates that the system thus crushes the staunchest humanists, reducing individuals to ciphers. Stark candidly admits, "There were others around/ to do our thinking for us" (158). The tales of Lili Tofler and Corporal Stark suggest that the exploitative nature of the fascist system, and not individual responsibility, determined their roles as victims or executioners.

Although the evidence against the accused is overwhelming, not one of them assumes individual responsibility for his actions. In an interview with Richard F. Shepard, Weiss discussed the refusal of the defendants to assume guilt: "I used their names, not to keep on trying them, but as symbols for the average, ordinary Germans who helped the machinery run."[39] The defendants feel exonerated because they were part of the normalcy of a socio-economic system that prospered in Germany at the expense of the victims. The play explores how individuals had no consciousness of their guilt because of the extreme abuse of power in a fascist government that is given ubiquitous approbation by its citizens–a system that alienated such people from their own actions. Weiss explained why the onus is on the fascist government rather than on the responsibility of the individual: "Why? Because their acts flowed inevitably from the nature of the society in which they lived."[40] For the victims, the destruction of their humanity became "normal" in Auschwitz. The Fifth Witness confides, "It was normal/ that everything had been stolen from us/ It was normal/ that we stole too/ Dirt sores and diseases/ were what was normal/ It was normal/ that all around us people were dying" (39–40). Equating victims with executioners, Weiss portrays the defendants as losing their humanity as well. Robert Cohen writes, "The system, designed to destroy any humanity in the *inmates*, also destroyed the humanity of the *camp personnel*."[41] Weiss goes to great lengths to portray the defendants as average citizens rather than as demons, sadists, deviants, or larger-than-life jackbooted perverts. Instead, Weiss focuses on the effective national brainwashing of the fascists and their ability to coerce human beings to surrender their humanity to conditioned thinking and total obedience to a system that has its own intrinsic rewards. Thus, although the witnesses argue that individuals could make choices, the defendants, politically conditioned, refuse to accept responsibility for the atrocities committed and instead make excuses for their actions: they were merely following orders (17, 152, 156, 193, 221, 272), never personally took part in the selections, hangings, or shootings (12, 26, 97, 163, 230), could not understand the accusations (19), empathized with the inmates (19, 25, 215), practiced passive resistance (27), could not recall any such brutalities (33, 49), had no authority to abuse prisoners (51, 91, 188), were strict but only did their jobs (52), conducted themselves the way everyone else did in the camp (54), maintained that witnesses lied about the atrocities (75), merely took severe measures against traitors and other enemies of the state (79), had responsibilities to one's own family (95), never heard any complaints from the prisoners (99), were being confused with someone else (174), and murdered only because patients were incurable and endangered the health of the entire camp (191). The witnesses were merely numbers in *l'univers concentrationnaire*, personified by the tattooed numbers etched into bodies that were removed of all personal possessions; the accused, although they have individual names, are given numbers by Weiss, for they are anonymous in their conditioned responses. Weiss wants to stress how the fascist system entices both victims and executioners into the normalcy of the quotidian.

Weiss wrote *The Investigation* not to castigate National Socialism for its racial ideology that precipitated the Holocaust, but to indict a capitalist system that alienated individuals from their own actions; in that sense, the play "investigates" the for-profit industrialized venture of Auschwitz. Weiss noted, "A large part of it [the play] deals with the role of German big industry in exterminating the Jews. I want to brand Capitalism which even benefited from the experiments of the gas chambers."[42] As Weiss traces the path of atrocities from the ramp to the crematoria, Auschwitz is depicted as a factory of destruction, a political and economic system of exploitation. Inmates were systematically relieved of their personal possessions, including jewelry and money. Gold was extracted from the teeth of the prisoners. Flesh carved from corpses was used in scientific experiments, while bones were pulverized into soap. Meanwhile, Weiss indicates that the Nazis, in the spirit of the commodification of entrepreneurship, kept careful inventories, including precise records of assets and production timetables; the only difference between the factory of Auschwitz and any other socio-economic system was the raw material used to manufacture the product: human corpses. In short, according to Weiss, under the fascist system of exploitation, racial oppression served economic purposes. Auschwitz is not an aberration for Weiss, since any fascist or capitalist system based on consumption and production could produce similar results. Thus, as Otto F. Best suggests, Weiss prefers to place the blame not so much on the regime that ran Auschwitz as a factory but instead on the society that produced such a system of exploitation.[43] Weiss corroborates what Best has concluded, clarifying the purpose of his "investigation": "It is capitalism, indeed the whole Western way of life, that is on trial."[44]

At Birkenau, adjacent to Auschwitz, factories were created to work Jews to death systematically. In the play, the First Witness specifies the names of these industries: "They were branch plants/ of I-G Farben/ Krupp and Siemens" (4). Moreover, the Degesch Company is specifically earmarked for supplying the gas, while Topf und Söhne are cited for building the crematoria, thus further linking private enterprise with the death factory. The symbiotic relationship between the Buna factories and the SS who ran Auschwitz made for unscrupulous profiteering in the name of capitalist industrialization. The Prosecuting Attorney, cross-examining the Second Witness, who was responsible for assigning prisoners to the factories, charges that huge profits were made by exploiting the deportees: "By the limitless grinding down of people/ you/ as well as the other directors/ of the large firms involved/ made profits/ that annually amounted to billions" (131–32).[45] The implication is that theft, brutality, torture, and murder were essentially excellent business propositions–and perhaps nothing out of the norm in any society based on accumulation of capital.[46]

During the Auschwitz trials, testimony frequently focused on the Adenauer and Walter Ulbricht administrations as a continuation of the frame of mind imposed by National Socialism. By keeping in tune with the spirit of factually oriented documentary theater, Weiss uses the trial testimony as a pretext for his attack on the Federal Republic of Germany circa 1965. After the war, I-G Farben, Krupp, and Siemens–the industries that profited during the Shoah–remained financially prosperous. The Prosecuting Attorney admits that the firms that did business with the fascists made billions and remain successful in capitalist Germany after the war: "Let us once more bring to mind/ that the successors to those same concerns/ have ended up today in magnificent condition/ and that they are now in the midst of/ as they say/ a new phase of expansion" (132).

Moreover, individuals who exploited victims during the fascist reign that produced Auschwitz were living in comfort and luxury during the postwar capitalist regime. The First Witness, responsible for delivering "freight" to Auschwitz via cattle cars, is now in an executive position as manager of the government railroads. The notorious Dr. Kaduk, feared for his ruthless beatings of inmates and for his stoical selections of prisoners for gassing, is now a hospital attendant beloved by his patients. The Second Witness, in charge of guards consigned to shooting prisoners who attempted to escape from the *lager*, is now the director of an insurance company. Knittel, a high school teacher who offered classes and entertainment for the SS officers in Auschwitz, has now been promoted to a principal. The First Witness, who worked prisoners to death as part of the war production effort of I-G Farben, currently holds a high advisory position in the government. Dr. Capesius, who operated the camp dispensary and was responsible for managing the use of the poison gas Zyklon B and the phenol used to inject prisoners in the heart, kept enough confiscated jewelry and extracted gold fillings to open his own pharmacy and beauty parlor after the war. A former chairman of the board of one of the Buna industries received a postwar pension that provided him with the luxury of collecting porcelain, paintings, and engravings while living in a luxurious castle. Weiss thus demonstrates how the exploitative nature of fascism made it easy for such criminals' transition into the capitalist society of the Federal Republic of Germany. The fascist system that created Auschwitz is not unique for Weiss; instead, it is as frighteningly "normal" as anything one would find in any modern industrialized capitalistic system. The irony, then, is that the play demonstrates that the capitalist-fascist systems exploit victims but allow mass murderers to flourish in splendor without reproach. Thus, as Catharine Hughes has perceptively realized, Weiss is concerned with the culpability of a system that, in the future, could again produce the same inhumanity in a "far more efficient guise."[47]

Weiss's premise that the victims and executioners are synonymous in a system that demands both for the purpose of exploitation has been challenged by Holocaust scholars. Primo Levi blatantly distinguishes between the executioners, who must be execrated, and the victims, who deserve help and pity: "We, the survivors, do not want confusions, blurs, morbidity, indulgences. The oppressor remains what he is, and so does the victim: they are not interchangeable, they do not overlap."[48] Moreover, Weiss's argument further breaks down when one realizes that the Jews were systematically worked to death in concentration camps, not for profit, but because the Nazis did not consider them to be part of the master race and thus were expendable as humans without any utilitarian value. In his analysis of *The Investigation*, Alvin H. Rosenfeld wrote, "Far from exposing a profit motive for Auschwitz, the evidence all points the other way: to gratuitous waste and needless elimination of human resources. The camps, far from existing for the primary purpose of exploiting slave labor for cheap production, murdered their slaves en masse and produced little more than corpses."[49] As a matter of fact, matters of economy did not dictate the fate of those interned in concentration camps; instead, labor without any productive purpose was the norm for those marked for genocide. Historian Daniel Jonah Goldhagen has done an extensive study on how the Nazis worked Jews to death in what appears to be an economically self-injurious manner and concludes the following:

> If the Germans had used all the Jews as slaves, which they could easily have done, then they would have extracted great economic profit from them. But they did not do so. They were like slave masters who, driven by frenzied delusions, murdered most of their slaves and treated the small percentage whom they did put to work so recklessly and cruelly that they crippled the slaves' capacity for work.[50]

If profit had been the primary reason for using Jewish labor, the SS would have fed and clothed these individuals properly in order to get from them the maximum productivity. Moreover, the Nazis murdered indigent Jews as well as wealthy ones; the impoverished Jews were executed certainly not because they were exploited (since there was little to exploit) but because they were Jews. Finally, Weiss's intention to glorify the virtues of socialism through a critique of fascism and capitalism makes for a spurious argument. Weiss admits, "The great thing about Socialism is its promise of complete human freedom once economic exploitation and class barriers have been eliminated."[51] Weiss conveniently chooses to ignore Jewish genocide during Stalin's socialist regime.

Weiss has certainly written a propagandist play, yet it is not without merit as effective theater of the Holocaust. During the play's early performances in West Germany, audiences sat mesmerized and exhausted before filing out of the theater, stunned but without applauding. The play was a profound educational experience, a no-holds-barred exposé of the carefully calculated bureaucracy of Nazi genocide. Roger Ellis claimed that the play has been successful despite the fact that audiences may have misunderstood Weiss's Marxist intentions: "It proved more important as a tragic oratorio on the horrors of Nazism than as a significant critique of Western capitalism."[52] Even today, when the play no longer has the same shock value that it had in 1965 when audiences were unfamiliar with the intricacies of the Holocaust, *The Investigation* offers a poignant reminder of a unique event that remains incomprehensible.

Tony Kushner's *A Bright Room Called Day* was first produced in a run of six workshops presented by Heat *&* Light Company and directed by Kushner at Theatre 22 in New York City during April 1985.[53] The first professional performances were staged in October 1987 at the Eureka Theatre in San Francisco. Oskar Eustis, who directed the production, substantially altered the original play staged during the 1985 workshops. In July 1988, *Bright Room* was performed at the Bush Theatre in London, where critics ravaged the play and its conflation of Nazism with the conservatism of Margaret Thatcher's prime ministry. Kushner substantially revised the play for the New York Shakespeare Festival, where it was produced at the Joseph Papp Public Theatre on 7 January 1991 under direction by Michael Greif. In the revised version, Zillah Katz, who Kushner envisioned as changing with the times, thereby allowing her to rant at will against any current political administration, is transplanted to Agnes's apartment in 1990s' Berlin, where her original diatribe against Ronald Reagan was then updated to include references to Iran Contra, Pat Buchanan, and George Bush. *A Bright Room Called Day* has also been presented by the Actor's Express Theatre in Atlanta (16 September 1995), the Connecticut Repertory Theatre in Storrs (27 February 1997), the Outward Spiral Theatre in Minneapolis (May 1999), and the Theatre of Note in Hollywood (April 2000).

Like Weiss, Kushner has been a disciple of Brecht, whose theoretical writings have provided guidance for the form and content of Kushner's plays. Kushner first encountered Brecht's plays during his freshman year at Columbia University when he read *The Good Woman of Setzuan* and *Threepenny Opera* in a modern drama survey course. During his sophomore year in 1976, Kushner, who was now reading Marx, went to see Richard Foreman's production of *Threepenny Opera* at least seven times at the Public Theater at Lincoln Center. Upon enrolling in a second modern drama course, Kushner became enamored with Brecht after reading the *Short Organum for the Theater*, *Brecht on Theater*, Walter Benjamin's *Understanding Brecht*, and *Mother Courage*; the latter drama Kushner has deemed "the greatest play ever written."[54] Turning his attention to directing after completing his degree at Columbia, Kushner mounted Brecht's *The Baden-Baden Play for Learning*. Kushner then applied to New York University's Tisch School of the Arts, largely because he envisioned a chance to work with director Carl Weber, Brecht's protégé from the Berliner Ensemble. His audition for entrance into the program included the staging of Brecht's one-act play, *The Beggar, or the Dead Dog*. During Kushner's graduate school work in the MFA program, Weber sharpened Kushner's directorial talents, made him more aware of the political responsibilities of the playwright, and inculcated him with the Brechtian notion that history teaches us vital lessons about the present. Kushner's recent directorial work with university and repertory theater groups has included productions of Brecht's *The Good Woman of Setzuan*, *Mother Courage*, and *In the Jungle of Cities*.

With regard to the structure of *A Bright Room Called Day*, Kushner borrowed much from Brecht. Eschewing traditional acts, Kushner, dividing the play into twenty-five scenes surrounded by a prologue and an epilogue, follows the German expressionist tradition of *stationen* that Brecht transformed into parables or gestus. Zillah's photo album, projected as a slideshow, becomes a narrating device derived from Brecht's use of newsreels that he himself borrowed from his own mentor, director Erwin Piscator. The mixture of verse and prose, while admittedly Shakespearean, is also very much like Brecht's epic theater. Zillah's interruptions are equivalent to Brecht's songs, as both devices reinforce the parable and simultaneously create a lull in the action to provide emotional distancing and an opportunity for the audience to think about the dialectic.

With regard to content, *Bright Room* was Kushner's attempt to write Brecht's epic theater. Kushner states, "I took a Brecht play that I have very little respect for, which is *Fear and Misery of the Third Reich*, and attempted when I started out to write *Bright Room* to do a sort of Reagan-era version of it."[55] The twelfth scene of the play, virtually in the middle of the text, is titled "Furcht und Elend" ("Fear and Misery"). The play imitates *Fear and Misery*'s pattern of showing the audience benign daily life while the world was disintegrating in Nazi Germany. Kushner also developed Brecht's model of invoking history to inform and shape the present; moreover, like Brecht, Kushner writes about broad historical developments and demonstrates how they inextricably affect individuals. In an interview with David Savran, Kushner acknowledged, "It's an interesting thing, because the more we know about history, the more we realize ... that it really does return, it never ends ... Even after the holocaust the monsters are still among us."[56] Whereas Brecht provided the structure for Kushner's plays, he, along with Kushner's reading of Marx, Leon Trotsky, and Walter Benjamin, shaped Kushner's Marxist ideology. Kushner told Wendy Arons that Brecht's conception of the dialectic enabled him to coalesce his utopian vision into the perfect union of politics and art.[57] *Bright Room* is essentially dialectical theater designed to make an audience think, argue, and galvanize politically, with the extended debate centering upon the choice between Agnes's withdrawal or Zillah's political activism. The synthesis of the dialectic is explained in Kushner's afterword to the play: "Better to be a Zillah than an Agnes."[58] Moreover, Zillah's political activism spawns a dialectic within the dialectic: whether Agnes's retreat is any different from the exile of her friends–a debate that Kushner personally would like to resolve because Brecht, his mentor, was in exile during the war.

The cynicism and fatalism of *Bright Room* derives from several despairing events in Kushner's life during 1984–1985. Weber, Kushner's mentor, left New York University to take a position at Stanford University at the same time that Kushner's alternate theater group, 3P Productions, disintegrated, leaving his prospects in commercial theater looking bleak. His best friend and frequent collaborator Kimberly Flynn[59] was seriously injured in a taxi accident, while his great aunt Florence, who became the model for Agnes, died suddenly. Kushner's personal woes coincided with what for him became an abysmal political situation with the reelection of Reagan in 1984. Kushner postulates that Reagan's reelection marked the end of any

Marxist hope for the future just as Hitler's rise to power designated the end of the Weimar Republic, when socialism briefly flourished. Kushner remarked, "And Reagan's reelection: Then as now, I see in Reagan's career a kindred phenomenon to Hitler's accession to power" (174). In retrospect, when Kushner wrote the afterword to the play, he still insisted that Reagan's policies of neglect with regard to the AIDS epidemic, the civil rights revolution, and the feminist movement were not only parochial and counter-revolutionary, but also could be compared with the genocidal indifference of the Nazis (176). In short, the personal and political conflicts that plagued Kushner at the time of writing became the focus of the play; Christopher Bigsby writes that *Bright Room* "is an account of those struggling to negotiate between internal needs and an external world which slowly begins to determine the parameters of that private realm."[60] The title of the play focuses on this "bright room," corresponding to a brief window of opportunity concomitantly representing the dual elections in 1932 and 1984 that could have rescued history from hopelessness. Kushner wrote the play as a warning signal, an omen about how contemporary society could slide into oblivion, much as it did in Nazi Germany, unless certain choices are made. Kushner, the political playwright, poses the fundamental question of why we elect individuals who misuse and abuse governmental power:

> In the grip of that knowledge, every human action, including the making of theatre, would have to be directed toward the abolition of such power and of the systems that maintain it. The brightest hope for the future would be any event, theatrical and otherwise, that presses this knowledge closer to home. (183)

Bright Room occurs in Berlin from 1 January 1932 to Hitler's rise to power on 12 November 1933, when the Nazis received a plebiscite during the Reichstag elections. Agnes Eggling, the center of attention and the only distinctly Jewish persona among her inner circle of friends, is surrounded by a stereotyped cast of colleagues who work with her in the German film industry. Several are communists, one is homosexual, and others may be Jewish, which makes all of them candidates for Nazi persecution. The communists are largely refugees in Germany–a situation similar to the German-born Weber's status in the United States. Moreover, the disintegration of 3P Productions was obviously on Kushner's mind when he wrote this play about the destructive effect of Nazism on the film artists of the Weimar Republic.

Agnes is persuaded to become a Marxist and to use her apartment as a meeting place for communist activities that are viewed as a deterrent to the imposing will of the Nazis. Gregor Bazwald (Baz), a homosexual who works for the Berlin Institute of Human Sexuality, was a socialist before he began to believe that Hitler provided Germans with orgiastic release of their frustrated sexual energies. Annabella Gotchling is a communist artist and graphic designer who makes posters that preach revolution against a capitalist system that she contends enslaves its artists while miring its citizens in inflation, unemployment, and monetary devaluation. She envisions a utopian society, where class does not matter: "The dreams of the Left/ are always beautiful. The imagining of a better world/ the damnation of the present one" (106). Vealtninc Husz, a cinematographer from Hungary, laments leaving his native country to come to such a barren artistic landscape as Germany. He is proud that he lost an eye during the communist revolution, and although the accident affects his camera work, he boasts that he gave part of his body to Trotsky. Paulinka Erdnuss, an actress in the German film industry, is the least radical of Agnes's inner circle of friends. A communist for only two weeks, merely because the Russians made the best films, Paulinka prefers to escape the rising tide of National Socialism by retreating into psychoanalysis and drugs. Like Faust, she dreams of doing business with the devil, which to her means prostituting herself to the Nazis so long as she can advance her film career.

As conditions deteriorate in Germany, Agnes's friends abandon her one by one. When the Nazis close the Berlin Institute for Human Sexuality and accuse Baz of printing pornography and promoting abortions, he goes into exile with a phony passport and visa. A slide representing the opening ceremonies at the Dachau concentration camp reminds us of the fate of many such homosexuals who remained in Germany. Gotchling flees to Switzerland without telling her friends.

When the fascists closed the electricians' union, Husz began filming the disturbance, only to be attacked by three Nazi thugs; although he supported resistance, Husz ultimately realized how futile it was and decided to exile himself to Chicago. Ironically, Paulinka, the least political of Agnes's comrades, after seeing Husz roughed up by the Nazis, decides to live in communist Russia.

Agnes's dilemma about whether to live in exile, revolt, or isolated fear is further complicated by the spectre of Die Alte, an enigmatic apparition who seems to haunt her throughout the play. Ostensibly residing in Agnes's apartment, Die Alte, a dead woman who vividly and lyrically recalls the destructive effects of war, is Agnes's alter ego. Die Alte is constantly hungry, pale, and clothed in a soiled dress that reflects the ravages of war; Agnes intuitively understands that she may ultimately become a war-blighted "old one." When Die Alte reveals, "I wound up all alone" (120) and then curses the Bolsheviks, Agnes goes into a fit of rage. Die Alte is able to calm Agnes momentarily but then re-cements the connection between the two of them when she states, "Time is all that separates you from me" (122). Die Alte frightens Agnes with her preference of retreat into isolation in lieu of commitment and responsibility. Die Alte remembers at the end of the war her inability to feel for the dead, arguing that she never pulled a trigger and was absent from the killing fields. Her only response was self-gratification: "and when they let us return to Munich/ I wonder what I'll find for dinner" (151). Her ominous warning to Agnes, "It's bad to be too much alone" (122), eventually falls on deaf ears.

Agnes Eggling, bit character actress of the German film industry, is influenced by her Marxist friends to aid and abet the communists. Agnes even writes an agitprop skit for a communist strike rally and struggles to read *Das Kapital*. However, when the Nazis outlaw the Communist Party and the Marxists decide to go into exile until fascism runs its course, Agnes puts personal comforts over the goals of the revolution. She admits that she has "a terrific apartment" whose low rent cannot be matched anywhere else (59). In refusing to go to Chicago with her lover Husz, Agnes laments her sense of conflict about exile: "I don't speak English. I can't function in strange places. It took me years to get a contract, what kind of work would I do in

Chicago? Traveling upsets me. Really. I can't move. I can't move. I'm sorry. Later, maybe ... " (129). Even when the film industry is incorporated by the Nazis and her political values are thus compromised, Agnes is still indecisive: "I don't know. I don't know what to do" (100). Kushner demonstrates the dilemma of many persecuted Jews in the 1930s who knew that conditions would worsen in Germany but feared the unknown factor inherent in exile. Refusing exile, Agnes makes one last defiant gesture. In response to Gotchling's request to use her apartment as a communist way station, Agnes reluctantly offers shelter to Rosa Malek for only one night.

Instead of resisting or going into exile, Agnes, living in paralyzing fear, isolates herself from the political upheaval. At one point in the play, Agnes exhorted her comrades to bond with the Social Democrats to unite against the Nazis; gradually, however, her lassitude leads to passivity. She confesses to Malek, "I'm afraid of living alone here, that something will happen to me. Stupid of me telling you this, you have such real things to be frightened of but ... I'm lonely. And years frighten me. I ought to do something to help but I'm simply not able" (145). James Fisher perceptively remarks, "Kushner warns that alienation, as depicted in his main character's agonizing inaction (her name, Eggling, suggests the protective shell–albeit easily broken– she creates around herself), leads to catastrophe, through an Orwellian depiction of the slow and steady closing in of her existence during the years 1932/33, in which the Weimar Republic falls and the Nazis seize power."[61] Since *Bright Room* is set entirely in Agnes's apartment, the room becomes a microcosm of life under the Weimar Republic for what will eventually be the victims of the Holocaust. As Christopher Bigsby realizes, the room "at first is an expression of stolid continuity, then the base for revolt, then a refuge and finally a cell."[62] Kushner comments on Agnes's retreat into fear, inaction, and powerlessness:

> I'm not advocating a politics of bipolar hysterical reactivity; but surely one of History's lessons, taught as eloquently and awfully through the Holocaust as any other event in human history, is that we must be wary of our attachment to the illusory comfort

of our rooms, the enormous familiar weight of everyday life– we must be wary of overvaluing stability. (179)

Without the inclusion of Zillah's interruptions, *Bright Room* could be considered a poignant Holocaust drama that depicts the tough choices of exile, isolation, or possible campaigning for socialist reforms within the Weimar Republic.[63] Kushner, through the voice of Agnes, expresses the dilemma of the powerlessness of benevolent individuals to combat the inexorable force of fascism. On this level, the play explores how the juggernaut of a political system destroys the dignity of the individual, which essentially is a major motif in Holocaust literature.

Zillah Katz is the protagonist of the play, connecting Kushner's seminal attack on contemporary American society with his need to explore his eastern European Jewish roots via the Holocaust. Living during Reagan's presidency, Zillah is first seen as a political activist who writes poisoned letters daily to the White House. Leftish in her political orientation, Zillah thrives on government acrimony and admits that the Watergate scandal was one of her happiest moments. Zillah senses parallels between the Reagan presidency and Hitler's dictatorship. In particular, Zillah equates Reagan's neglect of the AIDS epidemic with Hitler's mass murder of the Jews, spray painting on various walls, "REAGAN EQUALS HITLER! RESIST! DON'T FORGET, WEIMAR HAD A CONSTITUTION TOO!" (71). During eight interruptions, Zillah conveys the idea that history inevitably repeats itself and can be the best learning tool for the present in which the death of liberalism after Reagan's reelection parallels the vanquishing of socialism by the Nazis. In the production notes to the earlier version of the play, Kushner wrote, "To refuse to compare is to rob history of its power to inform present action."[64]

When Kushner revised the play for the New York Shakespeare Festival's production, Zillah, trying to reconnect with the past, moved into Agnes's apartment in Berlin. Now, in 1990, Zillah recalls how Agnes refused to give the Nazi salute fifty-seven years earlier. Zillah, like Agnes, feels frustrated by her inability to change a juggernaut of political oppression that makes individuals feel moribund and hopelessly inept. Zillah, however, totally removed from the haunting specter of Die Alte, is not passive like Agnes but instead actively seeks to learn from historical periods of cataclysm. Zillah believes that Reagan, and the Americans that elected him, ignored history and drifted into fantasy land. While experiencing at first hand the seeds of genocide in a nation where the lessons of the past are palpable, she goes on to compare Reagan, the Great Communicator, with Hitler, the master rhetorician: "Your Great Communicator spoke and created a whole false history, ours spoke and History basically came down with arteriosclerosis; from the Triumph of the Will to the Triumph of the Brain-Dead–from National Socialism to National Senility" (160). Zillah criticizes conservatives George Bush and Jesse Helms while asserting that Pat Buchanan would not have felt out of place in an intimate soirée hosted by the Goerings in 1942. After making contact with the ghosts of her ancestry, Zillah, unlike Agnes sequestered in her apartment, leaves the Berlin room with renewed enthusiasm, in a type of reverse exile, to reengage herself with life in the United States. Unfortunately, the association of the Reagan administration with Nazi Germany is tenuous, and Kushner assumes that there are parallels but focuses his attention exclusively on Germany. As Christopher Bigsby asserts, the American political culture that Zillah reviles "is never explored, dramatised or even explicated in the way that the Weimar Republic is."[65]

Kushner also links Hitler and Reagan with evil. Paulinka tells Agnes that Hitler's diabolical persona is infectious, for women who have slept with him become suicidal or are found murdered. After Paulinka accuses Hitler of being a coprophiliac, she asks, "Agnes, do you believe in evil?" (33). Zillah declares that Reagan is afflicted with Dupuytren's contracture, a disease that causes the hand to shrivel like a claw. Zillah argues that the letters in Ronald Wilson Reagan's name match 666–the mark of the Beast; moreover, the address of his retirement home is 666 Mayfair Road in Bel Air. Zillah finds Adolph Hitler's name to be more problematic because he has no middle name; however, she dismisses this small inconvenience by substituting Führer for the six letters that she requires. If the audience perhaps misses the implication that malevolent forces have infiltrated the United States after Reagan's reelection just as they did in Germany during 1933, Kushner hammers the point during scene thirteen, immediately before the intermission between the two acts of the play. Husz ushers the Devil onstage with a rendition of Mahler's Second Symphony. The Devil is a handsome blond Aryan named Gottfried Swetts, who recounts how he has become diffuse and invisible under the detritus of modern civilization. However, present conditions in Germany have given him renewed vigor, and he boasts, "I have taken up temporary residence in this country" (75).

Without delving into the causes of the demonic, Kushner adopts a simplistic Weltanschauung that postulates that the Nazis were evil. Immanuel Kant explained that evil occurs when a person deviates from moral law and revels in human degradation. Philosopher Kenneth Seeskin argues that evil is outside the bounds of rationality since philosophers throughout history have studied evil in depth and agree that it exists but cannot confirm its causes.[66] Holocaust writers like Kushner adopt the use of evil as a metaphor for primarily one purpose: to bring the world to its senses. Seeskin refutes the notion that the Nazis subverted morality; instead, their perverted values were the norm for a nation indoctrinated to vilify threats to the Reich. Seeskind writes, "On this view, the problem with the Nazis is not that they consciously affirmed evil, but that they had a highly distorted view of their own self-interest."[67] The Nazi view of morality affirmed that the Jews, communists, and homosexuals of Kushner's play were threats to the Volk; this ideology may be repugnant, yet because it was consistent with national laws, cannot merely be sloughed off as evil.

American and British theater reviewers criticized Kushner for equating Reagan with Hitler and for categorizing both regimes as evil; in his afterword to the revised edition of *Bright Room*, Kushner seemed to acquiesce, calling the play "immature" (172). However, when pressed for more information, Kushner, instead of relenting, reiterated that the Holocaust was not a unique event and that National Socialism, the paradigm for evil, has recurred in various forms: "I firmly believe in using the Holocaust model, promiscuously. I think we should be very liberal with likening people to Nazis."[68] In that same interview, Kushner claimed that Reagan was a Nazi because the indifference he had shown to the AIDS epidemic was genocidal.[69] What strikes Kushner as seminal in understanding *Bright Room* is the synthesis that results from the Brechtian dialectic, or what he expects audiences to learn from this piece of propaganda:

> And also, rather than make a sort of coy metaphor [between the Third Reich and Reagan era United States] and saying watch out it could happen here, the point of *Bright Room* is that the Holocaust is only useful as a standard of evil if you're actually willing to apply it, and if you don't apply it, if it's set up as a unique metaphysical event that has no peer, then those people really died for nothing.[70]

In the dialectic within the dialectic, we are led to understand that if the communists would have united with the Social Democrats and remained in Germany instead of withdrawing as Agnes did or going into exile like her colleagues, Nazism could have been defeated. Yet the play clearly acknowledges that although the Nazis lost votes after the second National Reichstag elections in 1932 while the communists gained seats, President Hindenburg nevertheless turned over the chancellorship to Hitler in 1933. Of course, there was no voting between 1933 and 1945. If the communists had stayed for a noble cause, their struggle, which would have been futile without a worldwide revolution, would have resulted in more communists interned and eventually murdered in concentration camps.

Thus, we realize that Kushner's only viable point is coded within the dialectic itself. Kushner likes to quote John Frohnmayer, the former head of the National Endowment for the Arts, who stated that in the Bush presidency during the years following Reagan, the United States was headed toward fascism.[71] Kushner wants us to understand that the Weimar Republic was a democracy that produced Hitler. Agnes, fully immersed in the cauldron of what Kushner describes as evil, admits, "What's so great about democracy?" (102). In short, voting, a basic tenet of democracy, becomes questionable because the results cannot be controlled. Elections may produce evil, for example, when political leaders such as Reagan or Hitler are chosen by the electorate. However, in socialist nations, where the wealth is more equally distributed among all classes, no voting is necessary, and thus evil, according to Kushner, cannot rear its ugly head. To Kushner, socialism is the means to stop the juggernaut of fascism and often equally ill-informed democracy. Like Weiss, Kushner therefore uncompromisingly and inappropriately rails against those "systems" that led to the exploitation of Jews, communists, and homosexuals, eventually supposedly leading to the genocide that was waged against them.

7 Aryan Responsibility During the Holocaust, I

During the trials of the perpetrators of the Holocaust, the existential notion of individual responsibility for one's actions was superseded by various excuses. The first defense for the Shoah was that rank-and-file Nazis were inculcated with absolute obedience to the principles of National Socialism. Indoctrinated with Nazi propaganda, inundated with the notion that Jews were primarily communists and thus were enemies of the Volk, intoxicated by anti-Jewish rhetoric of mass demonstrations, and threatened by the terroristic tactics of the Gestapo, perpetrators argued that individual responsibility was decided upon for them by the state. This philosophy also stems from the viewpoint that destructive acts are justified in terms of a higher good, much in the fashion that Christianity led to the Inquisition and the conquest of America led to the extermination of Indians. However, as Primo Levi realizes, the twelve years of the Third Reich did not form the sole educational experience of the perpetrators: "They were born and educated long before the Reich was openly 'totalitarian,' and their adherence to the regime was a matter of their free choice."[1] The overbearing nature of the Nazi propaganda machine, combined with a power hierarchy that molded bureaucrats into automatons and otherwise terrorized a civilian or military population refusing to conform, seemed to have made individual choices negligible. However, closer scrutiny of this argument finds that it is ungrounded. Even in the ranks of the disciplined *SS Einsatzgruppen*, defections were not uncommon. Daniel Jonah Goldhagen writes about the killing squads sent to exterminate Jews in Poland: "Offers and opportunities for removal from direct killing were accepted, both in front of the assembled battalion and in the intimacy of the platoons and squads."[2] Goldhagen acknowledges that SS men who professed a moral antipathy to the work they were doing in the execution squads were granted transfers if they requested them;[3] most of the perpetrators nevertheless continued to murder voluntarily.

Another seminal argument used by the perpetrators to justify their actions was that Germans, in the way their minds were shaped by educational institutions, were authoritarian personality types who gravitated to political systems such as fascism that demonstrated the power to captivate the masses. This type of thinking is warped, since millions of Germans voted for the communists before the Nazis gained power in 1933. Moreover, blaming the Holocaust on the pathological nationalism of the authoritarian personality precludes the possibility of individuals transcending the boundaries of institutionalized education. Furthermore, these same citizens who supposedly were obedient to state authority battled fiercely to rebel against the Weimar Republic in hopes of destroying it. Coinciding with the notion of the German authoritarian personality contributing to the Holocaust is the perpetrators' argument that they were merely following orders and had no other alternative. Obedience to the state was considered to be a virtue, and those who did not obey orders were deemed irresponsible troublemakers. Orders were absolutions that had to be obeyed for discipline to remain intact without breaking down. This attitude precludes the idea that humans have capabilities of making their own decisions and taking responsibility for their own moral actions. Examples abound during the Third Reich where orders were disobeyed on moral grounds without any repercussions to the guilty party. For example, no punishments were given to Reichbankdirektor Wilhelm, who refused to distribute second-hand goods to Jews, or to Sturmbannführer Hartl, who would not take command of a killing squad in Russia, or to Generalkommisar Kube, who interfered with an *Aktion* in Minsk.[4] Postwar trial defendant testimony indicated that the Nazis prosecuted merely fourteen cases of punishment for refusing to carry out an execution, and the penalties in most cases did not result in personal injury or death.[5] Protests among administrators of the occupied territories or in fascist regimes associated with the Nazis were often effective. For example, Italian military personnel, consuls, and police inspectors refused to cooperate with the deportation orders without enduring any repercussions. With regard to protests from the civilian population, the Nazis, not immune to public criticism, continued with their practices in secrecy when faced with individuals disapproving of their genocidal practices.[6] Bruno Bettelheim writes, "When ordinary German citizens witnessed utter brutality against Jews, some applauded, but among others there was at least some adverse reaction; and the Nazis were extremely sensitive to it."[7]

Another major contributor to the reason for denial of personal responsibility is that the perpetrators committed acts of atrocity primarily because of self-interest. The idea of advancing in career opportunities certainly does not justify murder or contributing to genocidal acts. Alarmingly, we are urged to accept the notion that the assumption of responsibility is defined individually, without regard for any empathy toward others. Yet this idea of exonerating oneself because of self-gratification is indefensible because most of the perpetrators were not angling for promotion or personal rewards as a result of their willingness to murder. This theory also does not explain why so many ordinary citizens in Nazi-occupied regions without recourse to advancement in the Third Reich aided the Nazis in identifying Jews and other politically undesirable persons, or why local police forces who were not part of the SS hierarchy, and therefore not promotable, assisted in the mass deportations. The other more benign excuses adopted by the perpetrators are obviously less tenable and suggest logical fallacies: defendants did not hate Jews and even had Jewish friends and acquaintances–they merely separated friendship from duty when involved in the killing operations; their crimes were mild compared to some of their comrades; they did not act alone, so if there is blame, the German people themselves, rather than any individual, must be responsible; they were powerless as individuals but felt fulfilled by the power fantasies of National Socialism; peer pressure was (undoubtedly) a strong influence for one to commit mass murder; and if one person refused to assume responsibility, another person would step up and do the job anyway.

What is omitted from the excuses of the perpetrators is any concept of morality or ethics.[8] Although morality is obviously based in individuals, because it is the result of concepts of shared values in the community, it is often not considered private. Ethics, although a matter of how individuals behave in society, provides community-based accepted rules, standards, and norms of conduct that people accept as inwardly experienced self-control that restrains the destructive power of humanity. With regard to the perpetrators, Raul Hilberg asserts, "To grasp the full significance of what these men did we have to understand that we are not dealing with individuals who had their own separate moral standards."[9] The Nazi policy makers were no different in their moral constitution than the average German citizen. The perpetrators represented a good cross-section of the German population, with every educational and skills level present at all points in the machinery of extermination. All of them were cultured people who had the ability to make decisions, take responsibility for their actions, and understand that moral responsibility was a legal duty to the German community. Eichmann, for example, pleaded guilty before God but not guilty according to German law. Nazis who also felt this way in assuming moral responsibility without the assumption of juridical guilt personified the arrogance of the high and mighty. As Giorgio Agamben astutely observes, many of these Nazis must have felt the burden of their own moral guilt, for they would not have committed suicide near the end of the war if they did not feel themselves to be legally responsible for their crimes.[10]

This chapter will explore the idea of whether moral choices could have been made during the Third Reich and what the consequences of those ethical decisions might have been. I will first examine the refusal of Nazi responsibility, which is best manifested in Richard Norton-Taylor's documentary drama, *Nuremberg*. Gilles Ségal's *All the Tricks but One* provides us with a stunning portrait of non-German yet Aryan lack of moral responsibility in the collaborationist Vichy government in France. Finally, Arthur Miller's *Incident at Vichy* provides a positive framework for the justification of moral values while indicting Western civilization for its inability to control its baser human impulses. This chapter focuses solely on Aryan responsibility, for Jewish commitment to moral values during the Holocaust must be judged in a different context amidst different, often more confining parameters, and thus will be dealt with in separate chapters.

British playwright Richard Norton-Taylor was born on D-Day, so he was not old enough to experience any aspect of the Holocaust first-hand. After writing for the *Washington Post, Newsweek, Financial Times,* and *Economist,* he joined the staff of the *The Guardian* in 1975. He eventually began crafting plays based upon transcripts of public inquiries, the most notable of which was *Half the Picture,* which focused on the arms to Iraq investigation.

Nicolas Kent, artistic director of the Tricycle Theatre in London, asked Norton-Taylor to adapt the Nuremberg trial transcripts for a possible play. The Nuremberg trials began in Berlin on 18 October 1945, and then shifted to Nuremberg, selected because of its symbolic value as the place of infamy for which the racist laws were named. An international military tribunal, consisting of American, British, French, and Russian judges, tried twenty-two Nazi political, military, and economic leaders on charges of crimes against humanity and the peace. The judgment, delivered on 30 September and 1 October 1946, after ten months of testimony, sentenced twelve of the defendants to death, three to life imprisonment, four to prison terms ranging from ten to twenty years, and acquitted three.

Norton-Taylor pared down the six million words of the trial's transcripts that included the testimony of thirty-three witnesses called by the prosecution and sixty-one by the defendants, bound in twenty-two volumes, into a one-hour one-act play. Using the actual words spoken at the trial, Norton-Taylor compressed more than fifty million pages of documents into the testimony of four defendants: Reichmarschall Hermann Goering, Chief of Staff Wilhelm Keitel, Reich Minister for Eastern Occupied Territories Alfred Rosenberg, and Albert Speer, Minister of Armaments and War Production; in addition, Rudolph Hoess (not to be confused with defendant Rudolf Hess, Hitler's deputy), who was the first commandant of Auschwitz, appeared as a witness for defendant Ernst Kaltenbrunner, head of the Reich Security Office.[11] Norton-Taylor seemed to include Hoess's testimony because it was most representative of the cold-hearted and unemotional, yet detailed, eye-witness accounts of the brutalities committed by the Nazis. *Nuremberg: The War Crimes Trial* was presented at the Tricycle Theatre in May and June 1996 along with three specially commissioned one-act plays (*Ex-Yu, Reel Rwanda,* and *Haiti*) that examined war crimes in Yugoslavia, genocide in Rwanda, and human rights violations in Haiti, respectively. During September and October 1996, *Nuremberg* was revived in a production that also featured Nicolas Kent's *Srebrenica,* an account of the International War Crimes Tribunal hearings held at The Hague to adjudicate transgressions committed in the former Yugoslavia and Rwanda. In an article published in *The Guardian,* Norton-Taylor noted that Kent, the director of *Nuremberg,* spent considerable time watching archival footage of the trial at the Imperial War Museum in order to capture the tone of voice and body language of the four defendants depicted in the play.[12] Kent also went to great lengths to ensure that the original courtroom in Nuremberg was recreated in detail at the Tricycle Theatre.

In his opening comments to the tribunal, Robert H. Jackson, chief prosecutor for the United States, stated, "These defendants will only deny personal responsibility or knowledge."[13] He also acknowledged that defendants who committed crimes against the state cannot take refuge in pleading a case of merely following orders, for the state, no more than a corporation, does not plot wars of aggression—individuals do. Sir Hartley Shawcross, chief prosecutor for the United Kingdom, reiterated the idea that morality supersedes political and military obedience, placing the blame squarely on individuals: "If these crimes were in one sense the crimes of Nazi Germany, they are also guilty as the individuals who aided, abetted, counselled, procured and made possible the commission of what was done" (6). However, after hearing these opening comments from Jackson and Shawcross, each of the defendants recites the oath swearing to tell the truth and then proceeds to lie about the extent of his involvement in crimes against humanity.

Goering, with his cleverness, flamboyance, and confident manner, provided the most intriguing testimony. As the man appointed by Hitler to head the Reich after the Führer's suicide, Goering could not readily abdicate responsibility. Goering initially told the tribunal that the concentration camps were created as a refuge for enemies of the state (9), a statement obviously appealing to judges who would not take too kindly to treason. Goering argued that the events in the concentration camps were kept secret, and not even Hitler knew to what extent the genocide was occurring. When asked about the millions of Jews and other enemies of the Volk who had been reported by the foreign press as exterminated, Goering stated that he did not listen to foreign broadcasts and did not read propaganda. Moreover, he had never killed anyone, never decreed murder, and never tolerated any such atrocities (53). Goering simply denied having understood that the Nazis adopted any policy to exterminate Jews. In feigning ignorance of the Final Solution, Goering, with his penchant for loquacity, refused to be responsible for any lack of morality. In response to General Rudenko's query about whether it was inconceivable for the second in command in Germany to be unaware of Hitler's plans to exterminate millions, Goering simply replied, "No, because I did not know anything about them and did not cause them … If I actually did not know them, I cannot be held responsible for them" (19).

Keitel argued that he was a career soldier who served for more than forty-four years under the Kaiser, President Friedrich Ebert, Field Marshall von Hindenburg, and then Hitler. Keitel claimed that Hitler's decisions were "unalterable" (22), which meant that it was his duty to carry out the Führer's orders. Insisting that he was a virtuous man who may have made mistakes but was never cowardly, dishonorable, or faithless to the state, Keitel refused to acknowledge any immorality or lack of ethics. Resolute in defending the need for unquestioned obedience to authority that stemmed from a Prussian code of discipline that Keitel suspected the prosecutors could not comprehend, the chief of staff adamantly and consistently professed that it was not possible for a soldier to disobey an order from the Führer. When pressed by his private counsel about whether he, as an individual capable of thinking and acting for himself, ever had personal doubts about committing immoral acts, Keitel reiterated that a soldier gives up his private life in the military (232). By following orders explicitly, Keitel refused to take responsibility for his actions and instead asserted that his position with regard to criminal activity was virtuous: "I am convinced that the large mass of our brave soldiers were basically decent, and that where even they overstepped the bounds of acceptable behaviour, our soldiers acted in good faith, believing in the military necessity, and the orders which they received" (21).

Rosenberg, who supervised the ideological education of the National Socialist Party and thus largely contributed to the propaganda against Jews, offered the least effective testimony. As the contributing writer and editor of virulent anti-Semitic documents, Rosenberg's comments, verifiable in print, were thus indisputable. At first, he tried to blame Himmler for creating concentration camps that, as Rosenberg politely put it, were benignly designed to "take action" against "nationals who refused to do war service" (37). With regard to statements he wrote about the extermination of Jews, Rosenberg resorted to semantic games about the meaning of "extermination": "It means to overcome in one sense and then it is to be used not with respect to individuals but rather to judicial entities, to certain historical traditions" (40). Rosenberg then went on to state that there is a vast difference in murdering individual Jews, ostensibly those who were traitors to the state, and exterminating Jewry. Ultimately, his defense deteriorated into a trivial denial of individual responsibility: "These accusations are described as 'genocide'–the murder of peoples. In this connection, I wish to summarise as follows. I know my conscience to be completely free from any such guilt" (54).

Speer was the only defendant who provided some semblance of moral culpability and appeared to be more interested in the fate of Western civilization than in his personal fear of retribution. As Minister of Armaments, Speer was responsible for Germany's industrial strength soaring after 1942, largely on the backs of slave labor. Speer admitted, "This war has brought inconceivable catastrophe to the German people and has started a world catastrophe. Therefore, it is my unquestionable duty to assume my share of responsibility for this misfortune before the German people ... In so far as Hitler gave me orders and I carried them out, I assume the responsibility for them" (42). Whereas the other defendants blamed Hitler–a dead man who could not counter the accusations– for their transgressions, Speer distanced himself from the Führer and even admitted to opposing his orders near the end of the war. Speer testified that in the latter stages of the war, he realized that the totalitarian system of unquestioned obeisance to those in the highest echelon of the Third Reich resulted in "tremendous danger" (46). Speer lamented the idea that, by disseminating propaganda through the technological advances of radio, telephone, teletype, and loudspeakers, Nazis were able to deprive citizens of independent thought. Assessing the gravity of what such implications meant to the future of Europe, Speer thus was able to argue that Nazi leaders must assume a larger collective or historical responsibility for the fate of Western civilization. Speer took the initiative to accept personal responsibility for a greater moral cause, stating, "Therefore, the more technical the world becomes, the more necessary is the promotion of individual freedom and the individual's awareness of himself as a counterbalance" (55). In his closing remarks, Speer intimated that the trial would be historically important in establishing a moral code for Western society: "The Trial must contribute towards preventing such degenerate wars in the future and towards establishing rules whereby human beings can live together" (55).

Nevertheless, Speer, like the other defendants in the trial, pleaded not guilty. In his final speech to the tribunal, Chief Prosecutor Jackson noted that all of the defendants had access to Hitler yet did nothing to alter the plans to commit crimes against humanity. Shawcross recounted an emotionally charged eyewitness account of the massacre of five thousand Jews at Dubno, which represented a small percentage of the twelve million deaths he attributed to the Nazis. Shawcross concluded that even in a totalitarian system, each person must assume individual responsibility for their actions. Finally, Shawcross implied that an individual's moral sense supersedes the notion of loyalty to any political system or to the demands of its leaders: "This trial must form a milestone in the history of civilisation, not only bringing retribution to these guilty men, but also that the ordinary people of the world (and I make no distinction between friend or foe) are now determined that the individual must transcend the State" (52).

French playwright Gilles Ségal's *Le Temps des muets* (*All the Tricks but One*), written in ten scenes spread over two acts, received its world premiere on 17 January 1992, in a production directed by Kenneth

Albers at the Milwaukee Repertory Theater. Born in Romania in 1929, Ségal's family immigrated to France in 1932. During the Nazi occupation in 1942, when Ségal, his mother, and father were arrested by the Nazis, thirteen-year-old Gilles managed to escape while his parents were sent to Auschwitz. Sheltered in safe houses with the assistance of members of the French Resistance, Gilles eventually managed to find asylum in neutral Switzerland. While studying philosophy at the Sorbonne after the war, Ségal also learned the art of mime after making his acquaintance with Marcel Marceau. Ségal, in working with Marceau and director Jean-Louis Barrault, became interested in theater, particularly choreography, acting, and pantomime. Ségal went on to appear in nearly fifty films, including *The Madwoman of Chaillot* (1969), *Mon premier amour* (1978), and *Black Light* (1994). His most notable accomplishment in film was writing the screenplay for director Jules Dassin's *Topkapi* (1964), in which he also played the role of Giorgio.

All the Tricks but One occurs in Limoges, France, during 1944, which was near the end of the Vichy government's collaboration with the Nazis. Little Slam, a Chaplinesque mime (sans Chaplin's white face and dressed in period attire rather than as "the little tramp") is actually a Jew named Blumenfeld who assumes the Anglicized French name Champfleury to hide his identity from the Nazis.[14] Champfleury goes by the stage name Little Slam, which is a term in bridge to indicate when you hold all the tricks but one; as an adept mime, Little Slam knows all the stage tricks, except how to effectively play the game of hide-and-seek from the Nazis. With a strong Yiddish accent, Little Slam avoids revealing his eastern European voice by posing as mute. Proficient at puppetry and mime, Little Slam is ostensibly hired by the theater director to increase the crowds during performances.

The Director and his wife invite Little Slam to live with them and their grandson Ludovic for the sole reason that it gives them the opportunity to act as good citizens by hiding a Jew from the authorities. Although the Director and his wife are both Nazi collaborators, the war is near its end, and if the Allies prevail, the couple hope to be rewarded for their benevolence toward Jews. In other words, with the outcome of the war irresolute, the Director hopes to placate both sides by using Little Slam as a pawn in the process. Initially, Little Slam thought the Director courageous for risking his life by harboring a Jew. However, Little Slam soon begins to feel uncomfortable in the home of a Nazi collaborator who listens to Vichy government radio programs that one moment spout propaganda about the "brave French troops" that have joined "the valiant Germans in their fight against the Red menace!" and then conclude with "Deutschland Über Alles."[15] At the same time, Little Slam must survive in a household where Ludovic's father is fighting alongside the Germans on the Russian front.

The Deputy Mayor of Limoges is also a shady character out for his own gain and nothing more. He exhorted Nelly, an actress in the theater, to fraternize with Maurice, the leader of the Resistance, in order for him to keep the Nazis abreast of any trouble brewing. However, the Deputy Mayor threatens to turn Nelly in to the Nazis unless she convinces Maurice, who has since become her lover, to understand that the "honorable" Mayor is actually a supporter of the Resistance. Thus, the Deputy Mayor covers all bases should either side prevail in the war. When the Deputy Mayor sees Little Slam's circumcised penis as Blumenfeld leaves the shower, the battle for possession of the Jew heats up. At this point, the play delves into black comedy as the dialogue between the Deputy Mayor and the Director for possession of the Jew becomes hilariously pathetic. The Deputy Mayor, hinting that he is looking out for the Director's welfare, mentions that he would not want anyone to reproach him for harboring a Jew; however, the mention of the transgression subtly indicates that the Director has not been true to Nazi principles and is thus in danger. To avoid having the Director shot by the Nazis, the Deputy Mayor offers to lodge Little Slam at his own house so that he, a fellow collaborator, will be in good stead with the advancing Allies. When the Director claims that Blumenfeld is his Jew, the Deputy Mayor offers to buy him, or at least rent him for a couple of days each week as a sort of pet. After the Director promises to find the Deputy Mayor a Jew of his own, the latter comments, "you can't find a single one ... I don't know where the bastards are hiding themselves." (46). Writing about this scene, Edward R. Isser praises the way Ségal indicts the Vichy collaborators for their irresponsibility and self-serving attitudes: "Ségal creates farce out of terror without undermining the historical narrative. It is one of the most effective and revealing scenes in all of Holocaust drama."[16]

The Jew is treated as a commodity in the play rather than as a human being. When the Director's Wife asks her husband to estimate the price for which he would sell Little Slam to the Deputy Mayor, the Director responds as if he is trading on the stock market: "Ah, no, this is not the moment to sell! ... not on the rise!" (51). He then admits that if he finds another Jew, he could sell Little Slam because there is "no need to accumulate them" (51). When the Director's Wife discovers that Jews can sell for a million francs, she hatches a plan involving the local priests who are harboring a Jew. She threatens to alert the Jesuits to a German raid on their school with the intention of having them entrust their Jew to the Director and his wife; then they can sell the Jew to the Deputy Mayor for a million francs. Moreover, if the war is won by the Allies, the Fathers would testify about the Director's good intentions to protect Jews. The Director and his wife need to shield themselves from the Allies because they sent their son to fight with the Germans in return for the favor to manage their own theater while the Nazis conveniently had the former director, Milhaud, arrested. We learn that the Director, once he became a sycophant for the Nazis, even turned in his own daughter-in-law as a member of the Resistance, leaving his grandson without parental supervision.

Although Little Slam is treated as an object by the Director, his wife, and the Deputy Mayor, he does establish a meaningful, trusting relationship with Ludovic. Their friendship is symbiotic: Little Slam becomes the boy's surrogate parent while the youngster truly cares for his mentor and treats him as an individual rather than as a member of an ethnic group. The games of charades and hide-and-seek that they play together reinforce Little Slam's artful resolve to remain mute and take refuge from the unrelenting pursuance of the Nazis. When Ludovic brandishes a real pistol and points it at the Nazi Colonel, thinking that it is merely a toy, Little Slam intervenes to prevent disaster, blurting out in his strong Yiddish accent, "Stop, he's only a boy, he doesn't know what he's doing! Stop, he's only playing!" (66). In protecting Ludovic, Little Slam has assumed enormous responsibility in risking his own life, which ultimately leads to his being deported to a concentration camp.

Ségal, with his background in mime and puppetry, had the inspiration to mesh a realistic portrayal of Aryan irresponsibility during the Holocaust with performance art. During the play, Little Slam performs five interludes that reflect his plight as a Jew fleeing the Nazis. In his audition for the job in the theater, Little Slam becomes a marionette who begs for mercy, receives none, and then cuts the strings to suggest possible suicide. Then Little Slam is reinvigorated by his puppet friend, mirroring the future situation in the Director's household in which Ludovic's friendship assuages Little Slam's despair. During other theatrical vignettes, Little Slam mimes being pursued by a spotlight, then tries to turn the tables by juggling with the beam of light , chasing it with a butterfly net, and attempting to seduce and trap it, always to no avail. Edward R. Isser observes, "This comic routine of Little Slam mirrors the situation of the Jew Blumenfeld who is always running in search of sanctuary and who loses his voice and identity in the process."[17] The implication of the interludes is also that the Jew is always in the spotlight in Vichy France while finding control of the situation to be futile.

After the Allies liberate France, the Director and his wife are forced to defend their acts of collaboration in a courtroom, which is reminiscent of the defense of the Nazis during the tribunal in *Nuremberg*. With regard to remorse over treating Jews as objects, the wife reluctantly admits to the President that her actions were regrettable: "Oh, certainly, yes! Oh yes! I surely tell myself that it wasn't right ... Since you say so" (70). When the President wonders whether the Director had any morality, the latter responds that he sided with German authorities, whose education led him to believe they must have had a moral sense. The former Deputy Mayor, previously a collaborator, now claims that he was a member of the Resistance and denounces the Director and his wife. Little Slam, newly liberated from the concentration camp to which he was sent, enters to testify. As he begins to speak, Ludovic bursts into the courtroom to reveal that his father was killed in battle. Now feeling the brunt of the *angoisse* derived from living in fear, exile, and desperation, being deported, and then learning of Ludovic's loss, Little Slam actually goes mute. As Little Slam stares at the Director, he mimes a terrible mute cry, and the circle of light that once pursued him goes black.

Like the Nazis who testified before the Nuremberg tribunals, the Director and his wife argue that individual responsibility was decided for them by the state. They sided with the Vichy government and thus believed that the state, represented by the majority of French citizens, was to be blamed, rather than individuals, for any wrong-doing. Ségal's play demonstrates how Aryans during the war often acted out of self-interest, displaying virtually no empathy for Jews. Significantly, the word "Jew" is never mentioned in the play, although the derogatory "yid" is used once; this suggests the qualms that the average French citizen had of even having the word on their lips for fear of repercussions. *All the Tricks but One* effectively indicates how Jews were treated as objects during the Holocaust as typical Aryan citizens refused to take responsibility and acted out of self-interest rather than making moral choices; all of this may explain the reluctance of the French to stage the play in France.

Arthur Miller's *Incident at Vichy* is also concerned with Aryan responsibility during the Vichy government. Moreover, the play ties in with *Nuremberg* since *Incident at Vichy* was written three years after the film debut of *Judgment at Nuremberg*, with "incident" substituted for "judgment" while the locations change. Furthermore, *Judgment at Nuremberg* was based on the International War Crimes Tribunal while the genesis of Miller's play derived from the 1964 Auschwitz trials that he attended in Frankfurt.

As early as 1941, in an essay published in the inaugural issue of *Jewish Survey*, Miller drew attention to the Nazi persecution of Jews even before the Final Solution had been implemented. Miller specifically mentions the fate of the French Jews in the Vichy government: "But even in the misery of French concentration camps a Jew or anti-fascist is not at the end of his journey, for Vichy confirmed on August 22 that the Gestapo has been allowed to enter those camps in search of enemies."[18] Miller pleads with diplomats in England, the United States, and South America to assist Jewish refugees in exile from Nazi persecution. As George W. Crandell remarks, Miller's essay puts the onus on apathy and indifference regardless of political or geographical boundaries, "and he therefore holds everyone responsible for the unchecked spread of Nazism."[19]

In 1964, Miller, having never seen a Nazi or a mass murderer and thus wishing to learn of their motives at first hand by covering the hearings in Frankfurt, contacted the *New York Herald Tribune*, which commissioned him as a special commentator on the Auschwitz trials. Whereas Peter Weiss was struck by the easy transition that the fascists made into capitalist society after the war and thus blamed the genocide on socio-economic systems, Miller's impression of the Auschwitz trials was focused on how civilized and cultured Germans could commit such atrocities without assuming responsibility for their acts. Miller realized that the defendants argued that they were following orders, yet he could not comprehend their ubiquitous moral collapse and lack of individual conscience. Miller concluded, "So the question in the Frankfurt courtroom spreads out beyond the defendants and spirals around the world and into the heart of every man. It is his own complicity with murder, even the murders he did not perform himself with his own hands. The murders, however, from which he profited if only by having survived."[20] These impressions of the Auschwitz trials formed the basis for the ideas that he would explore in *Incident at Vichy*.

After his return from Europe in May 1964, Miller, fresh from his visit to the former Mauthausen concentration camp and from covering the war crimes trial in Frankfurt, spent three weeks writing *Incident at Vichy*. The inspiration for von Berg came from Miller's friend and former psychoanalyst Dr. Rudolph Loewenstein, who told him of a Jewish man in Vichy who was saved from deportation when an unnamed gentile stranger substituted for him in a police line-up.[21] Ingeborg Morath, Miller's third wife, mentioned her former friend, Prince Josef von Schwarzenberg, an Austrian nobleman who refused to cooperate with the Nazis and thus was relegated to menial labor in France.[22] Von Schwarzenberg's worldly discernment and his pure moral code that reduced Nazism to enforced vulgarity became the second model for von Berg, whose name is a shortened version of that of the original Austrian aristocrat.

Miller, most likely adversely affected by the critical reaction to his previous play, *After the Fall*, which theater reviewers complained was too long, structured *Incident at Vichy*, a companion play to *After the Fall*, as a ninety-five-minute one-act drama. The form of the play is conventional realism in which Miller adheres to the unities of time, place, and action. Miller was fairly adamant about his purpose for the play, and thus only twenty lines of his original draft were altered for the first performances.[23] *Incident at Vichy* premiered on 3 December 1964 at the American National Theater and Academy (ANTA) Washington Square Theatre with performers from the Lincoln Center Repertory Company. The production, which subsequently alternated in repertory with *After the Fall*, was directed by Harold Clurman, whose strong cast included Hal Holbrook (the Major), Joseph Wiseman (Leduc), and David Wayne (Von Berg).

Incident at Vichy, which ran only for 99 performances, was given mixed notices by theater reviewers, who primarily felt that the play consisted of too much dialogue and not enough movement; the actors remain immobile while the audience ponders Miller's "sermon" on human responsibility.[24] Miller was thus accused of subordinating dramatic effect to polemics. The characters in the play were seen as one-dimensional typed figures, an unusual comment since Leduc and von Berg engage in a philosophical debate that alters their personae. Coming on the heels of Hannah Arendt's treatise on the banality of evil in *Eichmann in Jerusalem*, critics challenged Miller's premise that if all of us are complicit with Nazi crimes, then none of us can be held responsible; in short, Miller, like Arendt, was accused of removing the Germans from the burden of their Holocaust crimes. Obviously, most Holocaust dramas generate little entertainment value for American theater goers, but Miller's play offended international audiences as well. The Russians, seemingly upset over Miller's dismissal of the communist Bayard, banned the play for nineteen years, while the French, not wishing to be reminded of an anti-Semitic regime that collaborated with the Nazis, persistently prevented the play from being performed. Nevertheless, the comment from Martin Gottfried, Miller's biographer, that the play has never received a major revival at the time of his writing (2003) is false.[25] In 1966, Peter Wood staged *Incident at Vichy* at the Phoenix Theatre in a London West End production that featured Alec Guinness as von Berg. In 1973, Stacy Keach directed the play for a production presented on National Public Television in the

United States. In the early 1980s, the French finally relented, which allowed Pierre Cardin to produce the play in Paris, albeit resulting in weak theater reviews. Finally, in 1987, after Gorbachev eased the tight reins that the communists had on the arts, Miller's play was produced by Galina Volchek for the first time on the Soviet stage. However, Miller's remarks about Russian anti-Semitism forced the Soviets to close down the production shortly after its premiere.

During the initial controversy over the play's staging at Lincoln Center, Miller attempted to vitiate the vitriolic attacks by explicating his intentions in "Our Guilt for the World's Evils," published in the *New York Times*. Miller postulated that hostility and aggression lie hidden in every human and should be perceived as the norm rather than as the exception.[26] Miller stated that the rabbis who collected the Old Testament began with the story of Cain because they recognized its seminal contribution as a tale of fatal blindness to our own hostilities. Cain's question about whether he is his brother's keeper should best be framed by asking "Am I my own keeper?" Each person must accept the responsibility for one's actions. The Holocaust is thus viewed as viable because of the lack of commitment of so many who became complicit with universal evil. Guilt merely becomes the soul's remorse for its own hostilities. As Christopher Bigsby readily understands, Miller reminds us that we exist after The Fall and "It is necessary to reconcile ourselves to that fact instead of parading a specious innocence."[27] Thus, with regard to von Berg's position about feeling guilty over his affection for his Nazi cousin and for having been spared as a non-Jew, Miller writes, "Again, guilt can become a 'morality' in itself if no active path is opened before it, if it is not transformed into responsibility."[28]

The underlying model for the principles Miller espouses in *Incident at Vichy* can be found in Sartre's existential Weltanschauung. Sartre postulated that existence precedes essence; in other words, humans are born free and thus can create their own existence, and by doing so, they choose the type of person they will become. At the time of our deaths, we will be judged by the Other through our actions, which have created our existence. Sartre argued for human responsibility determining one's existence instead of relying on external forces, such as God, socio-economic conditions, environment, class structure, church, family, or state. Although we are defined by our past deeds, Sartre understood that the Self is fluid and keeps evolving. According to Sartre, most humans prefer never to make choices or to take responsibility for their actions—a condition that he described as *mauvaise foi* (bad faith). We may even have good intentions to act responsibly, but fantasizing about our actions is not equivalent to acting.

Incident at Vichy has much in common with Sartre's 1944 one-act play, *Huis clos* (*No Exit*). With regard to their structures, both plays are circular and follow the unities. *No Exit*, written at the time of the Nazi occupation of France, depicts hell on earth. Inez, Estelle, and Garcin are confined to a hellish room where there is no escape from the eyes of the Other and no chance of egress. All three characters are defined by their past actions; in hell, it is too late to take responsibility, so they must forever endure the gaze of the Other. As egotists, they have made the wrong decisions by believing that their actions had no meaning for others and thus have rendered their own lives meaningless. *Incident at Vichy* occurs in a similarly hellish room where eight men and a boy of varying classes and ethnicities (most are Jews) wait for Nazi interrogation with the possibility of "no exit." Christopher Bigsby describes the situation: "We are in the anteroom to hell, in limbo, where people are gathered together to learn their fate, a fate against which there appears to be no appeal."[29] Most of the detainees while waiting to be summoned to their deaths pretend, in the spirit of bad faith, that freedom will come or that they can rely on external forces for their salvation. Eric Sterling perceptively remarks about the detainees, "Their strong desire for self-preservation results in their attempt to mainstream themselves, to assume that the Nazis actually seek 'the other.' In their attempt to survive, these men shed their responsibilities as well as their consciences."[30] However, they are all in the detention center because of conscious choices that they have made, even though they do not understand that their fate is based upon free will. For example, Lebeau remains in Vichy because, although he had an American visa in 1939, his mother refused to abandon her furniture.[31] He laments, "I'm here because of a brass bed and some fourth-rate crockery."[32] Monceau stayed in Vichy to keep the lead in *Cyrano,* and Leduc ventured out that morning to obtain some codeine for his wife's toothache. Sheila Huftel remarks, "It was all avoidable. They were caught over nothing. Only the boy had a real reason for being out that morning. He was on his way to the pawn-shop with his mother's wedding ring, because there was nothing at home to eat."[33] Lawrence D. Lowenthal, who has written extensively about Sartre's influence on Miller's existentialism, states that Miller views original sin in a godless universe as an impulse residing in all of humanity. However, Miller believes in personal redemption because, as Lowenthal explains, "Miller shares Sartre's insistence on free will and the possibility of 'transcendence' or the recreation of self through a succession of choices."[34] Each of the characters in the play, whether detainees or Nazis, has the ability–and responsibility–to make choices that affect how they are perceived by the Other. The Nazis can deport Jews and Gypsies or rebel against such orders, while the detainees can resist or succumb to their oppressors.

Like the Nazi defendants in *Nuremberg,* the Major abdicates responsibility under the guise of following orders. The Waiter describes the Major as a benevolent, cultivated man who plays the piano beautifully and strives to better himself by taking French lessons. Although he is depicted as a decent person with good intentions who insists that his training is in engineering and artillery, not deportation, he understands that he must obey his superiors, including a professor of racial anthropology who admits that his methods of identifying Jews by circumcision are spurious. The Major rationalizes his role in the deportations, claiming that he is doing the job temporarily until an SS officer relieves him. He admits to Leduc that he has "feelings" about his duties and sympathy with the detainees (54), but he refuses to act because his life would be threatened in an absurd universe where ethics and responsibility are moot. The Major assures Leduc that even if he could help the detainees, his sacrifice would not change the evil in the world because new Nazis would be brought in the next day. Miller depicts the Major as a morally and physically tainted individual (he has a limp from combat at Amiens) who has resorted to alcohol as a crutch for his refusal to act. He practices bad faith through a self-inflicted defeatism that reinforces the notion that individuals are not responsible for the world's evil, so he believes that he might as well follow orders. Thus, the Major is defined through determinism rather than his own will. Lowenthal explains that the Major personifies the answer to Miller's query about how highly civilized and cultured individuals could commit such atrocities as experienced during the Holocaust: "Since essence is never given but rather chosen and constantly renewed, a man *is* what he *does*, and all the Major's civilized instincts are nullified by his uncivilized acts."[35] The Major hides behind the veneer of civilization and culture, which does not mask the fact that he *acts* inhumanely.

The Old Jew and the Gypsy are the most passive among the detainees. The Old Jew, in his seventies, spends his time praying, taking refuge in a decaying eastern European culture that reacted passively against the Nazi threat of genocide. Like those who practice bad faith, the Old Jew relies on external forces to combat the world's evil. However, as Janet N. Balakian has observed, "Although Miller claims that the Old Jew's eyes are watching God, there is a strong sense in *Vichy*, as in all of Miller's dramatic worlds, that this is a Godless universe."[36] June Schlueter and James K. Flanagan argue that the silent scream of this victim who refuses to act while praying that the dignity of Jews be respected makes the Old Jew, in Miller's eyes, as much the oppressor as the oppressed.[37] The Old Jew spends his time in detention clutching a bundle of feathers that scatter once he is forced from his seat. He was carrying his bedding like a refugee attempting to hold onto an Old World identity eventually made worthless by the Nazis. Miller admitted to Steven R. Centola that the scattering of feathers "does have an aspect of weakness, but also of domesticity, an uprooted domesticity."[38] The Gypsy, like the Old Jew, is inured to assuming any responsibility for his dilemma, and, like the Old Jew clutching his bundle of feathers, pays attention only to his copper pot. Preferring to ignore the reasons for his arrest, he becomes the ideal scapegoat. In his production notes for the original performances at Lincoln Center, director Harold Clurman described the Gypsy as "indifferent," "disconnected from the others, from their problems," one who "abstracts himself from his environment."[39] In isolating himself from the world, the Gypsy's abnegation of responsibility seals his fate.

Marchand, the wealthy businessman, is above the fray, believing that only those who are outcasts, like Gypsies, could possibly be detained. He is oblivious to the Holocaust, acting impatiently as if this "routine identity check" (4) has nothing to do with racial implications. Marchand's confidence rests with the order and efficiency of the Vichy authorities, so he assumes that his role in state government will preclude any possible deportation. Lowenthal states that Marchand is disgusted by the Jewishness of others while considering himself to be purely French.⁴⁰ This would indicate that he is practicing bad faith by ignoring his racial identity and thus obviously refusing to act because he believes the authorities need to reward their valuable businessmen, not murder them. Indeed, Marchand is given a white pass presumably because his release, for Miller's purposes, creates the impetus for the other detainees to provide excuses for their lack of responsibility and their inability to take action.

Bayard, the Marxist electrician, sees himself persecuted not as a Jew, but as a socialist who is a threat to the fascists. He blames the plight of the detainees on socioeconomics, explaining to Lebeau, "Big business is out to make slaves of everyone, that's why you're here" (6). Bayard views the German occupation as a result of the class struggle: "The bourgeoisie sold France; they let in the Nazis to destroy the French working class" (30). Bayard, who has learned that Jews are being worked to death in Poland, is only fooling himself when he states that the fate of individuals will be redeemed by the socialist revolution, "when the working class is master of the world" (32). He abdicates the existential notion of individual responsibility in favor of reliance on the theoretical notion that historical determinism will defeat Nazism. In his view, the proletariat "will destroy Fascism because it is against their interest" (34). Edward Murray depicts Bayard as a Rousseauistic "romantic": "He refuses to agree with Leduc that human nature has a propensity to evil as well as to good. No, argues Bayard, the Germans are bad because they are Fascists–if they became, Bayard implies, Marxists they would then be admirable fellows."⁴¹ Bayard's argument is countered by Leduc, who states that the communists refused to support France when the Nazis invaded. Moreover, von Berg assures Bayard that the Nazis and the proletariat are united in a common cause since "ninety-nine per cent of the Nazis are ordinary working-class people!" (33). Bayard's bad faith is exposed when he breaks off the handle of the Gypsy's pot to use as a wedge on the freight train doors– a precautionary measure if his communist revolution never materializes and he is thus deported.

Monceau, the actor who is accustomed to playing roles for audiences, believes that the means to avoid Nazi persecution is through more role playing. Monceau frames much of his argument in theatrical terminology. To Monceau, responsible action means the talent of creating one's own reality of self-assurance, thus relying on hiding behind a mask. Monceau confidently states, "The important thing is not to look like a victim. Or even to feel like one" (29). To him, if one plays the role of a valuable citizen, then one can, in a theatrical sense, act out an illusory identity that coincides with who your papers say you are. Monceau views the detention center as another stage illusion where the actor must perform. His audience is the cultivated intellectual that he performed in front of on German stages, people who "could not burn up actors in a furnace" (46) and whose culture demands an obeisance to laws that protect citizens. Monceau's immersion into the illusion of acting before audiences has made him blind to the reality of the impending Holocaust. He assures the detainees that his cousin dispatched to Auschwitz has found meaningful work as a bricklayer. The Waiter's announcement of bodies being burned by the Nazis in Poland is treated as "fantastic idiocy" (36) by Monceau, who insists that the Germans would not destroy their own labor force. He deludes himself into believing that the Nazis are doubling the rations for those who "volunteer" to work in Germany (16), while those in the Free Zone are immune from persecution anyway. In choosing the self-destructive role of victim, Monceau concedes not taking responsibility for his predicament and thus engages in Sartrean bad faith. When Leduc suggests that the detainees collectively attack the guard, Monceau defers, stating that he refuses to risk his life for no good cause; he plans to be released anyway, and even if the assault were successful momentarily, the Germans would catch the offenders within an hour. Dennis Welland contends that Monceau's "attitude is self-deceiving, his outward confidence masking an inner defeatism."[42] This defeatism is eventually exposed by von Berg, who tells the tale of how Monceau's "cultivated" Germans murdered an Austrian oboist after listening to him rehearse in the prince's orchestra. When Monceau persists in his role as non-victim, refusing to believe that his fate could be the same as this fellow artist's, Leduc, wondering how Monceau will play to his audience when the Nazis "point to that spot between [his] legs" (49), concludes, "Your heart is conquered territory, mister" (52).

Lebeau, the painter, deludes himself through immersion into a world of imagination. Working in abstract art, Lebeau is frustrated with people who insist on finding definitive meaning in his paintings. Lebeau states, "But you get tired of believing in the truth. You get tired of seeing things clearly" (50). He prefers invention and illusion to the horrid reality of the Holocaust and admits, "I could never paint what I saw, only what I imagined" (51). He assures himself that he is being detained and his nose measured so the Nazis can find laborers merely to carry stones. Lebeau assumes that since he has verifiable papers, he cannot be in danger, and if this spot check were more serious, the Nazis would have employed additional guards. Lebeau refuses to accept the reality that he is being detained because of his religion, so he, in his imagination, divorces himself from Judaism. He objects to being associated with the Old Jew, whose beard indicates an eastern European origin from which the Frenchman divorces himself. Lebeau, wishing to trade places with the uncircumcised von Berg, fantasizes, "Actually, I'm often taken for a gentile myself" (28). His sense of guilt for being a Jew makes him complicit with the evil preying upon him. According to Sartre, he is living an inauthentic existence reflected in the eyes of the anti-Semitic Other, becoming what the Nazis envision him to be instead of being himself. As Lowenthal suggests about Lebeau, "instead of transcending the Other's gaze, he allows himself to be paralyzed and destroyed."[43] Rather than struggle to avoid his imminent deportation, Lebeau, preferring to fantasize about how the Nazis arrested him "by mistake" (50), retreats into the passivity that Miller, the existentialist, abhors.

Leduc is the *raisonneur* of the play, the articulate voice of *bon sens*. As a psychiatrist who studied five years in Germany and Austria, Leduc analytically probes the intricacies of the human mind, like

Miller himself. He has learned about the absurdity of a world where humans are not reasonable and are instead murderous and evil. In remarks derived from Sartre's *Antisemite and Jew*, Leduc discusses how individuals use Jews as scapegoats for their latent hostilities:

> Part of knowing who we are is knowing we are not someone
> else. And Jew is only the name we give to that stranger,
> that agony we cannot feel, that death we look at like a cold
> abstraction. Each man has his Jew; it is the other. And the Jews
> have their Jews. (66)

Recognizing the evil inherent in all humans, Leduc, in response to Monceau's query about whether civilized Germans could commit genocide, says, "It's exactly because they are people that I speak this way" (20). Thus, Leduc understands that the first step in exchanging guilt for responsibility is accepting complicity with universal evil.

As a captain in the French army, Leduc is a motivator and a man who understands the need for action, applying the Sartrean concept that when one chooses for oneself, he or she chooses for all humanity. Fearful of acting passively, Leduc several times exhorts the detainees to take action and rush the guard. When the Major professes his sympathy for the detainees, describing the Nazi treatment of Jews as "inconceivable," Leduc prefers actions to words, expressing doubts about the Major's "condolences": "I'd believe it if you shot yourself. And better yet, if you took a few of them with you" (53).

Leduc, however, suffers from paralysis; on the one hand, he is an adept spokesman for the Sartrean call to action and assumption of responsibility, while, on the other hand, he hesitates to act himself. Leduc poses under the guise of a heroic army officer, but the reality is that he has spent the last couple of years hiding from the Nazis. Terry Otten notes, "Striking the pose of a hero, he tries to compel the others to act by overcoming the guard, yet Leduc himself does not initiate action and only follows the Boy when he bravely bolts for the door guarded by a lone soldier."[44] Leduc gives good advice to others about the dangers of complicity with the world's evil, but he fails to take responsibility for his own actions until his fate is sealed, and then, knife in hand, he approaches the corridor to escape. Miller comments, "But my own emphasis in everything I've done is the action of a person vis-à-vis himself. You can't be curing the world."[45] As Leonard Moss reiterates, salvation for Miller's characters lies first in self-knowledge, which Leduc seems to lack.[46] Leduc's willingness to psychoanalyze others may be a means to mask his own insecurities. Writing about Leduc, Benjamin Nelson infers, "Verbally committed to a perilous but imperative action, he never takes it, and his inability to do so defines him as accurately as all his probing analysis and eloquent rhetoric."[47] Leduc blames his wife for sending him out for codeine that morning and exhorts von Berg to tell her of his deportation to the furnaces to take revenge on her. Leduc thus refuses responsibility and instead operates through masochistic despair, whining to von Berg, "What scum we are!" (63). However, Leduc's philosophical rants will be put to the test after he is released, for he needs to assume responsibility on two accounts. First, he has promised the Boy to return his mother's wedding ring to her, a gesture that was of utmost priority for the youngster. Second, since von Berg has given him a white pass, Leduc must accept the guilt for the death of the prince. What is important is whether Leduc transforms this guilt and concomitant masochist despair into responsible action.

Wilhelm Johann von Berg, the only character in the play with a first and last name, is Miller's protagonist who becomes a paragon of virtue. He stands apart from the other detainees as a nobleman, and, although he is Catholic, he is the only individual in the group with a distinctly Jewish-sounding last name. As an Austrian, von Berg has had first-hand contact with the Nazis, whom he scorns as vulgar and vile for having destroyed human dignity. When the Nazis began murdering his musicians, von Berg contemplated suicide. Miller explained to Richard I. Evans how von Berg's guilt has been exacerbated by not being persecuted like the orchestra members he supported: "But he himself had always opposed the Nazis. Yet, as a Gentile they had spared him personally, and in his having survived by accident, so to speak, he now experiences an upsurge of guilt."[48] Von Berg also feels guilty about his cousin Baron Kessler, who assisted the Nazis in Vienna with deportation of Jews from the medical school.

To his credit, von Berg has already shown potential for acting responsibly, since he fled Austria rather than collude with a class that oppresses people. Yet his sympathy for the suffering of Jews and his hope for the triumph of cultural humanism over vulgarity reflects a naive type of idealism. Such faith in culture is only natural for von Berg since his name, which is a thousand years old, and his title derive from the European sense of *noblesse oblige*. Leduc, who, as a psychiatrist is trained to rid patients of their guilt, explains to von Berg that his sympathy for Jews and his guilt for the actions of Baron Kessler are irrelevant: "It's not your guilt I want, it's your responsibility–that might have helped" (67). Leduc asserts that von Berg's guilt for his cousin makes him complicit with the world's evil that he so readily condemns: "Baron Kessler was in part, in some part, in some small and frightful part–doing your will" (67). Whereas guilt is passive and induces self-paralysis (a condition with which Sylvia Gellburg is afflicted in *Broken Glass*), responsibility means acting existentially, or, to use Sartre's terminology, "engagement." Von Berg gives his white pass to Leduc in an act of salvation and martyrdom that eradicates his personal complicity with Cain and also with the perpetrators of the Holocaust whom he so despises. Moreover, von Berg now becomes the victim of the Holocaust and thus assumes the role of the Jew, the eternal Other; as such a victim, he learns about the responsibility in partaking of the world's evil. Kinereth Meyer's analysis of von Berg's conversion is noteworthy: "The self-sacrificing Christian, Von Berg, becomes Leduc's 'Jew' and, Christ-like, dies in his place–*imitatio Christi* taken to its logical conclusion."[49]

Lawrence L. Langer questions whether von Berg's gesture merely imposes the temporary idealism of self-sacrifice on a hopeless situation.[50] During the play's denouement, more detainees are brought in, and Leduc may not get far before he is rounded up again. Langer concludes, "But the magnitude of the sorrow and loss dwarfs the deed, however noble, of one man for one man; *Incident at Vichy* illuminates the difficulty, perhaps the impossibility, of affirming the tragic dignity of the individual man, when it has been soiled by the ashes of anonymous millions."[51] Miller's denouement indicates that absurdity is endemic to life, yet while the cycle of evil continues interminably, he refuses to believe that individual responsibility cannot redeem humanity. As Christopher Bigsby so aptly recognizes, Miller's epithet seems to be, "Not to rebel against the absurd is to succumb to it, to compound it."⁵² Unlike the Nazis tried for their crimes in *Nuremberg*, and the Vichyites who collaborated with the Nazis in *All the Tricks but One*, von Berg's moral act transcends self-interest, negates the absurd condition, and becomes the embodiment of responsibility among so many Aryans who claimed they could not refuse to cooperate with Nazi genocide.

8   Aryan Responsibility During the Holocaust, II

German playwright Rolf Hochhuth's *Der Stellvertreter* (*The Deputy*) has much in common with Miller's *Incident at Vichy*. Both plays indict the entire Western Christian civilization for its complicity with evil, and both offer the thesis that we must not be indifferent to the world's inhumanity. Miller and Hochhuth insist that the only moral response to the Holocaust is for the individual to act responsibly devoid of divine inspiration or, as the existentialists would acknowledge, without relying upon outside influence. Not to resist or doing nothing is sinful and is equated with acquiescing to those directly responsible for inflicting cruelty, oppression, and suffering on others. As such, Miller and Hochhuth make humans accountable for their own deeds in spite of the absurd or in deference to individuals who prefer to act as automatons in mass society. Miller and Hochhuth certainly share the view that only committed individuals can change society or even history. Thus, Hochhuth should have logically been paired with Miller in chapter 7. However, *The Deputy* warrants a separate chapter because it stands out as being the most controversial and the most cited twentieth century Holocaust drama, having been translated into more than twenty languages; as early as 1964, Egon Schwarz noted that the play was "probably the most discussed work in the history of German drama."[1] Furthermore, as Eric Bentley stated about the play's production history, "*It is almost certainly the largest storm ever raised by a play in the whole history of the drama.*"[2]

Although he was raised in an anti-Nazi household, as a ten-year-old in 1941 Hochhuth became a member of the *Deutsches Jungvolk*, a Hitler youth group; his father and brother fought in the

German armed forces. Marianne Heinemann, whom Hochhuth met at age ten and who later became his wife, recalls the traumatic experience when the Nazis arrested her grandmother, whom Marianne was only to learn years later had been decapitated in prison. In an interview in the *Saturday Evening Post*, Hochhuth remembered the end of the war: "I was 14 in 1945, and the total collapse of Germany was a great emotional shake-up for me. I considered it my responsibility to study the shameful history of the Third Reich."[3] After the war, Hochhuth was educated in the *Gymnasium* but decided against taking the traditional graduation exams and instead went on to work in bookstores in Munich, Heidelberg, and Marburg, where he became largely self-educated. He had read Gerald Reitlinger's *The Final Solution*, which provided accounts of actions by Roman Catholics on behalf of Jews during the Holocaust and an assessment of the pope's political penchant for neutrality and diplomatic immunity. Upon the death of Pope Pius XII in 1958 and his subsequent "canonization" through world opinion, Hochhuth decided to investigate the role of the papacy during the war.[4]

For three years, Hochhuth, who began his research in Rome in 1959, talked to ecclesiastics and carefully examined the memoirs, court proceedings, biographies, diaries, and letters pertinent to the Vatican's response to the Holocaust. Particularly germane was the memoirs of Baron Ernst von Weizsäcker, the German ambassador to the Vatican during the war years. Due to its controversial subject matter, *Der Stellvertreter* was denied publication by Rütten and Loening Verlag but was picked up by Heinrich-Maria Ledig-Rowohlt, a more courageous publisher, who recognized its timeliness in coinciding with the Eichmann trial. The play soon became a bestseller, with Rowolt printing over forty thousand copies during 1963 and approximately two hundred thousand copies a year later. For his efforts, Hochhuth garnered two literary awards: he shared the Gerhart Hauptmann Prize in 1962 and won the Young Generation Playwright Award in 1963.

Through Rowolt, German director Erwin Piscator received a copy of the play. As the recently appointed artistic director of the Freie Volksbühne in Berlin, Piscator was searching for a daring play that would become part of the new repertory season, and *Der Stellvertreter* accommodated him perfectly. The play premiered on 23 February 1963 at the Freie Volksbühne in West Berlin in an abridged production that reduced act five to a short epilogue. Within the next two years, international productions were mounted in Stockholm, Paris, London, Basel, Berne, Helsinki, New York, Vienna, Athens, and Odense, the most notable of which were Ingmar Bergman's 1963 staging at the Dramaten in Stockholm, Peter Brook's 1964 version at the Théâtre Athénée in Paris, the sensationalized, heavily condensed adaptation of Jerome Rothenberg and Herman Shumlin presented at the Brooks Atkinson Theater on Broadway in March 1964, and Clifford Williams's Royal Shakespeare Company performances in London during 1965. The play was also staged in the West German cities of Frankfurt, Essen, Düsseldorf, Hamburg, and Bochum, and when Hochhuth reconsidered his view that the communists might use the play as propaganda against West Germany, it was then performed in the East German cities of Dresden, Rostock, Leipzig, and East Berlin. Public protests often accompanied the productions, particularly in Berlin, Vienna, Paris, New York, and Basel. In Paris, members of the audience leaped on stage shouting, "A bas les juifs" and tried to interrupt the performances. In Basel, two hundred police officers restrained crowds of up to 2,500 protestors who tied up traffic for hours.[5] London audiences had to contend with demonstrators who handed out leaflets, defaced theater posters, and threatened the performers. In New York, Jewish organizations initially tried to dissuade Shumlin from producing the play; Catholics marched outside the theater during performances, and audiences were not allowed to leave the auditorium during intermission.

Accompanying the public protests was a furor that took place in the press. Never before in theater history was a play so vigorously debated among theater scholars, religious leaders, politicians, sociologists, historians, journalists, diplomats, and theologians. Hochhuth was personally attacked as being young (thirty-two years old when the play was staged and not old enough to have experienced the Holocaust first-hand), provincial, and, as a Protestant, uninformed about Catholicism or the papacy.[6] One source of contention was Hochhuth's interplay of historical material with fiction. Although he researched the material for years, the pope, the nuncio, Gerstein,

Eichmann, and Professor Hirt are the only historical figures in the play, which means that the majority of the characters are fictitious; moreover, the seminal confrontation between Riccardo and the pope and the Auschwitz scenes are fictitious, prompting critics to question the historical authenticity of the play. Another major complaint was that, as a German playwright, Hochhuth's objective was to shift the blame for the Holocaust from the German people to his scapegoat, the pope. Much of the criticism also revolved around Hochhuth's depiction of the pope as a cold diplomat whose primary purpose was to protect the institution of the Church. For example, Alfred Gong complained, "Even the negative hero of a tragedy deserves to be shown as a human being. The author, however, denies his pope any trace of inner conflict. Or is his dramatic talent not up to the job? The pope behaves like a talking marionette."[7] Religious leaders who intimately knew Pope Pius XII came to his defense. Francis Cardinal Spellman testified that the pope was "incapable of any base motive of personal cowardice" and instead acted compassionately toward people of all ethnicities; he feared that Hochhuth's play would only serve to drive a wedge between Catholics and Jews.[8] Cardinal Montini, who served Pope Pius XII from 1937 to 1954 and who was later to become Pope Paul VI, argued that the pope's "frail and gentle exterior," "sustained refinement," and the "moderation of his language" concealed "a noble and virile character capable of taking very firm decisions" that Hochhuth, with his inadequate understanding of "psychological, political and historical realities," failed to grasp.[9] Other theologians defended the pope as a man of peace who strongly believed that any protest against the deportations of Jews would further anger Hitler, thus exacerbating tensions between the Nazis and Catholics while possibly even causing more strife for the Jews.[10]

With regard to the form of *The Deputy*, Hochhuth eschewed theater of the absurd, as well as Brechtian epic theater and documentary drama with which his German colleagues were so enamored.[11] Instead, Hochhuth mixed several theatrical genres, including realism, tragedy, expressionism, morality plays, and melodrama. Attempting to maintain historical verisimilitude, Hochhuth tried to create historical drama in the Schillerian tradition of *Don Carlos*. Historical drama is often grounded in the techniques of realist theater, which, for Hochhuth, included the conventional five-act structure so dominant in the Renaissance and through the nineteenth century in Europe, cluttered sets, copious stage directions in the Shavian tradition, and contemporary dialogue. Hochhuth's subtitle of the play, *Ein christliches Trauerspiel* (*A Christian Tragedy*), is not meant to be taken as the Aristotelian concept of tragedy in which the protagonist falls due to a flaw in his or her character, inducing a purgation of pity and fear in the audience. Walter Kaufmann best clarifies Hochhuth's intentions about his conception of tragedy: "The play ends tragically, and the hero is not merely a nominal Christian or a man who happens to be a Jesuit, but one who tries desperately to become a Christian in the most demanding sense of that word. I doubt that a tragedy more Christian than that is possible."[12] Three monologues of deportees on their way to Auschwitz presented in act five, scene one, provide Hochhuth with the opportunity to experiment with expressionist poetry. Moreover, Hochhuth's almost Manichean sense of good versus evil, although found in Schiller's drama as well, invariably is derived from medieval morality plays. Hochhuth seems to regard the characters as allegorical, typed representatives of good (Riccardo and Gerstein) versus evil (the Doctor), or victims (the Jews) versus executioners (Nazis and church leaders who share complicity with evil). In his list of dramatis personae, Hochhuth states that characters in any one group can be portrayed by the same actor. As Rainer Taëni has noted, "even when they have historical prototypes, the characters are explicitly regarded as more or less interchangeable."[13] Finally, the melodramatic elements, including the conventions of shocking surprises, ill-planned escape attempts, mistaken identities, the unexpected saving graces of a *deus ex machina* contrivance, and violent sensationalism, all coalesce in the machinations of act five.

Hochhuth's use of a modified free verse with an iambic quality in lines of either four or five stresses served several purposes. First, verse drama gives Hochhuth's subject the requisite gravity of classical tragedy. Second, free verse allowed Hochhuth to use a heightened language that would transcend any notion that he was writing documentary drama that would appear to be similar to a naturalistic newsreel-type reenactment of history. Hochhuth observed, "Otherwise, it [the play] would often be likely to sound as if one were merely quoting from the documents."[14] Third, Hochhuth believed that poetry would produce more of an emotional response from the audience than would prose. Finally, as R. C. Perry realized, Hochhuth's verse, which many audiences confused with prose, functions as effectively as prose: "he is able to incorporate historical documents, facts and figures and logical arguments, as well as various realistic-sounding jargons and dialects, because his verse is not far removed from the sphere of everyday speech."[15]

The Jews in the play represent the victims whose secondary status affords them little psychological depth. Robert Skloot notes that Hochhuth depicts the Jews as representatives of all oppressed people, and, as such, they elicit the empathy of the audience.[16] When we first see Jacobson, he is hiding from the Nazis in Gerstein's Berlin apartment. He has recently learned of the deportation of his parents and understands that the elderly are gassed immediately. Although Jacobson is German, he is forced to flee his native country and thus becomes the wandering Jew without a homeland. Assuming the alias of Father Fontana, he is betrayed by his passport photo and shipped to Auschwitz. Carlotta, the Italian Jewess who converted to Catholicism, partly to conform to her husband's religion but also to avoid persecution, is nevertheless deported to Auschwitz. Upon learning of the deaths of her family members, Carlotta loses faith in humanity and has a nervous breakdown. Susan E. Cernyak-Spatz describes Carlotta's betrayal of her Jewish faith as she becomes merely another victim: "She is given, instead, all the attributes of a born *Untermensch* without dignity or even the basic instincts of moral preservation."[17] Finally, the Luccani family members, hastening to pack before the Nazis find them in hiding, are deported as well. The irony of the scene is that Luccani Sr. had converted to Catholicism years ago, but because of his Jewish heritage, he is not spared. When the Luccani children, eight and five years old, respectively, are carted off by the Nazis after arguing about which toy to take with them, the emotional impact of watching the plight of these helpless victims being deported beneath the windows of the Vatican becomes draining.

The Nazis are depicted as crass perpetrators typifying the banality of evil that Arendt characterized as the German mentality during the Holocaust. This behavior is best manifested in the *Jägerkeller* scene, which is reminiscent both of Auerbach's *Keller* in *Faust I* and the second scene of Carl Zuckmayer's *Des Teufels General*. The scene occurs in a clubroom in a suburban Berlin restaurant where the Nazis, several of whom have official duties in Auschwitz, are enjoying a night of bowling entertainment. In the spirit of *Gemütlichkeit*, the Nazis, drinking heavily, engage in a cacophony of derisive laughter and festive celebrating. Dr. August Hirt, an anatomist who collects skulls at the University of Strassburg, boasts about how the Final Solution is necessary from the scientific point of view. The comparison between his nonchalant gathering of skulls, as one might collect coins or stamps, and the bowling balls he handles is readily apparent, suggesting that even the educated are not immune from the banality of evil. Helga, the nineteen-year-old who transfers to Auschwitz to be near her fiancé working there, is the life of the party; later, in Auschwitz, we will see that she records the number of Jews gassed, performing as if she were carrying out any other type of mundane clerical assignment. Baron Rutta, a Ruhr industrialist, is oblivious to his use of slave labor and seems only to be concerned with the potential manpower the Nazis can supply to his factories. Of course, the host of the festivities is none other than Eichmann himself, whose overt vulgarity and brutality, combined with a latent desire to do whatever is necessary for advancement, makes him an icon for the other crass perpetrators.

The only noble Nazi in the play is Kurt Gerstein, who is based on an actual historical figure. Gerstein joined the Nazi Party in 1933, but because of his active involvement that included distribution of anti-Nazi pamphlets as a Protestant in the Confessing Church, he was dismissed from state service in 1936. After a brief prison internment followed by imprisonment in a concentration camp and subsequent to the death of his sister-in-law, a victim of Hitler's euthanasia program, Gerstein volunteered for the Waffen SS to learn more about Nazi genocide. As an engineer assigned to the Technical Disinfection Department, Gerstein witnessed the effects of Zyklon B gas during inspections in Treblinka, Belzec, and Sobibor. After August 1942,

Gerstein met with religious leaders, including the papal nuncio in Berlin, to expose the Nazis' plans for mass murder.

Gerstein represents, on the one hand, a Nazi sworn to fulfill his duties, and, on the other, the man of conscience whose Christian faith outweighs all other obligations. Hamida Bosmajian describes Gerstein's predicament: "In his case the ethical and psychological problem arises of how long one can commit crimes through the persona of the uniform before the uniform and the crimes touch one's real self."[18] Adhering to the teachings of Kierkegaard, the first existentialist to make the connection between religious faith and moral behavior, Gerstein's life is dictated by responsible moral behavior as a spy of God. When Riccardo presses him on the reason for his Nazi membership, Gerstein states, "You cannot drive unless you're at the wheel./ Dictatorships can be demolished only from within."[19] Gerstein shares Miller's view that humans must first assume complicity with the world's evil before they can take moral responsibility for it. When Riccardo asks Gerstein how cultured Germans, "the nation of Goethe, Mozart, Menzel," could be so barbarous (the question Miller pondered after the Auschwitz trials), Gerstein replies that the Germans are no worse than other Europeans, implying that evil is endemic to humanity. His existential sense of commitment is exemplary of the Aryan responsibility that Sartre and Miller advocate. Gerstein admits to Riccardo, "Those who keep silent are accessories to murder,/ and they imperil their immortal souls" (80). Emanuela Barasch-Rubinstein astutely remarks, "It seems that Hochhuth chose him [Gerstein] as a central figure in this play not only because he wanted to perpetuate his memory, but also because he embodied in his life the young German as Hochhuth would like him to be: brave, pure-hearted, with a deep sense of moral duty that governed his actions."[20] Throughout the play, Gerstein takes responsibility for changing an absurd, corrupt world. He informs the nuncio of the genocide that he personally witnessed in the extermination camps and exhorts him to tear up the concordat between the Vatican and the Nazis, pleads with the Abbot to use the Vatican radio station to broadcast a call for priests to rally for the rescue of Jews, urges Riccardo to intercede with the pope to condemn Nazi deportations, hides Jacobson from the Nazis, and persuades Salzer to slow Jewish arrests for fear of stirring up further international outcries against Germany.

The main focus of the play is on Riccardo's request to have Eugenio Pacelli (Pope Pius XII) break the concordat with Germany, ex-communicate Hitler from the Church, and sign a decree of protest against the Nazi treatment of Jews. As the spiritual leader of a half billion Catholics, including thirty-five million Germans that represented forty percent of the Reich's population, the pope's influence during World War II cannot be discounted. When Stalin facetiously asked how many divisions the pope could supply to counter Nazi aggression, Churchill replied, "A number of legions not always visible on parade." Friedrich Heer, who was professor of Catholic history at the University of Vienna, recalls that the American ambassador to Switzerland pleaded with the Vatican several times to protest Nazi atrocities, as did the Brazilian government–all to no avail.[21] The pope never spoke out against the deportation of Italian Jews, never ordered priests to pray for Jews, never threatened to excommunicate Reich leaders who had been baptized as Catholics, and did nothing to prevent Hitler from murdering three thousand priests.

Hochhuth, however, in his attempt to maintain historical veracity, indicates throughout the play that the pope and the Vatican made many overtures to help the Jews. Although *Mein Kampf* was probably not on the pope's reading list, the Vatican knew of Hitler's threats against the authority of the papacy, as the Cardinal indicates to Riccardo (119). Nevertheless, the Vatican hid Jews in schools and 115 monasteries, the latter being the destination of the Luccani family before they were deported. The pope acknowledges, "We have hidden hundreds of Jews in Rome/ Have issued thousands of passports!" (200). When the Nazis demanded a ransom of a hundred pounds of gold for the Jews, Salzer reminds us, "The Pope/ knows all about it. He was even willing/ to contribute gold if it turned out/ the Jews could not raise the full sum" (185). Papal workers also spent the equivalent of 16,700,00 marks over a three-year period in assisting, hiding, and emigrating Jews.[22]

There are several historical facts and incidents, many of which are documented in the play, that would indicate that the pope, had he taken responsibility to issue a decree against Jewish deportations, would not have had reason to fear Hitler. The nuncio tells Riccardo that the Nazis did not harm Bishop Galen when he denounced the Nazi euthanasia policy from his pulpit in 1941 (17). Professor Hirt confirms to Eichmann that the Nazis backed down when Galen challenged them: "I was fit to be tied, let me tell you, when the Führer/ called off the euthanasia program just ... / just because of the rabble-rouser of a bishop" (55).[23] Later in the play, Riccardo reiterates, "Hitler's prestige was at its height, but lo and behold/ they let the bishop speak out with impunity./ He did not spend a single hour in jail!/ And his protest stopped the extermination of the sick" (99). Moreover, the correspondence between Martin Bormann and Joseph Goebbels reveals that the Nazis were hesitant to arrest bishops for fear of stirring up negative public opinion.[24] Hochhuth noted that the papal nuncio of Bratislava was able to halt deportations from Slovakia when he spoke out against the murder of Jews near Lublin.[25] When Protestant Bishop Wurm and the Catholic clergy threatened to denounce the deportation of all Jewish spouses of mixed marriages, the Nazis relented and never enacted the legislation. Riccardo tells the cardinal that the king of Denmark, "a defenseless man," wore the yellow star when the Jews were forced to do so, and there were no Nazi reprisals (218).[26] Although Hitler was not religious and the Nazis' actions demonstrated contempt for Christian ideals, many of the Reich leaders were Catholics who feared antagonizing the Vatican.[27] When Hirt asks the doctor whether Goebbels was afraid of the Vatican, the latter replies about the former seminary student, "An old Jesuit never forgets the power of Rome." (55). Himmler was also in awe of the power of the Catholic Church, and Gerstein reminds Riccardo that the SS chief, whose uncle was Suffragan Bishop in Bamberg, "fashioned the Order of the SS/ according to the rules of St. Loyola" (76).

Nevertheless, Hochhuth offers several reasons why the Vatican refused to take responsibility for the fate of the Jews. The Vatican believed that Hitler provided a bulwark against the encroaching spread of communism throughout Europe. Count Fontana, counsel to the Holy See and obviously in agreement with his son's activism, tells Riccardo, "Whatever Hitler may be doing to the Jews/ only he has the power/ to save all Europe from the Russians" (104). The cardinal fears Stalin more than Hitler as a threat to the Church and predicts to Gerstein the results of a communist victory: "Can't you imagine what will happen:/ altars pillaged, priests murdered,/ women ravished?" (149). The pope himself considered Hitler to be a tool against Stalin, defending Europe against the Bolsheviks (206). Moreover, the Vatican insisted that the pope must remain a neutral diplomat who condemns all wars rather than take sides among the combatants. The pope viewed himself as a mediator who stands above the fray, explaining to the cardinal, "The Holy See must/ continue to shelter the spirit of *neutrality*" (213). If the pope does not remain neutral, he would lose his ability to act as an arbitrator and thus have little chance of expediting the end of the war.[28] Emanuela Barasch-Rubinstein suggests that the pope has a similar role to Christ, who was a mediator between God and man: "The Pope, who is Christ's deputy in this world, also has the role of mediator, not only between man and God but also between men."[29] Furthermore, as the cardinal affirms, the pope would make himself unpopular worldwide and lose prestige if he endangered his position for the Jews (120). Albrecht von Kessel, attached to the Vatican through the German embassy during the war, even goes so far as to argue that any protest against treatment of the Jews would have put the pope's life in grave danger.[30] In addition, the pope's refusal to assume responsibility rests with the notion that the fate of the Jews, like the fate of the war, is preordained. Count Fontana believes in Divine Providence, while the cardinal casts Hitler as the instrument of God. Riccardo asks his father whether the pope considers himself above the fray, untouchable in God's eyes: "Suppose God has elected, in these days/ unprecedented in all history,/ to let *him* perish too./ Would *that* not be ordained as well?/ Does no one in the Vatican grasp/ *this*? They still cling/ to the hope that *everything* is preordained." (98). E. Elaine Murdaugh asserts that here Hochhuth indirectly offers a critique of Hegel's view of history in which all events, no matter how catastrophic, are based upon a logical necessity and an adherence to a world spirit.[31] Hegel's philosophy gives positive meaning to history because it assumes the rightness of all events in the evolution of the spirit. Murdaugh writes, "Hegel's 'Grand Design' idea runs parallel with the Christian concept of Divine Providence, although with Hegel the transcendent God has become wholly immanent and the realization of 'paradise' lies wholly in the future."[32] Linking divine providence with the Hegelian notion of Grand Design further cements the strong ties that Pacelli had with Germany.

In the stage directions, Hochhuth specifies that the pope is to be perceived as a role player, a diplomat who represents the interests of the Church as an institution rather than as an individual who thinks and acts on his own (195). In the play, the pope signs checks, discusses stocks and securities with the cardinal, and seems to be driven with a lust for financial concerns of the Church. The pope relishes his role as a representative of the institution, striking recognizable poses and making grand gestures for photographers. Hochhuth remarks that the pope's language is also reflective of institutionalized behavior: *"Words, words, a rhetoric totally corrupted into a classic device for sounding well and saying nothing"* (212). Alvin H. Rosenfeld comments on the pope's language as grounded in the conventions of institutionalized diplomacy: "Language is always revelatory, as any good playwright knows, and the pope's language, marked as it is by high-sounding generalities and decorative but meaningless turns of phrases, shows him at once to be unfeeling and uncaring."[33] The implication of the pope as a product of institutionalized behavior is that he is shown to be more concerned with the temporal security and aggrandizement of the Church than he is with human rights. Critics such as Catharine Hughes and Rainer Taëni argue that one weakness of the play is that Hochhuth did not portray the pope as a complex individual faced with inner conflicts about the fate of the Jews.[34] Although making the pope less a product of institutionalized behavior and more introspective would have made for a more complex character study, Hochhuth insisted that his research was valid. Hochhuth's last words of his sixty-five-page "Sidelights on History" that he appended to the play maintain that the pope was "an over-ambitious careerist" who wasted time on "inconsequential trifles" instead of demonstrating "spiritual leadership" (352).

The concordat with Germany was signed in July 1933 by Pope Pius XI when it was apparent that the Nazis threatened Catholics in

Germany. The encyclical "Mit Brennender Sorge" ("With Burning Concern") of Pius XI clarified that there were no provisions for legal recourse should the Concordat be voided. The Concordat set legal limits on the Church's activities, including maintenance of seminaries, taxation standards, conduct of Catholic organizations, and states' rights to induct priests for military service. In order to maintain diplomatic neutrality, Pius XII saw no reason to abrogate the Concordat with the Nazis, despite the fact that Hitler's genocidal policies were well known. Pacelli, in protecting the rights of the institution first and foremost, was more concerned that if the Vatican voided the Concordat, Hitler would do more harm to the Church's constituents and finances. In the pope's opening words, he expresses his "burning concern for Italy's factories" (195). Hochhuth, by using the words of the pope's predecessor's encyclical, as James Trainer indicates, mocks the pope's maintenance of strict neutrality while accusing him of being preoccupied "with temporal affairs in the midst of a spiritual cataclysm."[35]

The pope's proclamation is essentially a generic platitude that does not even mention the plight of the Jews. When the pope signs the statement, he spills ink on his hands. By washing his ink-stained hands, the pope, Pontius Pilate-like, denies responsibility for his actions. The pope's refusal to take responsibility for the world's evil now recalls the reference to Cain in which the question, "Am I my brother's keeper?" should instead be, according to Arthur Miller, "Am I my own keeper?" The pope's comment after signing the proclamation, "We are–God knows it–blameless of the blood/ now being spilled" (220), is an ironic reference to the biblical tale of Cain and Abel. Hochhuth, like Miller, believes that innocent bystanders who refuse to act morally must share the guilt of the perpetrators. Alvin H. Rosenfeld summarizes Hochhuth's attitude toward the pope: "In Hochhuth's moral reading of history, the Pope's professed 'neutrality' implicated him directly in the Endlösung, for to remain silent before that event was effectively to condone it."[36] The play concludes ironically when the Russians liberate Auschwitz, implying that the Red Menace that the papacy so feared took the responsibility that the pope, like Cain, refused to assume.

Most theater critics, theologians, and historians misinterpreted the play as a vitriolic attack on the Vatican. Instead, a Jesuit priest, Riccardo Fontana, who accompanies Jews to Auschwitz, represents the pope as the deputy of Christ. Although the pope is excessively concerned about temporal issues instead of spiritual leadership, Riccardo casts aside earthly assets, such as career, finances, and family, to assume responsibility as the vicar of Christ. Riccardo's assumption of moral responsibility vindicates the Church, and viewed in this manner, his martyrdom is a tribute to, not an attack upon, Catholicism.

Riccardo is a fictitious character based on two other Christian martyrs: Provost Bernhard Lichtenberg and Father Maximilian Kolbe. As mentioned in chapter 7, Lichtenberg, the *dompropst* (chief priest) of Berlin's St. Hedwig's Cathedral, after publicly praying for the Jews and opposing the Nazi euthanasia program, was imprisoned and then died accompanying Jews on the way to Dachau in 1943. Kolbe was a Polish priest who extended help to refugees, including Jews, which resulted in his deportation to Auschwitz. In the extermination camp, a Polish man named Gajowniczek was chosen for gassing; when he learned of his fate, he cried out, "What will happen to my wife, to my children?" Father Kolbe declared that he wanted to take Gajowniczek's place. The Nazis moved Kolbe to a starvation cell, but when he took too long to die, they gave him a phenol injection. In October 1982, Father Kolbe was canonized as a saint of the Catholic Church.

Throughout the play, Riccardo consistently adheres to an existential notion of moral responsibility despite opposition from the Church, which dispatches him to Lisbon for six months. In an interview with Patricia Marx, Hochhuth commented on the central conflict in the play in which the existential notion of moral responsibility conflicts with social norms and values: "Man is meant to act, to be responsible. He should be the master of his fate. He should be moral, and history continually brings him into conflict with powers which condemn him to defeat, which are stronger than he and which destroy him."[37] Riccardo tells his father that as the deputy of Christ, the pope must protest the fate of the Jews; otherwise, he is acting as "a criminal" (102). Riccardo explains to the abbot, "Doing nothing is as bad as taking part" (155)–an acknowledgment, in the manner of Sartre's bad faith, that we are complicit with the world's evil when we refuse to act responsibly. Riccardo, who assumes the burden of that responsibility for the Church, comments to the abbot, "You must see that the silence of the Pope/ in favor of the murderers imposes/ a guilt upon the Church for which we must atone" (156). When the pope fails to mention the Jews in his decree, Riccardo pins the yellow Star of David to his cassock. By accompanying Jews to Auschwitz, Riccardo disregards the Christian-Hegelian view of blind obedience to historical determinacy and divine providence and shifts the focus to human beings acting morally according to the foundations of his own Christian faith. Christopher Bigsby sums up Hochhuth's sentiment for the need to act responsibly: "What concerned him [Hochhuth] was a refusal to accept responsibility for one's actions, a turning aside from human solidarity out of disregard, political or strategic calculation, a denial of that connection between the individual and that wider society of which he was a part."[38]

The denouement of the play should be at the end of act four, when Riccardo places the yellow star on his cassock. After much thought, Hochhuth decided to extend the play to one more act to allow Riccardo to debate with the Doctor in Auschwitz. This was a critical mistake because act five descends into melodrama, a contrived structure commonly associated with popular entertainment that is incongruous with the serious dramatic forms of tragedy, expressionism, naturalism, and the morality play that formed the foundation of the previous four acts. Moreover, setting act five in Auschwitz created for Hochhuth a major problem with regard to how the extermination camp should be represented on stage. Hochhuth writes in the stage directions, "*Documentary naturalism no longer serves as a stylistic principle. So charged a figure as the anonymous Doctor, the monologues, and a number of other features, should make it evident that no attempt was made to strive for an imitation of reality–nor should the stage set strive for it*" (222–23). Hochhuth claims that Auschwitz should be represented surrealistically (223), but, aside from bathing the stage in dusky lighting to reflect the smoke from the crematoria and suggesting that the setting should be *"dreamlike"* (i.e., nightmarish) because it defies imagination (228), Auschwitz is depicted realistically. Hochhuth vividly describes a realistic set of buildings in Auschwitz, and then the play proceeds conventionally with regard to dialogue, plot, and character development; in short, there is no hint of the random juxtaposition of images, as in a dream, that characterized surrealist drama. Furthermore, for Holocaust scholars, this act borders on absurdity because, as survivors of the extermination camps readily agree, the idea of having a philosophical discussion in Auschwitz, replete with literary references to Hegel, Nietzsche, Valéry, and Stendhal, would have been ludicrous, especially for anyone spending more than a few days in the camp. Jacobson, who had been in the camp for one year, would have been senseless, and even Riccardo's ten-day stay would have rendered him exhausted. Finally, by extending *The Deputy* to a fifth act, Hochhuth created the biggest problem for his play: depending on the production, the length runs seven to eight hours, which is totally unacceptable.[39] If Hochhuth had eliminated act five, the subplots and subordinate characters could also have been discarded without changing the main focus of the play. Several of the characters, including Jacobson, the doctor, Helga, Fritsche, the Luccani family, and Baron Rutta, appeared earlier only for the purpose of coalescing in Auschwitz; eliminating these scenes would shorten the play to a manageable playing time of four hours. Instead of focusing on the practical problem of staging such a lengthy play, Hochhuth preferred to include act five in order to associate Auschwitz with evil and to question God's role during the Holocaust; these two topics are not germane to the central notion of moral responsibility and even muddle the issue unnecessarily.

Act five deteriorates into melodrama as the doctor becomes the archetypal personification of evil descended from medieval mystery and morality plays. As the only major character in the play who is nameless, the doctor is a typed figure that Hochhuth describes in the stage directions as him having *"never been able to imagine as human"* (32). Although the doctor is based on Josef Mengele, who conducted experiments on twins in Auschwitz, he is referred to as "the devil" in the stage directions (32, 234), by Helga (234), who also calls him a "beast" (234), by Riccardo (244), and by his own admission (245).[40] In Auschwitz, this descendant of Mephistopheles and Lucifer is in complete command. Alvin H. Rosenfeld writes, "The Doctor's role, then, in Hochhuth's specifically Christian conception of *The Deputy*, is clear: he is 'the principle of evil in the flesh' (72), the anti-Christ who stands as a dramatic foil to the principle of good."[41] The doctor is the sly tempter of the morality play, now depicted as a melodramatic villain in a long black cape (in contrast to the white gowns that medical doctors traditionally wear) who spouts blasphemies. The doctor promises children "a tasty pudding" to calm their fears and asks new arrivals if they felt ill from their trip; then he dispatches them to the gas chambers. He satisfies his lecherous desires by tempting women who are willing to have sex with him because their families might be spared. The doctor, disguised as the tempting Devil, can assume different personae: charming dandy, theologian, nihilist, profligate, brilliant intellectual, or benevolent peacemaker, but as Hamida Bosmajian so aptly realizes, all persons who come into contact with him will soon die.[42]

The doctor recognizes that Riccardo is "an angel" (247), and as such, he is the antithesis of the devil (the angel cast out of heaven). The doctor explains to Riccardo that he reigns as the devil in this wasteland that God has decided to ignore, boasting, "The truth is, Auschwitz refutes/ creator, creation, and the creature" (248). The implication is that either God does not exist or is silent in heaven. The doctor brings up a salient point of contention, for if God is silent about the Shoah, why should we not expect the pope, his deputy, to demonstrate silence as well? Moreover, how can Auschwitz exist if there is a benevolent God? Riccardo refuses to believe in a world without God and counters with "Since / the devil exists, God also exists./ Otherwise *you* would have won a long time ago" (253). To test his faith, the doctor sentences Riccardo to incinerating corpses for ten days.

After undergoing this baptism by fire, Riccardo's faith is severely challenged. Riccardo admits to Gerstein, "I have been burning the dead ten hours a day./ And with every human body that I burn/ a portion of my faith burns also./ God burns" (270). By setting the last act in Auschwitz, Hochhuth has unintentionally muddied the waters by shifting the focus from the need for moral responsibility to a wasteland where God and the devil are allied, or where God has forsaken mankind for the devil. The play degenerates into a depiction of the absurd in the form of the modern wasteland known as Auschwitz. Leonidas E. Hill believes that Hochhuth's message is thus less than sanguine: "The play, then, is a series of reflections on a world gone mad–indulging in unbridled pillage and murder, in which the best, such as Riccardo and Gerstein, are so weak that they cannot affect the holocaust, but can and should nevertheless do what they must as men."[43] By setting act five in Auschwitz, where death and destruction are sovereign and there is little opportunity to demonstrate moral responsibility, Hochhuth inadvertently did his best to counter his own thesis. After all, as Alvin H. Rosenfeld mentions, on the surface, the devil seems triumphant since Riccardo is dead, Gerstein is defeated, the pope has long since "retreated into an empty spirituality," and the doctor sarcastically walks off, smiling, "with the text of Loyola's *Spiritual Exercises* tucked under his arm."[44]

Yet Riccardo is able to assume moral responsibility despite the fact that Auschwitz is the setting for an apocalyptic world where evil reigns supreme. As he bids goodbye to Gerstein after refusing the opportunity to escape Auschwitz, Riccardo says, "Don't let my father know/ where I am. Tell him my life/ has been fulfilled" (274). When Riccardo picks up Gerstein's pistol and aims it at the doctor, he is shot by the SS guard. Riccardo's actions speak louder than the pope's words, for his attempt to kill the doctor represents active opposition to Nazism, which sets a standard for the way the Church should have reacted. Riccardo's last words, "In hora mortis meae voca me" ("Call me in the hour of my death"), indicate that, in an affirmation of faith, he has followed his calling. Sharing the same Auschwitz number (16670) as his historical counterpart, Father Kolbe, Riccardo dies as a martyr, similar to Kolbe. Kolbe answered a calling to God, whereas Riccardo, still believing that even a silent God exists, responds existentially to the "call" of a Christian conscience. The doctor mocks Riccardo: "Amen. Did you really hear him calling–/ in the crematorium?" (283). Riccardo refuses to be tempted and will not compromise by striking a bargain with the devil, as many of the Auschwitz prisoners were forced to do. Instead, as Peter Demetz has remarked, Riccardo's assumption of moral responsibility has made him Christ's true deputy attempting to save the honor of the Church with "the resilient humility of a Christian whose beliefs have undergone the most cruel of tests."[45] Despite the fact that Riccardo murders, which is a mortal sin as far as the Church is concerned, he asserts a fundamental human morality that is essential to quashing the world's evil.

Christopher Innes sums up what Hochhuth hoped to gain by concluding the last act of the play in Auschwitz: "Evil triumphs as a consequence of the Pope's passivity, which stands for the apparent silence of God, while Riccardo's sacrifice as his, and so God's 'representative' is an affirmation which restores meaning to life."[46] Thus, act five seems to have been included mainly for the purpose of visibly demonstrating the evil that results when moral responsibility is ignored. Riccardo actually learns nothing in act five, for he dies in Auschwitz with the same knowledge that he had before he entered the extermination camp. The only element of the play that is added with the inclusion of act five is the question of God's existence in an absurd universe. However, this debate is extraneous to the play, for Hochhuth, like Miller and Sartre, is at heart an existentialist whose position on human responsibility does not change with or without God's presence. Even if Hochhuth believes that God can influence the course of history only through the actions of humanity, his position is the same as the existentialists. The implication is that the pope, who shunned his moral responsibilities, allowed the devil to run rampant at Auschwitz. In short, for Hochhuth, moral responsibility is one's calling, and accepting or refusing the call is what determined the extent of the genocide during the Holocaust.

9 Heroism and Moral Responsibility in the Ghettoes

Despite the deportation of Jews confined to the ghettoes of central and eastern Europe during the Holocaust, as Freud stated, no one believes in their own death. Although the Nazis deceived Jews and lied to them, playing games of cat and mouse with their prey, universal optimism and the instinct of self-preservation led Jews to believe in the deceptions. Once the ghetto was created, Jews frequently lost the opportunity to flee; moreover, by doing so, they would have had to leave loved ones behind. Furthermore, as Lucy S. Dawidowicz documents, open defiance of the Germans typically led to death, and "individual acts of resistance became nothing more than induced suicide."[1] Ghetto Jews frequently regarded armed resisters as irresponsible hotheads who would bring about reprisals from the Nazis. Thus, partisans and other resistors often faced the wrath of their brethren, who favored caution and prudence. Believing in the will of a God who loves the persecuted and not the persecutors, pious Jews elevated powerlessness into a virtue. Thus, Jews came from a tradition that practiced nonviolence, prudence, and moderation before active resistance was considered an option. Their preferred methods involved mediation, petition, and bargaining instead of meeting the Germans with brute force. With regard to the *Judenräte*, Dawidowicz asserts, "To say that they 'cooperated' or 'collaborated' with the Germans is semantic confusion and historical misrepresentation."[2] Despite the obstacles, Jews in the ghetto often acted existentially or heroically in attempting to control their fate. This chapter focuses on Jewish moral responsibility in four major ghettoes (Budapest, Vilna, Lodz, and Warsaw), where choices were limited.

Motti Lerner was born in Israel in 1949, so the Holocaust had no direct influence upon him.[3] After studying theater from 1975 to 1978 at the Hebrew University in Jerusalem and attending theater workshops in London and San Francisco, Lerner became director and dramaturg at the Khan Theatre in Jerusalem from 1979 to 1984. *Kastner* was produced by the Cameri Theatre under direction by Ilan Ronen in Tel Aviv during 1985 and won the Aharon Meskin Prize of the Israel Centre for International Theatre Institute for best play of the 1985–1986 season.[4] *Kastner* was next performed by the Chamber Theatre in Wiesbaden, Germany, in 1987. The play was then produced by the Heilbronn Theatre in Heilbronn, Germany, in 1988 and was broadcast on Hungarian Radio two years later. In 1994, Lerner wrote *Kastner's Trial*, a three-part drama directed for Israeli television by Uri Barabash. Presented over a three-night period beginning on 9 November 1994, the highly promoted broadcast became one of the most celebrated television dramas ever produced in Israel. Lerner's screenplay went on to win the Israeli Academy Award for best television drama of 1994.

When the Nazis invaded Hungary in March 1944, the 750,000 Jews there represented the largest Jewish community still intact in Europe. Hungary was the last nation to initiate the Final Solution, and as such, as Raul Hilberg notes, "Hungary was the only country in which the perpetrators knew that the war was lost when they started their operation."[5] Eichmann formed a *Judenrat* to carry out the German decrees in Budapest. The quisling Hungarian regime willingly enforced anti-Jewish decrees that initially imposed travel restrictions on Jews, closed Jewish businesses, and allowed the Budapest ghetto to be plundered and its property confiscated. Hungarian transports to Auschwitz began in April 1944. Dr. Rudolf (Rezsö) Kastner, as a Labor Zionist activist and vice chairman of the Jewish Relief and Rescue Committee of Budapest, already knew about the fate of the Polish Jews. Kastner, recognizing that the end of the war was imminent, negotiated with the Germans for the release of Jews and offered to testify on the Nazis' behalf in any postwar trials. At the end of June, Kastner managed to get visas for 1,684 Jews to immigrate to Switzerland; the train instead arrived in Bergen-Belsen. By December, all of those Jews were sent safely to Switzerland after Himmler ordered a halt to the deportations from Budapest. Although a half million Hungarian Jews were deported, Kastner tried to negotiate to save as many Jews as possible in a situation where resistance would have been suicidal in a country that lacked an underground movement. Holocaust historian Yehuda Bauer estimates that Kastner possibly saved as many as 15,000 Hungarian Jews.[6]

After the war, Kastner testified at the Nuremberg trials in defense of SS officer Kurt Becher, who, as Himmler's representative in Hungary, negotiated with Kastner for release of Jews. Kastner then moved to Palestine, settling in Tel Aviv. In 1954, Kastner sued Malkiel Grünwald, a Budapest survivor, who accused him of being a traitor, collaborating with the Nazis, and using his influence to save himself, relatives, and friends. The court ruled that Kastner "sold his soul to the devil" but exonerated him from any criminal offense. The most serious charge was that Kastner refrained from warning Hungarian Jews of their fates. During Kastner's appeal of the verdict in March 1957, he died after being shot in the back by a nationalist extremist. In 1958, the Israeli Supreme Court deliberated the final verdict, exculpating Kastner from charges of collaborating with the Nazis but finding him guilty of defending an SS officer from justice.

Kastner became a different type of Holocaust drama for the Israelis. Dan Laor notes that Kastner, the anti-hero, was a character diametrically opposed to the mythical heroic types, such as Hanna Senesh, that Israelis preferred to immortalize.[7] Lerner understood that great heroism is manifested by any Jew in the ghetto who stands in front of Eichmann, one of the major architects of the Final Solution, and negotiates with him. The debate that Lerner presents in the play about collaboration versus the moral responsibility to save lives became one of the most discussed Holocaust motifs in Israel.

Written in two acts consisting of sixty-one scenes, a prologue, and an epilogue, *Kastner*, which includes a cast of nineteen characters, can be difficult to stage. The play takes place during Kastner's 1954 trial in Jerusalem, where Grünwald seeks to determine the truth about Kastner's collaboration to clear the air in Israel "for the sake of our national conscience and honor."[8] Grünwald accuses Kastner of saving his family while keeping the truth about deportations to Auschwitz from his fellow Hungarian Jews. Grünwald also charges Kastner with arguing for the release without punishment of Eichmann's associates, (Becher, Hermann Krumey, and Dieter Wisliceny) at Nuremberg. The play flashes back to the events that occurred in Budapest from 19 March to 1 July 1944, as we, the audience, constitute the jury. As Glenda Abramson has remarked, *Kastner* is similar to documentary drama, where audiences typically are asked to judge some form of actual or symbolic trial.[9]

Although documentary theater can never be fully authentic because playwrights typically do not have transcripts of actual conversations, *Kastner*, for the most part, is historically accurate.[10] Kastner, a moderate Zionist, favored negotiating with the Nazis, delaying and stultifying the atrocities while stalling for time until the inevitable end of the war. As a physician, Kastner was committed to saving lives at all costs. Kastner at first offered money if the Nazis promised not to intern Budapest Jews in ghettoes or ship them to Auschwitz. Meanwhile, Jews from the rural areas of Hungary were being deported while the Nazis were fabricating postcards ostensibly sent by deportees who claimed to have found safe haven in labor camps. Kastner continued to negotiate for exit visas, promising Wisliceny, Eichmann's assistant, that he would vouch for him in any postwar tribunal. When Shamu Stern and Folöp Freudinger, two influential members of the *Judenrat*, urged Kastner to warn Jews of their fate, Kastner refused, arguing that he could negotiate for more visas and that panic among Jews would exacerbate Nazi violence. After the deal that Eichmann made with Joel Brand, to trade one million Jewish lives for ten thousand trucks, failed, Kastner offered to go to Switzerland to provide the war-depleted German army with heavy equipment in exchange for the release of one hundred thousand German Jews. His major successes were wresting a train of 1,684 Jews from Nazi claws, sending four additional trains to Vienna, and halting exterminations at Bergen-Belsen and Theresienstadt.

Kastner has good reason to believe that negotiating with the Nazis is more profitable than defying them. When Imre Varga declares war on the *Judenrat* and exhorts Jews to obtain weapons and go underground to subvert Nazi plans, the Hungarian police intervene, and

Varga commits suicide rather than face torture. Stern earlier warned Varga, "Provocation against the Germans is sheer madness" (202), while Kastner also told him, "Your blabbering does nothing but give excuses for the Germans to arrest and kill Jews" (201). Moreover, as Hermann Krumey, Eichmann's deputy, asserted and Kastner realized, Himmler, well aware of Germany's imminent defeat in the war, wanted to spare some Jewish lives for negotiations with the British and the Americans. Furthermore, Kastner's influence was directly responsible for saving the lives of several prominent Jews in the community, best demonstrated when the Hungarian police are ordered by Krumey to spare the life of Otto Komoly, head of the Zionist rescue committee.

However, Lerner, in making the play historically accurate, revealed that Kastner's decision to negotiate with the Nazis was highly problematic. Stern's assertion that the Hungarian government would protect its citizens from the Germans proved to be ludicrous. Kastner's trust in Eichmann's avowal not to harm a single Jew erroneously led him to believe that even Romanian Jews would ask for visas to emigrate to Hungary. Kastner mistakenly trusted Krumey, who assured the *Judenrat* that Jewish manpower was needed for the war effort, and thus sending Jews to Auschwitz would be counterproductive. Krumey even insisted to Kastner that the Jewish ghetto was created by the Hungarians, not by the Nazis because "They claim that you people are a security risk and must be isolated so you won't aid the Russians the way you did in 1918" (230). Meanwhile, Eichmann had been consistently lying about his plans for the Jews, most notably represented when he told Brand that Jews sent to Auschwitz will be placed "in the cooler for two weeks" (249) until the mission had been completed. Throughout the play, Stern represents the devil's advocate, putting the onus of responsibility on Kastner's decisions to negotiate rather than resist. Stern tells the audience that he knew the transports were not going to Krupp's labor camps: "I had no illusions about Krupp Industries: what would lawyers, accountants, doctors, journalists, actors, and opera singers do in a Krupp plant?" (219). Stern, questioning Kastner's willingness to deal with the devil (250), insisted that the *Judenrat* be dissolved and that Jews refuse to cooperate with the Nazis: "We've called their meetings for them, we've turned apartments over to them, and we have published their proclamations. Now we must stop" (243). Yet Stern also becomes the *raisonneur* who poses the question of whether Kastner's attempt to save Jews conflicted with his moral responsibility not to endanger lives in his negotiations with the enemy. Stern, speaking to the audience, reflects on Kastner's dilemma: "Common sense could supply no answers to these questions ... A moral sense? In the name of what morality could anyone call on 'moral sense' in those days?" (219).

In his introduction to the English text of the play, Michael Taub acknowledged that Kastner may be a controversial figure, but Lerner certainly did not romanticize him.[11] Modeled on the historical figure, Lerner's protagonist is cautious, pragmatic, and intelligent. He also enjoys life, and because of the enormous pressure placed upon him as a leader in the Jewish community who has to negotiate with his enemies, he finds emotional outlets for his frustrations. He goes to nightclubs frequently and socializes with the Germans by playing cards and drinking wine with them. Kastner's wife Bogyo accuses him of carousing with whores and is so fed up with his lechery that she leaves him to stay with his mother Helen. Living alone, Kastner, during a moment of intense solace, even invites Hansi, Brand's wife, to stay with him.

Despite the fact that he does not romanticize Kastner and structures the play as a trial that the audience must adjudicate, Lerner depicts him as a courageous humanitarian, not a collaborator. Kastner, convinced that physical defiance of Nazi decrees would mean death to Jews, risked his life by dickering with Eichmann; by doing so, he also alienated his family, friends, and fellow Zionists. With ample opportunity to desert his community, Kastner instead stayed in Budapest to negotiate until the dissolution of the ghetto and left only when the Germans granted him an exit visa. Speaking to the audience in the last scene of the play, Hansi refutes charges that Kastner collaborated with the Nazis: "Let them say what they will, it cannot be denied that Rezsö saved thousands ... maybe tens of thousands." (265). In what appears to be an implicit reference to the resistance fighters in Warsaw, Kastner, during his trial in the epilogue, questioned the notion of heroism by asking the court how many lives those Polish partisans saved.

Kastner testifies that he could not save everyone, including the families of some of his friends, such as Freudiger, but he did manage to get visas for 1,684 Jews, sent four other trains to Vienna, and intervened in exterminations in Bergen-Belsen and Theresienstadt. He concludes, "Your Honor, the only ghetto in all of Europe whose population stayed alive was the Budapest ghetto, despite the lack of acts which people would now consider heroic" (266).

Kastner forces us to reconsider the notion of heroism and moral responsibility under restricted conditions in the ghettoes of central and eastern Europe during the Holocaust. Prior to Lerner's play, the Israelis, in particular, glorified Hanna Senesh and the partisans of the Warsaw ghetto as the only worthy resistance heroes of the Shoah. However, not only did these resistance leaders fail to survive, they did not save a single soul. *Kastner* teaches us that heroism comes in different forms and that negotiation can be a moral form of responsibility. In the ghetto, where moral choices were limited, there is still a gray area between collaboration and active, armed resistance. Glenda Abramson observes, "This is the play's point: speaking to modern Israel, Lerner defends his rendition of Kastner's character by emphasising its lack of mythological or archetypal heroic attributes, and by proposing virtue in resistance other than by force of arms."[12] Kastner was concerned with saving lives even if it meant bartering for cash and goods. Although he was not the suicide martyr in the tradition of the mythical heroism of the Massada, Kastner becomes for Lerner's Israeli audience another form of resistance hero.[13]

Joshua Sobol's *Adam*, the second part of his Vilna triptych, premiered at the Habima Theatre in Tel Aviv in 1989. *Adam* has a realistic structure consisting of a prologue and eighteen scenes. Although Sobol sets the play in modern-day Tel Aviv where Old Nadya reminisces about life in the ghetto, the exact time and location of the flashbacks are never specified. The play focuses on the decision of Jacob Gens, head of the ghetto administration and *Judenrat* in Vilna, to turn Adam Rolenick, *nom de guerre* for Yitzhak Wittenberg, commander of the United Partisan Organization, over to the Gestapo or face the ghetto's liquidation.[14] Thus, by implication only, the audience can set the flashbacks in Vilna on the eve of 16 July 1943, which became known as

"Wittenberg Day." The play's exploration of the role of Jewish responsibility and moral obligation in the ghetto precipitated much debate among the Israeli public and press.

By July 1943, the Jews of Vilna had experienced the worst of the Nazi terror. Various *Aktionen* conducted from August to October 1941 resulted in the deaths of 33,500 of the 57,000 Jews living in Vilna.[15] From spring 1942 to spring 1943, there was a relative period of quiet where no *Aktionen* occurred, and the ghetto became productive in serving German interests. However, in spring 1943, several small ghettoes and labor camps near Vilna were liquidated, causing much fear among the remaining ghetto dwellers. The underground United Partisan Organization (UPO), established in 1942, remained relatively quiet until spring 1943, when they sensed the end was near. Gens maintained contact with the underground in the understanding that if the ghetto were to be destroyed, he would join them in an uprising; however, Gens also clashed with UPO leaders, fearing that smuggling weapons into the ghetto and inciting resistance would give the Nazis the incentive for liquidation.

Sobol depicts Gens as terribly frustrated, caught in a dilemma of trying to save as many Jews as possible yet having to kowtow to ghetto commandant Kittel's whims for fear that if he refuses, there will be reprisals against the Jewish community. Sobol does not portray Gens as a collaborator but sees him instead as an exhausted man of intense angst, constantly forced to make life-and-death decisions. Gens admits to Kittel the burden that he carries: "I'm the only person who can control the ghetto and give the people a sense of security, some hope for survival."[16] Gens is no patsy for Kittel, admitting that he would lead an armed revolt if Kittel decided to liquidate the ghetto. When Kittel commends him for being a natural leader and states that if he had been born German he would have been promoted to general, Gens, displaying his sympathy for his people, tells him that he prefers to be Russian. Actually, Kittel and Gens share the same goal of keeping the ghetto intact for as long as possible, for Kittel realizes that once the ghetto is liquidated, he will be sent to the Russian front; Gens hopes to keep people alive for another four or five months until the Russians can reach the city.[17]

Kittel is concerned that a partisan revolt, similar to the Warsaw uprising that occurred a few months earlier, could lead to orders to liquidate the ghetto. To abort a possible resurrection, the Gestapo kidnap Adam, but his fellow communist revolutionaries manage to overpower the kidnappers and return their leader to safety. When Kittel orders Adam's arrest, Gens claims that Rolenick is merely an administrator of the public baths and that no underground movement exists in the ghetto. As Kittel seeks to detain Adam's wife and children as hostages, Gens puts his life on the line when he lies to Kittel, claiming that Adam is a childless widower. Gens takes responsibility to protect the partisan movement and tells Kittel, "If you think there is an underground movement in the ghetto, and if you suspect that I'm concealing it, then arrest me, and put me on trial. If you find me guilty, punish me according to the laws of war" (288). Kittel gives Gens an ultimatum: deliver Rolenick within three hours or face the liquidation of the ghetto.

When Gens confers with the UPO members, he tells them the options and urges them to start an insurrection. However, with no sign of the ghetto's liquidation, the UPO leaders realize that an armed revolt of pistols, sticks, and stones would end disastrously against Nazi artillery, machine guns, and tanks. Moreover, the Jewish ghetto population did not favor armed resistance, which they understood would be suicidal. Gens, consistently portrayed as acting nobly, tells the revolutionaries to hide Adam's wife and children.

With the threat that the ghetto will be set on fire if Adam is not handed over to the Germans, the Jewish population turn against the UPO and begin to search for Adam's whereabouts. The UPO activists realize that turning Adam over to Kittel would be futile since they expect the ghetto ultimately to be liquidated anyway. The issue is further complicated by the fact that Adam is protecting his superior, Velvele Sharashevsky, a high-ranking official of the Communist Party, and thus puts his own life on the line to allow Sharashevsky to govern in secrecy.

Gens finally agrees that surrendering one life is more important than risking the lives of twenty thousand others. At first, the UPO resists handing Adam over to the Gestapo, claiming that Gens was conspiring with Kittel. They realize that Gens's gesture of accusing Adam of being a petty smuggler to be handed over to the *Judenrat* for punishment was a ploy the Nazis would never accept. Lachman, one of the partisans, succinctly expresses the moral dilemma faced by the UPO: "If we betray Adam, we betray ourselves;" he continues, "None of us can try to shake off responsibility" (319). Lev seems to speak for Sobol, whose point is that moral judgments have to be viewed differently in the ghetto:

> We're being forced to make an impossible decision. It's just as immoral to betray a friend as it is to cause the death of twenty thousand people. We are weak, and our enemies are strong. They've forced us into a situation that leaves us with no moral choice. It defies all moral teachings. (320)

Lev goes on to explain that no authority in the world could provide a definitive moral response to their dilemma. As a result, the UPO committee votes three to two to surrender Adam to the Germans rather than to opt for collective suicide.

Sobol goes to great lengths to indicate that the Jewish community was divided about the decision to deliver Adam to the Gestapo. Although the *Judenrat*, the Jewish citizens of Vilna, and three members of the UPO favored the decision, Gens and Rolenick disagreed. Gens was making plans for an attack on German headquarters while Adam fled, disguising himself as a woman to elude the sentries. Adam tells Gens that his plans to resist would have meant firing upon Jewish citizens who were adamant about the need for capitulation. Finally, Gens convinces Adam that it is better to sacrifice one person to save many. When Adam asks Gens what right he has to make such sacrifices, Sobol, in a blatant attempt to respond to critics who earlier chastised him for not putting the onus on the Nazis in *Ghetto*, allows Gens to respond with, "I'm not your hangman. It's the Germans" (329). Adam makes one last pitch to his comrades in arms, to no avail: "You think that sacrificing me will win you the support of the masses. You're wrong" (329). Instead of an armed revolt, the UPO is seen as the villain, and with their eyes lowered in shame, they turn Adam over to Kittel.

In surrendering himself to the Germans and therefore agreeing with his comrades in arms, Adam sacrifices his life to save many. Michael Taub has noted that Adam, who at first equivocated, ultimately turned himself in because he was a humanist who valued people over lofty ideals.[18] In his book on Jewish resistance during the Holocaust, Reuben Ainsztein reports that the Gestapo tortured Wittenberg by breaking his arms tied behind his back, torching his hair, and gouging his eyes before depositing the body on the street.[19] During the torture, Wittenberg was believed to have taken cyanide supplied by Gens. This view is corroborated by Israel Gutman, who, in his entry on Wittenberg for the *Encyclopedia of the Holocaust*, writes, "He [Wittenberg] apparently committed suicide in prison, by taking poison."[20] To glorify Adam as a martyr, Sobol creates a fictionalized account of his suicide. In an adjoining room, Kittel is torturing an innocent young woman as her daughter is forced to watch. Kittel explains to Adam that he will stop the torture if Adam cooperates with the investigation. Adam begins to bite his nails that have been coated with the cyanide that Gens supplied to him. Adam's suicide releases him and the anonymous woman from further torture. In choosing suicide as the best option, Adam, the humanist, releases an individual from suffering and simultaneously maintains his convictions by refusing to implicate his colleagues in the UPO.

The most controversial issue in the play concerns whether Gens's decision to save as many lives as possible by turning Adam over to the Gestapo was morally just or was unethical. As I mentioned in chapter 3 during the discussion of *Ghetto*, Sobol meticulously researched the subject of the Vilna ghetto; the result is that *Adam* is historically valid. However, Sobol, in setting the time period of the play close to "Wittenberg Day" (mid-July 1943), omits, perhaps intentionally, much of what historians know about Gens. Negotiating with Kittel, Gens was already aware that the Nazi leader had previously liquidated seven ghettoes, which probably meant that Vilna would suffer the same fate. Moreover, Gens had been warned earlier by four rabbis that his participation in selections during an *Aktion* of late October 1941 violated a Talmudic law that stated that individuals charged with specific offenses could be found guilty but not those whose only crime was being Jewish. Gens argued that by handing over a select number of Jews, he was saving the majority of them. The rabbis quoted the highly respected medieval Jewish philosopher Maimonides to him: "If a heathen said to you: Give us one of yours and we shall kill him, and if you don't we shall kill you, all shall die, but you shall not turn over one soul of Israel to them." Finally, the privileges that Gens was afforded are not mentioned in the play. As ghetto chief, Gens was allowed to carry a revolver, had access to plenty of food and drink, did not have to wear the Jewish star, and was able to acquire large sums of money and plenty of jewelry.

Eric Sterling argues that a true portrait of Gens would depict him as a misled Moses figure who hoped to lead the Jews out of the ghetto.[21] Gens duped the Jews in Vilna into believing that the Final Solution would not afflict the ghetto if their labor force became indispensable to the Nazi war effort. Sobol's play instead questions Gens's decisions but judges his motives to be pure. In an interview that Sterling conducted with Sobol, the playwright explained that Gens understood there was no moral justification for trying to save as many Jews as possible by surrendering a few of them: "He knew that he was the only person responsible for what he was doing and that he was functioning in a world in which morals didn't exist anymore. It was almost a foolish pretension to be moral."[22] Israeli Holocaust historian Yitzhak Arad concurs with Sobol's assessment of Gens: "Gens's belief that if the ghetto were productive its Jews would be saved proved baseless; but under the terrible conditions prevailing at the time, he did his best, as he understood it, to save as many as possible."[23] The issue of passive compliance calls into question whether Jews needed to cooperate with the Nazis in order to survive. Gens's sacrifice of Wittenberg, which stifled the armed resistance, also asks the audience to ponder whether Gens managed to save lives. The ghetto was eventually liquidated anyway. We will never know whether the utopian resistance movement would have saved any lives or if more people would have been killed. However misguided Gens may have been, he believed wholeheartedly in his mission, refusing to go into hiding or take refuge with Lithuanian relatives, choosing instead to remain in the ghetto on behalf of his fellow Jews.

Just as the title of the play would lead us to believe that the focus is on Adam rather than Gens, the time and location are misleading as well. The play is set in Tel Aviv in the present and occurs in Vilna in 1943 only in flashbacks. Old Nadya is present in eleven of the eighteen scenes, and, as Adam's lover and former unit leader in the UPO, she makes for the perfect witness. At the time of the writing of the play, Israel had experienced the war in Lebanon and the intifada, all of which is reflected by the artillery fire in the background as Old Nadya reminisces about the past to her husband Sep. In hearing her laudatory comments about Adam the hero, Sep notes that Adam is dead. Sep mocks his wife for distinguishing among different types of survivorship: "Adam's a first-rate survivor, I know. He's a national hero. You're a second-rate survivor, because you saved our honor. And I'm third-rate because I only saved myself. Say it!" (295). Sobol's subtle point is ironic: Adam, the national hero, is dead, his resistance movement noble in principle but having no effect on survivors. Gens's negotiating ability did manage to stall efforts until the liberation when 2,500 Jews survived, Old Nadya being one of them. In short, the play questions the nature of heroism and morality in an environment where these terms have quite different meanings than they typically would have when people are not imprisoned in a ghetto. Old Nadya and Sep spend their time telling school children about the Holocaust. Freddie Rokem notes, "This serves as the psychological motivation for the recollections of the ghetto at the same time as it creates a constant dialectical tension between now and then."[24] Sep, listening to the explosions in the background, laments the violence in the Middle East: "Barbarians. Primitives. Only fight. Only kill. Only murder one another. Booby-trapped cars. Arpigi's, Razookas, enough. I want calm" (311). Sobol links UPO resistance fighters with modern Israelis who are quick to sacrifice life for what they believe to be a noble cause. Michael Taub writes, "Ultimately, *Adam* is a plea for humanity and respect for the sacredness of human life."[25] Moreover, as a play of the late 1980s, *Adam* reflects a change of attitude among the Israeli public who were now beginning to view the Diaspora Jews with the newly acquired understanding that heroism, ethics, and moral responsibility of Jews in the ghettoes were concepts that were more heavily nuanced than previously understood.

Harold and Edith Lieberman's 1972 play, *Throne of Straw*, explores the motif of moral responsibility in Lodz, one of the largest of the occupied ghettoes. Like Israeli playwrights Lerner and Sobol, both born in Palestine, the Liebermans, both Americans, were indirectly affected by the Holocaust. Edith, in particular, was a Yiddishist who learned much about the Holocaust through tales told to her by her Old World Jewish aunts. Harold survived the Depression and was living in New York City during the Shoah. The Liebermans interviewed survivors of the Lodz ghetto and based much of *Throne of Straw* on Solomon Bloom's essay, "Dictator of the Lodz Ghetto," published in the February 1949 issue of *Commentary*. The play was first staged as a workshop in 1976 at the Odyssey Theater in Los Angeles, a production in which Kiefer Sutherland made his acting debut at age nine. The following year, *Throne of Straw* was presented again in a showcase production at St. Clement's Theatre in New York. The fully revised play, directed by Robert Skloot, premiered at the University of Wisconsin, Madison, in July 1978. Although Edith passed away in 1975, Harold, having moved to California, was able to see his play gaining popularity on the West Coast with productions at the Los Angeles Actors Theatre and at UCLA's MacGowan Hall.

In "A Note on Historical Accuracy" preceding the published text, the Liebermans reveal that although *Throne of Straw* is historically accurate, they are writing a play, not history, and therefore have exercised poetic license to create characters based upon survivor interviews. The Liebermans incorporated a number of techniques derived from Brecht's epic theater to create a play that engages the audience much more than most of the Holocaust ghetto plays, while still maintaining historical authenticity. Written in the episodic fashion that Brecht preferred, *Throne of Straw* is very symmetrical, with act one consisting of a prologue and eleven scenes and act two structured as twelve scenes. Yankele, a half-mad Hasidic teller of tales, functions as a Brechtian narrator whose songs break up the stage action and comment on events to give the audience time to think about the protagonists' moral dilemmas. Yankele's interruptions even have a metatheatrical presence, especially when he addresses the audience directly, putting the onus of moral responsibility on the spectators.

Most importantly, Yankele's songs and his comic satirism allow the audience respite from an otherwise highly tense and emotionally draining production; in other words, as Brecht preferred, the narrator's intrusions breach audience empathy with the characters, providing spectators with more time to ponder the moral issues. Brecht suggested employing Piscator's ideas concerning slide shows, posters, newsreels, captions, and films to explain difficult concepts to the audience; in the production notes to the play, the Liebermans write, "Slides may or may not be used depending on the aims of each particular production."[26] For example, in Skloot's production of *Throne of Straw* in Madison, he used slides primarily to provide historical information to an audience largely uninformed about the Holocaust and about Jewish rituals and customs, such as the Seder, which play a major role in the drama.[27]

On 8 September 1939, the Nazis occupied Lodz, and Jewish persecution began almost immediately thereafter. Jews were abducted into forced labor and deprived of all cultural and economic activities. Synagogues were destroyed, homes were looted, and Jewish shops were razed. The *Ältestenrat* (Council of Elders) was formed with Mordechai Chaim Rumkowski as its chairman, reporting to Hans Biebow, in charge of ghetto administration. Rumkowski's responsibilities included distributing rations, establishing factories, providing housing, and supervising ghetto services. Approximately 164,000 Jews were forced into the ghetto (the Balut section of the city), which increased to nearly 204,800 when Jews from Germany, Austria, Czechoslovakia, and Luxembourg were moved in during 1941 and 1942. Factories, the majority of which produced textiles by half-starved laborers who were forced to work twelve hours each day, were created to serve German interests and for a while insulated Jews from imprisonment or starvation. Jewish police, appointed by Rumkowski, helped maintain order in the ghetto. Shmuel Krakowski reports that 43,500 persons–approximately twenty-one percent of the ghetto inhabitants–died from starvation, cold, and disease.[28] Beginning on 16 January 1942, Jews, drawn from lists provided by Rumkowski, were deported to Chelmno, where they were executed in gas vans. Early deportations included the elderly, the disabled, and children–those who were infirm or too young to work. From September 1942 to May 1944, there were no major deportations to extermination camps. Although there were hunger strikes, the ghetto was relatively quiet during these years. By the end of this period, when the Warsaw ghetto was already liquidated, Rumkowski thus presided over the largest Jewish ghetto remaining in Europe. From spring 1944, when the Nazis decided to liquidate the ghetto, until August 1944, more than 81,000 Jews were deported, 74,000 to Auschwitz and the remainder to Chelmno.[29] When Lodz was liberated by the Russian army on 19 January 1945, approximately 5,000 to 7,000 Jews (the exact number remains inconclusive) were still alive.

Throne of Straw occurs from the time Rumkowski becomes *Judenrat* chief in 1939 until his deportation during the ghetto's liquidation in 1944. The Liebermans depict Rumkowski as a complex character forced to choose between survival of the ghetto and ruthless collaboration with the Nazis. Rumkowski rationalizes the Nazi threat, and like many Jews during the Holocaust who had previously experienced waves of anti-Semitism, believed that the Occupation was merely a passing phase. He assures Israel Wolf, "This is not the first place nor the first time someone has tried to do us harm. We managed before and we'll manage now."[30] Rumkowski stifles opposition to the Nazis, arguing instead that a productive labor force inside the ghetto will make the Jews essential to the war effort. When David Abramowitz suggests resisting, Rumkowski refuses violence as a viable solution: "We are not fighters. Let others use bullets. We are still a people of the word. We persuade. We argue. We petition" (136). Rumkowski alleges that these tactics have allowed Jews to survive for thousands of years among enemies who wished to destroy them. Acting dictatorial, Rumkowski not only disallows violence against the Nazis, but also forbids the workers to strike as well. In addition, he is ruthless when preparing the deportation lists, which he compiles without regard to friends or family. Finally, Rumkowski must be judged in the way he deceived Jews in boarding the trains, fully aware of their fates but assuring them instead that they were destined for a labor camp in Germany.

Much of the antipathy toward Rumkowski derives from the megalomania with which he pursued his job. In the Cast of Characters, the Liebermans describe Rumkowski as an egomaniac: "His wardrobe grew apace with his power, and he took to having stamps and coins made bearing his portrait" (119). Riding on a cart led by a half-blind white horse, Rumkowski, with his long white hair and at times wearing a cape, paraded himself through the streets of Lodz as a type of Savior of the Jews. Ellen Schiff astutely remarks, "The Chairman's careful grooming and his traveling about by horse-drawn cart appear insensitive denials of the squalor in Lodz, just as his drive to make the city's textile mills indispensable to the Germans seems to ignore the fact that ever-diminishing ranks of workers in them are starving and ill."[31] In the play, Rumkowski compares himself to Moses, a messiah leading the Jews to the Promised Land (143). Yankele describes Rumkowski as the Kaiser, "Listening to verses fashioned in his honor/ By his own poet laureate" (164). Rumkowski claims that he answers to no one except God, with whom he communicates routinely. When his authority is questioned, he arrogantly declares, "And if they dare to put me on trial, they'll have to try God too" (186). Yet much of the Jewish population's animosity toward him derives from the fact that he takes himself seriously when, as the title of the play suggests, his power is only illusory. Israel Wolf reduces Rumkowski to "a mailman for barbarians" (134) while Yankele chimes in with "Nothing is more corrupting that the illusion of power" (134). Rabinowitz, the unscrupulous chief of the Jewish police, is more blunt about Rumkowski when he says to Ada Wolf, "Haven't you learned yet his position is a joke? He can't even wipe his ass without their permission" (179). Rumkowski's tyrannical attitude, his vanity, his refusal to compromise, his opposition to insurrection, and his methods of manipulating and deceiving people result in widespread antipathy toward him in the ghetto. This hatred is best manifested when Miriam, Rumkowski's wife, smears excrement on her own husband's face.

Despite Rumkowski's personal whims and his transgressions, the Liebermans depict him as having noble intentions. In order to prevent starvation in the ghetto and to allow the Jews to survive, Rumkowski proposes the creation of factories that will serve the German war effort. Indeed, this ploy seemed to work effectively, for the ghetto population was relatively free of deportations for nearly two years, and because it was the last eastern European stronghold of Jews to be liquidated, thousands survived (the largest number in any of the cities in Poland) where elsewhere they were exterminated. Rumkowski also raises money to get the factories running so that Jews could avoid starvation. As Rumkowski tells Dr. Ari Cohen, who, as chief administrator for health services in the ghetto, has reservations about collaborating, "We work or we starve. There's nothing in between" (146). Rumkowski even provides ransom money to save select Jews from being shot. Acting in good conscience, Rumkowski explains to Dr. Cohen that Jews who refuse to move into the ghetto or those who resist will be committing mass suicide. Moreover, Rumkowski is seen as consistently negotiating with Biebow to supply more food in the ghetto, to reduce the number of individuals deported, and later, to deport only the elderly and the infirm rather than those who are productive. The order to deport children disturbs Rumkowski, who, having previously served as director of a Jewish orphanage, finds this assignment particularly repulsive. Rumkowski, speaking to God as a humble man torn between unpalatable alternatives, accepts the blame and the responsibility for sending Jewish children to their deaths: "Did You make me 'Father of the Orphans' to mock me now? When this is over, I will be one of Your most detested creatures" (175). For all of his attempts to collaborate with the Nazis, Rumkowski's major goal was to save as many lives as possible even if that meant giving up a few. Rumkowski justifies this credo as his *raison d'être*, explaining to the idealistic Cohen that he collaborates, "Because the price of survival is always right" (146). As the last Jews in the ghetto are being deported, Rumkowski defends himself: "I made a sacred promise that as long as one Jew needed my guidance, I'd be here" (194). Refusing to commit suicide, Rumkowski remains in Lodz until his ability to compromise no longer remains; then, with some semblance of dignity, he voluntarily joins his fellow Jews boarding the train to Auschwitz.

Communing directly with God, Rumkowski maintains that his goal of sacrificing many to save a few is morally righteous. He reminds Cohen, "Even God doesn't save all" (149). Yankele, however, like many of Brecht's narrators who reinforce the dialectic, provides an antithesis to Rumkowski's point of view. Just as the rabbis quoted Maimonides to Gens in Vilna, Yankele invokes the Code of Maimonides to Rumkowski, questioning the notion of offering up to enemies any Jew who is not guilty of a crime. Yankele poses the dialectic of survivorship versus the preservation of moral dignity: "Rabbi Maimonides, if we do as you suggest/ How will a remnant be saved?/ But on the other hand/ If we don't do as you say/ What kind of remnant will it be?" (148). Yankele also serves as a survivor, a witness of all of the horrible events that occurred during Rumkowski's five-year tenure as ghetto chief. Ellen Schiff writes, "Yankele functions essentially as the unsilenced, eternal voice of the Jew."[32] He is thus most qualified to pose the question of what constitutes moral responsibility in an environment where moral standards no longer apply. At the end of the play, Yankele, speaking directly to the audience, asks the spectators to judge Rumkowski for themselves: "Don't feed me your dinner table morals about how/ They should have behaved;/ Only say what you would have done" (196).

Although the focus of the play clearly is on Rumkowski, the Liebermans did not want to be confined to historical drama and thus included the Wolf family. By doing so, they altered the Holocaust experience from a simple historicization of facts and statistics to a personal tale in which audience members could empathize with the Wolf family, who represent characters of all ages. Moreover, including the Wolf family allows the Liebermans the opportunity to indicate that Jews other than Rumkowski collaborated with the Nazis, so the premise that Rumkowski's megalomania is the chief cause of his vile behavior becomes debatable. Finally, the inclusion of the Wolf family refutes the notion that individuals such as Rumkowski were chiefly responsible for the success of the Shoah and places the onus squarely on the Nazis for Jewish pain and misery in the ghettoes of eastern Europe.

Gabriel Wolf, Israel's grandson and Ada's son, joins the Jewish police to collaborate with the Nazis, much like Rumkowski did as chief elder of the *Judenrat*. Gabriel is the best representative in the play of how the Holocaust could turn family members against each other, much as it did to Rumkowski and his wife. At one point in the play, Gabriel searches his own sister Rosa, whom he accuses of attempting to smuggle a radio tube into the ghetto, while his infuriated grandfather protests. When given orders to surrender one member of each family for deportation, Gabriel nonchalantly chooses Hannah, his grandfather's niece, for selection. When Rabinowitz claims that Moshe is also listed for deportation, Gabriel confirms it without hesitation. After aiding and abetting Rumkowski in arresting his own family members, including his mother and sister, for deportation, Gabriel is told to accompany them. Biebow urges him to enter the train without resisting since a good policeman must do his duty. Throwing his cap at Rumkowski's feet, Gabriel retorts to Biebow, "But I don't think a good Jew would" (194) as he boards the train. As was true of many ghetto residents who were duped by the Nazis into assuming immoral responsibilities in order to survive, Gabriel, like Rumkowski, represents the penultimate tragedy in which humans were forced to compromise their values and turn against their own loved ones.

The Wolf family represents a cross-section of Jewish responses to Nazi atrocities in the ghettoes. Robert Skloot perceptively remarks, "One clear conclusion of *Throne* is historically verifiable: that for almost all Jews in Lodz, regardless of religious, political, or social affinity, *nothing* availed."[33] Israel Wolf, the patriarch of the family, is deeply religious and hopes that his humanism will endure in the pages of his diary. His widowed daughter, Ada, is the supreme compromiser trying to keep her family alive. She encourages her daughters to abandon their revolutionary zeal and instead engage in productive activity, such as selling armbands. In her nurturing fashion, Ada seeks to protect Gabriel from persecution by having him join the Jewish police as one of the persecutors. When Israel's niece Hannah, a Berlin lawyer considered useless for manual labor, seeks residence among the extended family members, Ada reluctantly takes her in only because she has money. Ada even agrees to submit to Rumkowski's lechery if, in doing so, she can gain privileges for her family. As Ellen Schiff has noted, Ada's resourcefulness is thwarted when children are ordered for deportation and she must decide which family member must board the train.[34] Moshe Lewin and David Abramowitz, two orphans who have been included into the Wolfs' extended family, try to survive by begging and stealing, respectively. Rosa Wolf, a Bundist and active Zionist who organizes strikes in the factories, embodies the spirit of revolutionary zeal that is morally responsible yet is snuffed out like all of the other responses to the Holocaust represented in the play.

If the Wolf family represents the myriad choices that were made to survive in the ghetto, and those options all resulted ultimately in deportation, the Liebermans ask us to reconsider Rumkowski's motives as well. Rumkowski cannot be excused for being an aggressive, ambitious, and lecherous megalomaniac who misused his authority. However, he was also an elder in the Jewish community forced into a no-win situation in which he did his best to prolong the imminent destruction of the Jews in Lodz. *Throne of Straw* poses important questions about the various alternatives available for Jews to survive in the ghetto and asks the audience to question the moral price individuals were forced to pay in making such choices.

Shimon Wincelberg's three-act realistic play, *Resort 76*, was originally written in 1962 under the title *The Windows of Heaven*. *Resort 76* is based on Polish writer and Auschwitz survivor Rachmil Bryks's novella, *A Cat in the Ghetto*, which chronicled his years spent in the Lodz ghetto before his deportation. Wincelberg was born in Kiel, Germany, in 1924, was raised in a religious household, and intended to become a rabbinical student before the Nazis ruined his plans. His family fled to the United States in the late 1930s when Nazi pogroms adversely affected their lives. During World War II, Wincelberg served in the army's 27th Infantry Division in combat intelligence. In the 1950s, he became a science fiction writer and later penned the first screenplays of the American television shows *Star Trek* and *Lost in Space*. Using the names S. Bar-David or Shimon Bar-David, Wincelberg was the screenwriter for many American television programs of the 1950s through the 1970s, including *The Rebel, Johnny Staccato, Combat!, Naked City, Gunsmoke, Route 66, Mannix, Logan's Run, Police Woman, The Paper Chase,* and *Trapper John, M. D. Resort 76* premiered at the Royal Dramatic Theatre of Stockholm in 1969 and has also been produced on French radio.

Resort 76 is a sardonic account of life in Lodz during an unspecified year in a brutally cold winter of the Nazi occupation of Poland. The play concerns ten Jews, eight of whom are confined to the cramped loft of a factory for the salvage of textile wastes. Starvation is the norm, and poverty is ubiquitous in this community; the setting is far removed from any resort. Throughout the play, these Jews are fully aware that at any time they can be deported to their deaths, and the sounds reverberating from the street, including police sirens, vibrations of heavy trucks, Nazis marching, and freight trains screeching, produce an ominous, yet all-too-familiar, effect. Wincelberg also describes the setting as bleak: "*The walls, the sky, the furniture, the people, the vegetation [as far as the latter two can be told apart] are all in shades of muddy gray, lightened only by an occasional touch of soot-black and tinges of phosphorescent green.*"[35] The dialogue in the play is coarse, brutally frank, sarcastic, and cynical, especially when delivered by Blaustain and Yablonka, a comic mountebank who laughs at the horrendous plight of his fellow Jews to prevent his succumbing to this inexplicable misery. Despite the overt pessimism, *Resort 76* is much more sanguine about the potential for moral responsibility in the Nazi-occupied ghettoes of central or eastern Europe than any other similar play dealing with the same subject.

The relationship between Schnur, a religious teacher, and Beryl, his fidgety teenage pupil, sets the standard for moral integrity in the play. Schnur is a righteous butcher, a "slaughterer" with a sense of morality that distinguishes him from the Nazi slaughterers. Schnur murders animals for food while the Nazis exterminate humans merely because they consider them to be vermin. Schnur teaches Beryl Talmudic law, a practice that is outlawed by the Nazis; as such, Schnur and Beryl make their miserable lives meaningful through spiritual understanding. When Beryl is caught by the Nazis and beaten bloody, he is forced to identify Schnur as his religious mentor and gives them the address of the textile factory. In abject misery and in frustration over having delivered his tutor into the hands of the Nazis, Beryl rejects Schnur's moral teachings: "Yes. I am finished with God! You have lied to me. He is not our father. If *this* is how a father loves his children ... then let me be an orphan!" (105). Beryl claims that he wants to be like the Nazis, who are well fed, unlike the Jews, who are miserable. Schnur, the butcher, counters with animal imagery: "Like them? Without the knowledge of having been made in His image? A beast of prey, without shame, without conscience, living for no higher pleasure than the smell of blood?" (106). Beryl is skeptical and challenges Schnur to explain why he thinks hunted Jews are more morally righteous than the hunters. Schnur responds, "Because you are a man! A man, and not an animal" (106). Robert Skloot's comment is particularly well stated: "According to Schnur, spiritual aspiration and humane behavior are what distinguishes a human being from the beasts and, in this case, the Jews from the Germans; the great challenge is to retain these qualities even in an environment of violence, bestiality, and senseless suffering."[36] Before Schnur is carted away by the Nazis, he proclaims, from a celebrated statement in the Talmud, the moral lesson that becomes the focal point of the play: "He who saves one life is counted as though he had saved an entire world" (108). Beryl is the first to understand the message, and as the Nazis besiege the loft, he retreats but not before taking the religious book from which he had been studying.

David Blaustain, an engineer in charge of organizing a workforce responsible for converting old garments, once worn by Jews who are now deceased, into carpets for the Nazis, is the key decision maker of the play. He is sometimes abrasive yet often cynical about his role as moral arbiter functioning as a lackey for the Germans. Blaustain is a pragmatist but also a humanist, most visibly manifested by the poetry he writes about the suffering in the ghetto. One of Blaustain's moral dilemmas concerns the fate of his sick pregnant wife, Esther, suffering from apparent fatigue and starvation that induce a lung-tearing cough that threatens her life. Blaustain wonders if getting Esther an abortion would solve her misery. He is pressured by his sister Anya, a member of the partisans, who urges him to flee to the woods and join the insurrection. Anya views Esther as Blaustain's crutch, a skeleton lying in bed all day, incapable of working but having to be fed nonetheless with part of her husband's rations. Blaustain insists, "Half-dead is still better than half-alive. At least she has something to look forward to" (85). Anya maintains that if Blaustain remains in the loft to tend to his sick wife, the only thing both of them can look forward to is following in the footsteps of their parents, who were incinerated by the Nazis. Moreover, Anya argues that it is unethical and immoral to bring a child into such a miserable environment. The child would be a major imposition for all those living in the factory loft and would mean another mouth to feed. When Esther later confronts her husband about wanting to abandon her and fight with the rebels in the forest, Blaustain admits, "Of course I wanted to. You think I'm made of wood?" (91). However, Blaustain, morally cognizant of Schnur's teachings, explains to his wife that he could not leave her to die, "Because I'm not made of wood" (92). In the denouement, Blaustain is offered the financial opportunity to get an abortion for Esther and is challenged about whether he wants to be a father. Esther asks Blaustain, "Do you *want* a child. (*She sees him avert his face.*) *Animal*! Do you want to be a father?" (111). As Esther calls her husband an animal, he reverts to Schnur's moral precepts that distinguish humans with a soul and conscience from animals like the Nazis. Aborting the baby would not be an act of conscience but instead would imply the barbarism of Nazis. Furthermore, as Eric Sterling comments, "Blaustain realizes that destroying the baby would also be an act of moral self-destruction, partly because it would deny his identity as a Jew. Jewish law, for example, strictly forbids abortion under any circumstances."[37] Minutes earlier, Schnur preached to Blaustain that preserving a single life is equivalent to saving many. Blaustain is also impressed by Schnur's willingness to risk his life for what is paramount to him: a moral obligation to continue spiritual study. Confirming that he wants to be a father and that he will not abandon Esther, Blaustain, emulating Schnur's moral sense, risks his own life in trying to save two others.

Blaustain's major dilemma in the play, its centrality represented by the title of Bryks's novella, concerns the fate of a cat. Madame Hershkovitch, a charwoman, reveals that anyone who brings the Germans a cat to fend off the rats and mice that have been infesting the food supplies will get a privileged job as a clerk at the Ration Board. Having caught a cat earlier, Hershkovitch is skeptical about taking it home with her, where fifteen other women that she lives with might steal it from her. She fears for her personal safety from her fellow boarders who would stop at nothing to get their hands on the cat, and if she is ever injured, there would be no one to care for her five children. As she entrusts Blaustain with the cat, he reluctantly agrees to share any profits accrued from the animal in a fifty-fifty split.

Several of the characters tempt Blaustain to surrender the cat for their personal benefits. Hupert, a charlatan who fancies himself to be a writer and film producer, pleads with Blaustain to sell the cat to a soup kitchen for fifteen pounds of potato peel, which would provide essential nutrients for the starving denizens of the loft. Hauptmann, a retired officer with a lapsed visa, offers to trade his most prized possession, a photograph of his son as a graduate of the Royal Military Academy, to Blaustain for a twenty-five percent share of the cat. Once his lawyer clears up the bureaucratic misunderstanding about his expired visa, Hauptmann plans to go to the United States and promises to negotiate free passage there for Blaustain as well. Krause, a German deported to Lodz, admitting that the nutritionally deprived need protein, suggests eating the cat. He states, "I mean, like any other meat, it contains all the essential amino acids necessary to regenerate muscle tissue, bone marrow, white blood cells" (100–101). Anya provides the most compelling arguments for Blaustain to surrender the cat. Anya argues that selling the cat will allow her and her older brother to obtain passports, work permits, and birth certificates for the two of them to flee the ghetto and join the partisans. When Blaustain defers, Anya promises to prostitute herself to one of the lecherous obstetricians who made advances to her in exchange for him performing an abortion on Esther. She reasons that if Blaustain did go into hiding in the forests, a crying baby would be a major hindrance anyway. Blaustain claims that the cat, belonging to Madame Hershkovitch, is not his to give away. Anya then poses the philosophical dilemma to her brother about whether it is more important to survive with his wife or to be morally responsible to a stranger he hardly knows.

Despite these many temptations, Blaustain accepts Schnur's notion that the overbearing suffering in the ghetto can be ennobled through moral behavior. When Blaustain complains that he does not want to accept any further responsibilities, Schnur replies, "What makes you think you have a choice?" (107). Blaustain then opens the window and releases the unharmed cat to its freedom.[38] Although the cat may have provided a chance for Blaustain's exit from the ghetto, the morally reprehensible notion of killing a defenseless animal outweighs any selfish notions the engineer may have had. Pressured from the undue daily grind of a miserable life of suffering, depression, and starvation in the ghetto, Blaustain's gesture of releasing the cat is life affirming and spiritually enlightening. Discussing Blaustain's humane behavior that distinguishes him from animals, Robert Skloot writes, "This is a truly existential creed, one which steals meaning out of the void and imposes reason on a world which insistently denies purpose and defies understanding."[39] By rejecting the murder of the cat, Blaustain affirms the dignity of life, unlike the Nazis who act as captors and oppressors. If Blaustain had killed the cat, he would have been imitating the behavior of the Nazis. Wincelberg attempts to convey that although the Jews in Lodz were destined for deportation, they maintained a sense of moral responsibility in order to survive, rather than descend to the level of soulless animals, like the cruel and inhuman Nazis.

Resort 76 goes beyond merely presenting a scenario in which moral responsibility is possible in the stifling atmosphere of the eastern European ghetto. Krause personifies the vast hypocrisy of a so-called moral nation that considers Jews to be subhumans without any values. Krause is a typical stocky, blond, pink-cheeked Protestant representing German society. After serving admirably in the German army during World War I, Krause was working as a pharmacist when he enlisted in the military to serve the Fatherland. During the mandatory background check, German authorities discovered that his maternal grandfather was Jewish. As a *Mischling* (with partial Jewish ancestry), Krause is not only denied military service, but also is deported to Lodz. Never having known his grandparents, Krause resents them, especially his grandfather, for having tainted his pure Aryan family history: "The dirty swine! Polluting an innocent Aryan girl with his bestial Asiatic lusts!" (74). Krause is so jingoistic that he refuses to blame his plight on Germany and instead disparages himself. He admits to Schnur, "We do, after all, have a bureaucracy which is the envy of the civilized world. And if *they* have decided I am not fit to live among human beings, they probably know what they're talking about" (75). When the topic of conversation turns to the thought of eating the cat for valued nutrients that have been determined by valid scientific experiments, Krause objects to such studies: "Vivisection. Any sort of experimentation that might inflict cruelty on a living animal ... We may have our faults as a nation, but thank God, we *are* civilized" (101). Eric Sterling has commented on the hypocrisy of Krause's nationalism: "The Nazis deem that vivisection is immoral but consider experimentation on Jews, such as the work of Josef Mengele, morally acceptable. Vivisection would challenge their sense of superiority, but anti-Semitism confirms their self-regard."[40]

As a respectable member of the National Socialist Party and a strict believer in its ideology, Krause is obviously anti-Semitic. Condescendingly referring to the Lodz ghetto Jews as "you people," Krause explains why the Germans are fighting a war of anti-Semitism: "That our Motherland at this moment is fighting a crusade, single-handedly, to preserve European civilization from the black barbarians of the Western world" (56–57). Krause stereotypes Jews as greedy businessmen out to make a profit at all costs. When he bites into a sausage, starving Hupert offers to buy a piece of it from him. Krause responds derisively: "If you don't mind my saying so, that is exactly the trouble with you people. Reckon everything in terms of money. Crucify our Savior, and then expect the world to share their sausage with you" (64). Yet Krause is in a situation where he must begin to question his own identity, for he is also a Jew according to Nazi law. Thus, by definition, Krause must be subhuman, a beast without any morals or ethics. To accept Nazi ideology blindly means that his identity as a moral human being must be called into question. Thus, despite his indoctrination as a Nazi, Krause is ripe for a change of heart.

Krause gradually discovers that the Jews in the ghetto are moral beings, not subhumans without a soul or conscience. Although he is an outsider to the community and considers himself to be an Aryan who loves his German Fatherland, Schnur and Blaustain empathize with his plight and treat him humanely. In spite of their debasement as a result of suffering, starvation, and persecution by the Nazis, the Jews demonstrate moral character by welcoming Krause into their community as a fellow comrade in pain. As Eric Sterling has acknowledged, "Krause comes to admire them [the Jews] because, in addition to empathizing with him, they maintain their dignity–their essential selfhood–even when being destroyed."[41] Blaustain's decision to support Esther, and his refusal to abort the baby as his sister advised, demonstrates moral character that impresses Krause. Schnur's adherence to Talmudic teachings when matters of sustenance and survival should matter most intimates to Krause that Jews indeed have souls. Blaustain's humane treatment of the cat also indicates that Jews can assume moral responsibility that the Nazis claim such subhumans could never achieve. Krause gradually begins to realize that the way the Jews treat animals should at least be a model for the way the Nazis treat subhumans.

At the end of the play, Krause receives a notice stating that his pastor has proven that his mother was illegitimate, so, as a full-blooded Aryan, he is allowed free passage back to Germany. Krause now has the opportunity to erase his Jewish heritage and return, cleansed, to his wife and daughter. However, Krause has realized that his attitudes toward Jews have been hypocritical and that he has been indoctrinated by Nazi propaganda. Krause's deportation to Germany has been obtained by deceit, and thus, virtually overnight, he has easily been transformed from Jew to Aryan. If there is no moral difference in character between a Jew and an Aryan and if one can move from Jew to Aryan so easily, Krause wonders why he should deceive himself into believing that Aryans are superior. He begins to empathize with his fellow Jews, most notably manifested when he gives Beryl, beaten and tortured by the Nazis, pain killers. Krause then commits suicide by ingesting arsenic. Krause's suicide represents his stoical stand against the hypocritical values of the Nazis. Krause would rather commit suicide than return to Germany and persecute Jews for no apparent reason. The Jews have demonstrated to him that they are not animals and that moral responsibility can be achieved despite the most adverse conditions imaginable.

American playwright Millard Lampell began his career in the early 1940s as a member of the Almanac Singers, a folk music group that included Pete Seeger, Woody Guthrie, and Lee Hays. Lampell wrote lyrics with Guthrie and adapted traditional songs into labor anthems with pro-union messages. His first screenplay was for the 1945 film, *A Walk in the Sun*; he later wrote for television, his most notable achievement being screenwriter for the 1976 miniseries,

Rich Man, Poor Man. Lampell was one of the screenplay writers for the 1989 film, *Triumph of the Spirit,* based on the true story of Salamo Arouch, who survived Auschwitz by becoming a successful boxer in bouts with other camp inmates on which the SS wagered. Directed by Robert M. Young, *Triumph of the Spirit,* which was filmed on location in Auschwitz, starred William Dafoe as Salamo, Robert Loggia as his father, and Edward James Olmos as Gypsy.

Lampell's *The Wall,* symmetrically structured in two acts, each containing six scenes, was inspired by John Hersey's 1950 novel, *The Wall.* Hersey's account of the events in Warsaw from September 1939 to the liquidation of the ghetto in April 1943 was largely modeled on Emanuel Ringelblum's *Oneg Shabbat,* an archived collection of thousands of pages of diaries, letters, notes, chronicles, descriptive accounts, photographs, underground newspapers, and posters about Jewish life during the Nazi occupation of Warsaw. The Warsaw Jews, apparently obsessed with the notion that they might be exterminated without leaving any record, left behind an immense array of diaries and letters. After the war, Henryk Rapaport and Rachel Apt (two characters in Lampell's play) were among a party of four ghetto survivors who unearthed the archives of Noach Levinson, hidden amid the rubble of Warsaw. Levinson had buried diaries, novels, notebooks, minutes of meetings, letters, plays, poems, and official *Judenrat* records in seventeen iron boxes wrapped in rags and old clothing. The archives featured more than four million words of notebooks that Levinson had kept about Warsaw life since 1935.[42] Hersey's novel is based on much of the Levinson material.

Lampell was intrigued by the compelling tale of six hundred Jews who fought Nazi artillery and tanks during the ghetto uprising and believed that Hersey's novel could be transformed into a play. Lampell, who had never written drama before composing *The Wall,* realized the difficulty of converting into a three-hour play a 632-page novel that spans four years and consists of fifty characters. Lampell began researching the original documents of Ringelblum's archives, as well as the Nazi military records, including the files of SS General Stroop, who, while he was in charge of liquidating the ghetto, documented the events of the uprising. Lampell then immersed himself into the culture of Polish Jewry and read Polish fiction, collections of Yiddish proverbs, folk tales, and songs. Lampell also learned quite a lot by interviewing Yitzhak Zukerman, a former commander of the Ghetto Fighters Organization, and two other ghetto fighters of the handful who still remained alive.

Produced by Kermit Bloomgarden, who had achieved success on Broadway with *The Diary of Anne Frank, The Wall,* directed by Morton Da Costa, premiered on Broadway at the Billy Rose Theatre on 11 October 1960. The cast included the relatively unknown George C. Scott (Dolek Berson), Yvonne Mitchell (Rachel Apt), Vincent Gardenia (Pavel Menkes), Marian Seldes (Symka Berson), and David Opatoschu (Pan Apt). Although the initial reviews were strong, the play closed after only 167 performances.[43]

After a brief run in Munich during 1961, in a production that featured a spare set that revolved on a turntable, *The Wall* was produced at Arena Stage in Washington, D.C. as part of its 1963–1964 season. Directed by Edwin Sherin, this production, set in Arena's open space, captured the teeming life of the ghetto much better than the cramped setting of the Broadway production, designed by Howard Bay. As Robert Franciosi contends, this revised version of the play, coming on the heels of the Eichmann verdict, the success of *The Pawnbroker,* the furor over *The Deputy,* and the Auschwitz trials, was more palatable for 1964 audiences than it was three years earlier in New York.[44] Since the 1960s, *The Wall* has been performed worldwide, particularly in Europe and Israel. In 1982, Lampell wrote the teleplay for the television film version, produced by David Susskind. Directed by Robert Markowitz, *The Wall,* which was filmed on location in Sosnowiec, Poland, starred Tom Conti as Dolek Berson.

Warsaw, the capital of Polish Jewry and internationally known as a major cultural, political, and educational Jewish center, surrendered to the Germans on 28 September 1939. Jews were almost immediately seized for forced labor, Jewish businesses were plundered, and Jewish professionals, journalists, teachers, social workers, and cultural administrators lost their positions without compensation. Anti-Jewish decrees were issued requiring the wearing of the Star of David, forbidding travel, banning radios, and blocking Jewish bank accounts. On 2 October 1940, the Warsaw ghetto was established in which approximately 550,000 Jews were contained within a wall sixteen kilometers long and three meters high, topped by barbed wire and broken glass.[45] Jews were crammed into rooms where the average density was thirteen people and given a daily ration of what amounted to 184 calories. Thousands soon died of hunger and disease, the latter spread mainly through epidemics of typhus and typhoid. Those fortunate enough to work labored for ten-hour days that often stretched to nineteen. During April 1942, the Nazis created panic in the ghetto by executing night raids in which they seized people in their homes and then took them out to be shot. In various *Aktionen* conducted from 22 July until 6 September 1942, the Nazis, with the help of the Jewish police, deported the majority of the Warsaw ghetto Jews, approximately 310,000, to Treblinka. When the deportations came to a halt in September, those remaining, a group that consisted mainly of women and young men, realized that resisting was the only viable option. Moreover, since their family members were now deported, these survivors had no qualms about the Germans holding their loved ones as hostages if they chose to resist.

When the second wave of deportations began on 18 January 1943, Jews ordered to assemble in the courtyards went into hiding. The *Judenrat* and Jewish police lost any power over the Jewish population. Preparing for the ghetto's liquidation, Jews built subterranean bunkers that had well-planned exits and entrances. On 19 April 1943, during the eve of Passover and Easter, the SS began liquidation of the ghetto. In the twenty-seven days of the Warsaw uprising, approximately seven hundred Jews, defending themselves with only pistols and clubs, held off a German military force of over two thousand men armed with tanks and artillery. The revolt ended when the Nazis systematically burned the ghetto building by building. The number of Jews remaining in Warsaw when the Russians liberated the city in January 1945 is unknown; Raul Hilberg estimates there were only two hundred left, while Israel Gutman states that between one and two thousand survived.[46]

Despite the obvious attempt to portray the leaders of the Warsaw uprising as heroic, *The Wall* depicts a microcosm of Jewish life in the ghetto. Jews of all ages, classes, and lifestyles are represented in the play. Lampell stated that he intended to stage a cross-section of a vibrant community: "I simply wished to present them as I believe they were–tragic, jealous, warm, frightened, tormented, cruel, courageous–in short, a mirror of the human race with all its failings and all its astonishing potential."[47] According to Dawidowicz, Jews in the ghetto faced destruction yet managed to preserve their humanity by "protecting the family, educating the children, feeding the hungry, caring for the sick, satisfying intellectual and cultural needs."[48] We see all of these multi-faceted aspects of ghetto life manifested in the play, including Jews caring for each other, enjoying concerts, dating, and attending weddings. In particular, the social and cultural life in the ghetto did as much, if not more, than any steadfast adherence to spiritual values did to maintain Jewish faith in a vibrant community.

Much of this vibrant community spirit of the Warsaw ghetto is conveyed through Jewish humor. When Lampell was preparing to write the play, Warsaw ghetto survivor Yitchak Zukerman gave him this advice: "Would you believe that in the worst days, when everything was burning, when we were hiding away in the bunkers, we drank and laughed, argued and sang, kissed in the shadows? You must know that, if you wish to write about the Ghetto."[49] Dawidowicz confirmed the existence of widespread humor in the ghettoes of eastern Europe: "Political jokes reflected the indomitability of the ghetto spirit and became the weapon of the powerless. Humor transformed the reality of power relations, its fantasy permitting the Jew to triumph over his persecutor."[50] Lampell seemed to model his protagonists on Zukerman's tough, resilient exterior that indicated a passionate thirst for life and a concomitant vocal ghetto peevishness expressed through humor. Lampell explained the type of humor he was aiming for when writing the play: "A life painted in bold colors. A life mirrored perfectly in their humor. Their wry, sardonic, bitter-sweet mockery of themselves. They did not tell jokes just to be funny. It was also a way of putting the harsh reality of their lives into a shape that was easier to deal with."[51] Fishel Shpunt, a peddler who displays comic wisdom, is much like the amusing figures of Yankele in *Throne of Straw* and Yablonka in *Resort 76*. Shpunt represents the eternal wandering Jew whose comic attitude toward life enables him to endure the misery of the ages. Shpunt's frog-like dances, his caustic wit, and his ability to mock his own abject condition not only provide much-needed comic relief in the play but also capture the exuberant spirit of survival in the ghetto.[52]

In his efforts to depict a stratified community in Warsaw, Lampell's play seemingly segments Jews into various categories, depending upon their reaction to the Holocaust. At the top of the hierarchy are the resistance leaders such as Katz and Rachel Apt, who are later joined by Dolek Berson and even Shpunt. In the middle of the hierarchy, we have most of the members of the Kogan family, who are victims of the Holocaust, and the Apt family, excluding Rachel, who are reluctant revolutionaries or selfish deserters. At the bottom of the totem pole are Reb Mazur and Stefan Apt, whose seemingly good intentions exacerbate the annihilation of the Jewish community.

Lampell's depiction of Rabbi Reb Mazur represents an indictment of the religious community that aided and abetted the Nazis by refusing to face the imposing threat of National Socialism to Jews. During the first scene, which occurs in 1940, Mazur states that the Germans will leave Warsaw by June without starting trouble because "World opinion wouldn't stand for it."[53] By spring 1941, the rabbi is passing along the information that the pope is arranging a meeting in Switzerland to bring the war to an end. When Katz reveals the news of Jews being massacred at Bialystok, Mazur claims that the Germans fired on a few drunken soldiers who had been unruly and assures the rebel that he has been nothing but a troublemaker since he was in diapers. Rabbi Mazur warns the partisans against any type of revolt for fear that "innocent people will pay for it" (65). The following winter, Mazur is still capitulating, arguing that the Russians have won a big victory at Kiev and the Americans are bombing Berlin. In late 1942, when conditions have vastly deteriorated in the ghetto, Mazur is still blind to the reality of the Holocaust, explaining to Rachel, "Why should they exterminate us? It doesn't make sense. We're working for them, no? Right here in the Ghetto, factories are making uniforms, gun holsters, knapsacks, God knows what" (98–99). Mazur places moral responsibility in the hands of God and biblical teachings instead of in the hands of humans. He tells Dolek, "It is nonsense to feel humiliated by the Nazis, because we are better than they are. Yes, I am calm–because I know that any faith based on love and respect will outlive any faith based upon murder" (108). However, when the Nazis choose who is to be deported and who is to be spared because of their ability to do useful work, Mazur, upon revealing that he is a rabbi, is sentenced to "resettlement." His morality and his steadfast adherence to religious faith mean nothing to the Nazis.

If Rabbi Mazur is a liability to the revolt and inadvertently aids the Nazis in genocide, his son Stefan overtly does so as a member of the Jewish police. Stefan violates the Code of Maimonides as he rounds up Jews initially for labor camps and later for deportation. Ostensibly believing that he could defer Nazi brutality as a member of the Jewish police, instead he contributes to it. Lampell depicts members of the Jewish police as abominations who not only suppress revolt, but also disrupt camaraderie and trust within the community and even within families. Stefan exhorts his own father to report for deportation, acknowledging to him, "You will be taken anyway. They'll get you one of these days. You can save me by going a few days sooner" (109–10). However, even the Jewish police cannot save themselves, and by refusing to take moral responsibility against Nazi tyranny, Stefan is deported as well.

The ineffective approach of refusing to react to the impending Nazi genocide instead of resisting is represented by the fate of the Kogan family. The Kogans are well-dressed, respectable bourgeois Jews deported into Warsaw from a small town in Poland. As the play progresses, Pan Kogan, once an established pharmacist, is reduced to selling his own clothes in order to survive. Each time we see the Kogans, they are more ragged and destitute, visibly represented by their disappearing and tattered wardrobe. Their eight-year-old daughter Regina winds up begging in the streets. After her parents are deported, Regina, *unkempt, a lost animal poking in the ruins* (143), is left to fend for herself. However, the subtle deterioration of the Kogan family is difficult for audiences to grasp because, since they are not on stage for much of the play, only an unusually perceptive spectator would notice their increasingly brutal fate.[54]

If Lampell fails to convey the devastating effects of the Holocaust on family members such as the Kogans, he surely succeeds in doing so through his portrayal of the secondary characters in the play. Symka, Dolek's wife, represents the thousands of victims who died of disease while hoping for some type of reprieve from their misery. Mordecai Apt adopts a nonchalant attitude toward the atrocities, refusing to get work papers and pretending the wall does not exist; instead, he prefers to retreat into his writing and focus his attention on Rutka. Rather than reacting to Nazi genocide, Mordecai rationalizes the Holocaust, arguing that although the Germans are uncivilized, they are still human; moreover, he believes that the destruction of the Jews would not economically benefit the Nazis: "We're valuable property. If Hitler wants to make peace, he can use us to bargain with" (99). Inevitably, Mordecai, helpless as he watches his father-in-law being deported, begins to learn the horrors of the Holocaust first hand, yet the uncommitted young man remains confused about what to do. Lacking common sense, Mordecai is finally told by Burson that his only chance of survival is to flee to the bunkers with the ghetto fighters. Mordecai's sister, Halinka, acts like a Jewish princess, focusing her attention on social concerns and maintaining her beautiful appearance. Halinka prefers to ignore news about the deportations, insisting that she is "not in the mood" (96) while fooling herself into believing that the transports have ended because "Stefan told me all they want is seventy thousand" (96). Near the end of the play, Rachel reports that Halinka, who has quietly disappeared like countless others in Warsaw, is dead. The patriarch of the family, Pan Apt, who owns a jewelry store, is assured that the solution to the Holocaust is to offer the Germans money that he contends will be the safeguard against Nazi brutality. Pan pays Berson to get him an identity card and offers bribes to the Nazis for his exit from the ghetto to live as an Aryan. He abandons his religion, but he never professed to be religious anyway. However, in fleeing the ghetto, he leaves behind his helpless family, including Halinka, who frantically begs her father to take her with him. Pan selfishly saves himself but abandons his offspring to their deaths. When he leaves behind several of his valuable gems as his legacy, Mordecai flings them away in disgust.

For much of the play, Dolek Berson is a lone wolf, a selfish person whose mordant sense of humor allows him to survive in an absurd world that he mocks. Rachel initially rebukes him for being, in her words, "So damned self-contained" (61). His attitude toward the Nazis is that to resist means suicide, and since survival is his priority, he believes it is best not to protest. Berson tells Rachel, "There's an old saying, if you can't bite, don't show your teeth" (30). During an incident when the Germans are beating a woman on the street, Berson looks the other way. He feels frustrated in his inability to help his sick wife, and when Reb Mazur assures him that God will punish the Germans, Berson retorts, "God? Is there a God? What is He? A practical joker?" (52). Rachel challenges Berson to make a commitment rather than drift through life aimlessly as a comedian: "Stand there with that little boy's grin. What is that idiot grin, what? Did someone once tell you it was charming? When will you get it through your head, childhood is over!" (100). After Symka dies, Berson gets his chance to flee from the ghetto and leave his Jewish comrades to fend for themselves. Berson's return to the ghetto to aid the resistance fighters is quirky. On the one hand, Berson realizes that he needs someone after Symka dies, and Rachel certainly fills that void; this scenario would devolve the play into a love story. Berson, however, has apparently been swayed by Rachel that his selfish attitude about survival at all costs was not morally responsible. When Rachel asks Berson why he returned to risk his life, he replies, "I walked along with the feeling that I ... had not survived. I always thought that just to live was enough. To live *how*? To live *with whom*?" (153). At the end of the play, when the Nazis have cornered the resistance fighters, Berson demonstrates true commitment to others when he plays the concertina, thus attracting attention away from Rutka's crying baby. In one sense, Berson's act of self-sacrifice is sheer martyrdom, but Lampell prefers to view Berson's distraction as an act of moral responsibility that one may inevitably choose to call heroism.

Rachel Apt, a schoolteacher who cares deeply about the effects of the Holocaust on her family and friends, turns commitment into action as a leader in the underground movement in a manner reminiscent of Hanna Senesh.[55] As the Nazis issue decrees and gradually deprive Jews of their rights, Rachel becomes the *raisonneur* for protest. Rachel urges the textile workers to mutilate German coats to make the Nazis freeze on the Eastern front. She represents the lone voice that alerts her fellow ghetto residents that Jews are being turned into ashes in the concentration camps. When Mordecai contends that the Germans may still have values, Rachel counters that they view Jews as vermin, not humans: "To them, killing one of us is like a butcher kills a chicken, without thinking twice!" (99). Moreover, unlike most of her ghetto brethren, Rachel assumes responsibility for preventing Nazi atrocities; she even accepts blame for not getting Reb Mazur to the bunker before his deportation. To counterbalance Jewish genocide, Rachel, delivering the play's most memorable line, tells Berson that she would like to have a child because "the only way to answer death is with more life" (156). During a motivating speech, Rachel urges the members of the underground to assume moral responsibility for the Holocaust:

> Why are we all so quiet? The most gentle bird does not go to death without a scream. This will be an eternal mystery: why didn't we resist when they began to resettle us? We should have run out, set fire to everything in sight, torn down the Wall! Now we are disgraced in our own eyes. And our docility has earned us nothing. You think talk will save you? You think work will save you? Bribery? *We must defend ourselves.* If we are too weak to defend our lives, let us at least defend human honor. (132)

Lampell views this existential commitment to take action even when the odds are daunting to be the major aspect of the Holocaust that he wished to convey in his play.[56] In the introduction to *The Wall*, Lampell wrote, "Out of all the horror of Hitler Europe, it is this that to me emerged as the most significant fact. A handful of Jews exposed the fullest potential of the human race. To resist death. To trust one another. To commit themselves. To endure."[57]

Erwin Sylvanus's *Korczak und die Kinder* (*Dr. Korczak and the Children*) was the first successful German Holocaust drama. During World War II, Sylvanus served in the German army and was wounded on the Russian front. After the war, he turned to writing

literature that focused primarily on heroic martyrdom against totalitarianism. *Korczak und die Kinder*, consisting of nineteen episodes
or *stationen*, premiered at the Schauspiel in Krefeld, West Germany,
on 1 November 1957. The Central Council of the Jews in Germany
awarded the play the Leo Baeck Prize the following year. In 1961, the
play received widespread visibility in a West German television production directed by Sam Besekow. *Dr. Korczak and the Children* was
particularly popular in West Germany, receiving 950 performances
from 1957 to 1980.[58] Since its premiere, *Dr. Korczak and the Children*
has been produced 120 times worldwide and has been translated into
fifteen languages.

The story of Dr. Korczak is one of the most remarkable tales
of heroism and moral responsibility depicted in any of the so-called
"ghetto plays" about the Holocaust. Janusz Korczak, the son of an
assimilated Jewish attorney in Warsaw, studied medicine at Warsaw
University. His early life was dedicated to practicing medicine to help
the impoverished, as well as writing books about children. In 1912,
he became director of an orphanage in Warsaw. During World War I,
Korczak served in the Russian army, and during his time on the military bases, he wrote his most important treatise on the social psychology of adult-child relationships, *How to Love Children*. After the war,
he continued his work in two orphanages, served as an instructor of
a boarding school, published a newspaper for children, ran summer
camps, and lectured at universities until anti-Semitic Polish decrees
of the 1930s curtailed many of these activities. When the German
occupation began, he refused to wear the yellow star and heed Nazis
rules, all of which led to a brief jail sentence. During the bleakest days
in the Warsaw ghetto, Korczak focused on the needs of the children in
the orphanage and refused to take asylum in the Aryan section of the
city. Facing the imminent deportation of the children in his orphanage, Dr. Korczak was given one final opportunity to escape. In his
diary entry of 1 August 1942, he wrote, "A casino. Monaco. The stake–
your head."[59] On 5 August, the Nazis rounded up Korczak and his
two hundred orphans for deportation. Korczak, who had anticipated
that moment, made sure the children, who were washed and neatly
clothed, proceeded in an orderly fashion, without crying, in rows of

four to the freight cars. Dr. Korczak then accompanied the children to their deaths at Treblinka. Dr. Korczak has been immortalized in books and plays, his writings have been translated into many languages, and several social work organizations throughout Europe and Israel have kept his memory alive by bearing his name.

In his introductory comments to the play, Sylvanus notes, "The author has not invented the events depicted in this play; he has merely recorded them."[60] Although Sylvanus generally maintains historical authenticity throughout the play, there are some minor transgressions. The destination of the children appears to be Maidanek in the play, whereas the children were actually gassed in Treblinka. Dr. Korczak's deeply religious faith is exaggerated by Sylvanus, ostensibly because he wants to link Korczak's sense of morality with a benevolent God who will sow the seeds of the dead into fertile Israel. Finally, as Edward R. Isser has revealed, Korczak, who served in the Russian army during the war, could not have been awarded the Iron Cross, a distinctly German honor.[61] The Iron Cross is introduced in the play to make the point that Korczak is not particularly proud of an award given to him by such a barbaric nation.

The experimental form that Sylvanus adopted for *Dr. Korczak and the Children* distinguishes the play from most of these naturalistic ghetto dramas. Sylvanus modeled *Dr. Korczak* on Luigi Pirandello's *Six Characters in Search of an Author* and *Tonight We Improvise*, in which actors rehearse a tale for public presentation. The actors are dissenting participants in this Holocaust drama, much like any modern German audience would be in their roles as spectators. The First Actor complains about the play's content: "Crying for the Jews— it's become the fashionable thing to do nowadays" (119) and states that the subject is boring. The actors reluctantly agree to rehearse because management has chosen the play, and the actors have no say about the matter. This play-within-the play device employed so effectively by Pirandello to conflate illusion and reality is used for the same purpose in Sylvanus's play. German society after the war accepted as reality the illusion of the Holocaust, making them guilty of collective amnesia. Throughout the play, the Narrator consistently reinforces the blurring of the lines demarcating reality and illusion.

Two of the five characters in the play assume more than one role, with the exceptions being the Narrator, the First Actor, who plays the Leader of an Elite Gestapo Squad, and the Second Actor, who plays Dr. Korczak. The Pirandellian ploy of having actors assume multiple roles is, as Sidra DeKoven Ezrahi has suggested, a means to implicate all humanity as potential accomplices in the Shoah.[62] The actors are ordinary people who are reluctant to engage in the roles that Sylvanus has chosen for them. Gradually, they warm to the play and assume the roles intended for them during the rehearsal. As this ordinary group of people become mass murderers, the implication is that the typical bourgeois German audience watching the play similarly assimilated into roles during the Third Reich that contributed to the genocide. In his introduction to the play, George E. Wellwarth writes, "These actors have the same background as the audience–they too had willingly functioned as cogs in the Nazi machine and they too had shifted the blame to cleanse themselves in the soothing waters of hypocrisy."[63] The refusal to accept responsibility for their actions after the war was so endemic to German audiences that Sylvanus attempted to assign guilt to the spectators vicariously through their identification with the performers as ordinary German citizens trapped into playing nightmarish roles.

Sylvanus meshed these Pirandellian devices with Brechtian alienation effects that disallow the audience to succumb to theatrical illusion or a theater of entertainment. A Brechtian-type narrator comments on the stage action and reduces suspense by revealing the outcome of the play: "This is the story of Janusz Korczak and his children and how they had to die because they were Jewish children in Poland" (117). Sylvanus's Narrator, as Brecht intended, explains parables to the audience so that their focus is not on what is happening but why, forcing spectators to think critically. Moreover, the Narrator functions as a metatheatrical device that consistently reminds the audience that it is watching a play, thus preventing empathy that might cloud one's judgment, particularly true of such an emotionally draining tale as the murder of innocent children. In exhorting spectators to leave if they are offended by the play or if they feel that their money has been wasted, Sylvanus's Narrator continually moves the audience away from empathy with the characters in order to preclude any catharsis. In addition, the removal of all makeup and costumes in a performing area of minimal props, similar to the effect Brecht obtained by having Russian farmers (read amateur actors) perform the Grusha story in *The Caucasian Chalk Circle*, reminds us that we are not in Poland during 1942 but in a theater where actors are rehearsing. Furthermore, the actors reiterate to the audience that they are in the theater watching performers who are merely playing Polish citizens. For example, the First Actor tells the Narrator, "Let's get going and give it a try, for goodness' sakes. The audience is sitting out there waiting" (120). At one point during the rehearsals, the Narrator interrupts and cuts a scene on the spur of the moment; later, the performers debate eliminating the begging scene and discuss whether they should run through various troublesome sections of the play, all of which serves to sever the audience from the traditional notion of plot. Finally, the protean change of personae prevents audience identification with any character, which also becomes for Sylvanus a device that precludes emotional involvement for the audience.

The dialectic that Brecht employed to frame his plays is also present in *Dr. Korczak and the Children*. As Brecht preferred, the dialectic was intended to create a debate that the audience could engage in objectively and intelligently. In Sylvanus's play, actors interrupt the action to disrupt audience empathy that might interfere with reason and intellect. At one point, the Actress tells the Narrator, "It might be a good idea to stop now in order to sit quietly for a while and just think about all of this" (141).

The dialectic focuses on the concept of lying: Sylvanus wants his German audience to understand that they have been living in lies about the Holocaust. At best, they have become morally irresponsible in forgetting German atrocities toward Jews; at worst, they have engaged in a conspiracy of silence that disengages themselves from their own complicity in the Holocaust. For instance, when the First Actor abnegates responsibility for Nazi theories that he did not create, the Narrator responds, "No, but they're tolerated by you" (126). Later, when the First Actor asks if this is a play about lying, the Narrator admits, "It's a play about the lie in our time" (143). The two opposing

sides of the dialectic are represented by the First Actor playing the
role of an SS soldier and the Second Actor playing Dr. Korczak. Both
actors are ordinary German citizens, one playing a Nazi and the other
a Polish Jew. The dialectic is embedded in the form of the play as well,
where the audience is asked to determine whether illusion (the play
itself) or reality (the Korczak story) represent truth or lies.

The First Actor, who has taken an oath of allegiance to the
Nazis, states, "No one can live without lying" (125). His *raison d'être*
is obeisance, and any reason for disobeying an order is equivalent to
lying. The First Actor's belief in the lie stems from a childhood incident when, as a member of the Hitler Youth, he and his comrades
stole apples from a farmer's field. After the farmer filed a complaint,
the First Actor acknowledged the misdemeanor to the Hitler Youth
commandant. When the camp commandant asked the young man
why he admitted his guilt, the latter responded, "Because it's the
truth" (143). The young man was punished for betraying the solidarity
of the regiment. The lesson that he learned was that a German exists
for Germany above all else. Thus, rather than accepting responsibility for any immoral behavior as an SS officer, the First Actor blames
the Jews for their plight. When the Narrator questions Nazi atrocity
against the Jews, evoking the spirit of Kristallnacht, the First Actor
responds, "Eye for eye and tooth for tooth. Why didn't they clear out
before that? Why do they always drag their feet so long? You can't deny
they assassinated a German diplomat" (127). The First Actor explains
atrocity as the norm during the ravages of war, but the Actress rebukes
him: "Tell me, aren't we all lying just a little bit? All of us–not just
us, but all of us" (129). However, when duty requires the First Actor to
deport Dr. Korczak and the orphanage children without any delay or
bargaining, he proceeds without hesitation. Sylvanus makes it clear
that the First Actor has difficulty accepting a moral code based upon
lies. Comparing his adherence to duty to Dr. Korczak's steadfast moral
obligation to the children of the orphanage, the First Actor experiences a sense of conflict about his hypocritical life and says to himself,
"Won't I ever be able to get rid of this feeling of being ashamed? It's just
like it was when I had to wear shirts that didn't fit because they were
cut out of my father's old ones. This goddam Jewish swine" (153). The

First Actor, thus, is lying to himself when he addresses the audience: "And then, of course, it won't be my fault. It isn't my fault in any case. Heaven is my witness: it wasn't my fault" (154). In short, the audience realizes that he doth protest too much.

In episode two, the Narrator explains the focus of the play to the Actress: "It's about Janusz Korczak, about a Jew who's supposed never to have told a lie" (119). When Korczak was eleven years old, his mother pawned his deceased father's gold-plated watch to earn money for the poverty-stricken family. The children saved their meager earnings accrued from doing odd jobs, but before they could buy the watch back, the pawnbroker sold it. Distressed over a watch that had sentimental value, Korczak conferred with his rabbi. Absorbed in the scriptures, the rabbi gave Korczak his own father's watch. According to Korczak, the rabbi, reading the Book of Law, saw only the truth and valued the watch as expendable compared to the holy books. Korczak understood why the rabbi gave him the watch: "Otherwise he would have had to lie. Otherwise he would have had to lie to me; and a man who knows God does not lie" (123).

The lesson that Korczak learned at that young age–never to lie– formed the principle that defined the way he lives his life. Korczak is ordered to prepare the children for deportation, making sure that they are not unruly and that no one gets frightened. When Dr. Korczak realizes what he must say to his wards, he asks the SS officer, "You mean ... you want me ... to lie?" (140). Korczak, a religious man of faith, unlike his Nazi tormentors, wonders why God tolerates this sacrilege from Nazis who scorn and blaspheme His name. As Korczak prays fervently, the Nazi officer is laughing in the background. Dr. Korczak decides that he will accompany the children to their deaths, just as Moses did not forsake his people. However, to comfort them, Korczak assures the children that they are journeying to the Promised Land, thus breaking his vow never to lie.

As the First and Second Actors face the audience and simulta- neously state, "I am ready" (150), the spectators are asked to judge who is lying: the hypocritical SS officer or Dr. Korczak, who lies for a noble cause. Contrary to what Brecht may have preferred, the argument is tipped in Korczak's favor by the emotional appeal to an audience that should sympathize with the victims rather than the perpetrators. Korczak accompanied the children to the gas chamber, where he told them to undress, and then undressed himself in preparation for gassing. The Narrator describes the extermination to the audience: "There were sixty-six children, boys and girls, all Jewish orphans. They were sixteen years old, fifteen, fourteen, thirteen, twelve, and eleven and ten years old. Nine, eight, seven, six, five and four years old. Three and two years old. The youngest ones had to be carried" (155). Korczak is depicted not just like Moses, but as the Jewish equivalent of Christian martyrdom. Edward R. Isser remarks, "Sylvanus presents Korczak as a pious figure who dies in a Christ-like sacrifice on behalf of his fellow man."[64] This piety is carried over to episode 19 in which the Narrator transforms himself into a rabbi citing the prophet Ezekiel. If the audience is not swayed by the emotional impact of Korczak's martyrdom, the Narrator as rabbi provides the synthesis to the dialectic about truth versus lies: "For I know that the prophet Ezekiel saw the truth; and what he saw will be fulfilled in us" (156). Quoting Ezekiel, the Narrator recites the prophecy that the resurrection of bones, sinews, and flesh of the Jewish victims of the Holocaust will transform into the state of Israel. Korczak's lie seems vindicated by the rebirth of his dead children as the Children of Israel.

The Narrator, speaking to the First Actor, says, "We're not asking you to talk here about how or why things 'went wrong.' We–all of us here–are trying to find the origin of the lie" (142). The origin of the lie can only be found in the audience. The performers who spout anti-Semitic aphorisms are no different from the typical bourgeois German citizens participating in the play as spectators. Thus, it is not clear whether the anti-Semitism stems from the performers' own beliefs or from the roles they are assigned in the play. Like Thomas Bernhard's *Eve of Retirement*, Sylvanus forces his audience to listen to echoes of its own anti-Semitic beliefs. When Dr. Korczak addresses the SS officer about the only lie he is about to tell in his life, the underlying implication is that the audience is being confronted directly: "I will lie–and yet I will not lie. You, Major, of course are incapable of understanding me" (151). Sylvanus implicates the German audience for refusing to accept their own roles in the Holocaust and for ignoring the latent anti-Semitism that precipitated the Shoah. As Robert Skloot has acknowledged, *Dr. Korczak and the Children* forces its German audience to recognize its "willful refusal to explore its recent history and presents a clear rebuke to the Nazi mentality and system."[65]

The plays discussed in this chapter focus on one of the most debated topics of Holocaust literature: whether moral standards could be applied in Nazi-occupied ghettoes. *Resort 76, The Wall,* and *Dr. Korczak and the Children* are perhaps idealistic in representing the idea that dignity and moral responsibility were not altogether lost in the ghetto. *Kastner, Adam,* and *Throne of Straw* are more realistic in delineating moral and humanitarian acts of resistance as equivalent to suicide or martyrdom rather than heroism. These plays are seminal in forcing us to reexamine our traditional notions of morality and ethics when applied to a unique situation never before encountered in Western civilization.

10   Dignity in the Concentration Camps

Maintaining dignity or assuming a sense of morality in the concentration or extermination camps was highly problematic. The degradation process typically began with an exhausting train ride that dehumanized the deportees, who were crammed into freight cars without food or water and with little air to breathe. Upon arrival, prisoners were robbed of their individuality, including all of their clothing, hair, and personal possessions; the SS never referred to them by their names, only by their tattooed numbers. The shearing of the inmates' hair and the conformity of the prisoners' garb reduced individuality to an indistinguishable mass. Moreover, the inmates were now bereft of any social identity, having lost their businesses, fortunes, homes, families, jobs, land, and religious affiliations. Without these social institutions intact, humans lose their sense of security. Jean Améry, who spent a year in Auschwitz, recalls, "If one has no home, however, one becomes subject to disorder, confusion, desultoriness."[1] The Germans essentially turned the prisoners into slaves, and, as such, they were socially dead beings. In other words, as discussed in chapter 4, *Häftlinge* were reduced to suffering bodies and nothing more. The Nazis, of course, found it easier to exterminate people if they looked and acted like subhumans or vermin.

These bodies could not feel good about themselves because they were constantly subjected to pain and indignity. Without proper nutrition, prisoners were typically ill and starving, thus further reducing them to subhumans. Bruno Bettelheim, a survivor of Dachau and Buchenwald, discussed the constant agony of the inmates: "They were inadequately clothed, but nevertheless exposed to heat, rain, and freezing temperatures for as long as seventeen hours a day, seven days a week."[2] Prisoners were routinely whipped, slapped, kicked, and tortured. Permission to defecate or urinate was often withheld, forcing inmates to soil their clothing regularly and live in filth. There was no way for anyone to satisfy their sexual desires in a normal way, which obviously frustrated the inmates. Furthermore, with the threat of gassing always lurking in the minds of the victims, fear led to perpetual terror. The result of this intense physical degradation was anomie and apathy. Auschwitz survivor Charlotte Delbo describes it thus: "Deep within me was a terrible indifference, the kind of indifference that comes from a heart reduced to ashes."[3] Améry corroborates Delbo's characterization of the body in *angoisse*: "The experience of persecution was, at the very bottom, that of extreme *loneliness*."[4] These conditions were carefully designed by the Nazis to debase and dehumanize the persecuted so that dignity was virtually impossible to maintain.

Life in the concentration camps was also a daily attempt to destroy the souls of the prisoners. *Häftlinge* were spiritually destroyed, robbed of their self-respect and the feeling that someone, somewhere, valued them as human beings. Bettelheim explains, "What happened to them impressed on them that nobody cared whether they lived or died, and that the rest of the world, including foreign countries, had no concern for their fate. One cannot meet catastrophic events and survive when deprived of the feeling that somebody cares."[5] As the SS constantly reiterated that the chances of survival were minuscule, inmates only had death to look forward to–a potentially viable chance for the release of a soul in agony. Typically, humans that die are accorded certain ritualistic procedures that confer meaning and dignity unto their lives. However, even death was denied dignity in the concentration camps, where, as Giorgio Agamben has noted, humans "do not die, but are instead produced as corpses."[6]

Is it possible for dignity to be established in such an environment in which individual autonomy is destroyed and personality disintegrates? As Primo Levi has indicated, even though the *lager* reduced humans to beasts or slaves without souls, the need to bear witness, to survive in order to tell the story, was paramount.[7] Disciplining the mind, keeping the body clean, and maintaining social contacts all created a semblance of dignity that could lead to survival. Dignity also meant establishing the one remaining element that would conflict with survival–the power to refuse consent. Terrence Des Pres remarks, "To oppose their fate in the death camps, survivors had to choose life at the cost of moral injury; they had to sustain spiritual damage and still keep going without losing sight of the difference between strategic compromise and demoralization."[8] This chapter focuses on two plays that examine whether the preservation of dignity and morality in the concentration camps outweighed survival: Martin Sherman's *Bent* and George Tabori's *The Cannibals*.

American playwright Martin Sherman, whose parents were Russian Jewish immigrants, began writing drama in 1968 after studying with Harold Clurman as a member of the Actors Studio. Most of Sherman's plays, which have been performed in more than forty-five countries, were staged in small theaters in Scotland, Great Britain, and Off-Broadway before he wrote *Bent*. Inspired by the Berlin nightclub sequences in Noël Greig and Drew Griffiths's 1977 play, *As Time Goes By*, Sherman wrote *Bent* for staging by Gay Sweatshop in London.[9] When Sherman sent Griffiths a draft of the play, the latter urged him to seek a larger theatrical venue. Sherman, having had negative theater experiences in New York, was determined that a London theater would first stage the play. After the Hampstead Theatre had difficulty finding a gay director for *Bent* (the script had already been rejected by the Eugene O'Neill Memorial Theater Center), the draft was sent to Ian McKellen.[10] McKellen, who was a closet homosexual and not a major theatrical drawing power, agreed to take on the daring role of Max. *Bent*, directed by Robert Chetwyn, opened at the Royal Court Theatre in London on 3 May 1979. The production, which also starred Tom Bell, transferred to the West End's Criterion Theatre before the end of its run so the Royal Court could accommodate the already-scheduled Neil Simon play, *The Last of the Red Hot Mommas*. London theater reviewers gave the play negative notices, with only Michael Billington (*The Guardian*), Steve Grant (*Time Out*), Sheridan Morley (*Punch*), and Benedict Nightingale (*New Statesman*) offering positive commentary. The major complaints were that Sherman's play was sensationalized and also glamorized homosexual love in the inauspicious setting of a concentration camp.

Bent, in a production directed by Robert Allan Ackerman, had its American premiere in New York at the New Apollo Theatre on 2 December 1979. Richard Gere, who had recently finished starring in the successful film, *American Gigolo,* gave the play widespread appeal in his performance as Max. Although the British critics were reserved in their appraisals of the play, American theater reviewers lauded it. *Bent,* which ran for nine months (241 performances) on Broadway, was nominated for a Tony Award for Best Play and won the Elizabeth Hull-Kate Warriner Award from the Dramatists Guild in 1979. The play has since been one of the most popular Holocaust dramas, having been staged in more than thirty countries. The most noteworthy of these productions was the January 1990 London revival at the National's Lyttleton Theatre, again starring Ian McKellen. Subsequent to the AIDS crisis of the 1980s and its resulting homophobia, the 1990 production of the play resonated with audiences rather differently than its original staging in 1979. John M. Clum notes that the revival was so successful that it moved to the West End, closing only because of prior commitments that McKellen had to keep.[11] Sherman also wrote the screenplay for the 1997 British film version directed by Sean Mathias. *Bent* starred Clive Owen (Max), Ian McKellen (Uncle Freddie), Lothaire Bluteau (Horst), and Mick Jagger (Greta).

Although Paragraph 175, which outlawed "lewd and unnatural sexual behavior," had been on the books since its inception as part of the Bavarian code established by King Wilhelm in 1871, homosexuals were left relatively unscathed through the Weimar Republic. In the early days of the Nazi movement before the establishment of the Third Reich, gay people perhaps constituted ten to thirteen percent of the Party membership.[12] Hitler felt that gay people were degenerate, effeminate, and could infiltrate the military and thus constitute a secret order of a Third Sex; consequently, he initiated a propaganda campaign against homosexuals that began in 1933.[13] Ernst Roehm, Hitler's friend since his early days in Munich in 1919 and chief of the SA, was openly homosexual and never hid from public view his forays into gay bars or his drunken orgies with gay brownshirts. When Nazi officials were trying to attract mainstream German citizens to the Party during the late 1920s and early 1930s, they warned Hitler that

Roehm was a detriment to their cause. Hitler, however, would roll his eyes, admonish Roehm, but at the same time defend him, arguing that the SA members were soldiers, not choir boys, and had to let off steam occasionally. Roehm, who refused to relinquish power to Himmler and the SS, was murdered during the Night of the Long Knives (28 June 1934), not because of his homosexuality, but for political reasons. With Roehm and his gay cohorts purged from power, the Nazis began to enforce Paragraph 175 and passed laws condoning the sterilization of homosexuals. In 1935, Paragraph 175 was revised to include such punishable offenses as homosexuals kissing, embracing, and even fantasizing about each other. The *Völkischer Beobachter*, published as part of the 1935 Nuremberg Laws, included specific measures to cleanse Germany of sexual deviants.

Himmler was the chief architect of the Nazi policies against homosexuality. In his book on the Nazi extermination of homosexuals, Richard Plant noted that Himmler believed that because gay people did not beget children, they would lead to the destruction of the Reich's future.[14] Moreover, gay people represented a threat to the warrior mentality that Himmler envisioned for his SS troops. Homosexuality needed to be eradicated to ensure the purity of the master race. Hans Peter Bleuel reports that between 1937 and 1943, the Nazis castrated 990 homosexuals.[15] As early as 1933, homosexuals were interned at Dachau. Although the figures vary, approximately 50,000 to 63,000 gay people were sentenced from 1933 to 1944; many of them were shot by firing squads.[16] There were between 10,000 and 15,000 homosexual people wearing the designated pink triangle in the concentration camps.[17] During the 1930s, before the extermination of Jews, the pink triangle represented the lowest rung of the hierarchy in the concentration camps, which made homosexuals the targets for even further abuse among the *Häftlinge*. Many kapos in the *lager* vilified homosexuals particularly, giving them the most ferocious beatings and even shaving their pubic hair, not just the hair on their heads. Homosexuals in the concentration camps were often segregated in special blockhouses and work units while being singled out for brutal torture as well.

Bent, written in eleven scenes that span two acts, begins in Berlin during 1934 and ends in Dachau in 1936. The play is historically verifiable, which is surprising when one considers that information concerning the Nazi treatment of homosexuals was sparse when Sherman wrote the play in 1979.[18] *Bent* is the study of a crass and selfish gay man who eventually develops a sense of pride and dignity when faced with persecution inside Dachau. Moreover, the play is the most significant Holocaust drama to call attention to the persecution of homosexuals during the Third Reich. Even after the Holocaust, Nazi anti-gay laws remained on the statute book in West Germany until 1969 and in East Germany until 1957, the suffering of homosexuals went uncommemorated in concentration camp memorials, and the West German government denied homosexual Holocaust survivors financial compensation until the 1990s; *Bent* breaks this conspiracy of silence.

Maximilian Berber is an unsettled, egotistical thirty-four-year-old gay man who has no self-respect. Max, who worships "storm-troopers" decked out in leather and chains that he picks up in bars, admits that he likes rough sadomasochistic sex with these Nazi men.[19] Max acknowledges to his jealous partner Rudolf Hennings (Rudy), "I'm a rotten person. Why am I so rotten?"[20] Max, an alcoholic and a cocaine peddler, is mainly interested in personal gratification but has little sense of self-worth. In scene one, Max has picked up Wolfgang Granz (Wolf), a young blond that he met the previous night in a bar, tempting him with lies about his wealth as a baron and a promised trip to his fantasy house in the country. Max is so insensitive that he insults his lover Rudy by bringing home another male. Eric Sterling writes, "This humiliation is exacerbated by the fact that Wolf walks through the apartment totally nude. Wolf's nudity suggests to the audience–and to Rudy–that Max has no respect or concern for Rudy's feelings."[21] Scene one seems innocuous until officers come in and slit Wolf's throat. A slide from a projection screen reads "Berlin–1934," for the first time revealing to the audience the time and location of the play. *Bent* occurs after the Night of the Long Knives, when Nazi persecution of homosexuals began in full earnest.

Greta, a drag queen who employs Rudy as a dancer in his sleazy nightclub, informs Rudy and Max that Ernst Roehm was murdered the previous evening. Roehm and his SA storm troopers acted as protectors of gays in Berlin, but now with his death, the SS plans open warfare on homosexuals. Wolf was one such storm trooper planning a coup, and his trail has led the SS to the residence of Max and Rudy. Max goes on the run with Rudy for two years until he asks his uncle Freddie, a middle-aged respectable citizen who is secretly a "fluff," for two train tickets to Amsterdam. When Freddie produces only one ticket, Max, who perhaps feels as if Rudy can incriminate him, needs to make sure his friend is properly "chaperoned." Max, who at the end of the play tells Horst that he cannot remember the "dancer's" name, admits that he does not love Rudy (24) and then crassly tells Freddie, "Once we get to Amsterdam, I ditch him" (25).

Arrested by the Gestapo, Max and Rudy are deported to Dachau. En route, Rudy, singled out as an intellectual for wearing horned-rimmed glasses, is beaten until he is semi-conscious. When the officer brings in Rudy's limp body, Max, like Mother Courage who refuses to identify the dead body of her son Swiss Cheese, feigns indifference. Max is then forced to pummel his friend until he is dead. Nicholas de Jongh asserts that by refusing to recognize his friend, Max, interested only in saving his own life, repudiates his homosexuality and thus his dignity as well.[22] Moreover, since Rudy and Max are sexual partners, Max's crass rejection of his friend further demonstrates his own callousness and lack of self-esteem.

In Dachau, Max tells Horst, who wears the pink triangle, that he angled a deal with the Gestapo in order to substitute his pink triangle for the yellow star. The contention, which became the play's most controversial element, is that Jews were treated better in the concentration camps than homosexuals.[23] Horst believes this is true, visibly demonstrated when the kapo stirs the soup for Jews and criminals, bringing the nutrients to the top, but refuses to do so for gays. Max even contends that he received meat in his soup, while pink-triangled Horst did not. Nevertheless, Max has abandoned his identity and thus his soul in converting from gay to Jew. He is only fooling himself, for the Nazis love to watch the prisoners wallow in self-abasement. As Eric Sterling astutely comments, "Although Max feels that he has outsmarted the Nazis by obtaining a yellow star rather than a pink triangle, the soldiers realize that he is a homosexual, not a Jew; they merely provide him with a yellow star in exchange for the pleasure of watching him humiliate himself and lose his dignity."[24]

In his early days at Dachau, Max still remains crass, selfish, and undignified. Questioned about Rudy's death, Max tells Horst, "He wasn't my friend" (39). He also reveals that on the train, he prostituted himself and abandoned his sexual identity to have sex with a dead girl, thus proving that he was not homosexual. To Max, necrophilia becomes merely another sexual activity that fits into his lifestyle of debauchery. Max's denial of his own sexuality has become for him a means of survival, albeit a denigrating one that robs him of his dignity.

Max begins to develop a sense of dignity and change his persona as a result of Horst's presence. John M. Clum views Horst as a stock character in gay drama and film: "the proud gay who is the teacher, foil, and lover of the ambivalent hero."[25] Horst's message to Max throughout the play is "You should be proud of *something*" (48). Max and Horst toil meaninglessly as they shift rocks from one place to another and then back again–work designed to drive the prisoners insane. Every two hours they are allowed a rest period of three minutes in which they must stand erect without looking at or touching each other. During one such encounter, Horst initiates a sexual liaison with Max as they stand at attention. Horst begins by mentioning that he finds Max's body sexy. Horst and Max fantasize about kissing and touching each other, then having oral sex, all of which culminates in a dual orgasm. In short, Max, whose idea of sex previously had been sadomasochistic pain, now begins to appreciate intimacy. By bonding with Horst, Max reawakens his gay sexuality and begins to affirm an identity that he previously denied in order to survive under Nazi law. During the sexual fantasy, Max repeats the word "strong" as his mantra, implying that the sex act has given the two of them strength to survive. Horst proudly tells Max, "We did it. They're not going to kill us. We made love. We were real. We were human. We made love. They're not going to kill us" (57–58). As Kia Hammermeister acknowledges, "Sex emerges as the signifier of human dignity, especially since this kind of sex is what brought Max and Horst to the camp in the first place."[26]

Despite the sexual fantasy shared by the two men, Max, who hates himself, is slow to respond to Horst's gestures toward social responsibility and his outward display of pride in his own sexual identity. Two months after their mutual orgasm, Max still resists Horst's advances because, as he says, "I can't love anybody back" (60). Max, himself crass and unemotional in his gay relationships, prefers to abide by Paragraph 175, which states that intimacy with another man is a crime. Max explains to Horst, "Queers aren't meant to love. They don't want us to" (61), and then, in a recurrent moment demonstrating his lack of self-esteem, tells Horst to reconsider his sexual advances: "Hate me. That's better. Hate me. Don't love me" (61).

As the play progresses, Horst's message that Max should give up his hypocritical values reflected by his posing as a Jew, his steadfast egotism, and his willingness to ignore his gay identity seems to alter the latter's persona. Max becomes more empathetic toward Horst, urging him to get help for his cough and exercise to avoid turning into the haunting specter of a "Moslem." Another sex fantasy is interrupted when Max imagines biting Horst's nipple, prompting Horst to admonish his friend for engaging in rough sex instead of intimacy. Max retreats from self-abasement and abides by Horst's wishes: "I'm touching you softly ... gently ... You're safe ... I'll keep you safe ... and warm" (67). Max even performs oral sex on an SS captain to obtain cough medicine for Horst.

In the last scene of the play, the SS captain, jealous about Horst's power over Max, forces Horst to take off his cap, throw it on the electric fence, and then retrieve it. This sadistic game was understood by the prisoners to mean a death sentence. If Horst refuses to obey the order, he will be shot; retrieving the cap means electrocution. Before going to his death, Horst rubs his left eyebrow, a secret signal that Horst and Max created to indicate their mutual love. In an act of protest, Horst screams and then rushes to attack the captain. Horst, understanding full well that death was imminent, chose to die with dignity by resisting instead of going to his death as a compliant victim of the Nazis. Earlier, Horst explained to Max, "It doesn't mean anything if a moslem kills himself, but if a person who's still a person commits suicide, well ... it's a kind of defiance, isn't it? They hate that—it's an act of free will"

(58–59). Max embraces Horst's dead body and begins to take pride in his gay identity and rue his dishonesty with Rudy. He speaks to the corpse: "I think I love you. [*Silence.*] Shh! Don't tell anyone. I think I loved … I can't remember his name. A dancer. I think I loved him, too" (75). Horst's death creates an epiphany for Max, who jumps into the pit, dons Horst's jacket with the pink triangle on it, and then commits suicide as an act of defiance by walking into the fence. The stage directions indicate, "*The fence lights up. It grows brighter and brighter, until the light consumes the stage. And blinds the audience*" (76). Robert Skloot has described the blinding light as a highly theatrical method that validates the "brilliance" of Max's love for Horst while concomitantly accentuating Max's revelation that he has ignored his sexual identity.[27] Horst has taught Max that spiritual and emotional intimacy are more meaningful than sadomasochism and that Max should exhibit gay pride.

We have seen how Holocaust drama is often literature of the body in which National Socialism reduced humanity to bodily functions. *Bent* explores the dilemma of whether identity can be maintained once the body deteriorates in *l'univers concentrationnaire*. Max has not been true to himself throughout his life; instead, he has been living a life of lies, first as a sadomasochist incapable of love, then by denying his homosexuality, and finally, posing as a Jew. Max learns first hand that even the Nazis are hypocritical about their treatment of homosexuals, for the SS captain treats gays as subhumans and punishes them for a crime in which he himself participates. Meanwhile, Horst, who has been true to his own identity, provides Max with a model for living a life of dignity. Horst has taught him to be proud that he is a gay man. By running into the electrified fence, Max defies the Nazis and adopts an identity for himself. This self-awareness and newly found respect for others provides Max with a sense of dignity for the first time in his life. In choosing the pink triangle over the yellow star, Max, by "coming out," evades a life of lies and, in an empowering act of self-immolation, proclaims his true identity. A key debate that the play poses is whether maintaining a sense of dignity in the concentration camps outweighs survival, an issue that also becomes the focal point of George Tabori's *The Cannibals*.

George Tabori was born into a family of nominal Jews in Budapest on 24 May 1914. His father Cornelius was an agnostic who had his sons baptized and sent them to a Protestant school. George's mother Elsa was Catholic, so she raised George in that tradition and made him go to confession regularly. George grew up in a bilingual household in which his parents spoke Hungarian while his nanny spoke German. In 1932, he left Hungary to work in a luxurious Berlin hotel and then as a bartender in a cafe that was raided by the SA. After returning to Budapest briefly, Tabori, frustrated with the rise of fascism in his native country, fled to London in 1935 and became a British citizen in 1947. As his fluency in English increased, Tabori began working as a foreign correspondent and for the British Broadcasting Company in Cairo and Jerusalem, where he married Hannah Freund, the first of what was to be his four wives. During the Holocaust, his father Cornelius was arrested in 1941 and eventually deported to Auschwitz, where he died. Tabori felt terribly guilty about not sharing with his father the danger signs for Jews living in fascist Hungary.[28] George's mother Elsa, arrested in Budapest in 1944 and deported to Auschwitz, managed to escape death by telling the Germans that she had a pass issued by the Swedish Red Cross; her remarkable tale is documented in Tabori's 1979 play, *My Mother's Courage*. George also had two uncles, two aunts, and several cousins who perished at the hands of the Nazis.

In 1949, after writing two novels, Tabori moved to the United States to write screenplays for MGM and Warner Brothers, none of which were ever produced. During his residence in California, Tabori met Brecht, in exile from the Nazis, who drew him away from prose writing and into playwriting. Tabori translated several of Brecht's dramas and co-directed with Gene Frankel a collage of excerpts from Brecht's plays, including biographical data, that was staged as *Brecht on Brecht* at the Theatre de Lys in New York on 14 November 1961. His second wife, Viveca Lindfors, introduced Tabori to Lee Strasberg's Actors Studio, where George acquired much of his theatrical acumen. Although several of his plays were staged in the United States, including *The Cannibals*, Tabori's theater was foreign to Americans, so he returned to West Germany in 1971 after nearly twenty years in America. In Europe, Tabori rediscovered his Jewish heritage and began writing his Holocaust dramas: *Mutters Courage* (1979), *Der Voyeur* (1982), *Jubiläum* (1983), and *Mein Kampf* (1987). In 1978, he became resident director of the Munich Kammerspiele, founded his own theater (Der Kreis) in Vienna in 1986, and then directed fourteen productions, including plays by Shakespeare, Beckett, Lessing, and Elfriede Jelinek, mostly at the Burgtheater in Vienna from 1990 to 1999. During the latter part of the twentieth century, Tabori became one of the most important playwrights/directors in Germany and Austria, most notably represented by his receipt of the Georg Büchner Prize in 1992, the only non-German dramatist ever to receive the prestigious award.

Tabori wrote the first draft of *The Cannibals* when he was living in New York during the mid-1960s in an attempt to envision a typical day that his father experienced as a prisoner in Auschwitz. Apparently guilt-ridden about not doing enough to warn his father of the Nazi threat to Hungarians, Tabori labored over these drafts, writing several of them before the play, eventually structured in fifteen scenes, was ready for staging. *The Cannibals*, directed by Martin Fried, premiered Off-Broadway at the American Place Theatre in New York City on 17 October 1968. When the play received mixed notices from the New York reviewers, Tabori then seriously considered returning to Europe.[29] After Tabori revised the play for German audiences, *Die Kannibalen*, which he codirected with Martin Fried, debuted in Berlin at the Schiller Theater on 13 December 1969. The play did much better in Germany than it did in New York; the Germans were intrigued yet there was consternation about Tabori's depiction of the Holocaust. Germans audiences, accustomed to the sentimental treatment of the Holocaust depicted in plays such as *The Diary of Anne Frank*, or the soporific documentary theater of Weiss and Hochhuth, were fascinated yet confused about how to react to Tabori's grotesque drama.

Tabori, as Brecht's disciple, employed several Brechtian techniques in *The Cannibals*.[30] The two survivors of Auschwitz, Healtai and Hirschler, join ten other sons or nephews of those who perished in the camp to reenact an act of cannibalism. As Brecht preferred, this narrating device moves away from mimesis so that the audience cannot empathize with concentration camp prisoners because the spectators are constantly aware of the performative nature of the play. At the start of the play, Tabori emphasizes that we are witnessing laymen without theatrical expertise who reenact, or improvise, what they envision to be the events leading up to the cannibalism. The stage directions indicate this disparity between the real and the performative as the survivors and the offspring of the deceased change from their street clothes into "costumes": *"The guests enter and climb up the mountain to pick out pieces of clothing that might have belonged to their fathers or uncles."*[31] At times, the "actors" step out of their roles to address the audience directly, thus creating a Brechtian alienation device that distances the performers from the audience, thereby minimizing empathy; and since we know that these characters are merely performing Auschwitz, we do not fear for their lives. Tabori's play-within-the play thus even allows two characters, Puffi Pinkus and the Ramaseder Kid, to die and return to the cast. Moreover, realizing that Auschwitz would be difficult to represent realistically on stage, Tabori uses a nearly bare stage with minimal props to create a stylized effect; this movement away from realism is essentially another Brechtian alienation effect that produces a disjunction between the audience and verisimilitude of plot. Tabori's goal in reducing emotional reactions from the audience is to allow the spectators to focus on the moral question of whether dignity can be maintained under the most extreme conditions of human existence.

Another experimental aspect of the play is its improvisational element, which works because, as Edward R. Isser reveals, "The scenes that are dramatized are not flashbacks, but reconstructions."[32] As if we are watching an amateur production, sound and action are often improvised rather than realistically staged. For example, the performers imitate the sound of gas, "Sssssssss," instead of the audience witnessing any inmates actually being gassed. Other sounds, such as the roaring of an overhead airplane, are stylized as well. The surrealistic dialogue also gives the impression that words are delivered in an impromptu fashion rather than as part of a carefully crafted text. Actors morph into God, snow, wind, liverwurst, fat men, and insects. Tabori often writes his plays in English, translates them into German, and then fine tunes the text during rehearsals. As such, Tabori's plays, rather than adhering to rigid texts, offer opportunities for improvising within certain parameters. Jack Zipes remarks, "In short, Tabori's writings are like works in process. He is constantly translating, rewriting, rehearsing, and reproducing his plays."[33] No doubt Tabori's use of improvisational techniques derived from his work with Strasberg and the Actors Studio. However, Tabori was also likely to be familiar with Joseph Chaikin's Open Theater, which, in the mid-1960s, experimented with transformational techniques that were essentially exercises in actor training. Chaikin used transformational techniques, which required actors to change who or where they were instantaneously in mid-scene, as a means of moving performers away from Method training. Tabori's transformational techniques are structured in a different way from what Chaikin had in mind, yet Tabori apparently recognized the similarity, for he attempted to get Chaikin to direct *The Cannibals* for its New York premiere.[34]

The play-within-the play recreates the atmosphere for the moral dilemma that permeates the play: whether dying with dignity or doing whatever it takes to survive in *l'univers concentrationnaire* is the right choice. Upon the death of inmate Puffi, the starving *Häftlinge* decide to eat his body in order to obtain nourishment. However, after much debate, they realize that they have a moral obligation to bury the body and refrain from cannibalism. When SS officer Schrekinger, the Angel of Death, gives them the choice to eat the body or face the gas chamber, only Healtai and Hirschler comply and thus become the only survivors. As the nude prisoners are taken for gassing, Schrekinger mocks Healtai and Hirschler for following orders, just like any good Nazi would do: "There is a Fuehrer in the asshole of the best of us" (262). However, Healtai and Hirschler lived and thus were able to bear witness; if they had refused to eat Puffi's body, the tale of cannibalism would have been nonexistent.

Anat Feinberg points out that in Tabori's 1981 autobiographical account, *Unterammergau*, he referred to *The Cannibals* as a black mass or what Feinberg equates with "a subversive ritual which calls to mind Jean Genet's theatre."[35] In Genet's theater, marginalized individuals, such as maids, homosexuals, blacks, prostitutes, and Arabs, engage in a ritual or black mass in which the celebrants are defiled as they participate in acts of self-immolation and then elevated to deities; the ritual ultimately functions as an exorcism, a purging of the demons plaguing the celebrants.[36] In the last lines of *The Cannibals*, the Loudspeakers proclaim the purpose of the ritualistic cleansing:

> The practice of devouring dead kinsfolk
> As the most respectful method of disposing
> Of their remains is combined with the custom
> Of killing the old and the sick.
> But some savages eagerly desire the body of a murdered man
> So that his ghost may not trouble them. (265)

The "savages" in the play are all outcasts who were victims of the Nazis: Jews, Gypsies, and homosexuals. They engage in a reunion celebration in which eating becomes the mechanism to exorcise the ghost of Auschwitz that haunts their lives–a specter that was daily characterized by starvation, a denial of eating.[37] As Robert Skloot notes, the topos of eating seems appropriate as a Holocaust motif since survivors attest to the enormous amount of time the inmates spent fantasizing about obsessive visions of food.[38] The tale begins with Puffi eating bread that he has hidden under his armpits. As the prisoners pounce on him for his transgression, he dies. Ultimately, Puffi's body becomes the means of survival, the savior for Healtai and Hirschler when Schrekinger forces them to eat or die. In this sense, the play is also a black mass, an inversion of the Eucharist in which eating condemns the survivors to living in a godless world, a wasteland.

The Cannibals begins with a dedication to Tabori's father, Cornelius, who "perished in Auschwitz, a small eater" (197). In exorcising the ghost of Auschwitz, the survivors and sons of the deceased become what we could call "big eaters." The ritualistic reunion is to culminate in a veritable feast–the eating of a fat man's body. The appetizer to the feast occurs in scene one, as Healtai discusses eating at Howard Johnson's with Hirschler, who says, "Anything to start with? A club sandwich? A cheeseburger? (*Screams:*) Breaded veal cutlet?" (202). The remainder of the play is essentially a dinner party, a communal ceremony or totemic feast as the twelve celebrants wait for Puffi's flesh to cook. Anat Feinberg perceptively observes, "The number of diners, twelve, is hardly accidental: the Last Supper was attended by the twelve apostles, and in Jewish tradition the number is associated with the twelve sons of the biblical forefather Jacob, the twelve tribes of Israel."[39]

Food fantasies become the life force in Auschwitz. Uncle chastises the Ramaseder Kid for worming his way to the head of the chowline when he should know that it is preferable to be at the end of the line, where "the best of the soup is on the bottom of the pot" (205). In Uncle's eulogy for Puffi, he mentions that Puffi raised geese, to which the Gypsy responds, "Never mind, speak to me about goose liver" (206). In a mock version of the Eucharist, the Gypsy mimes eating Lang as if he were the Host and chants "Christ has risen" as Healtai compliments him for being "One of the most talented eaters I've ever seen" (223). When Uncle objects to carving up the body, Hirschler says, "You know you'd make a lovely roast pig, with an apple in your mouth!"(209). Weiss, the cook, dreams of Puffi's sautéed kidneys while Hirschler, claiming that he is not a vegetarian, compares Puffi to a roast pig. Uncle, calling on God for inspiration, puts the prayer in the form of a food fantasy: "'Who shall give us flesh to eat? We remember the fish/ In Egypt which was free of charge, and the cucumbers/ And the melons, and the garlic'" (214). Klaub is more pragmatic about his potential cannibalism, asserting, "Meat is meat, and fuck my father in heaven" (248), while remembering, again in food imagery, how God seemed indifferent when he was stuffed in the cattle car like sardines. Puffi even rises from the dead and provides instructions, which seemingly derive from a cookbook, on how to prepare a proper festive meal; similarly, Weiss, in a mad Hassidic dance, offers guidelines for frying fritters in sautéed butter. While they wait for what appears to be an eternity for Puffi's body to cook properly, the celebrants dream of cheese soufflés, peaches, liverwurst, toasted English muffins, omelettes, garlic toast, carrots, turnips, milk, various types of coffee, chocolate éclairs, candy, hot soup with matzo balls, roast beef, fettucini, and fine wine.

The Cannibals would then seem to be a paean to eating. However, in the Brechtian spirit of creating a dialectic (to eat or perish), Uncle provides the counter-argument, the antithesis of the black mass. Uncle challenges the immorality of cannibalism as the credo of a wasteland that postulates that one man's death is another man's bread. Uncle states to the *Häftlinge*, "You have sodden your father, and he is your food/ I will oppose this abomination till my dying breath!" (210). Despite the inexplicable, absurd world of Auschwitz, Uncle maintains his pride, a sense of dignity. Uncle views cannibalism as an immoral act that is the first step to the destruction of civilization: "Goodbye the Age of Reason, goodbye certitude/ Goodbye hardhats and high hopes, goodbye/ Baggy trousers, the pain in the side, and/ The resigned sigh before falling asleep, goodbye/ The fullness of time" (240). Uncle even cites Deuteronomy 12: 23–24, which prohibits Jews from eating blood, considered the sacred part of the biblical soul: "'Only be steadfast in not eating the blood;/ For the blood is the life; and thou shalt not/ Eat the life with the flesh'" (216).

Uncle's appeal to morality would be sensible in normal circumstances but assumes a different meaning under the extreme conditions of life in the concentration camp. Uncle's ethical conviction is synonymous with the maintenance of dignity in an extreme situation where death is imminent. Perusing Tabori's archived papers, Anat Feinberg quotes the playwright as saying that what mattered to the prisoners was their manner of death: "Their resistance, the affirmation of their own humanity was, I believe wholly efficacious. One would read St. Augustine, another insisted on shaving even on the day of his murder, and my father was seen entering the shower room with a gesture of extreme courtesy as though saying, After you, Alphonse.'[40] Indeed, Ghoulos aims for this semblance of dignity, urging the inmates to clean the barracks in order to create an environment that would make the feast a festive occasion: "Let's sweep the floor and wash the window. Everybody please shave. And let there be music" (238). However, this belief is countered by disillusioned Klaub, who bets Uncle and the audience that they themselves would abandon morality in similar extreme circumstances: "I give you five to one that you will join the meal,/ And what's worse, you will ask for a second helping" (217). Klaub, mocking God who might frown on such cannibalism yet who favors the Chosen People as victims, states, "Resist not evil. Turn the other cheek./ Blessed are those that men revile, those that/ Wash the sidewalk, blessed, blessed the dead./ And damn the living that want to eat" (251).

Dignity in the concentration camps may be efficacious, as Tabori has indicated, but he leaves debatable and open ended the question of whether morality can be maintained under such extreme situations. At the end of the play, Schrekinger, who eats with Healtai and Hirschler in an extravagant display of wolfing, gulping, and licking each bowl clean, derides the victims for obeying orders and not resisting. The Loudspeakers echo Schrekinger's mock cannibalism and recommend to the audience a tasty tidbit: "The Jew's heart, in aspic or with sauce vinaigrette,/ So soft it will melt in your mouth" (265). The Loudspeakers may have the last words, but those words mean nothing when inmates sacrifice their own lives for a concept that has to be reconsidered in extreme situations. While Martin Sherman researched the Holocaust thoroughly and understood the concept of dignity in the *lager* to be a vision of fantasy, Tabori knew from intimate experience that dignity meant death. Like Tabori's father who maintained his pride in an absurd wasteland, ten of the inmates in the play who refuse cannibalism also go to their deaths. Healtai and Hirschler, two of the least likable characters in the play, are alive because they refuse to be efficacious. *Bent* and *The Cannibals* are seminal Holocaust dramas, for they explore the ethics of human behavior in a unique environment where maintaining dignity surely meant death.

11 Holocaust Survivors in the United States and Israel

About half of the Jewish survivors (120,000) interned in Displaced Persons camps in Germany, Austria, and Italy after the liberation emigrated to Palestine, which was to become Israel in May 1948; another 80,000 to 90,000 of those interned went to the United States.[1] After the war, approximately 140,000 survivors fled to the United States while nearly 350,000 embarked for Palestine.[2] A large majority of the remaining Jews, which represented a small portion of the total number of survivors, emigrated to Canada, Australia, South Africa, or Argentina. Most survivors suffered from depression and anxiety, as well as various psychological and psychosomatic disorders resulting from the traumas associated with the Holocaust–a subject that will be examined in chapter 12. This chapter will focus on the plays that probe the difficulties that survivors had in adjusting to their new lives in the United States (Barbara Lebow's *A Shayna Maidel*) and the problems that Sabra Jews (native-born Israelis) had in accepting Old World Diaspora Jews into Israeli culture (Leah Goldberg's *Lady of the Castle* and Ben-Zion Tomer's *Children of the Shadows*).

Survivors who emigrated to the United States, many of them suffering from severe psychological trauma, had to accommodate to a much more complex lifestyle, learn a foreign language, adapt to new laws and customs, and build a new support structure. English, in particular, exacerbated problems for survivors. Individuals who were fairly well versed in their native language could try to find appropriate words to articulate the Holocaust experience, but their English vocabularies now failed them miserably. The result was that they had to keep silent, internalizing their frustrations. Survivors who fled to the United States were advised to look to the future instead of dwelling on the past. Eva Fogelman confirms, "Immigrants to the United States were strongly encouraged by their relatives to abandon their European culture, language, religious practices, and so on, and to suppress the memory of their experiences."[3] Native-born American Jews, feeling guilty about their inability to help their brethren Jews in Europe, did not want to hear about the concentration camps and instead offered tales about deprivation during and after the Depression as palliatives. Aaron Hass remarks, "These offensive parallels further contribute to the survivor's alienation from the mainstream of the American Jewish community, for they confirm a complete lack of understanding of the nature of their ordeal."[4] Besides, survivors, limned as "green-horns" who were physically maimed and psychologically marred by the Holocaust, were considered to be tainted outsiders in an afflu-ent, progressive, sanguine postwar society that glorified success. As such, survivors were depicted as the Other by Americans who sub-liminally wanted to suppress their own feelings of vulnerability; by scapegoating the European Jew as Other, American Jews denied their own insecurities: the Holocaust happened to these pathetic "green-horns," not to us. In order to compensate, survivors in the United States, persecuted as the Other, desperately attempted to assimilate into American culture. However, survivors who were forced to betray their memories, forget the past, and hide their emotional scars found it nearly impossible to do.

Many of the survivors, eager to leave the countries of their persecution and destruction behind, emigrated to Palestine, hoping that there they could begin life again with a renewed spark of vitality. Although these "refugees" were welcomed into Israel, they were not provided with adequate psychological support. Sabra Jews viewed the Holocaust survivors as victims who went to their deaths like sheep going to the slaughter. This downtrodden view of the Old World Diaspora Jew was in conflict with the Zionism of the new state of Israel, which rejected defeatist ideology. Eva Fogelman reports that the Sabras, in their need to eradicate the negative image of the Jew as vic-tim, developed a collective ego of denial, avoidance, and repression of the Holocaust.[5] Israelis were essentially ashamed of these "refugees" who had been tortured, starved, and victimized by the Nazis; no one wanted to endure their tales of suffering but wondered instead why they did not fight back. Geoffrey H. Hartman writes, "For a long time Israel rejected the ethos of the refugees who flooded in, while legitimizing itself (as it still does, and increasingly) through Holocaust memory."[6] The Holocaust was essentially muted during Israel's formative years, as memorial services were rarely held, and the history of the Shoah was left out of the schools' curriculum. This overt suppression of the Holocaust did not allow survivors to mourn their personal and communal losses effectively, and, along with the stigma of being victims, prevented them from feeling the same national pride and sharing the same security accorded to the Sabra Jews. Yael Danieli, who studied postwar adaptation of families of Holocaust survivors, concludes, "The resulting 'conspiracy of silence' proved detrimental to the intrapsychic wellbeing of survivors and to their familial and socio-cultural integration."[7] As a result, thousands of Holocaust survivors returned to Germany after failing to assimilate into Israeli society.

American playwright Barbara Lebow's venture into theater began when she moved to Atlanta in 1962 and joined the Academy Theatre's developmental workshop, eventually leading to her becoming its playwright in residence. Lebow has had nearly thirty plays produced, including ten for children. She has been primarily involved with a number of human service projects designed to bring theater to disadvantaged populations, such as women in prison, the homeless, patients in drug and alcohol rehabilitation programs, and physically disabled persons. She has been a Susan Smith Blackburn finalist for several of her plays and won the prestigious Guggenheim Fellowship for Playwriting in 1997.

A Shayna Maidel, written in fifteen scenes spread over two acts, premiered as part of the Academy Theatre's First Stage New Play Series on 18 April 1985, under Lebow's direction. After a brief production run staged by Robert Kalfin of the Hartford Stage Company in November 1985, the play had its New York debut on 20 October 1987, at the off-Broadway Westside Arts Theatre. Mary B. Robinson directed a cast that featured Melissa Gilbert as Rose, in a production that ran for 501 performances, closing on 8 January 1989. In 1992, Anna Sandor adapted Lebow's play, now retitled *Miss Rose White*, for a Hallmark Hall of Fame television presentation. The television drama, directed by Joseph Sargent, featured a stellar cast that included Maximilian Schell (Mordechai), Kyra Sedgwick (Rose), Maureen Stapleton (Tanta Perla), and Amanda Plummer (Lusia). This production won an Emmy Award for Best Television Film in 1992. After the success of the television drama, *A Shayna Maidel* was performed regularly by repertory theater groups; the most notable of these performance runs were Melanie Martin's production for the Minnesota Jewish Theatre Company in Minneapolis in 1995, Laurie T. Freed's staging at the Vanguard Theatre in Fullerton, California, during spring 1998, and as part of the Colony Theatre Company's repertoire for the 2000–2001 season (Burbank, California).

   A Shayna Maidel is essentially concerned with the overbearing difficulties that Holocaust survivors had in adapting to postwar life in the United States. Mordechai Weiss, an Old World Jew from Chernov, Poland, who is now nearly seventy, left Europe in 1928 with his daughter Rayzel (Rose). When the play opens in New York City in 1946, Mordechai, despite keeping Old World Jewish customs, has adapted to life in America. Rose is fully assimilated into American society and has long since left her former life in Poland behind. If Mordechai, a practicing Jew who is set in his ways with regard to Jewish customs, can assimilate, one wonders why his daughter Lusia cannot. Lusia, a survivor of Polish concentration camps, has witnessed the effects of the Holocaust at first hand. The loss of loved ones during the Shoah has seared her consciousness, for her mother and infant daughter Sprinze were gassed while Hanna, her dear friend, died of typhus shortly after the liberation. Moreover, her sense of loss and grief continue after the war since she is unsure of the whereabouts of her husband Duvid Pechenik. Lusia thus fails to assimilate into American culture, not because she is ingrained in Old World Jewish customs like her father, but because her Holocaust experience precludes accommodation to postwar American life.

   Mordechai, born in a Polish shtetl in 1876, still maintains his strong Yiddish accent, keeps kosher, observes the Sabbath, and is proud of his heritage; despite his Old World background, he has sought to assimilate into American culture. For example, he admonishes Lusia for speaking Yiddish and boasts about his own ability to fit into a New World lifestyle: "Here we should speak American always. You, like your sister Rayzel. You become real American. Your *taten*, he does pretty good, but not so much as children."[8] Mordechai comes from a strong family background, reminding his daughters that his grandfather lived to be 102 and until the day of his death still walked three miles delivering milk; Mordechai himself seems to have been born with his own stoicism, represented in scene one when, as an infant, he intuitively refrained from crying when the pillaging Cossacks threatened his family's home. In short, he believes that assimilation is merely a matter of will power. Upon first entering the United States without even knowing a word of English, Mordechai took a job as a stock boy working for his relative, Greenspan. He rapidly moved up through the ranks and now holds a well-respected position in the company. Mordechai's opinion is that Old World Jews can assimilate into New World culture if the effort is made to do so: "No matter how much you suffer, what [sic] you lose your family, you don't hardly know no English, you still can be a person with respect, which is worth more than all the tea in China" (43).

Mordechai failed to bring his wife to the United States due to his paucity of resources during the Depression; this omission resulted in his wife's death in an extermination camp. Yet he does not allow any feelings of guilt to hinder his assimilation into American culture. Mordechai rationalizes his grief, explaining to his daughters, "What? I knew was coming the Depression? I knew the doors would be closed here? I had a crystal ball showed ten years ahead to Hitler?" (59). Mordechai does not experience the Holocaust at first hand, and thus, by feeling a disconnect with what happened in Europe, he does not allow the Holocaust to affect his assimilation into American society.

In her effort to assimilate into American culture, Rayzel Weiss has changed her name to Rose White "to sound like everyone else" (29). Moreover, she has abandoned all traces of a Yiddish accent. Although her father lives in Brooklyn, which Rose perhaps associates with Old World Jewry, she instead prefers to reside on the upscale Upper West Side of Manhattan. In the stage directions, Lebow notes, "*Rose, while modernizing and assimilating, is neither ashamed of, nor hiding, her heritage"* (5). However, Rose, who follows strict Orthodox Jewish law only when she is around her father, views keeping kosher and maintaining the Sabbath as merely impediments to her assimilation. Rose dresses in the latest stylish wardrobe, treasures the modern kitchen appliances in her apartment, monograms her towels and washcloths, coifs her hair fashionably, and treats herself to fancy bubble baths. Rose explains to Lusia that she was only four years old when she left Poland, so the Old World is foreign to her, unlike America: "That I was born in another world. I don't remember any of it. Just a feeling, maybe. Sometimes there's a particular smell when something's cooking or a song comes on the radio and all of a sudden I feel different, like I'm in another place" (21). After Duvid returns to his wife, Lusia even describes Rose to him as "A hundred percent American, she is" (65), exhorting her husband to speak only English when Rose is in their presence.

A Shayna Maidel is not a dialectic about whether Old World Diaspora Jews can assimilate into U.S. society in the same manner as Jews, like Rose, who are fully acculturated; instead, the play posits the idea that Holocaust survivors could never be fully assimilated into postwar America. Lusia has survived an unnamed concentration camp experience in Poland, having lost most of her family members to the Shoah, including her baby daughter, her mother, and, although she suspects otherwise, perhaps her husband. Despite the fact that, as Lebow suggests in her stage directions, Lusia is a strong, stoical person who is not self-pitying and refuses to see herself as a victim (5), she is psychologically scarred by the Holocaust and thus cannot assimilate into American society.

Lusia cannot adapt to the material comforts of postwar America, for, as a Holocaust victim, she does not belong and must learn how to live again in this type of modern society. Lusia is first seen as a greenhorn wearing worn-out hand-me-down clothing that sharply contrasts with Rose's stylish dress. Her only possessions consist of an old black handbag, a worn suitcase, and a child's stuffed clown doll. Even when Rose fits her elder sister with a modish dress and fashionable shoes to make her feel at home in her new environment, Lusia is uncomfortable in the dress, wobbles on her feet, and claims that she "belongs" in Poland. Lusia cannot understand buying such a thing as a dress that no one has yet worn, cannot fathom the concept of a price tag, and after going to the cinema, can only be amazed at how much it costs to attend. Even such an idea of simply wearing a coat to ward off the cold weather is foreign to her Holocaust experience, as she admits to Hanna in a dream sequence, "And I don't want a warm coat. I want to be cold like the dead ones" (48). Rose's modest 1946 accommodations are immaculate to Lusia, who marvels at such "amenities" as carpeting, electricity, heaters, bathtubs, hot water, and garbage collection, all of which were foreign to her in the concentration camps. Moreover, her lack of fluency in English exacerbates the alienating experience of an Other, and she listens intently to the radio, hoping to assimilate by learning the language: "I got a right to study, listen the music, the words, so can talk more better" (38).

In his study of Holocaust survivors, Aaron Hass states, "Survivors who immigrated to America encountered a culture which glorifies success, optimism, and happiness, while shunning failure, pessimism, and suffering. To be accepted into that society, survivors were urged to 'put all of that behind you.' In a sense, survivors were asked to betray their memories. They were also forced to hide their pain."[9] The Holocaust has scarred Lusia physically and mentally to such an extent that she cannot possibly betray her memories or hide her pain, thus precluding any smooth transition into postwar American life. Lusia is physically scarred by the tattooed number on her forearm and by the fact that her menstrual periods had stopped after the trauma, thus lamenting to Hanna, "We're not women anymore. We don't have women's bodies" (48). In a series of flashbacks to her former life in Poland, at times represented as nightmares, Lusia reveals the guilt of losing her daughter and mother to the Nazis, the desperate need to find her lost husband, the agony of witnessing the death of her close friend Hanna, and the mournful loss of her once-idyllic life in Chernov where she was joyously surrounded by friends and family. The doll that Hanna gives her after the liberation is her talisman, a gift that she cherishes in New York, the constant reminder of the loss of her daughter and her inability to save Sprinze from gassing.

Moreover, Lusia internalizes the guilt because, had she not contracted scarlet fever, she would have been able to emigrate with her father and Rayzel to America, thus saving herself and her daughter.

Writing about the omnipresence of the Holocaust experience in the play, Alvin Goldfarb remarks, "The Holocaust past intrudes on and reflects each present moment, and frequently Lusia exists in moments of duality, literally moving from her fantasy into the 'real' world and back again."[10] Lusia remains paranoid about the possibility of continuous persecution as a Jew, explaining to Rose that changing her name will not prevent future genocide: "Even you should wear a cross around neck, they know who you are. Always with Jewish, they find out the truth" (30). Lusia feels embarrassed and confused about suddenly having too much food to eat, unlike her former internment where food meant rationing. Trying to fend for herself in an attempt to return to the Immigration Office to seek the whereabouts of her husband, Lusia is lost and expresses her confusion in the context of the Shoah: "I think big world hates Jewish" (24). In his study of Holocaust survivor syndromes, William G. Niederland noted, "There were anxieties and fears of renewed persecution such that some even feared New York City's uniformed police officers."[11] During Lusia's escapade into New York to find her missing husband, her encounter with what turns out to be a helpful police officer is initially a frightening situation because Lusia subliminally linked the police uniform with a "suit like army" (20), which seemingly recalls memories of the SS.

Moreover, not only is Lusia unable to assimilate into American society because of her Holocaust past, but she adversely affects her sister and father, who have already effectively melded into American culture. For Rose, Lusia's presence creates guilt about surviving while her immediate relatives perished. Now becoming more introspective, Rose muses to herself, "It could've been you, Rose" (13). Her Polish background is constantly being reinforced by Lusia, who refers to Rose as Rayzel Weiss. In her fantasy confession to Duvid, Lusia admits that she seems to have tainted Rose, who now feels like a stranger in her own home. Lusia senses that the Holocaust has created a schism that cannot be breached between the two sisters: "But Rayzel is afraid of me. She tries to hide it, avoids looking at me as one avoids a cripple" (18). Rose tells Lusia that she has watched newsreels about the Holocaust and now wants more information about what happened. After she receives a letter and her baby spoon from her mother, Rose identifies with Lusia and other family members who were Holocaust victims; she even goes so far as to use a pen, and, as if she were carving a tattoo, imprints a number on her forearm. In short, the Holocaust mars the image of Rose as "a shayna maidel" (a pretty girl seen as untainted by her mother).

Although Mordechai is stoical, dignified, and self-assured, his hidden secrets about the Holocaust are unearthed by Lusia. In the play's most emotional moment, Mordechai and Lusia take an inventory of their dead relatives. As Mordechai repeats the names of his dead family members, a reading that takes on a ritualistic quality, Lusia corrects him: she says that they were "murdered" and intones the exact places of the exterminations (Maidanek, Auschwitz, Belzek, Chelmno, Treblinka, and Birkenau). This list includes Mordechai's wife, granddaughter, nephews, aunt, uncle, brother-in-law, sisters, brothers, father-in-law, cousins, and mother-in-law. Mordechai, who had a chance to bring his family to the United States but refused to do so because of poor economic conditions after the Depression, all of a sudden feels guilty about his past and tries to assuage his guilt by showing Rose photographs of the Old World family for the first time. Lusia's presence reinforces the guilt because she urged her mother to leave Poland when a Polish countess offered her the opportunity to emigrate; however, Mordechai's wife refused to go because she was distraught about leaving her daughter behind to care for the ill Sprinze. Lusia reminds Mordechai that when a philanthropic group in Brooklyn offered to pay for his wife's passage to America, he was too proud to accept the money. Lusia's reaction, "From shame. From shame" (59), obviously unnerves her father to the extent that we realize that she will forever be a visible reminder that his past can never be separated from the Holocaust, no matter how effective his assimilation has been.[12] Although Lusia's concentration camp experience remains unspecified and the audience is left to fill in the details, spectators, as Bette Mandl suggests, will certainly gain "a tacit acknowledgement of the 'unspeakable' nature of the Holocaust" as the root cause of the difficulties of postwar Jewish assimilation in the United States.[13]

Israeli poet and playwright Leah Goldberg is not known primarily as a Holocaust writer, for her only noteworthy musing on the Shoah was the 1955 play, *Lady of the Castle*. Born in Königsberg, East Prussia, in 1911, she spent her childhood years in Russia and then, after the Revolution in 1917, her family settled in Kovno, Lithuania. She studied philosophy at the University of Kovno and then earned a doctorate in Semitic studies at the University of Bonn in 1933. In 1935, she emigrated to Palestine, where she initially worked in Tel Aviv as a school teacher, a literary advisor to Habimah (the national theater), and as a theater critic for the *Al Ha-Mishmar* journal. On the eve of World War II, Goldberg announced in an essay published in *Hashomer Hatsa 'ir* that she had no intention of writing Holocaust poetry, a vow that was briefly broken by her 1950 poem cycle, "Keneged arba' ah banim," in which she pondered what it meant to be wise, wicked, simple, or unquestioning in the post-Holocaust era. In 1952, she was appointed lecturer in European Literature at the Hebrew University in Jerusalem and then went on to chair the Comparative Literature Department from 1963 until her death in 1970. Her work in comparative literature included translating modern European poetry and drama, as well as Russian and Italian classics, into Hebrew and writing twenty books for children, ten books of poetry, two novels, and three plays. *Lady of the Castle* premiered in 1956 at Israel's largest playhouse, the Cameri Theatre in Tel Aviv; Carolyn Swift adapted *Lady of the Castle* from T. Carmi's translation of the play for its international debut at the Gate Theatre in Dublin on 22 January 1963.

Goldberg does little in the way of experimenting with form, and thus *Lady of the Castle* cannot be considered to be innovative Holocaust drama. The play follows a traditional three-act structure that was popular among similar realist playwrights that preceded Goldberg in the late nineteenth and the first half of the twentieth century. Moreover, the play adheres to the unities, occurring in three hours, in one setting, and with no subplots. Critics have compared Goldberg's focus on the search for Truth in a haunting, brooding atmosphere of lies, deceit, and self-delusion to Ibsen's plays, particularly the late realist dramas.[14] Robert Skloot even goes so far as to define Goldberg's realist tradition as a blending of Ibsen's melodramatic plot structure with the traditional Chekhovian theme of the replacement of the old order and the concomitant embracing of the new.[15]

Lady of the Castle is Goldberg's attempt to delineate the differences between the free-spirited Sabras who looked to the future and the downtrodden Old World Diaspora Jews who were victims of the Holocaust. The play occurs in 1947, two years after the Shoah that resulted from the Nazi occupation, in what Goldberg depicts as a nebulous part of Central Europe. Dr. Dora Ringel, a social worker and member of Youth Aliyah in Palestine, is searching for Jewish children who may have survived the Holocaust. She is accompanied by Michael Sand, a former librarian who has embraced the Eretz Israeli concept of socialism for the collective good of the country, willingly adapting himself to diverse roles such as farmer, soldier, and teacher. His mission is to recover books that the Nazis stole from Jewish libraries. Sand's role in the play is to allow Dora an audience for her progressive views on modern Palestine while playing devil's advocate as Goldberg's *raisonneur*, albeit unsuccessfully, for the notion that the refined culture of the Old World, despite the Shoah, is not without merit. Dora and Sand discover that, although the war has been over for two years, Lena Brabant, a nineteen-year-old Jewess, has been hiding from the Nazis for the past three years in an old castle run by a gentile aristocrat named Zabrodsky. The play develops into a battle of wills between Zabrodsky, who represents the Old World European notion of *noblesse oblige*, versus Dora, the Sabra Jew, for control of Lena's spirit and soul. Given the fact that Zabrodsky is fifty-seven years old and Dora is nearly one generation younger at forty, the conflict thus becomes a generational battle of Old World (Europe) versus New (soon-to-be Israel) for the soul of the Jew. Moreover, Goldberg's portrayal of Lena indicates that the Old World Diaspora Jews will have to change their personae to fit into modern Israeli culture.

The first words of the stage directions, *"An old castle in Central Europe,"*[16] represent Count Zabrodsky's Old World European lifestyle and reinforce the notion that this world is the antithesis of Palestine, where no castles existed. Zabrodsky is a caretaker of the castle, which has been turned over to the state in post-Nazi Europe, but he longs for what appears to be an idyllic past when he and his ancestors ruled the manor. Zabrodsky's castle is the epitome of the great cultural tradition of Europe: the castle has now literally been turned into a museum lined with paintings and books marking Zabrodsky's residence as a repository for Old World culture and grace. Zabrodsky lives in a civilized past in which an educated, cultivated European, like himself, can quote St. John's Revelation at will. Sand admits, "His voice is from the past. His past. He lives in it. He loves it" (44). As an aristocrat, Zabrodsky epitomizes the humanist tradition of European civilization, replete with the nobleman's respect for refinement, beauty, elegance, and erudition. Zabrodsky's motive for hiding a Jewess from the Nazis appears to be noble, but the reality is that he detested National Socialism, for its vulgarity, ignorance, and arrogance caused a breach in his link to civilized European culture. With regard to the Nazis, Zabrodsky states, "Always, it is always the scum of humanity, those who cannot grasp the ancient tradition and the true culture, who prophesize a new life, build another culture, and meanwhile they riot, murder, rape, and spit on the carpets" (41). Glenda Abramson further explains Zabrodsky's motive for his overprotectiveness of Lena: "He loves her, but even more than that he reveres her as a symbol of youth and the past which he is unable to relinquish."[17] Zabrodsky views Lena as an icon of an idyllic past when he was a scion of the manor–a savior of young women from the barbarians who tried to destroy central European culture–rather than merely the aging, reclusive caretaker of a castle.

Zabrodsky has immersed himself into what ostensibly appears to be the treasured beauty of nineteenth-century European gothic romanticism. Glenda Abramson remarks that the nineteenth-century gothic atmosphere is palpable: the play is set during a stormy evening, replete with lightning and thunder, in a castle buried in a forest; a decadent nobleman lives a charmed existence with a young beauty as his inspiration; the castle contains secret doorways and passageways; Lena wears a poisoned amulet that serves as a talisman; and Dora plays the role of a melodramatic villain who seeks to rob the reclusive nobleman of his illusory existence by removing the young maiden, fairy-like in her existence, from the castle.[18] Zabrodsky displays the manners of an aristocrat, even refusing to sit down in front of Dora and Sand, who implore him to do so. This Old World European courtesy and the love of a beautiful, idyllic past seem to coincide with his heroism as a noble-man who saved a young Jewess from the hands of uncouth barbarians. This sense of beauty, nobility, and elitism coupled with a reliance on the mysticism of the Bible is how Goldberg once remembered the Europe of her past. Michael Taub notes that Goldberg conceived of Zabrodsky idyllically: "Her German background and dedication to teaching the masterpieces of European literature could explain the positive, even perhaps, tragic portrayal of the Count, whose intellectu-alism, conservatism, nobility, and high aesthetic sense, are what, after all, produced the Goethes and Schillers of European culture."[19]

However, Zabrodsky's gothic romanticism degenerates into European decadence, loss of dignity, and pathos after the Holocaust. Notions of a modern Europe based upon the beauty, elegance, and pur-ity of the past became a sham after 1945. Aaron Hass explains this loss of faith in a privileged European culture that has virtually vanished after the Holocaust: "The *best* did not survive, many survivors admit-ted. The pious passively placed their fate in God's hands. The intellec-tuals placed their faith in the enlightened, rational part of man and the cultured German citizen of Goethe, Heine, and Mendelssohn."[20] The beauty and elegance of Zabrodsky's nineteenth-century gothic roman-ticism is now immersed in decadence and decay in postwar central Europe. The castle that once represented the purity of nobility and the aristocracy has now been occupied by the Nazis. Dora mocks how the great European cultural tradition has changed since the Holocaust: "If you had to deal with children hiding in strange families, in mon-asteries, you'd see how this 'beauty' still grips them!" (44). Moreover, Zabrodsky, the representative of a glorified past immersed in the great cultural tradition of Europe, is shown to be a sham, a patina. As a result of his need to hold onto the dream of the purity of the past, Zabrodsky has imprisoned Lena in a world of deception, for the war has been over for two years. Zabrodsky confesses to Lena, "I did not want to hold you by force, Lena. I did not want to deceive you. But I did deceive you ... I held you by force" (70). The Old World European's romanticism has thus degenerated into deceit, depravity, and repression; the noble aris-tocracy has died after the Shoah. Dora describes Zabrodsky to Lena in this way: "He's dead, he's a corpse. That's the truth. He belongs to the world of the dead" (63). At the end of the play, the stage directions describe Zabrodsky sitting alone in the castle as the lights symbolically dim: *"He sits motionless in an armchair, as if he were one of the museum pieces"* (78). Goldberg has some degree of pathos for Zabrodsky, who reminds the playwright of her own European culture that she fondly remembers and still respected at the time of the writing by teaching classical literature to her Israeli students; however, that culture exacerbated her suffering as a Jew and is now dead to her.

Dora, the Zionist, rejects the Old World European values as the culture of a dead past and looks to Palestine as the hope for the future. In contrast to the dark, cold, and "stormy" atmosphere of the European gothic, Dora's land represents sunshine, purity, and rejuvenation. The decaying and decadent aristocracy of Europe conflicts with the egalitarian socialism of her kibbutz. Matti Megged contrasts the moribund world of Zabrodsky's treasures, charm, and nobility with Dora's materialistic world, "focused around the primary and simple concerns of life, work, and food for *all* its inhabitants and not only for the select few, a world which gazes with justified suspicion upon all the ghost castles with their guards and fascinations."[21] The once-picturesque notion of counts living in castles is now a tainted past to Dora because that environment has morphed into the locale for Nazi headquarters. Dora explains to Sand, "I'm scared, simply scared of being sentimental about this whole vanishing world. I was closer to it than you. And I know that its dangers aren't yet past" (44). For Dora, Europe reflects the idea of the Jew as victim in which a culture of beauty and erudition ultimately resulted in the Shoah; Palestine, however, is a country where the Jews are accepted as the dominant majority rather than as victims. Dora tells Lena that in Palestine Jews do not have to hide from Nazis and are free to do as they please, perhaps going to the theater or movies if they wish. Palestine represents a world where Jews can be healthy, free, and prosperous, unlike Europe, where Jews, frightened and paranoid, must hide in castles under the benevolent auspices of gentile benefactors.

Like Goldberg, Dora grew up in Europe but emigrated to Palestine at an early age. Count Zabrodsky's aura subliminally reminds Dora of her suffering as a Jew in the Old World; moreover, she consciously conflates his glorification of a romanticized, pure European past with his association with the Nazis and with his deception of a young Jewess. Dora acknowledges that Zabrodsky makes her "nervous" (28) as she reacts negatively to the refined culture of Europe's past, which she dismisses as "all these old things … " (31). Even when Lena confesses that Zabrodsky formerly played Chopin for his Lady of the Castle, Dora mocks the choice of music (55).[22] Whereas Sand the librarian finds Zabrodsky's old books, including a first edition of Voltaire's works, fascinating, Dora reacts with contempt as she now views classical Europe as tainted: "Castles and ruins are always found side by side! Perhaps I have no aesthetic sense. Perhaps I've witnessed too much sorrow and anguish and poverty during these years, tracking down these poor children, homeless, delinquent, infected with vermin and TB. I hate all this old stuff, all this useless ash!" (32). Dora's emphasis on the future of Israel as the hope of a Promised Land for the Jews equates with the notion that Europe, the place of degeneration and victimization, is dead for the Jews. Furthermore, Glenda Abramson insightfully remarks that Zabrodsky "believes firmly in the individual and is therefore the natural opponent of the bright young socialism and its welfare state, the mass-life which is symbolised by Dora."[23] Thus, Dora considers Zabrodsky to be nothing more than a relic from a dead past, exclaiming to Sand, "This old man! I'm afraid of him. It's as if he–rose from the grave!" (28).

Lady of the Castle seems to be a tug of war for Lena's soul in a battle of wills between Zabrodsky and Dora. However, the alarming subtext of the play is the way Goldberg, a Sabra Jew, negatively stereotypes Lena as the paranoid, humiliated, and victimized diasporic Old World Jew. After the Nazis took her parents and siblings to be murdered, Lena hid alone in the forest until she was rescued by the Count. When Dora and Sand first confront Lena, she is obviously paranoid, confusing the thunder of the electrical storm with a Nazi air raid. Her condition of hiding from the Nazis two years after the war has ended can only be described as laughable and pathetic–black humor, to be sure, similar to the ludicrous cliché of war films in which Japanese soldiers fought on remote Pacific islands long after World War II was over. Lena at first believes that Dora and Sand are Nazi spies, making her recalcitrant and reticent in their presence: "You came here to interrogate me … yes, yes, now I know. You won't get a single word out of me! You want to find out about me and the Count! But I won't tell you. I won't talk, you can kill me. I won't talk!" (52). Lena even foolishly offers solace to Dora and Sand so as to help them avoid extermination by the Nazis. Dora, aware that Lena is a prisoner in a poorly lit castle, describes Lena as literally "pale" (48) or figuratively "in the dark" – a definite contrast to the sunlight and freedom experienced by the Sabras who have rediscovered their souls in the warmth of the desert of Palestine. Dora makes explicit the comparison between Sabra Jews like her and diasporic Jews such as Lena: "Don't you see: we're free and we're not afraid" (49). Lena even wears around her neck an amulet of poison to be used as a last resort if she is captured by the Nazis. The implication is that these "refugees," instead of looking to the future as would the Jews in Israel, are so warped as ghosts or the "walking dead" that they constantly think of death–they are intricately linked with the poison.[24] In short, Lena, content to rely on Zabrodsky's Old World gentile culture as protection for the Jews, takes on the role of the eternal victim.

At first, Lena hesitates to abandon the safety of the European castle to leave with Dora and Sand for the secure life in Palestine. However, Goldberg makes it clear that Lena's decision to immigrate to Palestine is the only rational choice. In the denouement, Lena, much like Nora in Ibsen's *A Doll's House* who symbolically changed her dress before dancing the tarantella, alters her costume, her clothing, before embarking on a new life. She then leaves the confining, stormy atmosphere of the Old World to seek a new life in Palestine, the land of sunshine and fresh air. Sand describes the conversion as moving from death to life (77). The implication is that the Israelis have rescued the refugee from her dead past, allowing her to start life anew in the Promised Land. Robert Skloot notes, "The curtain falls at midnight–the beginning of a new day, a new life, and, a year later, a new nation: Israel."[25]

In her discussion of *Lady of the Castle*, Rachel Feldhay Brenner remarks upon the conflict of views the Sabras had about the Old World diasporic Jew:

> At the unconscious level, the rescuers recognize the survivors as their alter-egos and, at the same time, reject them as such. In

order to gain confidence in Jewish potency, the Israeli Jew must eliminate the past of Jewish helplessness. The survivor, who embodies Jewish weakness, represents therefore a threat to the group whose *raison d'être* is rooted in an internalized image of the free, powerful, and future-oriented 'new' Jew.[26]

Dora returns to the place of her childhood only to discover Lena as a paranoid version of herself as a young girl–her alter ego. Like Goldberg, who wrote the play as a catharsis (Leah transmutes to Lena), Dora seeks to destroy the self-image of the Jew as victim that threatens the existence of the Sabras and is similar to a constantly haranguing archetype that they are trying to repress. Goldberg herself is well aware that had she refused to emigrate to Palestine, she probably would have been part of the "dead" European culture with which Zabrodsky is associated. Thus, the survivor, who, as the walking dead, lives with the nightmare of the Holocaust long after the war has ended, exacerbates the guilt that Sabra Jews have over the Holocaust, and for that reason, survivors need to be ostracized unless they can conform to the norms of modern Israeli society. Thus, for Goldberg, the play becomes a need to validate Israel as her only home while eradicating all ties to a European past that is intricately linked with the bleakest period in Jewish history.

Israeli playwright Ben-Zion Tomer was born in the small village of Bilgoraj, Poland, in 1928. When World War II erupted, the family fled to Russia, where they were expelled to Siberia. After the German invasion of Russia in 1941, his relatives were freed and moved to Samarqand. To avoid having his son starve, Tomer's father placed him in an orphans' home. From there, Ben-Zion became one of the 830 children who were shipped to Eretz Israel in 1943; they were known as the Tehran Children because they had to wait in Tehran for a permit to emigrate to Palestine. During the War of Independence in 1948, as an officer in the Palmach, Tomer was captured by the Jordanians and sent to a prisoner of war camp for eleven months. In 1962, *Yaldei ha-Tzel (Children of the Shadows)*, Tomer's largely autobiographical play, premiered at the Habimah Theatre and has since been performed in the United States and Canada, as well as having been translated into English, German, Spanish, and French. After studying philosophy and literature at the Hebrew University, he became editor of the literary magazine *Masa* and taught literature at various kibbutzim and teachers' colleges. From 1966 to 1968, he was Israel's cultural attaché in Brazil, and from 1969 to 1977 was an advisor to the Ministry of Culture and Education. Tomer spent much of his time until his death in 1998 translating poetry from Russian and Polish into Hebrew.

Unlike Leah Goldberg, who does very little with the structure of the play, Ben-Zion Tomer, like Joshua Sobol, is a sophisticated innovator in experimenting with form. *Children of the Shadows* appears to be traditionally symmetrical in structure, with act one comprised of six scenes and act two of equivalent length of time in only five scenes. Although the major characters in the play are meticulously crafted, each with a distinctive past that evokes realism, there is no linear plot, for the action is broken up by expressionistic dream sequences that invalidate any notion of unity of time or place. The most notable breaks with realistic structure occur in scene six at the end of act one, where Yoram and Sigmund are immersed in a dream sequence that takes them back to their Holocaust memories in Poland, and a segment in act one, scene five, in which a typed character named Guiltfeeling, derived from German expressionist drama, rants about nihilism and acts briefly as Yoram's alter ego. Furthermore, poems and songs interrupt the play, allowing the spectator to disconnect from any realistic narrative framework that would otherwise lead to audience empathy with protagonists.

Children of the Shadows focuses on Yoram Eyal, who arrived in Palestine from a small town in Poland in 1941, and now, at age twenty-eight in 1955, has spent fourteen years futilely attempting to assimilate with the Sabras. Yoram is a classic Diaspora Jew who feels guilty about leaving his family behind in Poland to face the Holocaust, and because of his Old World European past as a victim of the Shoah, albeit indirectly, he cannot fit into an Israeli culture that looks to the future and seeks heroes instead of to a downtrodden Jewish past of which Sabras were ashamed. Guilt is essentially defined as the embodiment of anger directed not outwardly (i.e., toward the Nazis), but inwardly toward the self. In his ground-breaking study of Holocaust survivors, William G. Niederland identified "a severe and persevering guilt complex related to the fact of having survived when so many others had perished,"[27] as one of five major symptoms of the survivor syndrome. The Holocaust survivor often empathizes with beloved family members whom he or she feels obligated to unite with in death. Moreover, as Yael Danieli asserts, guilt presupposes the presence of choice and the power to exercise it; in other words, the Holocaust survivor believes that he or she chose wrongly and could otherwise have prevented the deaths of family members.[28] This passivity in the face of the Holocaust was often devastating for Holocaust survivors. Guilt thus served as a commemorative role in displaying fidelity to the memory of the dead. In her analysis of Holocaust refugees in Israel, Eva Fogelman concludes, "The inability of Holocaust survivors in Israel to confront the real destruction they had experienced during the Holocaust combined with their inability to truly mourn their personal and communal losses functioned to keep survivors from feeling true security and identification with the other Israelis–the 'Sabras.'"[29] Yoram, who throughout the early part of the play believes his parents and siblings have perished during the Shoah, personifies this sense of guilt that prevents him from acculturation.

Yoram has tried to assimilate into Israeli culture, albeit unsuccessfully. After he fought in the War of Independence, he entered a kibbutz. He abandoned his native Polish tongue and tried to speak only Hebrew. Attempting to create a new identity for himself, he changed his Polish name Yossele to Yoram and began to model himself upon his friend Dubi, whose father was a powerful figure in the immigration department. To Yoram, Dubi was the Sabra to be emulated: a good tractor driver, an excellent speaker, captain of the soccer team, the finest dancer in the kibbutz, and attractive to women. Yoram describes his conversion through an imitation of Dubi: "The prince of the valley. And Naomi was his girl. Inside me, I began to murder Yossele. Yossele is dead! Long live Yoram! A year later, I was king, Naomi was in my arms. I learned to dance the polka. I learned the ropes."[30] Yoram tells his wife Nurit that through assimilation he tried to cleanse himself from his Holocaust past: "I burned my lice-infested clothes along with myself. Along with Yossele ... And when I was through being disinfected, I was a new man, a superman like Dubi by the name of Yoram!" (155). Yoram, haunted by nightmares related to the Shoah, particularly admires Dubi's ability to sleep soundly because he obviously is at peace with himself.

Similar to Tomer's own history, Yoram's impoverished parents had difficulty feeding the family and thus placed their son in an orphanage. After the arrival of the Nazis in Lvov, Yossele and the "Tehran children" made the trek to Palestine. Yoram's brother Yanek stayed behind and became a resistance leader in the Warsaw ghetto uprising. Ultimately, Yoram's parents, two sisters, and brother were deported to various extermination camps; all of them managed to survive with the exception of his sister Esther. Yoram was enjoying life in the kibbutz while his family endured the agony of the Holocaust. Haim Shoham notes that Yoram's guilt is a result of trying to emulate Sabra Jews who live in the present but want to obliterate the Jewish past associated with the Shoah. Shoham writes, "Jewish identity in *Children in the Shadows* is a direct product of the two realms of Jewish existence in the twentieth century: of *here* and of *there*."[31] Yoram lives in the "here," in the safety of modern Israel where Jews are the confident aggressors, but he has nightmares about the "there," dreaming of the hunger and typhus of Lvov, as well as the death of his sister. Yoram understands that his abandonment of his formerly lice-ridden clothes for Israeli garb and his change of name are nothing more than a facade, a mask. He laments to his wife, "I don't feel any hatred, Nurit, only contempt, the contempt that a clown feels for his costume and his mask" (155). The Holocaust disallows Yoram from ever identifying himself with modern Israeli culture. For example, while bussing tables with Dubi and Naomi, Yoram, who experienced starvation at first hand in Europe, cannot fathom the idea of Jews leaving food on their plates. He complains to Nurit that Dubi and Naomi laughed when he refused to throw out the leftovers: "Suddenly I started to hate myself. Them. Myself. The memories that kept me from being one of them" (140). Yoram considers himself to be a "stranger" in modern Israel and is even estranged from his wife, who cannot possibly comprehend the difference between "here" and "there." He cannot even adjust to family life, stammering to Nurit, "Look, I ... I'm just not used to ... since I was eleven, all I ever thought about was a bed to sleep in, a roof over my head" (144).

271

Yoram's guilt about the "here" versus the "there" is exacerbated by the arrival of his family in Israel. Yoram refuses to allow his brother Yanek and his wife Helenka to stay with him in his apartment, as he tells Nurit, "So as not to have to see Helenka's eyes every day, as if I'd stolen something from her, as if it were my fault that I didn't go through what she went through, my fault that I came to Israel before she did, that I'm *here* (my italics)!" (162). The presence of Yanek and Helenka disturbs Yoram, for they keep referring to the Holocaust in Poland and remind him, "it's easy for you to talk, you were never *there* (my italics)" (165). When Yanek and Helena visit, tensions increase for Nurit and Yoram, the latter confessing to his wife, "Their tales of horror make me the guilty one. Guilty without having done anything" (168). Yoram is made to feel guilty around his brother because he recalls sitting comfortably in a cafe and then going to the movies during the Warsaw ghetto uprising. Glenda Abramson astutely comments, "Yoram is the representative of a general guilt caused, in his case, by the fact that he was powerless to assist his parents and friends, for while they were suffering the tortures of the Holocaust, he was thousands of miles away and comfortably secure in his new life."[32] Trying his best to acculturate to Israeli society, Yoram considers his family to be outsiders, the victims, the downtrodden Diaspora Jews, who now threaten his own security in the Promised Land. He becomes a marginal man—one who cannot be a Sabra but who is also alienated from his brethren in Poland since he did not share the responsibility for the death of his sister nor for the suffering of his siblings and parents. As such, Yoram becomes neurotic, even paranoid, often blaming his Sabra wife Nurit for patronizing him or defending his innocent family members, which only serves to increase his self-immolation.

The other Holocaust survivor in the play who is guilt-ridden and cannot accommodate to the culture of the Sabras is Yoram's brother-in-law, Dr. Sigmund Rabinowitz. Before the Nazi invasion, Sigmund was a doctor of philosophy, a professor of Renaissance art at the University of Lvov. In the ghetto, he was a member of the *Judenrat* and thus collaborated with the Nazis in selecting Jews for deportation, one of which was his wife Esther. Sigmund was quite possibly deported as well, for he refers to himself as a tattooed number, a designation that only marked the inmates of the concentration camps but never the denizens of the ghetto. Dr. Rabinowitz is particularly jaded about faith in the humanist tradition, for his best friend, a German he studied with at the prestigious University of Heidelberg, became a commandant in one such concentration camp. Thus, there is a deep fissure between Sigmund's training in the humanities and the brutal reality associated with the Shoah. Unlike Yoram, who was "here" (in Palestine), Sigmund was actually "there," and as such, he experiences the guilt of having witnessed the results of Jewish family members and friends suffering at the hands of the Nazis.

In the early years of Israel's statehood, Sabras praised the heroism of Jewish resistance during the Holocaust while condemning collaborators and those who went to their deaths as sheep. Michael Taub comments, "While partisans and resistance movement heroes received all the attention, with streets and buildings named after them, figures like Sigmund, characters who occupied those difficult, gray areas of morality, were either shunned or roundly demonized."[33] Sigmund realizes that he is so alienated from mainstream Israeli postwar culture that he engages in withdrawal and self-flagellation. He has changed his name to Benjamin Apfelbaum from Vilna in order to disguise his identity and to obliterate his notorious past in Lvov, for as he says metaphorically to the Balloon Seller, "The sheep are a funny nation, they forgave the tigers, but they never forgave the tiger's stooges" (172). Sigmund has reduced himself to any anonymous, indigent beggar confined notably to a bench on the beach–an outcast living on the outskirts of Tel Aviv. The lugubrious poetry that he recites is tinged with verses that echo "the sound of railcars/ Emptied of the children as of coal" (157). He describes himself to Yoram as a cipher, once a distinguished professor of the humanities reduced by the Nazis to a victim, a tattooed number: "My name? 155370, and kindly note that the last digit is zero" (176). Sigmund is a member of the walking dead, similar to a zombie, who cannot fit into the aggressive Sabra culture that looks to the future instead of an unheroic past. He is suicidal (128) largely because he suffers from nightmares that reinforce the guilt he has for refusing to resign from the *Judenrat*, a fate that directly resulted in his complicity with Esther's death. Instead of the pride that Sabra Jews feel, guilt-ridden Sigmund retreats into self-flagellation, continually referring to himself as a medusa (a type of jellyfish) (170), a rat (171), a corpse (173), a fish in the jaws of a pelican (171), and a dog (173) – all far removed from the vestiges of the human soul that he once was. His only hope to preserve his sanity in a culture that hardly supports his guilt-ridden persona is to adopt his own mask of madness, and as such, he compares himself to suicidal Hamlet whose antic disposition provided a mask to alleviate his own guilt for failure to act.

Children of the Shadows, then, is noteworthy in presenting the difficulty that diasporic Jews had in adapting to life in Israel after the Holocaust. Like Rose in *A Shayna Maidel*, Yoram suffers from the guilt of surviving while family members in Europe perished or suffered scars that will last for life, making it nearly impossible for him to coexist with Sabra Jews. Like Lusia, who experienced the effects of the Holocaust directly and thus could not assimilate into American society, Sigmund, the survivor, also bears the guilt directly and will always remain on the outer fringes of the Promised Land.

12 The Survivor Syndrome and the Effects of the Holocaust on Survivor Families

Holocaust survivors admit that luck was a major factor in whether they remained alive, while having a social support system in the extermination camps certainly also helped, for loners often perished. However, the most important concerted effort that enabled the victims to survive was the will to bear witness to the atrocities. Terrence Des Pres, himself a survivor of the *lager*, recalls, "For most survivors the chance to speak comes later. To bear witness is the goal of their struggle."[1] Despite the fact that SS guards relished telling prisoners that they had no chance of living and that even if someone miraculously survived to tell the tale, no one would believe that such persecution was possible, many prisoners struggled to survive to enact revenge as witnesses.

Immediately after their liberation from *l'univers concentrationnaire*, survivors were in no shape to bear witness. Former Ravensbrück inmate Simone Veil, interviewed by Annette Wieviorka, revealed, "For several days after my return I had such difficulty reading that I was afraid I would never again be able to take up normal intellectual activity."[2] Charlotte Delbo, who survived Auschwitz and Ravensbrück, stated that upon her return home after her internment, she tried to recall the gestures necessary to assume the shape of a living being: learning again how to talk, walk, answer questions, dream, imagine, laugh, and think for yourself.[3] Gradually, she began to redevelop her senses of smell, taste, sight, and hearing, while later becoming accustomed to recognizing colors and sounds. Delbo confirms, "I was not in despair. I was absent."[4] Survivors often were so disoriented that they lost the will to have any initiative, feeling as though they were no longer alive. Auschwitz and Bergen-Belsen survivor Jean Améry writes, "We emerged from the camp stripped, robbed, emptied out, disoriented–and it was a long time before we were able even to learn the ordinary language of freedom."[5]

Bruno Bettelheim made the first serious attempt to psychoanalyze the mentality of survivors. Trained in Freudian psychoanalysis, Bettelheim seemed committed to explaining the Holocaust exclusively in Freudian terminology, arguing that Jewish compliance with Nazi orders had been a result of Jews losing their will to live, allowing the death drive to dominate in its continuous battle with one's instinct for life.[6] Bettelheim insisted that prisoners, who were abnormally preoccupied with sustenance and excretory demands in the concentration camps, regressed to the oral and anal stages of childhood. Bettelheim, a survivor of Dachau and Buchenwald, stated that concentration camp inmates regressed to infantile behavior not only through a childlike preoccupation with food and incontinence, but also through a pre-adolescent need to impersonate the aggressor. Bettelheim concluded that survivors thus had limited potential for ego development beyond this psychosexual regression. Des Pres challenged Bettelheim's findings, insisting that Freudian psychology is inapplicable in determining human behavior in such unique circumstances that Freud could not have envisioned. In the extreme condition of the extermination camps, adults soiled their clothing and dreamt of food out of the need to stay alive, which is totally unlike their behavior would have been in civilized society. Des Pres infers, "The psychoanalytic approach is misleading because it is essentially a theory of culture and of man in the civilized state."[7] Moreover, Bettelheim based his analysis of survivor mentality on his life in the German concentration camps–truly a dismal experience but far different from the utter devastation shared by survivors of extermination camps in Poland. Furthermore, Leslie Berger comments that Bettelheim failed to account for the fact that most of the prisoners he referred to were German criminals, who, unlike Jews or political prisoners, were selected for positions as camp functionaries and thus were forced into a role imitating Nazi behavior.[8]

In 1961, William G. Niederland, a psychiatrist and a refugee from Nazi Germany, coined the term "survivor syndrome" to indicate that Holocaust survivors, previously thought to be merely depressed, suffered from a host of psychological disturbances. Niederland found that, besides feelings of apathy, insecurity, and anhedonia (an inability to experience pleasure), which often led to withdrawal or seclusion, survivors suffered from guilt complexes, feelings of valuelessness and persecution anxieties that often resulted in paranoia, and personality variations that led to psychotic disturbances, complete inertia, or morbid brooding.[9] Leo Eitinger, who studied concentration camp survivors in Israel and Norway, confirmed Niederland's findings and further stated that survivors frequently demonstrated a crass, mistrustful attitude toward life and, as such, had difficulty establishing interpersonal contacts.[10] Virtually all Holocaust survivors were found to have conflicting feelings: their overwhelming desire to bear witness, which sustained them through the agony of life in the concentration camps, was now intricately linked with articulation of the horrors of the Holocaust, thus coinciding with the anguish of remembering a painful past. Other clinicians researching the survivor syndrome after Niederland and Eitinger focused on psychosomatic disorders that included fatigue, restlessness, inability to concentrate, insomnia, and nightmares.[11] Although many Holocaust survivors found solace during the day by focusing on work and in the evening by concentrating on family matters, the Holocaust was omnipresent in their lives at night when insomnia or nightmares interrupted any semblance of a normal existence.[12] By 1980, when the American Psychiatric Association recognized post-traumatic stress disorder as a major psychological illness, Freudian analyses of survivor trauma were no longer viewed as relevant.

Of particular note among the characteristics of Holocaust survivor syndrome is guilt. H. Krystal and Niederland reported that guilt was a major pathogenic factor in ninety-two percent of the Holocaust survivors that they studied.[13] Holocaust survivors frequently experienced guilt because their lives were spared while friends or relatives perished. Moreover, since their survival largely depended upon luck, the spared individual may feel guilty about being saved while millions died. This feeling of guilt may be exacerbated if the survivor acknowledges that he or she was forced to watch the extermination of friends or relatives without attempting to intervene. As a result of a study of families of Holocaust survivors, Yael Danieli writes, "Being totally passive and helpless in the face of the Holocaust is perhaps the most devastating experience for survivor/victims."[14] Guilt accrues when the individual realizes that choices could have been made during incarceration in the camps, but either nothing was done or the wrong decisions were made.

With the inability of language to express the deeply rooted *angoisse* of the Holocaust, coupled with the fact that immigrants were forced to learn a new language that contributed to problems communicating, most survivors, realizing that those who had not experienced the Shoah could never understand their angst, kept silent. Aharon Appelfeld, an adolescent survivor in 1945, later admitted, "So we learned silence. It was not easy to keep silent. But it was a good way out for all of us. For what, when all is said and done, was there to tell? To us as well it began to sound like something imaginary, which ought not to be believed."[15] However, silence did little to alleviate the survivor syndrome. Charlotte Delbo cites her colleague Mado, a survivor who kept silent for years, even to her husband: "People believe memories grow vague, are erased by time, since nothing endures against the passage of time. That's the difference; time does not pass over me, over us. It doesn't erase anything, doesn't undo it. I'm not alive. I died in Auschwitz but no one knows it."[16] To avoid internalizing the frustration of keeping silent and to make up for lost time that was denied them, survivors tried to keep busy in their work or by immersing themselves in married life and raising children to replace the extended family that was now dead. Aaron Hass's seminal study of Holocaust survivors reveals that although a few prominent Holocaust survivors, such as Jean Améry and Primo Levi, committed suicide, most survivors were strong individuals who were determined to trudge through life rather than to give the Nazis satisfaction of another death.[17]

Gilles Ségal's one-act realist drama, *Le Marionnettiste de Lodz* (*The Puppetmaster of Lodz*), provides a frank yet startling portrayal of the survivor syndrome. Written in 1980, the play was first performed in France in 1983, with Ségal, who trained in mime and puppetry with Marcel Marceau and Jean-Louis Barrault, playing

Samuel Finkelbaum, the puppetmaster. The following year, during a theatrical run that began on 10 January 1984, Jean-Paul Roussillon staged *Le Marionnettiste de Lodz* at the Théâtre de la Commune in Aubervilliers. In 1988, *The Puppetmaster of Lodz* had its American premiere at the Milwaukee Repertory Theater, which was under the auspices of managing director Sara O'Connor, who had translated the play into English. Since its debut, Ségal's drama has been widely performed in the United States, which is unusual because, although the play seems easily stageable with only four characters and a single set, Finkelbaum must be played by a master puppeteer, which precludes many actors from attempting the role. The Empty Stage Theatre in Seattle mounted the play for its 1988/89 season, and within the next two years, productions were given at the Studio Theatre in Washington, D.C., the American Jewish Theater in New York, and the Wilma Theater in Philadelphia. In May 1993, in Port Jefferson, Long Island, Jerry M. Friedman directed Jeffrey Samzel as Finkelbaum in a Theater Three staging that was presented in conjunction with the opening of the Holocaust Museum and the fiftieth anniversary of the Warsaw ghetto uprising. *The Puppetmaster of Lodz* also ran from 20 January to 14 February 1999 at the Marin Theater in Mill Valley near San Francisco; for this production, director Lee Sankowich brought in Holocaust survivor and Warsaw puppeteer Henryk Hajwentreger as an artistic consultant. The play was subsequently performed in March 2000 at the Actors Alley of the El Portal Center for the Arts in North Hollywood and at the Mum Puppettheatre in Philadelphia from 26 October to 20 November 2004. The most heralded production in the last twenty years has been Jimmy McDermott's direction of Larry Neumann, Jr., as Finkelbaum at the Writers' Theatre in Glencoe, Illinois, from 27 March to 8 July 2007. The Chicago community was particularly in awe of puppetmaster Michael Montenegro's design of the Ruchele marionette, which was realistic enough to look as if Finkelbaum's wife were actually alive, yet simultaneously was abstract enough to make the audience realize the extent of Finkelbaum's traumatization.

The Puppetmaster of Lodz takes place in the apartment of Berlin resident Samuel Finkelbaum, who, in 1950, has been living a secluded life for the last five years since the end of the war. Finkelbaum, a Jewish puppeteer from Lodz, was deported to Auschwitz with his pregnant wife Ruchele. In Birkenau, Finkelbaum worked as a member of the *Sonderkommando*, where he burned corpses, the most notable of which was that of his own wife. He reveals to his fellow survivor friend Schwartzkopf, "Lord knows, I've tried ... tried with all my might but ... you see when I found Ruchele, that October day ... in the pile of corpses we had to burn, I thought I was going to go mad ... Ruchele with our child in her belly ... "[18] Before the liberation of Auschwitz, Finkelbaum and Schwartzkopf bolted from the camp. Since then, refusing to believe that the war is over, Finkelbaum has sequestered himself in his Berlin apartment. His landlady, who provides him with food and shelter, is his only contact with the outside world.

Finkelbaum displays the classic symptoms associated with trauma plaguing many Holocaust survivors. Suffering from feelings of valuelessness and persecution, he has withdrawn into seclusion and morbid brooding. After experiencing the horrors of Auschwitz, Finkelbaum distrusts others to the point where his paranoia keeps him secluded like a hermit. Finkelbaum's behavior is consistent with the findings of Maria Rosenbloom, who studied long-term trauma-tization effects on Holocaust survivors and concluded, "distrust of the world, isolation, and withdrawal from relationships" appeared to be typical symptoms.[19] Convinced that no one can empathize with the ordeal with which he has suffered, Finkelbaum ostracizes himself from all social contact. This withdrawal from society corroborates Elie Wiesel's statement that at Auschwitz, not only man died, but also the idea of man. Aaron Hass writes, "Survivors' profoundly mistrust-ful attitude toward those around them resulted not only from their persecution and betrayal, but from the recognition that pleas from one's fellow man will fall on deaf ears."[20] Moreover, as psychological studies of Holocaust survivors have shown, those who were left with-out any family members, like Finkelbaum, were frequently the most depressed and therefore more withdrawn.[21]

The Concierge tries to convince the paranoid Finkelbaum that the war is over, but he perceives it to be a Nazi conspiracy to get him arrested. When she exhorts him to read the newspaper to learn about current events in Berlin, he is dubious and surmises that it is merely a fake publication that she has printed herself. The Concierge then tries to lure Finkelbaum out of seclusion by having a colleague play various roles: Russian infantryman Mikhail Popov, American Sergeant James W. Spencer, and Hyman Weissfeld, who later transforms into a doctor. Finkelbaum, not confident that the Russians are in Berlin, even after accepting an authentic Russian cigarette that would indicate proof of Popov's identity, casually dismisses him by saying, "It's hard to survive when you trust people!" (20). Spencer claims he is from an American battalion that liberated the camps and wants Finkelbaum's assistance in identifying SS adjutants. Finkelbaum, wondering how an American can speak fluent German, refuses to believe the ruse. Hyman Weissfeld tries to convince Finkelbaum that, as a Jew, he is able to walk Berlin streets freely now that the war is over. Moreover, Weissfeld claims to be a lawyer who will help Finkelbaum get reparations from the German government. After the way Finkelbaum was abused by the Nazis, he finds Weissfeld's assertions to be incredulous: "You're trying to make me believe that they lost the war and that they've kept lists of all the people they've arrested, deported, gassed, in order to pay them damages with interest afterwards. Is that it?" (39). The doctor is the last to try to coax Finkelbaum out of hiding, citing the fact that he needs the survivor's help to identify two SS guards who fled Birkenau before its liberation. Realizing that the doctor has come in previous disguises, Finkelbaum refuses to budge from the safety of his seclusion, blatantly associating the physician with the notorious Auschwitz murderer, Doctor Mengele.

The source of Finkelbaum's paranoia and depression is the guilt accrued from his conduct during the Shoah. As Edward R. Isser verifies, "Finkelbaum is hounded by the guilt of his own survival and by his actions in the death camp."[22] Finkelbaum, who describes himself in the pre-Holocaust years as " a spirited young stallion" (36), was helpless in Birkenau to save the life of his wife and soon-to-be-born son. Giorgio Agamben reminds us that guilt is a *locus classicus* of the literature on the camps, recalling Bettelheim's claim that survivors inevitably felt guilty about being lucky when so many perished, and then citing Wiesel's apothegm, "I am here because a friend, an acquaintance, an unknown person died in my place."²³ Finkelbaum realizes that he survived through luck but cannot understand a senseless universe directed by an indifferent God who allowed his wife to die pregnant. Moreover, Finkelbaum subliminally realizes that mourning over the dead is an ascribed ritualistic process in the Jewish religion, and by not even allowing him to view how his wife died, Auschwitz has subverted that process. Since Finkelbaum is in denial about his wife's death–talking to her puppet likeness as if she were still alive– his ability to mourn, as Eva Fogelman has documented among similar Holocaust survivors, will be even more impaired.²⁴ Moreover, Finkelbaum feels guilty about his pathetic behavior while in Birkenau. He vowed to do anything to survive in order to see his son, so he stole bread from his friend Schwartzkopf and performed an erotic puppet show with corpses in order to placate a Nazi officer.

Ségal has created a masterful play that superbly captures the survivor mentality. Finkelbaum's consciousness is forever grounded in the Holocaust experience that shaped his life. When he cooks for himself, he is very economical with the ingredients, weighing them as precious commodities typical of someone accustomed to rationing. Insisting that God deserted him during the Shoah, Finkelbaum makes up for lost time by recreating and refashioning his own world: the puppeteer as Creator. Finkelbaum makes the comparison to God explicit as he talks to himself: "Finkelbaum, the rival of God, since he too creates beings to whom he gives life, and from whom he can withdraw it at will, and, since God does not exist, the sole Creator of Creation!" (22). The *raison d'être* of the play is made viscerally clear to any audience through the visual effects: there is something macabre, pathetic, and demented about a man who talks to himself through puppets. The pathos of the survivor mentality is apparent when during most of the play, Finkelbaum is talking to the full-size puppet Ruchele as if she were alive as his wife and confidante. Other puppets of various sizes are torn from the arms of their mothers, line up for roll call, or try to flee from the Nazis, suggesting that the Holocaust is the only scenario, and one without any chance of egress, that pervades his consciousness.

At the end of the play, Finkelbaum opens the door only to greet his former comrade Schwartzkopf, as if to suggest that the agony of a

Holocaust survivor can only be understood by another survivor. The stage directions state, *"The two men look at one another for a long moment and, immobile, weep without sound"* (48). Their understanding of the horrors they experienced is intuitive, and nothing they can say to nonsurvivors could explain what they lived through, no matter how articulate they could be. Schwartzkopf convinces Finkelbaum to leave the Berlin apartment, so the puppetmaster realizes he cannot take the marionettes with him. Thus, the denouement in which Finkelbaum begins to burn the puppets in the stove sends a mixed message: he is willing to try to start life anew, but the burning implies that he will forever be a member of the *Sonderkommando* in Auschwitz. After burning the puppets, only Ruchele's likeness remains. Finkelbaum clutches the puppet, refusing to burn her with the others. When the Concierge asks Finkelbaum to confirm that the war is over, his last words end the play: "So they say, so they say ... " (53). For survivors, the Holocaust can never end, for the trauma cannot be turned on or off at will.

British playwright Peter Flannery's remarkable 1989 drama, *Singer*, is one of the most poignant portrayals of Holocaust survivorship written in the twentieth century. *Singer* is Flannery's only noteworthy venture into Holocaust portrayal. Flannery is best known for the plays he penned during his residence as playwright for the Royal Shakespeare Company during the late 1970s and early 1980s: *Savage Amusement* (1978), *The Adventures of Awful Knawful*, with Mick Ford (1978), and *Our Friends in the North* (1982). After 1983, he wrote mainly for film and television, where his work was known to a wider audience, particularly through the nine-part television adaptation of *Our Friends in the North*, produced by the British Broadcasting Company in 1996. During the British Academy Television Awards ceremony in 1997, Flannery received the Dennis Potter Award for outstanding achievement in television writing.

Singer premiered on 27 September 1989 at the Royal Shakespeare Company's Swan Theatre in Stratford. Terry Hands directed a wonderful cast that featured Mick Ford as Stefan and Antony Sher's protean, electric performance as Singer. In 2004, director Sean Holmes revived the play at the Oxford Stage Company's Tricycle Theatre in London from 10 March until 10 April. Ron Cook, who captured Singer's vibrant wit and pathos in this production, was ably supported by John Light, who played Stefan as a mellow contrast to Singer's vigor. Unfortunately, *Singer* has not been widely staged outside the United Kingdom, perhaps because of its nearly three hours running time and its cast of seventy-five characters (many of whom obviously need to be doubled or tripled in performance).

 Singer is written as epic theater that encompasses a time period that spans forty years from World War II to the Margaret Thatcher administration. The play consists of thirteen scenes in five acts framed by a prologue and a short epilogue. The chorus seems to be more of an Elizabethan device than Brechtian, providing exposition at the beginning of each act yet far removed from the Brechtian narrator interrupting the action to "alienate" the audience from empathizing with the characters. *Singer* is also reminiscent of Jacobean drama, as Singer himself seems to be a witty, erudite tragicomic protagonist bent on revenge while ranting against an unjust world.

 The prologue, set in Auschwitz, is the focal point for the play. Flannery used Primo Levi's *If This Is a Man* to supply background information to set the stage for this scene. Two Jews from Lvov, Poland (Pyotr Zinger and Stefan Gutman), and one German gentile political prisoner known as Manik have been deported to Auschwitz. Zinger's parents have been gassed, so now his remaining family consists of his nephew Stefan, who also considers his relative to be like an older brother. Zinger is an educated person who wanted to be a dentist and had cultivated tastes in music, art, and theater. In Auschwitz, Zinger is reduced to engaging in the black market to stay alive, rationing food, and surviving in the "cold," an operative word that later functions in the play to remind him of the misery of the Holocaust. Stefan works as Blockchief, whose job it is to run the children's brothel while choosing which of his minions will be selected for the gas chamber. Stefan is forced to supply Mirchuk, a particularly vicious Ukrainian kapo, with children in exchange for favors. Stefan suffers from intense guilt and shame for his work in the Children's Block and speaks blatantly about his remorse: "We'll all be whipped along the Road to Heaven; two thousand six hundred and eighty-one children will be waiting there for me and *they* will sit in judgment on *me.*"[25] In this scene, Manik, a high number and thus a relative newcomer to the camp, has just traded his shirt for Zinger's coupon, forcing Mirchuk to hit him repeatedly in the head for being shirtless. Mirchuk then forces Zinger to admit that he is worthless, nothing more than "A piece of Jewish shit" (7). When Mirchuk inadvertently steps in excrement, he forces Zinger to eat it. Zinger, who is submissive in Auschwitz, contrary to his natural predilection for wit and vigor, follows orders, and thus, at Mirchuk's command, goes on to beat his friend Manik.[26]

After the liberation of the camps, Zinger, Stefan, and Manik flee to England. An immigration official gives them advice about how to cope in postwar Britain: "Forget: forget the past. You've had terrible experiences. But there is nothing to be gained by dwelling on the past. The future's what counts; you must make up your minds who and what you want to be" (11). These words reverberate throughout the play as the three Holocaust survivors try to cope with their traumas. Zinger, attempting to put the past behind him, changes his name to Peter Singer and promises the immigration officer, "We'll forget. We all want be English. God save the Kink!" (11). Stefan, however, realizes that Holocaust memories will forever sear their lives. He pleads with Singer to understand that they are ultimately different people now than they were before their lives were destroyed: "I don't want to be told: forget. Nobody should forget; we should all sit down now and write down everything that has happened. Don't you see?" (12). Manik, his mind arrested by the beating he received, accompanies Singer, as Stefan makes his way in postwar British society on his own.

In the 1940s and 1950s, Singer, like many Holocaust survivors, took his mind off the trauma by absorbing himself in work. Writing about his frustration with his Holocaust past, survivor Jean Améry noted, "Self-confessed man of resentments that I am, I supposedly live in the bloody illusion that I can be compensated for my suffering through the freedom granted me by society to inflict injury in return."[27] Like many nihilistic survivors, such as those studied by Leo Eitinger, Singer develops into a crass, ruthless individual trusting virtually no one. In his study of Holocaust victims, Aaron Hass remarks about the ruthlessness of survivors: "The breast of nurturance, the breast of

285

succor, the breast that brings with it a primal assurance was replaced with seething coals. Survivors learned that goodness is an aberration, malice the norm. Survivors saw the impotence of piety and the tenacity of evil."[28] In such a spirit, Singer becomes a vicious slum landlord who relishes the idea of profiting from the ignorance of refugees in London. Thus, Singer, forced to be submissive in Auschwitz, now relishes the chance to become the aggressor and dominate subordinate ethnic groups who have immigrated to England. Theodor W. Adorno posed the question of whether any Holocaust survivor can go on living with the inevitable guilt that one feels about being alive while loved ones died in the camps. Adorno, strangely enough, frames his response in the metaphor of coldness that Flannery employs throughout the play; "His [the victim's] mere survival calls for the coldness, the basic principle of bourgeois subjectivity, without which there could have been no Auschwitz; this is the drastic guilt of him who was spared."[29] Singer, constantly suffering from cold in Auschwitz, instead of internalizing his frustrations, now sublimates his anxieties through socially acceptable channels of the cold reality of entrepreneurship.

Singer begins his crass brutality as a wisecracking con artist operating out of a public telephone booth in Bayswater. He confirms to Manik that since the two of them are no longer hungry nor subject to beatings, then "nothing *matters*" (16). Singer's first venture into business involves renting dilapidated apartments to West Indian refugees. Gaining more confidence in his shady dealings, Singer plans to buy overcrowded slum properties and turn them into individual apartments for rent. When Singer is told that his scheme cannot work because sitting tenants refuse to leave their properties, he laughs at the idea. Singer gets results; for example, he turns off the water in Mrs. Daley's apartment and then offers to buy her out. When the offer is refused, Manik, Singer's strong-arm, bites Mrs. Daley's dog, and while bleeding from the mouth, he strangles the animal and then throws her belongings out into the street. When Manik has second thoughts about the eviction, claiming that his mother was forced out of her home, Singer exhorts him to act ruthlessly without pity: "Don't *think* Manik. It's suicidal for you" (31). Furthermore, Singer's penchant for young girls keeps him preoccupied when he is not working, effectively operating as another means of blotting out the Holocaust. For instance, we see Singer engaging in fellatio with a whore and learn about his playing tennis, "the love game," with Lord Earner's wife. He even admits to Manik that he toys with his mortgage lenders: "And in the afternoons I screw their wives which they also cannot be bothered to do. I borrow their money and I borrow their wives" (49).

Meanwhile, Stefan has taken a job as a photographer but has had no pretensions of forgetting his Holocaust past. As a constant reminder of his life in Auschwitz where trains represented the omnipresence of death, Stefan lives near a railway in Clapham. He refuses to obscure the tattooed number on his arm. Taking up painting as a hobby, he declines to draw English landscapes and tells Singer that he paints solely "Polish subjects" (38) to remind him of his former life. In particular, Stefan is obsessed with painting images he remembered from Auschwitz, especially the fear-stricken faces of children that he led to the gas chamber.

Singer's efforts to obtain British citizenship become a means to eradicate his Polish past and concomitantly to give him an identity. Singer boasts to Stefan, "I'm British. I'm British! I'm not a stateless person anymore! I have a home!" (41). Singer invites the cream of British society to a soirée to celebrate his citizenship. In a style reminiscent of Groucho Marx taunting the upper class with his prickly wit, Singer, a Holocaust refugee lacking social graces, manages to insult his guests, albeit unknowingly. His crass attitude toward tenants who crash the party to testify to his brutality has the British nobility "gobsmacked." When Mrs. Daley accuses him of killing her dog, Singer's nonchalant query, "Anyway, what's a dog" (53), results in universal condemnation. Instead of celebrating citizenship, the party results in violence: Manik, who regresses to speaking German when he is agitated, physically attacks Pepper and Shallcross when they threaten Singer with incarceration. Stefan, improperly dressed for the fancy occasion, is even subjected to Singer's caustic barbs. However, Stefan, not to be intimidated, responds to his fellow survivor, saying, "Perhaps you can't forgive me because I remind you of what we really are!" (50). Stefan speaks to Singer in Polish and then gives him a gift for the occasion: a bowl from the camp.

Singer's attempts at citizenship, his prodigious work ethic that has made Singerism a household term associated with greed and evil,[30] and his penchant for young women are all ruses that divert his attention from remembering his Holocaust past. Aaron Hass explains this aspect of the survivor mentality:

> Just as many survivors spurned an abnormal self-image, they also *insisted* that their ability to enjoy life has not been impaired by their ordeals. Despite feeling angry, guilty, sad, or fearful, these survivors refused to acknowledge further debilitating effects of their past. They want to live a normal life and they are determined to enjoy it. Yet, they are often more accomplished at experiencing joy in response to what they *have* than at attaining any inner contentment. Internally, the struggle to keep so much of themselves from awareness is a never-ending one.[31]

However, although he would like to avoid awareness, Singer latently understands that his identity is defined by the tattoo that marks him for life. In truth, Singer realizes that his past has been obliterated, for he tells his banker's secretary that he was once a concert pianist but cannot return to Lvov because the city no longer exists. His inability to sleep, despite the daytime distractions, proves that the Holocaust forever haunts his consciousness. Moreover, Singer's crass business practices and his fascistic attitude toward his servants, dismissing them from service at the slightest indiscretion, emulates Nazi behavior in the camps. For example, when Singer notices what he thinks is dirt on one of the plates, the servant corrects him, stating that the mark is part of the china's design. Singer, reverting to the type of behavior he witnessed in Auschwitz, smashes the plate over the servant's head and then fires him after screaming, "It's not the pattern. It's filthy shit! Are you trying to get me to eat shit?" (45). In 1960, realizing, "My life was a waste of time because I was worthless" (56), Singer attempts suicide by drowning. However, the immersion into water can also be perceived as Singer's baptism–the purification needed to confront his Holocaust past directly.

Eight years after his attempted suicide-baptism, Singer seeks revenge for his Holocaust past by seeking to confront Mirchuk. Mirchuk's daughter Ruby tells Singer and Stefan that her father was in Auschwitz and feels guilt for having lived when so many others died, but Singer has no compassion for him. Before meeting Mirchuk, Ruby's performance group stages a pantomime, similar to an Elizabethan masque, of Auschwitz. When Singer asks one of the performers the meaning of the pantomime, the latter responds with a reference to Marshall McLuhan: "No meaning, man. No explanation. 'The medium was the message'" (67). After a prolonged period of sex in which Singer uses Ruby to gain access to her father, the meeting between Singer and Mirchuk is arranged. Waiting for Mirchuk to arrive, Singer again feels Auschwitz: "Cold. Cold. Cold" (71). Flannery makes a wise decision to confine Mirchuk to a wheelchair so that he is unable to walk away from his tormentors. Singer has to restrain himself when he hears Mirchuk talk about the frigid weather, immediately associating the voice with the extermination camp: "That voice. Cold. Cold. The weather is very cold" (72). Mirchuk, a pathetic, broken man, claims he cannot remember Singer nor his own number in the camp. Singer is livid, explaining to Ruby, in a voice echoing Primo Levi, that her father was the personification of the evil that was the Holocaust: "it's a voice that doesn't have to raise itself because it can never be opposed, it belonged to a man who could snuff out our lives any moment he felt like it and nobody in the world would know or care" (76). Singer implores Mirchuk to explain the reason that he was reduced to a nonentity: "I was a human being. You turned me into nothing. I was solid, I was real. I demand to know the reason why. *Why* was that done to me?" (76). The pantomime earlier offered a clue to Mirchuk's lack of response: there is no meaning; the Holocaust was senseless.

After the encounter with Mirchuk, Singer, attempting to assuage his Holocaust guilt by redeeming his past sins, spends the next twenty years helping the homeless. Singerism is transformed into saintliness as Pyotr/Peter assumes his new persona as St. Peter of the South Bank. He has also become celibate, which is quite a contrast from his former womanizing. When Singer is invited to lunch with the prime minister, he is tempted to return to his days as a ruthless slumlord. In Flannery's critique of the Social Darwinist profiteering of Thatcherism, Minister Nicholas de Knop tries to convince Singer that his ruthless desire to make money was much more meaningful than his charitable efforts.[32] Adhering to his principles, Singer initially replies that no one deserves to be homeless but then realizes that his life as a slumlord did indeed make him feel more alive.

The last scene of the play, the encounter between Manik, Singer, and Stefan in the latter's art studio following lunch with the prime minister, is riveting. The ministers have come there to persuade Singer to lead a consortium that will do what Singer did so well years ago–buy old properties and then rent them out to make huge profits. Stefan tries to convince Singer that his recent work with the homeless has proved invaluable and that he need not revert back to his former crass behavior. Singer becomes cynical and jaded, claiming the world is interested only in lies, not the truth. He attempts to explain the truth about himself to Stefan, finding it impossible to separate his new persona from his former life in Auschwitz: "I am worthless. I am nothing" (93). Stefan, unable to convince Singer to rejuvenate himself as he was before the Shoah, parts company with his lifelong friend. However, when Singer learns that people with mental health problems are going to be renting the properties, he associates their persecution with the infamy of Auschwitz. When de Knop describes their residences as "camps" and the need to "whip" any recalcitrants to get them to comply with camp regulations, the connection is clear to Singer. His reaction, "I feel cold. Cold. Cold" (95), places him squarely back in Auschwitz. As de Knop blames British immigration problems on the lack of enforcement from previous administrations to control blacks and Jews, Singer regresses to his former status as Holocaust victim. Meanwhile, Manik, who is shocked by Stefan's painting of a young Manik in the camp, is reborn as a starving inmate trading coupons for food in the prisoners' market. For the first time in the play, Manik remembers that he once had a vibrant life as a human being–Otto Vanselow from Düsseldorf–not a whipping boy.

In his rejection of the need to change his persona again, Singer learns the great truth that he has been avoiding: survivors should not attempt to shun the historical event that forever altered their lives. Speaking to himself, Singer concludes, "You were right, Stefan. It wasn't a mistake to remember. The mistake was not remembering enough" (97). Stefan, the great rememberer who could paint only the faces of the children he led to the gas, commits suicide. Flannery has taken Primo Levi's tale and dramatized his dilemma for audiences to ponder: it is disingenuous for survivors to think that they can escape the trauma of the Holocaust, but to confront the Shoah directly is a flirtation with nihilism that can be suicidal. Indeed, in a 1989 study (published the same year of the debut of *Singer*) of Polish concentration camp survivors conducted by Arie Nadler and Dan Ben-Shushan, two Israeli scholars, they reported that two-thirds of the subjects could not enjoy life while one-third were suicidal.[33] At the end of the play, after Singer views the dead body of Stefan, he is faced with the life-in-death struggle that all Holocaust survivors must endure and wonders whether life is worth pursuing, given his complete loss of faith in mankind. Singer's words end the play: "When someone builds a machine the size of half a continent, employing a cast of thousands, just to make you into soap, it's hard to take entirely seriously the idea of progress. But it's necessary to go on trying" (97). *Singer*, although not a well-known play internationally, is emotionally taut and intellectually stimulating–undeniably one of the most meaningful psychological portrayals of the paradoxical dilemma of Holocaust survivorship.

A play that demonstrates with panache the effects of the Holocaust on the surviving families of the victims is French playwright Jean-Claude Grumberg's *L'Atelier* (*The Workroom*). Born during the start of World War II in 1939, Grumberg was not yet four years old when his father Zacharie, who never became a French citizen, was arrested by the Vichy police in 1943. As a Romanian Jew, Zacharie was sent to Drancy for internment before his deportation to Auschwitz, where he was gassed. Jean-Claude's mother, a French citizen, was spared. She took her two sons to hide from the Nazis in the Free Zone in south-central France. After the war, Jean-Claude's mother supported the family by working as a seamstress, and although she tried to get a pension from the French government, the authorities refused to grant it because of her husband's Romanian ancestry. In the 1960s,

Jean-Claude worked at various odd jobs before writing his first play in 1967. He has since written more than twenty-five plays and a half dozen screenplays, the most notable of which was the one he co-wrote with François Truffault for the film *The Last Metro*, but he is certainly best known for his Holocaust triptych: *Dreyfus* (1974), *L'Atelier* (1979), and *Zone libre* (1991). *Dreyfus* is a pre-Holocaust drama about the Jewish response to anti-Semitism; set in Poland in 1931, a group of Jewish actors rehearse the Dreyfus story, allowing Grumberg to make parallels between French anti-Semitism and the persecution of Polish Jews in the 1930s. *Zone libre* portrays the tribulations of French Jews during the Holocaust as the Zilberberg family flees from the Nazis and are sheltered by an elderly gentile farmer in the Free Zone. The plight of the Zilberbergs–hungry, frightened for their lives, forced to deny their Jewish identities–depicts the extent to which Jews were willing to go to ensure their survival.

L'Atelier, the third part of the "trilogy," delineates the predicament of Jewish survivor families in post-Holocaust France. *L'Atelier* premiered at the Odéon Théâtre in Paris on 18 April 1979 in a production that Grumberg co-directed with Maurice Bénichou and Jacques Rosner. The notable feature of this production was Grumberg assuming the role of Léon, the owner of the sweatshop. In 1980, French drama critics awarded *L'Atelier* the Prix du Syndicat de la Critique for best play, the Molière prize for best new drama, and the Prix Ibsen for outstanding theatrical achievement of the year; *L'Atelier* has since been prescribed as required reading for the baccalauréat program in France. Also in 1980, *L'Atelier* was staged at the Théâtre du Gymnase in Marseilles and was translated into English and performed as *The Workroom* during the 1979–1980 theater season of the Milwaukee Repertory Company in Milwaukee, Wisconsin. In November 1981, Philip Minor mounted the play at the Trinity Square Repertory Company in Providence, Rhode Island, with Cynthia Carle as Simone. Using a translation by Tom Kempinski, Nancy Meckler, in January 1982, directed *The Workroom* at the Long Wharf Theater in New Haven, Connecticut, with Marcia Jean Kurtz playing Simone. The New York premiere of the play occurred that year, based on a new translation by Daniel A. Stein and Sara O'Connor; these performances were directed by Aaron Levine for the American Theater Alliance at the South Street Theater. Another notable production was Gildas Bourdet's staging at the Théâtre Hébertot in Paris during 1999, where the play won the Prix Molière again. The most recent noteworthy run of the play was Israeli director Moni Yakim's production for the Unbound Theater from 19 February to 12 March 2005 at the Manhattan Theater Source in Greenwich Village, featuring Anna Guttormsgaard, founder of the Unbound Theater, as Simone; Yakim had an intimate knowledge of the play, having personally known Grumberg since the 1970s.

In the tradition of Michel Vinaver, Grumberg has been characterized as a practitioner of quotidian theater who presents the minutiae of ordinary events in everyday life.[34] Eschewing portrayal of the survivor experience in experimental form, which would negate the realism of a postwar French sweatshop, *The Workroom* is instead structured in ten naturalistic scenes. To reflect the ennui of the world of work, the setting never changes, although the play spans the years 1945 to 1952. The language spoken is literal and direct, never metaphorical or evocative, with Grumberg showing a flair for reproducing the small talk of working class women in postwar France. Grumberg himself worked as a tailor's apprentice and thus was intimately familiar with postwar French sweatshops.

The women in the sweatshop who labor as seamstresses are non-Jews who work with Simone, who is the only Jew among this closely knit group. Gisèle, at times frustrated over her own domestic life, is down to earth, caring, and entertains the others with her singing. Prim, proper, privileged, and prudish, Madame Laurence is the wife of a police officer who may have collaborated with the Nazis in rounding up Jews for deportation. Mimi is young, unpretentious, and outspoken, often speaking her mind no matter how vulgar or bawdy the language. Marie, the coquette of the group, spends much of her time talking about her impending wedding. The women are joined by an unnamed Jewish presser who survived the extermination camps; after he quits the job unexpectedly, he is succeeded by Jean, an activist with communist affiliations. Léon, the Jewish owner of the shop, is a crass businessman who constantly urges the women to work overtime to meet deadlines for getting the fabrics stitched. His ruthlessness is tempered by his peacemaker wife Hélène, whose sister was deported in 1943.

The focal point of the play is Grumberg's semi-autobiographical account of how his mother, through the persona of Simone, adapted to the hardships of postwar life in France as the wife of a deportee struggling to raise her two sons. Her Romanian husband was deported because he had no French citizenship, yet Simone, due to her French ancestry, was spared the agony of the horrors of the Shoah. Simone, like Grumberg's own mother, works as a seamstress all day, taking whatever time off that she can to go through French bureaucratic channels to search for her missing husband. Simone seeks to receive a widow's pension from the French government if they will grant her a certificate that officially confirms the death of her husband. Without such a document, Simone, who has hopes that her husband is still alive in some type of camp for refugees, looks to the Red Cross for help with the search to trace him. Leo Eitinger, who did pioneering work on the psychology of Holocaust survivors and their families, explains Simone's mentality: "An extreme sense of insecurity resulted in the need to search for someone, somewhere, who might by a miracle still be alive."[35] In the early part of the play, Simone's *raison d'être* is her search for her missing husband.

Simone tells the presser that she often dreams of finding her husband among the innocent bystanders in the street, and the fact that the police will not issue her a death certificate confirms her hope that he remains alive. When Simone reveals that her husband was on a transport destined for Lublin-Maidanek, the presser's silence indicates his intuitive understanding of the fate of her husband. After Simone confirms that her husband was thirty-eight but looked slightly older, wore glasses, and was balding, the presser, without malice, calmly explains the fate of those who appeared to be unfit to work in the camps. Simone, unwilling to accept an unbearable truth, responds, "Everyone says that he'll still return, that they're everywhere–in Austria, Poland, Russia–that they're being nursed and put back on their feet before being sent home! (*The presser nods his head in silence.*) Thirty-eight isn't old, it really isn't old."[36]

As I mentioned earlier, survivors often immersed themselves in their work and families to diffuse the traumas associated with the Holocaust. Simone preoccupies herself during the day with work and at night with raising her two sons. When asked by her colleagues when, if ever, she takes her mind off her agony, Simone replies, "Here, with you ... " (215). In his essay on *L'Atelier*, Robert L. King characterizes Simone's immersion into the community of work as "psychic numbing" to assuage the horrible truth about a trauma that overwhelms any sense of rational understanding. King writes, "Through Grumberg's artistry, an audience is caught up in the rhythms of the work place, of its speech and of its silences until we see their totality as a code of social conduct, a set of unwritten rules for coping."[37] As the seamstresses talk of their family lives, their working conditions, and the political landscape in France, they bond together in such a way that Simone is provided with a support structure and a new family to replace the husband that she lost. The mutual goal of these women–to sew garments that will enable them to fill orders for clothing–provides Simone with the compensation necessary for survival and a means of psychological sanctuary from the traumatic effects of the Holocaust. Commenting about the repetitive nature of the work the women do, which King referred to as psychic numbing, David Bradby wrote that the play's "mood remains broadly nostalgic, emphasising the simple contradiction that although the workshop was experienced as a treadmill, it also gave respite from the anguished loneliness of those who had survived the holocaust."[38]

Despite the conviviality in the workroom, the specter of the anti-Semitism that allowed French citizens to collaborate with the Nazis sets the undertone for the play. Simone's attitude toward her colleagues is consistently generous, and although she maintains an aura of stoicism and sews without complaining throughout her trauma, the strictures of latent anti-Semitism work against her as a survivor in postwar France. As was discussed in chapter 11, Holocaust survivors learned to keep silent about their misery because their periods of depression were often callously and inappropriately compared to any layman's typical misfortunes in life. Upon meeting Simone initially, Mimi, who immediately recognizes her as a Jew, confides to Gisèle that Simone deserves no sympathy: "So? We all have our misfortunes. I lost my shoes" (141). Gisèle and Marie have their own social world to worry about and cannot relate to Simone's problems. When Gisèle finally learns that Simone is Jewish, having conversed intimately with her for two years, she is incredulous about the revelation, then insensitively asks, "By the way, then maybe you could tell me what was the problem between you and the Germans during the war?" (173). Simone actually breaks down in tears at work twice during the play for no reason apparent to her co-workers. Mimi even suggests an antidote: "A good screw from time to time would do you a world of good and chase away the blues" (213).

Léon's crass attitude toward life, coupled with his unsympathetic regard for Jewish suffering, also extends to the Holocaust and demonstrates how the misery of survivors and their relatives was exacerbated by ubiquitous insouciance. Léon admires the presser merely for his work ethic, realizing that surviving the concentration camps made him a man of iron, tough as nails, one who never complains, an excellent worker because of "natural selection" (163). When Hélène confesses that she cannot look at the presser, implying that he reminds her of the fact that her own sister was deported while she survived, Léon caustically says, "He's no different from anyone else, is he?" (163). After the presser confides to Simone that her husband is probably dead, Simone leaves, and Léon, without tact, says to the presser about Simone's missing husband, "On the shelves of German housewives, in their stock of black soap, that's where he is, that's where you should look for him, not in offices, not on lists, not in files" (183). Léon explains to the presser that during the war, replete with fake papers, he posed as a gentile under the name of Léon Richard and had to "suffer" the pangs of hiding from the Nazis. After hearing this patronizing tale of "survival," the presser, fed up with his boss's vulgar attitude toward those who have experienced the survivor syndrome at first hand, quits the job. Léon, refusing to recognize the agony of the survivor, shouts as the presser is leaving, "But you're not the only ones who suffered, damn it, not the only ones! I also had to do despicable things in order to survive" (189).

Léon is oblivious to Simone's suffering as well. He refuses to give Simone time off from work to go through the extended bureaucratic procedures necessary to locate her missing husband, and when he suggests that she run those "errands" on Saturday, Simone, in tears, blurts out, "But offices are closed!" (197). When Mimi defends Simone, stating that in her free time she must also buy groceries and cook for her children, Léon mocks the notion of paying reparations to surviving family members: "She's entitled to zilch! Zilch! Pensions are given to the French, not to stateless persons of Rumanian extraction" (198). Moreover, Léon asserts, those who returned from the concentration camps were all "nut cases" that the French had to accommodate, like the presser. When Simone receives the death certificate she has been seeking, Léon can only comment that he will be able to get more work out of her: "Fine ... Fine. Now she won't have to run around from office to office, maybe she'll stay put from time to time" (202). Even after Simone's son announces that his mother is being hospitalized from exhaustion, Léon's only concern is that office productivity will suffer with her absence. Léon's crass attitude also extends to the victims of the Holocaust, for he argues that they died without proper burial and thus are not fit to be memorialized: "I don't want to have anything to do with the dead, the dead are dead, no? And these dead are a thousand times deader than the other dead because they weren't even ... " (232).

Simone's misery is also due to the latent anti-Semitism of a French bureaucracy that is uncaring and unsympathetic to the needs of Holocaust survivors. The French authorities for years allow Simone to chase from one bureaucratic office to another, refusing to provide compensation or a pension to her simply because her husband, deported by French police, was not a French citizen. When Simone finally receives the death certificate, she reads on it that her husband mysteriously perished at Drancy, even though Simone learned that he left the internment camp on 3 March 1943 on a train destined for Lublin-Maidanek. Hélène's comment to Simone about such certificates that trace all Jewish deaths in Vichy France to Drancy reflects the crassness of a government that refuses culpability, hoping to put the stigma of the Holocaust behind them: "In that case, no one went there, no one got into their boxcars, no one was burned; if they simply died in Drancy or Compiègne, or Pithiviers, who'll remember them? Who'll remember them?" (203).

At the end of the play, Simone, inundated with a constant barrage of anti-Semitism through the shared culpability of an uncaring French bureaucracy, an insensitive employer, and caring yet careless colleagues, winds up being hospitalized. After seven years of harassment, including years searching in vain for her missing husband under the burden of realizing what her husband must have suffered simply because he was Romanian, the cumulative effects take its toll: Simone is ill because of exhaustion.

The Workroom not only provides audiences with an understanding of survivor family mentality, but also offers a portrait of the psyche of the children in survivor families. In the last scene of the play, which occurs in 1952, Simone's youngest son, age eleven or twelve, visits the sweatshop to announce that his mother has been hospitalized. Born in 1939, Grumberg would have been virtually that same age in 1952, and thus, the play in part becomes a memoir for Grumberg of the harsh realities of adolescent life in a Holocaust survivor family.

Studies of the children of Holocaust survivors confirm that they matured quickly and felt overprotective of their parents. Janice F. Bistritz, who conducted research on pathology in Holocaust survivor families, discovered, "The pressures of conformity and 'parenting the parents' contributed to a sense of guilt in the children, who were constantly struggling with their own development while also being urged to be all and do all in their power for their parents."[39] Two different studies conducted by J. Sigal and L. Podietz, respectively, confirmed that because children in Holocaust survivor families considered their parents to be depressed, paranoid, and withdrawn due to the trauma they experienced, offspring became very protective of their fathers and mothers.[40] Moreover, in writing about the psychological consequences of the Holocaust on the offspring of survivors, Leslie Berger noted, "Children of the survivors express greater responsibility for preventing their mother from emotional upset."[41] Estranged from their parents while they were in the Free Zone, Simone's children grew up virtually independent. Subsequent to being reunited with their mother after the war, they became overprotective of her. When Léon wonders why Simone will not search for another husband, she counters, "The children are too old, they would be miserable, they're used to being the men in the house" (222). During Simone's rendezvous at the Thermometer Café with a potential mate, her sons, fearing their mother would be hurt, were so obnoxious to her suitor that he later abandoned the courtship. After revealing that he and his older brother took their mother to the hospital, the child tells the other seamstresses that he and his brother will manage because they are self-sufficient as the men of the household. The child dispels any notion that he is soft and cannot be the man of the family: he regrets having to wear a girl's coat supplied by the Americans, dislikes being called a lamb by Gisèle, refuses to take money as charity, declines accepting candy as if he were a boy being rewarded for good behavior, and is rebuffed by Jean's willingness to give him a kiss because, as he tells the socialist, "Men don't kiss each other" (238). Moreover, to stress that Simone does well under the protective care of her sons, the child admits that his mother never cries at home, even though we know that she does so at work. The child leaves the seamstresses with the notion that his traumatized mother will always remain safe in the hands of her offspring: "Later on, me and my brother will work and she won't have to work ever again" (238).

Unlike *The Puppetmaster of Lodz* and *Singer,* two plays that focus on the palpable traumatic psychological effects of the Holocaust on survivors, *The Workroom* delineates the often intangible results of the Shoah on family members of Holocaust victims. All too frequently, the Holocaust is delineated in terms of the number of dead or by the impact the trauma has had on the walking dead. Grumberg's achievement in *The Workroom* is the way he frames the effects of the Holocaust on ordinary survivor family members who must learn to integrate their otherness in an uncaring and thoughtless postwar society in which individuals were concerned primarily with renewing their own lives. By focusing on the quotidian, Grumberg challenges audiences to view the workroom as a microcosm for the difficulties shared by survivor families in coping with life among indifferent Jews and gentiles during the postwar era.

13 Holocaust Survivor Memory

History is not merely shaped by historians but is also created by Holocaust memory shared by survivors and the families of those who survived. After the war, memorials in the form of statues, museums, or concentration camp sites to honor the dead were built throughout Eastern Europe. However, as Geoffrey H. Hartman remarks, these monuments not only served to close the book on a shameful past, divesting us of the obligation to remember, but also, as profiteering, exploited and trivialized the Holocaust.[1] Moreover, the individual angst of the Shoah became lost in these communally prescribed public rituals associated with collective memory. Collective attempts at national healing can even lead to false memory and forgetfulness. At the other extreme for many Holocaust survivors was the need to keep silent instead of commemorating the dead through monuments, for there was a strong desire to forget the trauma and to avoid being associated with a shameful past. Aharon Appelfeld commented, "So we learned silence. It was not easy to keep silent. But it was a good way out for all of us. For what, when all is said and done, was there to tell? To us as well it began to sound like something imaginary, which ought not to be believed."[2] However, keeping silent, as Elie Wiesel has acknowledged, only strengthens the voices that wish to deny the Shoah or those that prefer not to be reminded of its horrors.

Holocaust memory was evident after the war through testimonials and memoirs of survivors. Initially, the primary aim of Holocaust memory was to provide historical information and knowledge about the genocide. Sidra DeKoven Ezrahi reminds us of other reasons for preserving Holocaust memory: to bear witness, to commemorate the dead, to absolve individuals from any notions of complicity, to seek justice, and to warn humanity of its future potential for similar genocide.[3] Commemorating the dead is particularly significant, for the victims were robbed of everything they owned–their culture, possessions, and family members–and thus remembrance is the only thing that we can grant them. One of the most salient reasons for preserving Holocaust memory is that it allows us to understand the mentality of survivors, whose essence was reduced to nothingness. As Lawrence L. Langer states, "When memory imprints on us the meaning of the presence of 'absence' and animates the ghost that such a burden has imposed on our lives, then the heritage of the Holocaust will have begun to acquire some authenticity in our postwar culture."[4] Certainly, the most vital purpose of Holocaust memory is to bear witness. As Annette Wieviorka realizes, "All the testimonies of the deportees respond to one imperative: to remember, not to forget."[5] For Jews, as Wiesel reiterates, forgetting means not only denying the self, but also denying the Nazi attempt to eradicate all Jews.

Memory, by its very nature, is always fallible and therefore tainted. When writing or speaking from any present vantage point, memory is particularly unlikely to recall what was truth twenty, thirty, or forty years ago, when, as a young person, one viewed the world differently. There is always an abyss between the reality of an event and its recurrence in memory years later. Moreover, memory may fade with time, shift as a result of brain or bodily traumas, fragment, remain selective or modified, be challenged by competing memories, or be repressed. When memory is transferred to a play, we are then dealing with represented rather than unmediated reality. Oral testimony is memory communicated directly; however, as Lawrence L. Langer notes, "Writing invites reflection, commentary, interpretation, by the author as well as the reader."[6] Memory that is dramatized onstage is therefore invariably tainted by the playwright and consequently must be even more suspect.

In addition to typical problems associated with memory, there are specific questions endemic to the nature of Holocaust memory. Charlotte Delbo addresses the issue of how concentration camp survivors typically lost their sense of self, which included a loss of memory: "First, human beings are stripped of what makes them human, then their memory leaves them. Memory peels off like tatters, tatters of burned skin."[7] Survival in *l'univers concentrationnaire* may have even depended upon memory denial; moreover, the conscious mind had difficulty processing what seemed to be incomprehensible in the camps, marring the possibility of accurate memory retrieval in the future. The SS in the concentration camps did not make memory retrieval any easier, constantly reminding the deportees that no one would believe the tales of any survivors, most of which would have to be considered unbelievable. As Primo Levi explains in *The Drowned and the Saved*, "At any rate, the entire history of the brief 'millennial Reich' can be reread as a war against memory, an Orwellian falsification of memory, falsification of reality, negation of reality."[8]

Holocaust memory is intrinsically related to loss, violence, suffering, and degradation. Survivors often cannot recognize themselves as the nonentities or dysfunctional human beings that they became during their incarceration, nor do they want to remember, for doing so leads to guilt and shame; often, survivors realized that the self that inhabited the camps was nearly impossible to access. Human nature tends to dwell on pleasant memories and bury painful ones in the inner recesses of the mind, and since the Holocaust produced such an imposing burden on any survivor, memory inevitably becomes diminished, suppressed, or selective. Writing about Holocaust memory, Karein K. Goertz stated, "As Sigmund Freud, Joseph Breuer, and Pierre Janet observed more than a century ago, the brain cannot process traumatic experiences as it does other experiences."[9] Such memories of trauma are not stored in words and symbols as normal memories would be but instead are retrieved through somato-sensory levels, such as during nightmares or in response to certain stimuli.

Being possessed by such horrid memories can conflict with the necessity to bear witness. Thus, Holocaust survivors are almost always torn, for as Lawrence L. Langer recognizes, "Memory can be a palliative as well as an avenue to a darker reality."[10] Moreover, when survivors are urged to dredge up their experiences through conscious memory and then articulate them intelligently, language intrudes. When one is asked to explain what is essentially senseless, one's words inevitably fail because the old language cannot do justice to a traumatic event of such magnitude that resists articulation. As Ellen S. Fine astutely remarks, "Survivors of the Holocaust are torn between the mission to bear witness and an equally compelling fear of betraying the sanctity of the subject."[11] Thus, Holocaust survivors may taint memory further by trying to find the appropriate words to convey the proper way to memorialize the dead.

This chapter focuses on the fallibility of Holocaust memory. Two plays that will provide a useful framework for examining the inherent problems associated with Holocaust survivor memory are American playwright Emily Mann's *Annulla: An Autobiography* and French dramatist Armand Gatti's *La Deuxième existence du camp de Tatenberg (The Second Life of Tatenberg Camp)*.

After receiving her Master of Fine Arts degree from the University of Minnesota in 1976, Emily Mann became a directing fellow for the Guthrie Theater in Minneapolis and served there as associate director for the following two years. She then did a stint as resident director for the Brooklyn Academy of Music Theater Company from 1981 to 1982 before becoming the artistic director of Princeton University's McCarter Theater. Since 1990, she has directed or supervised over eighty-five productions there, and was largely responsible for a 1994 Tony Award designating the McCarter for excellence as a regional theater. Mann's theatrical achievements have been well rewarded with six Obies, a prestigious Guggenheim Fellowship, two National Endowment for the Arts grants, a Helen Hayes Award, the Dramatists Guild Hull-Warriner Award, the Rosamond Gilder Award, and a McKnight Fellowship; she was also the co-winner of the Great American Play Contest in 1985.

Mann's plays focus on historical or sociological issues. Her father, Arthur Mann, was a distinguished professor of American history who taught first at the Massachusetts Institute of Technology (MIT), then at Smith College, and finally at the University of Chicago. During Emily's senior year in high school, her father, as head of the American Jewish Committee's Oral History Project, recorded the memories of Holocaust survivors. While listening to the transcripts, Emily was emotionally moved by the testimony of a Czechoslovakian survivor of Treblinka interviewed by her daughter. When the precocious teenager was told by her father that the tapes could not be made public, Emily became determined to explore history by conducting her own testimonials. She was spurred on by the fact that her grandmother's family on her mother's side was virtually wiped out by the Nazis in Ostrolenka, Poland.[12] In 1974, while she was doing an oral history project as an undergraduate at Radcliffe, Emily went to Europe to visit her grandmother's village in Poland and to interview Annulla Allen, a Holocaust survivor who was her college roommate's aunt, living in Hampstead Heath, London. After Mann graduated from college in 1974, she was awarded a Bush Fellowship at the Guthrie Theater. While there, she saw actress Barbara Bryne in *Tartuffe* and realized that she was perfect to play Annulla in the stage play Mann was thinking of writing. After reading the transcript of Mann's interview with Annulla, Bryne agreed to play the role.

Annulla: Autobiography of a Survivor premiered at the Guthrie Theater's Guthrie 2 in 1977 in a two-act production starring Barbara Bryne and directed by Mann herself. In 1978, Bryne revived the role of Annulla at Gregory Mosher's Goodman Theater's Stage 2 in Chicago. This version was recorded in the late 1970s for Earplay as part of National Public Radio. After Annulla's death in 1978, Mann revised the play's title and, as a result of her friend Timothy Near's suggestions, changed the monologue by adding a disembodied voice as a second character. The retitled one-act version, *Annulla: An Autobiography*, directed by Near, debuted during the 1984–1985 season of the Repertory Theater of St. Louis. This version of the play was presented at the Alliance Theatre in Atlanta in 1986 under direction by Near, and was produced at the New Theater of Brooklyn during a brief run in late October and November 1988 with Mann directing Linda Hunt as Annulla. *Annulla: An Autobiography* made its West Coast debut during a staging by the Eclectic Company Theatre in West Hollywood, California, in January 2005. The play's New York premiere was a production directed by Pamela Hall that ran from 14 May to 11 June 2006, off-Broadway at the Theatre at St. Luke's.

Annulla: An Autobiography is written in the form of a testimonial or oral history similar to documentary drama. Instead of transcribing and then editing courtroom testimony, which typifies the nature of documentary drama, Mann edited a transcript of an interview that she conducted, adding herself as a disembodied voice questioning and prompting the interviewee. Mann stated that she wanted to capture the unique voice of Annulla: "I am a purist. I feel it's my job to conduct an interview well enough that, through editing and boiling down, I will get all the poetry of that person's speech. I will get what they want to say. I'm very careful about not changing what they want to say."[13] According to Mann, the technique of writing good testimonial drama involves careful listening and then allowing the audience to share the same direct interaction experience that she had as an interviewer/listener.[14] Mann's goal for this type of theater is to allow real-life characters to act as witnesses to history–essentially carrying on the oral tradition that her father was enamored with as a historian. Attempting to be objective as one who observes and then records historical testimony, Mann adopted Brecht's alienation techniques that became a model for so many German documentary dramatists. In her "Playwright's Note," Mann writes, "For the most part, these are Annulla Allen's own words told to me during the summer of 1974, in London. And my own words told to Timothy Near during the winter of 1984–1985 in St. Louis."[15] The audience is alienated from empathizing with Annulla, whose monologue is interrupted by the disembodied voice; furthermore, the Holocaust tale is twice removed from 1940s real time, as it is narrated by Annulla in 1974, who is questioned by Emily Mann in 1985. However, the objectivity supposedly gained through this type of testimonial theater is misleading, for as Christopher Bigsby has demonstrated, the "shaping hand of the playwright is present even in the questions asked and hence in the answers elicited," and the conversation itself has a template chosen by the author.[16]

Unlike Brecht's major plays, which are rarely set in a domestic environment because they are essentially historical dramas that were parables for current events in Germany, Mann's play occurs in Annulla's north London kitchen. Annulla discusses her past life during teatime and afterwards, while she prepares dinner. Mann views the kitchen as the perfect learning environment where women will loosen up to speak about their historical backgrounds. Speaking to Alexis Greene, Mann acknowledged, "I find that you can talk about the horrors of life and that, in domestic situations, people will listen. Much more than if you put that in an austere setting where people put up their guard. People's guard comes right down in the kitchen. Putting those plays in a kitchen was a very conscious choice."[17] In an interview conducted on 18 May 1995, Mann confirmed, "As I've said a number of times, I think I've learned more in the kitchens of wonderful older women that I've known as a child than I learned at Harvard, from my grandmother, my aunts, and neighbors. Just sitting around the kitchen table while they're cooking and listen."[18]

A vibrant woman whose charm, humor, and resiliency make her appear to be much younger than her seventy-four years, Annulla recounts her life story to the Voice. Annulla was born in Lvov, Galicia, which, at the time of her birth, was part of Austria but was eventually incorporated into Poland and then Ukraine. She later settled in Germany, Italy, and finally England. As the Wandering Jew of Europe, she managed to learn seven languages in her lifetime. When the Nazis invaded Vienna in 1938, Annulla's brother, a budding biochemist, had to flee after his laboratory was destroyed. During Kristallnacht, her husband was taken from Vienna and sent to Dachau, but Annulla, who was thought to be too beautiful to be Jewish and was able to fool the Nazis with a Czech accent, was spared deportation. Posing as an Aryan who needed her husband's approval in order to sell her house to the Gestapo, Annulla brazenly went to Dachau to secure his signature. Eleven months later, her husband was released for good conduct. Meanwhile, her eight-year-old son was hidden from the Nazis by a charitable organization in Sweden. Annulla's mother and sister Czecha were not so lucky, for they were shot by the Nazis in Poland. In 1939, disguised as an Aryan, Annulla rejoined her husband in England, where her spouse had managed to take refuge by means of an exit visa.

Despite the fact that Annulla has the ability to recall the minutiae of her life with regard to certain dates and specific events, her age, combined with the trauma of the anti-Semitism endemic to eastern Europe that led to the Holocaust, have tainted her memory. Mann confirmed to Alexis Greene that all of her plays focus on how an individual confronts some type of traumatic event.[19] *Annulla: An*

Autobiography is structured much in the manner in which the brain deals with trauma–Annulla's memory is fragmented, askew, disjointed, and thus her autobiography is told haphazardly without any discernment of chronological order. Moreover, with regard to Annulla's age, Christopher Bigsby perceptively comments, "In a play about the necessity of remembering we have a central figure for whom continued life seems to turn on the ability to forget."[20] Alvin Goldfarb noted that when the play was staged by the Repertory Theater of St. Louis, the sound of a clock ticking in the background underscored the idea that time will further obliterate memory and thus obscure comprehension.[21] There are numerous times in the play where Annulla demonstrates faulty memory. Placing herself in Berlin during the 1919 workers' riots, Annulla admits, "You know, I was so frivolous that I can not even remember that. All I remember is that everyone spoke Russian to me" (11). Annulla recalls a family trip to Heist when she was eleven, but she forgets the age of her sister Mania at that time, claiming "I don't remember" (2). Annulla even mentions how trauma has adversely affected her memory: "I remember almost nothing of *my* childhood, but I had such an unhappy childhood I *want* to forget it" (3). With regard to the *Anschluss* in Vienna after Kristallnacht, Annulla confides, "The SS came to our house. I can't remember, it was so fast" (4). When Annulla's husband was in Dachau, a Jew who also posed as an Aryan wanted to emigrate illegally across the Czech border with her. Annulla's memory of the incident is vague: "The cheek of that man. He lost a job when the Nazis came. I can't remember what" (13). The Voice, recalling her grandmother's funeral, where her daughter (Mann's mother) expressed regret at how quickly time passed during life, stresses the importance of memory when life is so transient. Annulla's faulty memory reinforces the need to record and preserve the past, which, concomitantly, was also the purpose of the Voice's trip to Poland.

Annulla's utopian view that females are superior to men is challenged by the reality of her own disparaging opinions of the women closest to her, making us wonder if whatever she claims to have remembered can be trusted as the truth. Annulla's view of women is terribly conflicted. She is writing a six-hour play titled *The Matriarchs*, which argues that global matriarchy would absolve the world of its barbarism and tyranny. Annulla states, "You see, only women know mother-love. It is the most powerful response in the world of a positive kind. Men have strong feelings too, but they are violent. They should not be allowed to rule. A woman's *natural* instinct is loving" (16). Meanwhile, Annulla seems to forget that her own family history contradicts her view of women as consistently benevolent and loving. Speaking of her mother, Annulla recalls, "I hated my mother. She hated me" (7). Later, she reveals, "Ach, you know I *abused* my mother. I called her names. I was so bitter about her. My mother was a tyrant" (8). Annulla also expresses negative feelings about her sister Ada: "You know, it's difficult not to call Ada gruesome. She's terribly gruesome. A terribly gruesome person" (11). Mann herself has commented on the inconsistency of Annulla's adoration for female political leaders coupled with her distrust of men: "And she talks about how the one really destructive relationship in her life was with her mother and how she adored her father and always wanted his approval. She hated Indira Gandhi. She's not exactly consistent in her political theory."[22]

Mann, speaking through the Voice, challenges Annulla's historical memory: "I'd love to believe that women are the civilizing force in the world but I don't believe they are. And I don't believe that historically they have been. I think women are just as capable of brutality and murder as men" (100). Indeed, perhaps the most salient point underlying the text of the play is how the traumatized, tainted mind can be relied upon to reflect the truth associated with the Shoah accurately. How can someone traumatized by the Holocaust be a reliable witness? Research conducted by Claudia Koonz on the role of women during the Third Reich contradicts Annulla's assertions that women did not have fascist tendencies. Koonz writes that in 1939, there were three million girls in the Hitler Youth and eight million women in organizations sympathetic to the Nazis.[23] In large numbers, women attended Nazi rallies, and when the Nazis color-coded the ballots during elections held in the early 1930s, they discovered that women voted to support National Socialism in nearly the same percentages as men.[24] Female social workers, teachers, and nurses who worked for the Reich turned over those people with mental health problems, Jews, socialists, and other "undesirables" to the authorities to face

deportation. There were more than three thousand female concentration camp guards, and many witnesses claimed the women were
more brutal than the men; some of these adjutants, like the notorious Irma Griese at Auschwitz, took cruel sadomasochism to its most
extreme level. In summing up the roles that women had in the Third
Reich, Michael Burleigh and Wolfgang Wippermann noted, "Like men,
women were simultaneously victims of and participants in National
Socialism, with some of the latter equalling their male colleagues in
inhumanity and cruelty."[25]

Mann's play calls into question the precarious nature of
Holocaust memory. What are we to believe from a traumatized woman
who constantly contradicts herself, stating, for example, "I am a
woman who never has any time" (2), and then, one hour later, tells
the Voice, "I have so much time now, I am alone" (17)? Can we trust
the memory of a seventy-four-year-old woman whose depression and
recurring Holocaust nightmares once led to her cancer? Can we take
seriously Annulla's assertion that the Americans, British, and French
treatment of Germany after World War I caused the rise of Nazism
that led to the persecution of Jews (13), especially when she has experienced first hand the anti-Semitism ubiquitous in many European
countries in which she has lived? Finally, how can we validate the
play she is writing and the Women's Party she seeks to create when
her own behavior seems contradictory to her utopian ideals? In short,
Mann's play asks us to examine the often-tenuous nature of traumatized Holocaust memory, which, in this instance, is perhaps even less
suspect coming from a feisty survivor with a zest for life.

Armand Gatti was born on 24 January 1924, in Monaco; his
parents were French and Russian immigrants who raised their child
in the Catholic tradition. In 1942, he joined the maquis, the French
Resistance in the Corrèze. The following year, Gatti was arrested
by the Vichy police and condemned to death, but because of his
youth, he was sent to the Neuengamme concentration camp near
Hamburg. As Number 713 in the labor camp, Gatti was assigned to
construct submarine shelters two hundred meters below ground. He
managed to escape the camp when a diving bell accident momentarily distracted the guards. After the war, Gatti worked as a journalist

for fourteen years–a career that provided him with the opportunity to travel to China, Korea, and Latin America to report on social and political struggles. In 1955, marking the tenth year since the end of the war, Gatti visited Mauthausen in Austria and was astonished to discover that the former concentration camp was still home to displaced persons who had nowhere to go. Influenced by French director Jean Vilar, Gatti embarked on a career in theater in 1959. Since then, the Holocaust has figured prominently in his writings. His first film, *L'enclos*, which Gatti himself directed in 1960, was set in Mauthausen; Gatti selected former deportees to play the prisoners. His first play about the Holocaust was *L'enfant rat* (1962), which, deriving from his own memories of deportation, focused on the obsessions haunting six survivors, referred to as numbers, who labored in the salt mines of a concentration camp. In 1967, Gatti directed an allegorical play with a science fiction plot, *Chroniques d'une planète provisoire*, which was about Eichmann's plan to trade one million Hungarian Jews for ten thousand trucks that were to be supplied by the Allied Forces. In 1978, Gatti wrote and directed six one-hour films about Roger Roussel, a member of the French Resistance who was executed by the Nazis in 1944. Finally, in 1989, Gatti composed *Le Chant d'amour des alphabets d'Auschwitz*, rewritten as *Adam quoi?* in July 1993 as a Talmudic reading of excerpts, or ten "Alphabets," from the literature on Auschwitz composed by survivors who had written about their experiences in the camp.

Gatti's most well-known Holocaust drama is *La Deuxième existence du camp de Tatenberg*, which he began composing in 1959.[26] Three years later, on 13 April 1962, the play premiered at Lyon's Théâtre des Célestins in a production directed by Gisèle Tavet. On 22 February 1967, the play, under direction by Jean Hurstel, began a run on a small experimental stage at the Institute of Theatrical Research at Strasbourg University. In this production, Hurstel choreographed beams of light to reflect the various levels of the shades of memory. Outside France, the play was staged by Joachim Fontheim in Essen on 9 January 1965; in productions at the Gulbenkian Theatre in Canterbury in 1979 and at the Lyric Theatre in Belfast during April 1979, both of which were directed and translated by Joseph B. Long; in a German version directed by Klaus Höring at the Akademie Theater in Vienna in 1984; and by Eric Salama at the Théâtre du Garage in Geneva during 1993.

The Second Life of Tatenberg Camp is stylistically the most convoluted Holocaust drama written to date. The form of the play is unlike any type of Western theater and has little in common with realism, naturalism, symbolist theater, epic theater, expressionism, surrealism, or even theater of the absurd. In her book on Gatti, Dorothy Knowles credits Gatti's experience with Chinese theater as contributing to his desire to free his plays from all confining limits and create action situated in several simultaneous frames in different time scales.[27] Gatti's fragmented plot, viewed from diverse consciences, and his use of multiple perspectives occurring in the past, present, and future, are far removed from any realist structure. Gatti's theater is based upon a radical transformation of time and space, an imaginary universe that has no limits but is created by the actors from one moment to the next. Gatti explains, "My theatrical search consists, however, in trying to live in *several parallel worlds at the same time*: to create theatrical simultaneity."[28] As John Ireland has indicated, for Gatti, the individual experience of the Holocaust is bound up in a collective experience that forces memory to be continually in flux, hence the need to portray on stage this radical intermingling of multiple representations of time and space.[29] Bettina Knapp notes that Gatti believes that since each person possesses hundreds of lives but is aware of only one existence at a time, the restrictive nature of memory must be restructured so that individuals can live in different planes at different times.[30] Richard N. Coe has described Gatti's technique as similar to Cubist art in which space breaks down, identity is depicted as fragmented, and then symbols are used to reconstitute this reality into an immanent form that endows characters with a more profound significance.[31] This innovative type of theater works extremely well for Gatti, who is seeking to convey the abstract unreality of the memory of *l'univers concentrationnaire* among survivors who are consequently fragmented in time and space.

The Second Life of Tatenberg Camp is set in the town of Grein, Austria, and in Vienna; the Danube River flows between the two cities and into each of them. As Agnieszka Tworek has noted, the play begins with a "Presentation-Aide Memoire" followed by four scenes that take place in the present, four flashbacks, and four episodes ("Alternation," "Ballad of the Parallel Parades," "Hypcrmnesia," and "Flash-Forward") that occur in the future.[32] The fictional Tatenberg, the "hill of death," becomes a composite image of the concentration camp that haunts the play's protagonist, Ilya Moïssevitch. In his introduction to the English translation of the play, Joseph Long explains the connection between Tatenberg and Mauthausen, the site of Gatti's visit in 1955, the subject of *L'Enclos*, and now the specter that haunts the play:

> Tatenberg is a fictitious name which represents all of the camps, but its location refers more specifically to the infamous camp at Mauthausen, in Austria, with its granite quarries, close to where the river Enns meets the Danube. Some 200,000 people are believed to have died at Mauthausen, between 1938 and 1945.[33]

The past in the play corresponds to the life of the deportees at Mauthausen/Tatenberg and the period after 1945 when refugees remained on the campsite's railway station as squatters without a homeland. The railway station was a facade, replete with signs indicating exits, entrances, restrooms, ticket offices, restaurants, waiting rooms, and even a broken clock that read twelve o'clock, all of which was created to calm the nerves of the deportees. The world of the past is envisioned through the consciousness of Baltic Jew Moïssevitch, who, as a survivor of several concentration camps, including Birkenau and the fictional Goldpilz, now works as a carny at the fairgrounds in Grein and at the Prater in Vienna.

Also working the fairgrounds is Hildegard Frölick, whose husband, Corporal Wolfgang Frölick, was killed during the war. Starving on the Russian steppes, Wehrmacht Corporal Frölick left his post with two of his comrades to chase a snow hare; when he returned, he was court-martialed and then shot for deserting. Every evening, Frau Frölick reenacts her husband's death via a puppet show that she performs with her husband's two comrades, Captain Ludwig von Basseville and Private Johann Steltenkamp, and another puppet who represents Corporal Frölick. Since she was not present on the Russian steppes, Frau Frölick can only imagine the death of her husband. Moïssevitch, however, is haunted by past memories, vividly reenacted daily as he lives with his fellow former survivors who now work the fairgrounds with him: the Cracovian Jew Abel Antokokoletz, the Ukrainian boxer Gregori Kravchenko, and the Republican soldier from the Spanish Civil War, Manuel Rodriguez. The dramatic tension of the play revolves around whether Frau Frölick and Moïssevitch can share a life together in the future. However, just as the Danube divides Austrian cities, Frölick and Moïssevitch will forever remain separate. Frölick lives in the present and is forced to recreate a past she has never known, thus making memory a strictly imaginative experience of what her husband must have suffered. Moïssevitch's concentration camp experience means that the past dominates his life in the present and thus blurs the two realms. The establishment of any common ground between the two characters is impossible since Moïssevitch's past becomes his present while Frölick's present consists merely of an imagined past. John Ireland astutely comments about the dichotomy between the mind-sets of the two protagonists: "This different temporal insertion is made clear on the stage: the individuals who haunt Moïssevitch's memory are portrayed as 'real' characters from his past; the characters who haunt Hildegard Frölick's past enter her universe, and therefore the dramatic universe, in the form of marionettes, puppets produced by her imagination."[34] The stage directions of the play indicate that communication between Moïssevitch and Frölick is insuperable, as both walk in concentric circles that never meet.

The major motif explored by Gatti in *The Second Life of Tatenberg Camp* focuses upon the vagaries of Holocaust memory. Holocaust memory cannot be divorced from present consciousness, the former's intrusiveness in the present reflecting the "second life" of the camps. Gatti blends time and space to reflect the tenuous nature of Holocaust memory. In an interview with Hélène Châtelain, Gatti explained how present-day Vienna merges with the Holocaust past: "The second story is set in Vienna, one of the places we simply could not ignore—because Vienna is the capital of Austria, and Austria equals one single place: the Mauthausen concentration camp."[35]

Moïssevitch's Holocaust experience is based on memory that is tainted and therefore illusory. Obviously, his experience in the Buna factories of Auschwitz was real, but that reality intermingles with the fictional Goldpilz camp; Tatenberg is fictional also, yet it coexists with the reality of Mauthausen. Mauthausen itself was a humbling reality once the prisoners passed through a facade railway station. All typical train stations have departure gates, yet Mauthausen, defying rational comprehension, had none. Even the time on the clock eternally representing midnight suggests a pathetic carnival that the mind finds to be illusory. This unreal carnival atmosphere also insidiously enters the present (its second existence), as the play takes place in Vienna, the city of illusions, during Carnival.

Moïssevitch himself personifies the tenuous nature of Holocaust memory. John Ireland discusses the focal point of Gatti's play: "But what is the truth of the past, what really did happen? Moïssevitch is no longer sure and, in tortured dialogue with other figures who emerge from the gloom of Tatenberg, he desperately confronts his own guilt as a survivor."[36] Moïssevitch's internment in Tatenberg is also confused with the four years he spent on the site as a displaced person. As Richard N. Coe points out, "Everything about Tatenberg is hazy, uncertain, and unreal. Even the menaces inside the camp itself are dream-enshrouded and difficult to visualize–not the all-too-real hutment-blocks and gas chambers, but the 'Buna.'"[37] Moïssevitch and his surviving comrades have memories that constantly conflict, thus calling into question the truth associated with the reality of the camps. Moïssevitch comments on the nature of tainted Holocaust memory as he tells Frau Frölick, "Each one rummaged through his stock of memories–when there was nothing left, he turned to what others remembered–after that, he made things up" (46). Moïssevitch is not sure whether he experienced the horrors of the camp or whether they were so unreal, so illusory, that he invented them. Moïssevitch is particularly tormented by his memory of Antokokoletz, a kapo at Goldpilz who brutally beat the prisoners. Yet Antokokoletz is envisioned as a nightmarish composite of kapos in other camps as well, as Moïssevitch tries to remember what is the truth: "He turned up again at Tatenberg. That's who Antokokoletz was (or else a Polish double of his

evacuated from the Buna at Birkenau–at least that's what he said)" (52).
Throughout the play, Gatti uses these parentheses to indicate uncer-
tainty in situations where characters do not trust their own memories.
Although Moïssevitch participated in stoning Antokokoletz to death,
he is still unsure why he did so. Moïssevitch and his fellow survivors
perhaps are repelled by Antokokoletz's sanctimonious use of scripture
and his rude demeanor. Antokokoletz's behavior in the camps provides
no answers, for Moïssevitch's memory is conflicted: "Us: He's a traitor!
Them: He's a hero! Us: He beat the prisoners with the utmost brutality.
Them: He saved fifteen lives at the risk of his own" (52). Moïssevitch is
so confused that he is unsure whether Antokokoletz was even a kapo
at Goldpilz, and when he questions the Cracovian Jew about his past,
Antokokoletz responds, "Will you ever know, Ilya?– Will I ever know?"
(57). Furthermore, Moïssevitch and Rodriguez share conflicting memories about their experiences in Tatenberg. Moïssevitch claims that
the Spanish prisoners refused to allow the Jews to take part in the
camp revolt. Rodriguez recalls a different experience, remembering
that the Jews were slow to organize and thus were late when the decision to revolt was made by the international committee.

The tainted memory of the Holocaust as a blur, an illusion, carries over to the scenes in the present that occur in Grein and Vienna.
The tableaux in the present reinforce the notion that Moïssevitch's
illusory vision of the camps continues to haunt him in the present.
The amorphous carnival that was Tatenberg is now transformed to
the tawdry stalls and lights of the carnival in Vienna, the city of illusions, where Moïssevitch, surrounded by his survivor comrades, is
forever reminded of how nebulous his Holocaust past has been. Ellen
Schiff further enlightens us to the comparison between Vienna and
Tatenberg: "Subjective perceptions are orchestrated with extravagant
lighting and sound effects–barking rifles, blaring music, truck horns
and turning wheels–appropriate to the grotesqueries both of a fair-
ground and of a concentration camp."[38] These Holocaust survivors
are fully immersed in the world of illusion that is the carnival at the
Prater, where they rub shoulders with others engulfed in a world of
charades, such as Reuter, the fire eater. Moïssevitch supposedly operates a musical robot whose facade is actually manned by a crippled

fifteen-year-old named Guinguin. The young man, carried from one concentration camp to another by his mother who hopes to find the remains of her two deported sons fifteen years after the Shoah, is thus himself a product of conflicting Holocaust memories. Antokokoletz, the animal trainer, and Rodriguez, disguised as a bear, have their own charade as the former manages the boxer Kravchenko in his staged battles with the bear. Antokokoletz even cautions Rodriguez: "Keep silent!–I've already told you that a bear must never speak, or else our future customers may discover the trick" (70). And when speaking of the women who appear to be easy marks for the men during the Carnival, Antokokoletz and Rodriguez agree that it appears to be a facade, nothing more than "Illusion! Illusion!" (71).

In an episode that takes place in the future, Moïssevitch, hoping to achieve "hyper-amnesia," seeks to unite with Frau Frölick; since Moïssevitch cannot dispel his own memories from the camps, he murders Frölick's puppets, thus relieving her of a past she never experienced. He even murders Kravchenko, convincing himself and Antokokoletz, "I've no regrets for the boxer.–The long lines of the imaginary life of the camp killed him; they'll follow him where he has gone. They'll be no past anymore, Abel (no past any more)" (77). Moïssevitch then shoots Rodriguez and Antokokoletz, hoping that the murders will put his Holocaust past behind him.

Holocaust memory has confused Moïssevitch; Dorothy Knowles has noted that while committing the murders, Moïssevitch is unable to distinguish the living from the dead.[39] Hildegard Frölick realizes that by destroying her puppet show that redeems the past for her, Moïssevitch has destroyed her illusory life that she cannot live without: "The present is enough for me–without my puppets I feel I have lost all the reasons which gave me the illusion of living" (79). For Ilya, however, he is fated to live on with his tainted memories of the Shoah no matter how often he tries to murder the relics from his past. Time for Moïssevitch will always be fixed as the immutable twelve o'clock in the railway station, and space will forever be the world of the camps.

During the last tableau, Moïssevitch, surrounded by former Baltic Jews who perished in the camps, tries to make sense of his conflicting memories. He wonders how he was able to get a work permit that saved his life while others were not as lucky, how he recovered from septicaemia when others became too ill to work, how he survived dysentery on the march to Estonia in 1943, and how an SS doctor spared him from selection in Goldpilz while the Rabbi of Vilna went to his death. Characters from the past completely surround Moïssevitch, creating an inseparable barrier between him and Frau Frölick. Moïssevitch dons a German helmet as if to frighten the ghosts of the past away; the gesture is futile. Ellen Schiff eloquently explicates how Moïssevitch will forever be confined to his Holocaust memories: "For Ilya Moïssevitch, to be a Jew means to suffer guilt and solitude entrapped by memories as incomprehensible as they are faithful."[40] Frau Frölick's words end the play: "Come back among the living, Ilya.–I am waiting for you" (85). Instead, Moïssevitch is condemned to be part of the walking dead, forever confined to his recurrent Holocaust memories. He will never be liberated from the camps. Holocaust memory, however tainted and incomprehensible, will always intrude on the present; survivors will forever remain in the "second life" of Tatenberg.

14 The Holocaust and Collective Memory

The uniqueness of the Holocaust has left us with a legacy in the form of a collective response to the trauma of atrocity. The Shoah has called into question the nature of humanity and civilization in a way fundamentally different from any other historical event. As Geoffrey H. Hartman has suggested, we, the nonparticipants, share with the survivors a type of trauma or breach in our traditional conception of human and civilized nature.[1] This emotional burden, the capacity to act as a witness to the Holocaust, is something with which we are complicit. Marc Silverstein has described the notion of acting as witnesses for "the dead, the deported, the disappeared, the disenfranchised" as a challenge to live beyond ourselves, the only viable response to the ravages of our "post-traumatic century."[2] Nobel Prize-winning British playwright Harold Pinter's *Ashes to Ashes* best demonstrates how the Holocaust has been seared into our consciousness as collective memory and thus serves as a fitting conclusion to this book.

Pinter's first brush with the Holocaust was in his early teen years, growing up in East Hackney, London, during the air raids of World War II. Pinter recalls his backyard in flames from the bombings, forcing his family to evacuate the area frequently. As a Jew, Pinter understood the dark consequences of a German victory over the British and Allied forces. However, the Holocaust per se does not enter the early "comedies of menace" nor even the political plays that he began to write in 1984 with *One for the Road* (although some critics, and even Pinter himself, might argue that his use of language as a weapon of domination even in the early plays is political). Pinter's first theatrical achievement related to the Holocaust was directing Robert Shaw's

The Man in the Glass Booth at the St. Martin's Theatre in London during July 1967. Twenty-eight years later, in May 1995, Pinter directed Ronald Harwood's *Taking Sides* at the Minerva Theatre in Chichester. This date is significant, for Harwood's play must have rekindled Pinter's interest in the Holocaust; Pinter began reading Gitta Sereny's biography of Albert Speer and wrote *Ashes to Ashes* after composing four drafts during ten days in 1996.

Ashes to Ashes, a fifty-minute one-act play, had its world premiere in Dutch by Toneelgroep in Amsterdam and then was staged by the Royal Court Theatre at the Ambassadors' Circle in London on 12 September 1996. Pinter directed Stephen Rea as Devlin and Lindsay Duncan as Rebecca. This version, with Pinter again directing Rea and Duncan, was performed during the Pinter Festival at Sala Beckett in Barcelona during fall 1996 and in April 1997 at the Gate Theatre in Dublin. Pinter then went on tour with the play to Italy (Palermo and Genova) in November 1997 and to the Salle Jean Vauthier in Paris during spring 1998. A Czech version of the play was soon mounted at Prague's National Theatre, the Narodni Divadlo, in 1998. *Ashes to Ashes* debuted in New York at the Roundabout/Gramercy Theatre in a production directed by Karel Reisz and starring Lindsay Duncan reprising her role as Rebecca, playing opposite David Strathairn as Devlin; it ran from 7 February to 9 May 1999. *Ashes to Ashes* has since been staged worldwide: in a production directed by Katherine Burkman at Ohio State University in late October 1999; at the Nea Skini Theatre in Kypseli, Greece, during October 2000; at the Culture Café, British Council Conference Hall, in Chennai, India, during March 2001; as part of the Lincoln Center Festival in 2001 in honor of Pinter's seventieth birthday; at the Garage Performance Space in Seattle, Washington, from 15 February to 9 March 2002; in a twin bill with Pinter's *The Lover* at the 6th @ Penn Theatre in San Diego during March 2004; and in a production directed by Natasha Mytnowyd at the Alumnae Theatre in Toronto during November and December 2005.

In *The Life and Work of Harold Pinter*, Michael Billington reported that Pinter's source material for *Ashes to Ashes* was Gitta Sereny's biography, *Albert Speer: His Battle With Truth*.[3] Speer, who was Hitler's favorite architect and Minister for Armaments and

Munitions from 1942, was responsible for the slave-labor camps and factories of Nazi Germany. As one who considered himself to be educated and cultured, Speer was outraged by the horrible working conditions, particularly the lack of sanitary facilities, that he encountered during a visit to Dora, one of his own work camps established to build V-2 rockets with labor supplied by Buchenwald inmates. Pinter remarked, "Reading the book also triggered lots of other associations. I've always been haunted by the image of the Nazis picking up babies on bayonet-spikes and throwing them out of windows."[4] When Speer was arrested after the war, he did not view himself as a criminal. However, during his trial at Nuremberg, Speer began to have a change of conscience and gradually began to debate taking responsibility for the Holocaust and for crimes he did not commit and of which he had no direct knowledge. Speer's admission of guilt becomes the collective memory that Rebecca responds to in *Ashes to Ashes*. D. Keith Peacock believes that Pinter's conception of Rebecca may have been inspired by an unnamed German woman, mentioned in Sereny's "Postscript," who was married to an Englishman, had two children, and resided in England.[5] At age seventy-five, Speer had an affair with this woman who was nearly forty, approximately the same age as Rebecca. She was particularly impressed by Speer's book, *The Secret Diaries*, which dramatically altered her guilt feelings about her German past and about her own persona. The idea that collective Holocaust guilt is transformed into personal guilt through memory that becomes metonymic is what forms the principal component of Pinter's play.

Amazingly, critics have made erroneous assumptions about *Ashes to Ashes*. Like Pinter's early plays, distinguished as comedies of menace, *Ashes to Ashes* occurs in a room, and like these early plays in which an intruder posed as the menace to the security of the room, in *Ashes to Ashes*, the intruder is the Holocaust. Although some critics assume that the room in this country house is in England, Pinter does not specify so anywhere in the play, and the mention of Dorset and Wembley does not necessarily mean that the couple reside in England. Rebecca does live with her lover Devlin, who may be her boyfriend or her husband–again Pinter leaves it to the audience to decipher, even though several critics have concluded that Devlin is Rebecca's husband. Rebecca may be a Jewish name, as some critics have argued, but there is no evidence of her ethnicity presented in the play, and the name could just as easily be Anglo-Saxon. Devlin obviously seems to be of Irish or Anglican origin, and not your typical Jewish name. What we do know is that Rebecca and Devlin, both in their forties, move further apart during the course of the play, and much of this separation seems to relate to Rebecca's repulsion toward her lover's authoritarian personality, which she associates with the Holocaust. In the stage directions, Pinter notes, *"The room darkens during the course of the play,"*[6] which refers to the increasingly somber mood of the two characters as tensions begin to mount. Yet Pinter also writes, *"The lamplight has become very bright but does not illumine the room"* (1). Susan Hollis Merritt's interpretation is useful here: "This is a crucial stage direction. Pinter suggests that, whereas 'the room' is not being 'illumine[d]' by the lamplight, *something–something else–*is being illuminated–or understood–in a new way."[7] Moreover, as Marc Silverstein has mentioned, this intense lamp light has transformed the quiet of a country room into an interrogation center reminiscent of the setting for several other of Pinter's political plays.[8]

Despite the fact that the play never mentions Nazis or Jews directly and history is referred to allusively, *Ashes to Ashes* evokes the Holocaust. During the Pinter Festival in Barcelona, specifically, on 6 December 1996, Mireia Aragay asked Pinter whether *Ashes to Ashes* was about Nazism, and he responded, "No, I don't think so at all. It *is* about the images of Nazi Germany; I don't think anyone can ever get that out of their mind. The Holocaust is probably the worst thing that ever happened, because it was so calculated, deliberate and precise, and so fully documented by the people who actually did it."[9] During that interview, Pinter mentioned that he had been haunted by images of the Holocaust for many years and thought many others shared the same collective memory.[10] This is essentially Rebecca's dilemma in the play.

Rebecca reminisces about her former lover, a "guide" who "had something to do with a travel agency" (19). Manuela M. Reiter reminds us that one translation of the German "Führer," besides "leader," is also "guide," which ironically may refer to his role in deportations, or making "travel" arrangements.[11] The generic term "Führer" can be ascribed to all high-ranking Nazis, including Speer, who as Oberstgruppenführer in the SS, was responsible for travel, including the railway system. This "guide" took Rebecca to a type of factory where all of the laborers doffed their caps in deference to his authority. Michael Billington comments, "The image, inspired by the Speer book, is of a cowed workforce and an autocratic controller."[12] Rebecca acknowledges the respect that the workers displayed for her former lover: "Because he ran a really tight ship, he said. They had total faith in him. They respected his ... purity, his ... conviction. They would follow him over a cliff and into the sea, if he asked them, he said" (25). "Purity" and "conviction" are euphemisms or code words that call to mind the justification for Nazi genocide. Rebecca recalls that the factory was exceedingly damp, the workers were not dressed for the weather, and the facility seemed to be devoid of restrooms. The images of the gruesome working conditions in the factory bring to mind Speer's visit to Dora, the slave labor camp that lacked sanitary facilities.

Rebecca tells Devlin about one of her former lover's chief duties: "He used to go to the local railway station and walk down the platform and tear all the babies from the arms of their screaming mothers" (27). The image of tearing babies from their mothers obviously can only refer to the chaos that ensued on the arrival ramp of the *lager*, thus cementing Rebecca's imaginative vision as Holocaust memory. These manifestations of the Shoah were prompted by Rebecca hearing a police siren that made her "terribly upset" (29). Strangely enough, Holocaust survivors often have mentioned that police sirens can be prompts that elicit latent or repressed visions of life in the concentration camps.

Rebecca also claims to have passively witnessed "guides" ushering crowds of people into what appears to be a mass suicide at Dorset: "They walked through the woods and I could see them in the distance walking across the cliff and down to the sea" (49). The notion of sycophants following their "guides" into the ocean derives from the tale that Rebecca told of her former lover's mastery over the slaves who doffed their caps and "would follow him over a cliff and into the sea."

The factory at Dora now transforms into England, for the visions of the Holocaust have become universal and metonymic.

Since Pinter designates that the play occurs "now," which at the time of the writing was 1996, Rebecca, in her forties, could not have personally experienced the Holocaust; even if she were forty-nine years old, her birth would have been in 1947. Rebecca admits that she has had no personal contact with the Shoah: "I have no such authority. Nothing has ever happened to me. Nothing has ever happened to any of my friends. I have never suffered. Nor have my friends" (41). Martin S. Regal writes, "Rebecca, in remembering someone else's past, illustrates that certain atrocities haunt all our minds and that she needs no 'authority' to be the mouthpiece of the present moment."[13] Rebecca, through her imaginative vision, has adopted the collective memory of the Holocaust as her own. She has taken on the role of bearing witness and commemorating the dead, becoming the mouthpiece for remembering the Shoah from generation to generation, or from ashes to ashes. Rebecca is very much like Sylvia Gellburg in Arthur Miller's *Broken Glass*, who felt spiritually connected to Jewish persecution like a wire that stretched around the world–a consciousness to which most people were oblivious. Rebecca feels the Holocaust as our inheritance through an atavistic sense of emotion, imagination, and collective memory. As Charles Grimes has commented, "Rebecca embraces a kind of historical determinism in which everyone's life is connected with everyone else's."[14]

Throughout the play, Devlin progressively becomes more like Rebecca's former Nazi lover, which allows Pinter to mesh the personal with the political.[15] *Ashes to Ashes* begins with Rebecca recalling her former sweetheart standing over her with a clenched fist, putting his hand on her neck, and then asking her to kiss his fist, which Rebecca agreed to do willingly. Rebecca's admission of having her legs open intimates that the relationship was a rape. Devlin proceeds to question Rebecca about her past, and despite Craig N. Owens's assumption that the relationship seems to be one of psychotherapist and patient that albeit becomes repressive,[16] most critics agree that it degenerates into an interrogation.[17] Devlin's Socratic method of probing seems innocuous at first, but his persistence soon becomes fascistic; as Geoffrey

Hartman has noticed, Devlin's "very questioning becomes another kind of violence."[18] Ann C. Hall agrees that Devlin becomes more abusive as the play progresses: "Whatever the case, the play solidifies Devlin's position as interrogator. He is frequently standing over Rebecca, and he attempts to direct the conversation at all times."[19] Devlin demands to know concrete details about Rebecca's past, but as Hanna Scolnicov has mentioned, when Rebecca recounts the atrocities, Devlin, like a good Nazi without memory or guilt, is impervious to such tales of genocide.[20] Rebecca even accuses him of "mental elephantiasis" and places the onus of responsibility for the genocide squarely on his shoulders, telling him, "You are not the *victim* of it, you are the *cause* of it" (51). His authoritarian personality precludes empathy for others and intimates that following orders carries more weight than moral responsibility. Devlin portrays this fascistic attitude as his language indicates to Rebecca his blatant abuse of power: "Fuck the best man, that's always been my motto. It's the man who ducks his head and moves on through no matter what wind or weather who gets there in the end. A man with guts and application. *Pause.* A man who doesn't give a shit. A man with a rigid sense of duty" (47). Katherine H. Burkman clarifies for us the connection between Devlin and Speer in their attempts to gain power: "Like Speer, who also regarded people as objects as he strove to fulfill Hitler's grandiose dreams and to secure his own power as he rose in the Nazi ranks, Devlin treats Rebecca as less an object of love or even desire than as an object to be dominated."[21] Rebecca reacts to his abuse, calling him a "fuckpig" (9), a name that could equally be applied to her former lover as well, and then adamantly confirms, "I'm not your darling" (15).

Varun Begley argues that Devlin, representing an authoritative desire to fix and control, to glorify assertion while disguising its violence, and to express an absolutist desire for fullness devoid of contradiction, battles with Rebecca, whose metonymy suggests interconnectedness and independence.[22] Devlin struggles to control the conversation and assert his dictatorial power over Rebecca by divesting her of Holocaust memory and diverting her instead to mundane domestic issues. As Rebecca relies on her imaginative vision of Holocaust atrocities, Devlin, hostile to metonymy, deflects the conversation to marital infidelity, relationships with her sister Kim and her children, trips to the cinema, and suburban life. Devlin attempts to ground Rebecca in a concrete past or present and pull her away from the nebulous articulation of collective memory. For example, when Rebecca cites the atrocities she supposedly witnessed at Dorset, Devlin undermines the political by focusing on the quotidian: "We live here. You don't live ... in Dorset ... or *anywhere else*. You live here with me. This is our house. You have a very nice sister. She lives close to you. She has two lovely kids. You're their aunt. You like that" (65). Thus, when Rebecca sings about "ashes to ashes," which to her relates to the Holocaust, Devlin can only think of the mundane. As Charles Grimes indicates, "To Devlin, they ["ashes to ashes"] are simply the cue for a popular (also misogynist) song, worthy of no more thought than one gives to any cliché."[23]

Emulating Rebecca's unnamed former fascistic lover, Devlin, near the end of the play, asks Rebecca to kiss his fist and then presses his hand on her throat. However, Rebecca's legs do not pry apart since she now realizes that this violation is equivalent to a rape. Rebecca declines to kiss his fist and instead invokes Holocaust imagery as she imagines babies being taken from their mothers on the railway platform. Wrapping her baby into a shawl and making it into a bundle, Rebecca tries to hide the child from the fascists. However, the baby cries out, and Rebecca is forced to relinquish her child. With Devlin's voice silenced, Rebecca is left only with an echo that reverberates throughout the theater the Holocaust imagery associated with loss: "the trains," "the babies away," "a bundle," and "my baby."[24] Rebecca earlier stated that she hoped that the siren, one of the Holocaust stimuli, would be with her always as an echoed image of her newly discovered consciousness: "I hate it fading away. I hate it echoing away. I hate it leaving me. I hate losing it. I hate somebody else possessing it. I want it to be mine, all the time" (31). Her now-echoed voice, as if repeated through time, solidifies her wish to be at one with the collective memory of the Holocaust and thus its witness. With regard to the echo, Craig N. Owens comments, "Its presence suggests that Rebecca speaks from a larger consciousness that encompasses an entire culture's memory and guilt in a voice unrestricted by the psyche of the individual who is its medium."[25] The echo, repeating Rebecca's words, underscores the significance of a raw, emotional vision of the Holocaust that effectively drowns out and ultimately silences Devlin's fascistic interrogation.

Recounting her tale of the bundle given up at the railway station, Rebecca begins in the third-person "she" and then ends in the first person "I," clearly indicating that she does not merely imagine the Holocaust but also, from collective guilt, identifies herself as one of the victims. However, Rebecca's last words of the play, "I don't know of any baby" (85), repeated for the third time, further extend her collective Holocaust memory to the personae of the perpetrators. Rebecca adopts the role of the passive German bystander who, like Speer, originally claimed to be guiltless for not having actually witnessed the genocide. Speer, later admitting responsibility for the genocide, struggled with the notion of assuming guilt for murder he never committed or witnessed. Rebecca's collective memory of the Holocaust encompasses her assumption of roles as the victim and victimizer. As Francis Gillen has realized, Devlin is more than capable of playing the authoritarian victimizer but fails to understand the role of the victim.[26] He also, like Speer, refuses to accept guilt for the authoritarianism that produced atrocities under the guise of "purity" and "conviction."

In the denouement of the play, Rebecca has rejected Devlin as synonymous with the voice of fascism who, like her former lover, is associated with rape, and, more specifically, with the rape of the century. The implication is that Rebecca recognizes the Holocaust as being rooted in the authoritarian personality personified by Devlin, thus conflating the personal with the political.[27] Rebecca is left with her echo, imprinting her as the voice of victim and perpetrator–the conscience of the Holocaust. As Katherine H. Burkman has commented, *Ashes to Ashes* bears witness to the Holocaust and reminds us of our complicity in the world's suffering.[28] Moreover, the play makes us aware that such genocide could begin again if we do not recognize that the personal is meshed with the political. Michael Billington writes, "The play gets under one's skin precisely because it is not dealing with some alien or distant world: it acknowledges the potential for oppression and resistance that lies within all of us."[29] The play's title suggests the circularity of such genocide, "echoing" Rebecca's comment that as one form of genocide ends, another begins: "Again and again and again. And we can end again. And again and again. And again" (67). As the voice of metonymic memory, Rebecca attempts to alert us of Elie Wiesel's plea not to forsake the lessons of the Holocaust–"Never again." Rebecca, through her imaginative vision of the Holocaust, has been able to make herself aware of the lessons of the past, allowing her to refuse to be victimized again and again.

Notes

1 Introduction

1 Daniel Jonah Goldhagen, *Hitler's Willing Executioners: Ordinary Germans and the Holocaust* (New York: Alfred A. Knopf, 1996), 167.

2 The term was first coined by David Rousset as a microcosm distinct with its own vocabulary and sinister connotations. See Rousset, *The Other Kingdom*, trans. Ramon Guthrie (New York: Reynal & Hitchcock, 1947).

3 See Berel Lang, "The Concept of Genocide," *Philosophical Forum* 16, nos. 1–2 (1984–85), 8. Bruno Bettelheim notes that East German sources consider eleven million to be the lowest estimate of the total number of deaths while "well over" eighteen million seems to be the best gauge of the high number; he also writes that the *Encyclopedia Britannica* (15th ed.) places the total number of deaths in the concentration camps to be between eighteen and twenty-six million. See Bettelheim, *Surviving and Other Essays* (New York: Alfred A. Knopf, 1979), 46–47.

4 This is the thesis of Goldhagen's extensive research on the Holocaust. See also Lang, "The Concept of Genocide," 13.

5 Michael Burleigh and Wolfgang Wippermann, *The Racial State: Germany, 1933–1945* (Cambridge: Cambridge University Press, 1991), 306.

6 Leni Yahil, *The Holocaust: The Fate of European Jewry, 1932–1945*, trans. Ina Friedman and Haya Galai (New York and Oxford: Oxford University Press, 1990), 39.

7 Robert Skloot, ed., *The Theatre of the Holocaust*, vol. 1 (Madison: University of Wisconsin Press, 1982), 3.

8 Elie Wiesel, *Legends of Our Time*, trans. Steven Donadio (New York: Holt, Rinehart and Winston, 1968), 190.

9 Alvin H. Rosenfeld, *A Double Dying: Reflections on Holocaust Literature* (Bloomington and London: Indiana University Press, 1980), 3.

10 Giorgio Agamben, *Remnants of Auschwitz: The Witness and the Archive* (New York: Zone Books, 1999), 72.

11 See Zev Garber and Bruce Zuckerman, "Why Do We Call the Holocaust 'the Holocaust'?: An Inquiry Into the Psychology of Labels," *Modern Judaism* 9, no. 2 (1989): 202.

12 Agamben, *Remnants of Auschwitz*, 29.

13 Garber and Zuckerman, "Why Do We Call the Holocaust 'the Holocaust'?" 207.

14 Mary Fulbrook, *German National Identity After the Holocaust* (Cambridge: Polity Press, 1999), 32, 34, 49.

15 Convicted *Einsatzgruppen* SS officers, assigned to kill Jews in the Eastern territories, often only received less than ten years of hard labor. For example, Dr. Otto Hunsche, Eichmann's legal expert, who ordered the deaths of six hundred Hungarian Jews, received five years of hard labor, while Dr. Otto Bradfisch, responsible for the murder of fifteen thousand Eastern European Jews, was sentenced to ten years. Joseph Lechthaler, chief administrator for the liquidation of the Russian Jewish community in Slutsk and Smolevichi, served three years and six months. Many other such examples of lenient sentences for crimes against the Jews could be noted as well.

16 Other Holocaust literature began to appear sporadically but had little impact on the public. For example, John Hersey's novel *The Wall* (New York: Alfred A. Knopf) was published in 1951, a year before the publication of Anne Frank's diary in the United States, yet despite its success as a best selling novel, its overall impact was slight.

17 Lawrence L. Langer, "The Americanization of the Holocaust on Stage and Screen," in *From Hester Street to Hollywood: The*

Jewish–American Stage and Screen, ed. Sarah Blacher Cohen (Bloomington: Indiana University Press, 1983), 214.

18 Bettelheim, *Surviving and Other Essays*, 251.

19 Haim Shoham: "Here and There: The Israeli Playwright and His Jewish Shadow," *Modern Hebrew Literature* 10, nos. 1–2 (1984): 32.

20 Anat Feinberg, "The Appeal of the Executive: Adolf Eichmann on the Stage," *Monatshefte* 78, no. 2 (1986): 205.

21 See Hannah Arendt, *Eichmann in Jerusalem* (New York: Viking Press, 1964), 252.

22 Anton Kaes, "The American Television Series *Holocaust* Is Shown in West Germany," in *Yale Companion to Jewish Writing and Thought in German Culture, 1096–1996*, ed. Sander L. Gilman and Jack Zipes (New Haven and London: Yale University Press, 1997), 783.

23 Peter Demetz, *After the Fires: Recent Writing in the Germanies, Austria and Switzerland* (New York and San Diego: Harcourt Brace Jovanovich, 1986), 29. Demetz also notes that each showing of the miniseries was followed by a midnight discussion and that a quarter of a million people requested a government-produced documentary brochure containing additional historical information about the Holocaust.

24 Theodor W. Adorno, "Kulturkritik und Gesellschaft," in *Prismen* (Frankfurt: Suhrkamp Verlag, 1955), 26.

25 See Theodor W. Adorno, "Engagement," in *Noten zur Literatur III* (Frankfurt: Suhrkamp Verlag, 1974), 422–23.

26 Theodor W. Adorno, *Negative Dialectics*, trans. E. B. Ashton (New York: Seabury Press, 1973), 366, 367, respectively.

27 Irving Howe, "Writing and the Holocaust," *New Republic*, 27 October 1986, 27.

28 Michael Wyschogrod, "Some Theological Reflections on the Holocaust," *Response: A Contemporary Jewish Review* 25 (Spring 1975): 68.

29 See Lawrence L. Langer, *The Holocaust and the Literary Imagination* (New Haven and London: Yale University Press, 1975), 3.

30 Jean Améry, *At the Mind's Limits: Contemplations by a Survivor on Auschwitz and Its Realities*, trans. Sidney Rosenfeld and Stella P. Rosenfeld (Bloomington and Indianapolis: Indiana University Press, 1980), 30.

31 Terrence Des Pres, *The Survivor: An Anatomy of Life in the Death Camps* (New York: Oxford University Press, 1976), 182.

32 Langer, *Holocaust and the Literary Imagination*, 185.

33 Sidra Dekoven Ezrahi, *By Words Alone: The Holocaust in Literature* (Chicago and London: University of Chicago Press, 1980), 1.

34 Michael Taub, ed., *Israeli Holocaust Drama* (Syracuse: Syracuse University Press, 1996), 3.

35 Agamben, *Remnants of Auschwitz*, 99.

36 George Steiner, "K," in *Language and Silence: Essays on Language, Literature, and the Inhuman* (New York: Atheneum, 1967), 123. See also similar comments Steiner made in *In Bluebeard's Castle: Some Notes Towards the Redefinition of Culture* (New Haven: Yale University Press, 1975).

37 Elie Wiesel, "One Generation After," in *One Generation After*, trans. Lily Edleman (New York: Random House, 1970), 10.

38 Langer, "Americanization of the Holocaust," 213.

39 Elie Wiesel, "Art and the Holocaust: Trivializing Memory," trans. Iver Peterson, *New York Times*, 11 June 1989, sec. 2, 38. Wiesel's dictim seems to coincide with his own writing on the Holocaust, for *Night* is a literal account of what happened–the unencumbered truth. Alvin H. Rosenfeld describes *Night* thusly: "It has no symbolic dimensions, carries no allegorical weight, possesses no apparent or covert meaning." See Rosenfeld, *Double Dying*, 24.

40 Bettelheim, *Surviving and Other Essays*, 97.

41 Primo Levi, *The Drowned and the Saved*, trans. Raymond Rosenthal (New York: Simon & Schuster, 1988), 11.

42 Rosenfeld, *Double Dying*, 14.

43 Elinor Fuchs, ed., *Plays of the Holocaust: An International Anthology* (New York: Theatre Communications Group, 1987), xxvi.

44 Skloot, *The Theatre of the Holocaust*, 14.

45 Wiesel, "Art and the Holocaust," sec. 2, 38.

46 Taub, *Israeli Holocaust Drama*, 4.

47 Langer, *The Holocaust and the Literary Imagination*, 43.

48 Richard N. Coe, "Armand Gatti's Carnival of Compassion: *La Deuxième Existence du camp de Tatenberg*," *Yale French Studies*, no. 46 (1971): 70. Also note that Martin Esslin did not include Gatti in his seminal study on absurdist theater, not even in his chapter "Parallels and Proselytes." See Esslin, *The Theatre of the Absurd* (Garden City: Doubleday, 1969).

49 Documentary theater, the gathering of information through historical reports, statistics, government documents, newspapers, diaries, journals, and media reports, seems particularly apropos to represent the Holocaust and has become a favorite tool of the German playwrights. Documentary theater does not invent; instead it presents authentic material on stage, ostensibly unchanged in content but now integrated in a different form. The documentary dramatist essentially acts as a scientist uncovering facts in an understanding that reality, no matter how seemingly irrational or impenetrable, can be explained. Facts are stated, discussed, and interpreted, usually in a courtroom setting that offers opportunity for debate typically modeled on Brecht's dialectical theater. The goal, then, is to make people think and ultimately to educate the audience. For more information about documentary theater, see Jack D. Zipes, "Documentary Drama in Germany: Mending the Circuit," *Germanic Review* 42, no. 1 (1967): 49–62.

50 See Edward R. Isser, *Stages of Annihilation: Theatrical Representations of the Holocaust* (Madison, NJ: Fairleigh Dickinson University Press, 1997), 14, and Alvin Goldfarb, "Select Bibliography of Holocaust Plays, 1933–1997," in *Staging the Holocaust: The Shoah in Drama and Performance*, ed. Claude Schumacher (Cambridge: Cambridge University Press, 1998), 298–334.

2 Staging the Banality of Evil

1 Hannah Arendt, *Eichmann in Jerusalem* (New York: Viking Press, 1964), 33.

2 Ibid., 49.

3 Ibid., 276.

4 In a 1990 staging of the play at the Milwaukee Repertory Theatre, Lillian's name was changed to Hannah to make the connection between Freed's drama and Arendt's study clearer to anyone who ignored the play's subtitle.

5 Donald Freed, *The White Crow: Eichmann in Jerusalem* (Imperial Beach, CA: VRI Theater Library, 1985), 26. All subsequent citations from the play are from this edition and will be enclosed within parentheses in the text.

6 See Joseph H. Stodder's review, "The White Crow," *Theatre Journal* 37, no. 2 (1985): 234.

7 Robert Skloot, "Stage Nazis: The Politics and Aesthetics of Memory," *History and Memory* 6, no. 2 (1994): 68.

8 For a brief overview of the critical assessment of the play in London and New York, see William W. Demastes, "C. P. Taylor," in *British Playwrights, 1956–1995: A Research and Production Sourcebook*, ed. William W. Demastes (Westport, CT: Greenwood Press, 1996), 401.

9 C. P. Taylor, *Good* (London: Methuen, 1983), unpaginated "Author's Note." All subsequent citations from the play are from this edition and will be enclosed within parentheses in the text.

10 Taylor needed to edit the play a bit more carefully. At one point, he tells Maurice that he has three first-class children (18); then, in a second conversation with his best friend, states that he has two children (46).

11 Halder's situation parallels Taylor's own domestic life, for Taylor had two wives, four children, and a blind mother; eventually, like Halder, he left his family for a younger woman. Moreover, Taylor was constantly hustling as a freelance writer, trying to make ends meet. His output was prodigious, writing seventy plays in thirty years. Although he concentrated on writing sophisticated drama for the proletariat and worked arduously as a playwright-advisor with community and youth theater groups, he never turned down even a meager opportunity (like Halder), even if it meant prostituting himself to write for television.

12 Taylor seems to be overly fond of ellipses. In every quotation that I have cited from the play where an ellipsis is indicated, it represents Taylor's way of representing a pause in the dialogue rather than any omissions from the text.

13 Susan Friesner, "Travails of a Naked Typist: The Plays of C. P. Taylor," *New Theatre Quarterly* 9, no. 33 (1993): 54. Friesner writes that *Good* originated from a request from Michael Bogdanov, Taylor's colleague at the Tyneside Theatre Company, for an adaptation of Goethe's *Faust*. The project never materialized, but the early drafts of *Good* reveal the connection with Goethe's play, as Halder is called Faust while Mephistopheles morphs into Hitler. The second draft of the play even begins with a quotation from *Faust* about the dangers of self-conceit.

14 Edward R. Isser, *Stages of Annihilation: Theatrical Representations of the Holocaust* (Madison, NJ: Fairleigh Dickinson University Press, 1997), 54.

15 Robert Skloot, "Teaching the Holocaust Through Theatre," in *What Have We Learned? Telling the Story and Teaching the Lessons of the Holocaust*, ed. Franklin H. Littell, Alan L. Berger, and Hurbert G. Locke (Lewiston, NY: Edwin Mellen Press, 1993), 318.

16 Robert Skloot, *The Darkness We Carry: The Drama of the Holocaust* (Madison, WI: University of Wisconsin Press, 1988), 55.

17 Susan Friesner, "The Plays of C. P. Taylor," *Contemporary Review* 255, no. 1487 (1989): 310.

18 Bernard F. Dukore, "People Like You and Me: The Auschwitz Plays of Peter Barnes and C. P. Taylor," *Essays in Theatre* 3, no. 2 (1985): 114.

19 Harriet Margolis, "'Nur Schauspieler': Spectacular Politics, *Mephisto*, and *Good*," in *Film and Literature: A Comparative Approach to Adaptation*," ed. Wendell Aycock and Michael Schoenecke, *Studies in Comparative Literature*, no. 19 (Lubbock: Texas Tech University Press, 1988), 86.

20 See Robert R. Calder and Silvia Mergenthal, "Hitler on the Ballachulish Beat: The Plays of C. P. Taylor," *Revista Canaria de Estudios Ingleses* 41 (November 2000): 50.

21 See Dukore, "People Like You and Me," 123–24.

22 Benedict Nightingale, "C. P. Taylor," *Stand* 23 (1982): 32.

23 Barnes's mother was Jewish, and his father converted to Judaism when they married. Although Barnes was nominally religious, during the war he was understandably concerned about the consequences for Jews in England if the Nazis were to be victorious.

24 Peter Barnes, *Auschwitz*, in *Plays of the Holocaust*, ed. Elinor Fuchs (New York: Theatre Communications Group, 1987), 107. All subsequent citations from the play are from this edition and will be enclosed within parentheses in the text.

25 John Lahr, "*Laughter!*," *Plays and Players* 25 (March 1978): 27.

26 See Dukore, "People Like You and Me," 109. Also see Bernard Dukore, *Barnestorm: The Plays of Peter Barnes* (New York and London: Garland, 1995), 44; Bernard Dukore, "Peter Barnes," in *Essays on Contemporary British Drama*, ed. Hedwig Bock and Albert Wertheim (Munich: Max Hueber Verlag, 1981), 104; and Bernard Dukore, "Peter Barnes and the Problem of Goodness," in *Around the Absurd: Essays on Modern and Postmodern Drama*, ed. Enoch Brater and Ruby Cohn (Ann Arbor: University of Michigan Press, 1990), 164.

27 Vivian M. Patraka, "Fascist Ideology and Theatricalization," in *Critical Theory and Performance*, ed. Janelle G. Reinelt and Joseph R. Roach (Ann Arbor: University of Michigan Press, 1992), 344.

28 Eric Sterling, "Peter Barnes's *Auschwitz* and the Comedic Dilemma," *European Studies Journal* 17–18 (Fall 2000–Spring 2001): 199.

29 Peter Barnes, "On Class, Christianity, and Questions of Comedy," *New Theatre Quarterly* 6, no. 21 (1990): 8.

30 Robert Skloot perceptively notes that the phrase "root it out" is repeated eight times in the play, "each time as a conclusion to a serious scene that has veered off track into a kind of bizarre vaudeville." See Skloot, *The Darkness We Carry*, 64.

31 W. B. Worthen, *Modern Drama and the Rhetoric of Theater* (Berkeley: University of California Press, 1992), 170.

32 For more information about black comedy in the contemporary theater, see Gene A. Plunka, *The Black Comedy of John Guare* (Newark: University of Delaware Press, 2002).

33 Peter Barnes, *"Laughter!,"* in *Collected Plays* (London: Heinemann, 1981), 343. All subsequent citations from *Tsar* are from this edition and will be enclosed within parentheses in the text. Barnes's attitude toward laughter and the Holocaust is similar to that of Terrence Des Pres, who contends that laughter is hostile to the world it depicts and subverts the respect on which Holocaust representation depends. See Des Pres, "Holocaust Laughter?" in *Writing and the Holocaust*, ed. Berel Lang (New York and London: Holmes & Meier, 1988), 216–33.

34 For an in-depth discussion of the influence of Jonsonian comedy on Barnes's plays, see Brian Woolland, "His Very Own Ben: Peter Barnes and Ben Jonson," in *Jonsonians: Living Traditions*, ed. Brian Woolland (Hampshire, UK: Ashgate, 2003), 153–66. Also see Dukore, *Barnestorm*, 16–18.

35 Barnes, "On Class, Christianity, and Questions of Comedy," 24. Also, Barnes has made similar comments about how laughter grounds reassurance but is actually for losers, assisting them to accommodate to defeat. See Jim Hiley, "Liberating Laughter," *Plays and Players* 25 (March 1978): 15; and Nick Curtis, "Barnes Stormer," *Plays and Players* 440 (July 1990): 13.

36 Christopher Innes, *Modern British Drama, 1890–1990* (Cambridge: Cambridge University Press, 1992), 305.

37 Brian Woolland, *Dark Attractions: The Theatre of Peter Barnes* (London: Methuen, 2004), 67.

38 Sterling, "Peter Barnes's *Auschwitz*," 209.

39 Mark Bly and Doug Wager, "Theater of the Extreme: An Interview With Peter Barnes," *Theater* 12, no. 2 (1981): 45.

40 For a more detailed analysis of the venom and madness in Bernhard's drama, see Martin Esslin, "A Drama of Disease and Derision: The Plays of Thomas Bernhard," *Modern Drama* 23, no. 4 (1981): 367–84.

41 Stephen D. Dowden, *Understanding Thomas Bernhard* (Columbia: University of South Carolina Press, 1991), 2.

42 For information about Bernhard's reception in literary circles, see Amity Shlaes, "Thomas Bernhard and the German Literary Scene," *New Criterion* 5, no. 5 (1987): 26–32.

43 See Martin Esslin, "Beckett and Bernhard: A Comparison," *Modern Austrian Literature* 18, no. 2 (1985): 67–78.

44 Nicholas Eisner has described Bernhard's characters as "verkörperte Funktionen" (personified functions), instruments for an exposition of ideas that are subordinate to the form of the play, which works via highly repetitive language that overshadows plot, character, and genuine dialogue. See Eisner, "*Theatertheater/Theaterspiele*: The Plays of Thomas Bernhard," *Modern Drama* 30, no. 1 (1987): 104–14.

45 Rüdiger Görner, "The Excitement of Boredom–Thomas Bernhard," in *A Radical Stage: Theater in Germany in the 1970s and 1980s*, ed. W. G. Sebald (Oxford and New York: Berg, 1988), 164.

46 For a thorough analysis of the Filbinger affair as impetus for *Eve of Retirement*, see Gitta Honegger, *Thomas Bernhard: The Making of an Austrian* (New Haven and London: Yale University Press, 2001), 131–37.

47 Thomas Bernhard, *Eve of Retirement*, in *The President and Eve of Retirement*, trans. Gitta Honegger (New York: Performing Arts Journal Publications, 1982), 204. All subsequent citations from the play are from this edition and will be included within parentheses in the text.

48 William E. Gruber, *Missing Persons: Character and Characterization in Modern Drama* (Athens and London: University of Georgia Press, 1994), 113.

49 Jeanette R. Malkin, "Pulling the Pants off History: Politics and Postmodernism in Thomas Bernhard's *Eve of Retirement*," *Theatre Journal* 47, no. 1 (1995): 105–19. Also, see Jeanette R. Malkin, *Memory-Theater and Postmodern Drama* (Ann Arbor: University of Michigan Press, 1999), 192–205.

50 Joseph A. Federico, "Millenarianism, Legitimation, and the National Socialist Universe in Thomas Bernhard's *Vor dem Ruhestand*," *Germanic Review* 59, no. 4 (1984): 145.

51 Hellmuth Karasek states that the original Stuttgart audience, well aware of the latent reference to Heydrich and his violin playing, laughed uncomfortably at this point in the play. See Karasek,

"*Vor dem Ruhestand*," *Thomas Bernhard Werkgeschicte*, ed. Jens Dittmar (Frankfurt: Suhrkamp Verlag, 1981), 216.

52 Federico, "Millenarianism, Legitimation," 147.

53 Malkin, "Pulling the Pants off History," 110.

54 Gitta Honegger, "Acoustic Masks: Strategies of Language in the Theater of Canetti, Bernhard, and Handke," *Modern Austrian Literature* 18, no. 2 (1985): 61.

55 Honegger, *Thomas Bernhard*, 141.

56 Vivian M. Patraka, *Spectacular Suffering: Theatre, Fascism, and the Holocaust* (Bloomington and Indianapolis: Indiana University Press, 1999), 38.

57 Donna L. Hoffmeister, "Post-Modern Theater: A Contradiction in Terms? Handke, Strauss, Bernhard and the Contemporary Scene," *Monatshefte* 79, no. 4 (1987): 433.

58 Görner, "Excitement of Boredom," 169.

59 Malkin, "Pulling the Pants off History," 117.

60 In an interview with *Der Spiegel*, Bernhard, referring to the Filbinger affair, explained that the Nazi spirit remains in all of us. See Erich Böhme and Hellmuth Karasek, "'Ich Könnte auf dem Papier Jemand Umbringen': Der Schriffsteller Thomas Bernhard Über Wirkung und Öffentlichkeit Seiner Texte," *Der Spiegel*, 23 June 1980, 178.

3 Culture and the Holocaust

1 Lucy S. Davidowicz, *The War Against the Jews, 1933–1945* (New York: Bantam, 1975), 241.

2 Sidra DeKoven Ezrahi, *By Words Alone: The Holocaust in Literature* (Chicago and London: University of Chicago Press, 1980), 16.

3 Yehuda Bauer, *A History of the Holocaust* (New York: Franklin Watts, 1982), 179.

4 Primo Levi, *Survival in Auschwitz: The Nazi Assault on Humanity*, trans. Stuart Woolf (New York: Macmillan, 1993), 112–15.

5 Charlotte Delbo, *Auschwitz and After*, trans. Rosette C. Lamont (New Haven and London: Yale University Press, 1995), 171.

6 Rosette C. Lamont, "Charlotte Delbo, a Woman/Book," in *Faith of a (Woman) Writer*, eds. Alice Kessler-Harris and William McBrien, Contributions in Women's Studies, no. 86 (New York and Westport, CT: Greenwood Press, 1988), 252.

7 For information about the play's reception in Germany, see Michael Handelsaltz, "The Levin-Sobol Syndrome: Two Faces of Modern Israeli Drama," *Modern Hebrew Literature* 1 (Fall/ Winter 1998): 21, 23.

8 Elie Wiesel, "Art and the Holocaust: Trivializing Memory," *New York Times*, 11 June 1989, sec. 2, 38.

9 For information about the Ball State University production, see Judy E. Yordon, "More Than a Sense of the Other: An Account of the Events Surrounding a Production of Joshua Sobol's *Ghetto*," *Text and Performance Quarterly* 12, no. 4 (1992): 372–76. Sobol and his wife attended on opening night in Kobe. For more on the Japanese production, see Tomokazu Nakatani, "A Theater in a Graveyard," *Look Japan* 41, no. 477 (1995): 30–32.

10 Joshua Sobol, "Postscript: A Theatre in the Wilna Ghetto," in *Plays of the Holocaust: An International Anthology*, ed. Elinor Fuchs (New York: Theatre Communications Group, 1987), 228.

11 The theater was by no means the only cultural activity in Vilna. An active library had a readership of 4,700. Competitions in music, poetry, and playwriting were held. Lectures, symposia, and morning assemblies were widely attended, and even cafe theaters were proliferating.

12 Alfred Cismaru, "*Ghetto*: A Recollection of Vilna," *Cimarron Review* 87 (April 1989): 34.

13 Mervyn Rothstein, "When Art Becomes a Matter of Life or Death," *New York Times*, 30 April 1989, sec. 2, 1.

14 Sobol, "Postscript," 230.

15 Srulik is a fictional character based upon Israel Segal, the director of the theater. Weiskopf is a fictional portrayal of other profiteers common in Vilna. All of the other major characters in the play, including Kittel, Herman Kruk, and Jakob Gens, were modeled by Sobol on their real counterparts.

16 Perhaps one reason for the international success of *Ghetto* is that the play is about theater people–always a popular subject for theater troupes.

17 Joshua Sobol, *Ghetto*, trans. Kathleen Komar and Jack Viertal, in *Plays of the Holocaust: An International Anthology*, ed. Elinor Fuchs (New York: Theatre Communications Group, 1987), 167. All subsequent citations are from this edition and will be included within parentheses in the text.

18 Rothstein, "When Art Becomes a Matter of Life or Death," sec. 2, 8. Sobol also made similar comments concerning the Jews in Vilna resisting the Nazis "spiritually and morally" in order to survive not only as living creatures, but "mainly as human creatures." See Joshua Sobol, "Interview," *Index on Censorship* 14, no. 1 (1985): 25.

19 Joshua Sobol, "Theatricality of Political Theatre," *Maske und Kothurn* 33, nos. 3–4 (1987): 108–9.

20 Vivian M. Patraka, *Spectacular Suffering: Theatre, Fascism, and the Holocaust* (Bloomington and Indianapolis: Indiana University Press, 1999), 100.

21 Douglas Langworthy, "When Choosing Good Is Not an Option: An Interview With Joshua Sobol," *Theater* 22, no. 3 (1991): 16.

22 Although Sobol's main intention in *Ghetto* is apolitical, the dialectic between Kruk and Dr. Paul politicizes the play. Kruk, the Bundist, is a socialist, a representative of the Old World Diaspora Jew; on the other hand, Dr. Paul is the New World Jew from Palestine, looking forward to the future of the Jewish homeland, not back to the misery of the Holocaust. Kruk believes in passing on knowledge through the culture while Dr. Paul frames his Weltanschauung around the aggression of the Israelis. Kruk is associated with the suffering of the Old World Jews who have gone through two thousand years of pogroms and persecutions. Dr. Paul instead looks to the Zionist Jews, an effective military force that makes preemptive strikes instead of waiting to be attacked. Since Kittel and Dr. Paul are played by the same actor, critics have associated the scholarly views of the doctor with Nazism. For example, see Yael S. Feldman, "'Identification-With-the-Aggressor' or the 'Victim Complex'? Holocaust and Ideology

in Israeli Theater: *Ghetto* by Joshua Sobol," *Modern Judaism* 9, no. 2 (1989): 175. Moreover, Dr. Paul reminds Kruk that Freud's concept of the death instinct is related to aggression; the implication is that the Nazi killing machine has been transplanted in the Zionist Jews of Palestine. Thus, the cultural viability of the Diaspora Jews so emulated by Kruk is clearly contrasted by the fascist, messianic Zionism of the Israelis so endearing to Dr. Paul. There is no doubt that this political subtext to the play was in Sobol's mind at the time of writing. In an interview published in the *New York Times*, Sobol discussed the genesis of the play: "The war in Lebanon was going on, and I was very strongly opposed to it. I felt that everything I could do to raise my voice against it, I would do." See Rothstein, "When Art Becomes a Matter of Life or Death," sec. 2, 8. Furthermore, Sobol has agreed that Martin Buber's anti-Zionism position against nationalism and ego building is commendable, which is why Sobol went back to the Shoah to understand what he calls Israeli colonialism. See Sobol, "Interview," 25, 54. The politicizing of *Ghetto* may send modern audiences squirming or wondering what lies beneath the subtext of introducing Freudian psychology into the debate. Thus, as was true in the Broadway production of the play, several directors chose to eliminate much of the Kruk–Dr. Paul dialectic, which makes the play more palatable for Jewish audiences. Yet Sobol could not escape Israeli criticism of the play. Rachel Shteir writes, "Because Sobol has linked Nazism and Zionism, some Israeli critics have accused him of ignoring German culpability." See Shteir, "In Search of Sobol," *Theater* 21, no. 3 (1990): 41. Sobol must have taken the criticism to heart, for he wrote two more plays (*Adam* and *Underground*) about the Vilna ghetto. *Adam*, clearly the most political play of the triptych, is examined in chapter 9 of this book.

23 Langworthy, "Choosing Good Is Not an Option," 15.

24 Sobol did his best to portray Gens as a person with foibles and conflicts, rather than as a saint. Gens's goal of saving as many Jews as possible is certainly laudable, yet he is also at times self-aggrandizing and contemptuous of opposing views. Robert Skloot

forces us to consider his ulterior motives: "Of course, there is a self-serving point to Gens's anger, too: a more passive population will reduce the threat to his authority." See Skloot, *The Darkness We Carry: The Drama of the Holocaust* (Madison, WI: University of Wisconsin Press, 1988), 40.

25 Sobol notes that Gens was in the Lithuanian army before the war and thus understood that there was no chance of an armed resistance. His policy, then, of selectively choosing which Jews to save meant sacrificing others, such as the infirm and the elderly. See Langworthy, "Choosing Good Is Not an Option," 13. Gens also realized that although choosing who shall live and who shall die is against Talmudic law, in a wasteland ostensibly abandoned by God, he had to make his own decisions. These moral and ethical decisions will be examined in more detail during the discussion of *Adam*.

26 Freddie Rokem, "On the Fantastic in Holocaust Performances," in *Staging the Holocaust: The Shoah in Drama and Performance*, ed. Claude Schumacher (Cambridge: Cambridge University Press, 1998), 47.

27 See Levi, *Survival in Auschwitz*, 125, 180, and Bruno Bettelheim, *Surviving and Other Essays* (New York: Alfred A. Knopf, 1979), 280, 287.

28 Terrence Des Pres, *The Survivor: An Anatomy of Life in the Death Camps* (New York: Oxford University Press, 1976), passim.

29 Bettelheim, *Surviving and Other Essays*, 25.

30 Christopher Bigsby, *Remembering and Imagining the Holocaust: The Chain of Memory* (Cambridge: Cambridge University Press, 2006), 198.

31 Arthur Miller, *Playing for Time* (Woodstock, Il: Dramatic Publishing, 1985), 33. All subsequent citations are from this edition and will be included within parentheses in the text.

32 Jay L. Halio, "Arthur Miller's Broken Jews," in *American Literary Dimensions: Poems and Essays in Honor of Melvin J. Friedman*, eds. Ben Siegel and Jay L. Halio (Newark: University of Delaware Press, 1999), 130.

33 Obviously, the idea of establishing one's identity through the collective historical experience intrigued Miller. The title of his autobiography, *Timebends*, published two years after his adaptation of the television script, reflects the notion of establishing autobiography through memory, just as Fania's life after Auschwitz will always be colored by her reflections about the Holocaust.

34 Christopher Bigsby, *Arthur Miller: A Critical Study* (Cambridge: Cambridge University Press, 2005), 313.

35 Judy Mann, "Art Is Long, But Life, Politics Are Short," *Washington Post*, 26 September 1980, B6.

36 Kimberly K. Cook, "Self-Preservation in Arthur Miller's Holocaust Dramas," *Journal of Evolutionary Psychology* 14, nos. 1–2 (1993): 107.

37 Susan C. W. Abbotson, "Re-Visiting the Holocaust for 1980s Television: Arthur Miller's *Playing for Time*," *American Drama* 8, no. 2 (1999): 71.

38 Bigsby, *Arthur Miller*, 316.

39 Abbotson, "Re-Visiting the Holocaust," 68.

40 Edward R. Isser, *Stages of Annihilation: Theatrical Representations of the Holocaust* (Madison, NJ: Fairleigh Dickinson University Press, 1997), 70–71.

41 Abbotson, "Re-Visiting the Holocaust," 72–73.

42 Bettina Knapp, ed., *Off-Stage Voices: Interviews With Modern French Dramatists* (Troy, NY: Whitston, 1975), 198. See similar comments Liliane Atlan made in Kathleen Betsko and Rachel Koenig, eds., *Interviews With Contemporary Women Playwrights* (New York: William Morrow, 1987), 25.

43 Atlan based Grol on Janusz Korczak, an orphanage teacher and physician in the Warsaw ghetto who, in 1942, accompanied children to their deaths in Auschwitz. During the deportation, he told the children stories to ease their tensions. There is no evidence, however, that Atlan knew of Erwin Sylvanus's 1957 play, *Dr. Korczak and the Children*, when she wrote *Mister Fugue*.

44 Knapp, ed., *Off-Stage Voices*, 200.

45 Bettina Knapp, *Liliane Atlan* (Amsterdam: Rodopi, 1988), 21.

46 Liliane Atlan, *Mister Fugue or Earth Sick*, trans. Marguerite Feitlowitz, in *Plays of the Holocaust: An International Anthology*, ed. Elinor Fuchs (New York: Theatre Communications Group, 1987), 58. All subsequent citations are from this edition and will be included within parentheses in the text.

47 Judith Morganroth Schneider, "Liliane Atlan: Jewish Difference in Postmodern French Writing," *Symposium: A Quarterly Journal in Modern Foreign Literatures* 43, no. 1 (1989): 277.

48 Vivian M. Patraka, "Feminism and the Jewish Subject in the Plays of Sachs, Atlan, and Schenkar," in *Performing Feminisims: Feminist Critical Theory and Theatre*, ed. Sue-Ellen Case (Baltimore and London: Johns Hopkins University Press, 1990), 170.

49 See Bettina Knapp, "Collective Creation From Paris to Jerusalem: An Interview With Liliane Atlan," *Theater* 13, no. 1 (1981–82): 50. Atlan also wrote *Un Opera pour Terezin* (1984) about the cabaret performances in Theresienstadt.

50 Isser, *Stages of Annihilation*, 112–13.

51 Skloot, *The Darkness We Carry*, 32.

4 The Holocaust as Literature of the Body

1 Lucy S. Dawidowicz, *The War Against the Jews, 1933–1945* (New York: Bantam, 1975), 22.

2 Michael Burleigh and Wolfgang Wippermann, *The Racial State: Germany, 1933–1945* (Cambridge: Cambridge University Press, 1991), 201.

3 See Hans Peter Bleuel, *Sex and Society in Nazi Germany*, trans. J. Maxwell Brownjohn (Philadelphia and New York: J. B. Lippincott, 1973), 137–38.

4 See Bruno Bettelheim, *Surviving and Other Essays* (New York: Alfred A. Knopf, 1979), 287.

5 Daniel Jonah Goldhagen, *Hitler's Willing Executioners: Ordinary Germans and the Holocaust* (New York: Alfred A. Knopf, 1996), 167, 286.

6 Ibid., 320.

7 Charlotte Delbo, *Auschwitz and After*, trans. Rosette C. Lamont (New Haven and London: Yale University Press, 1995), 7.

8 Jean Améry, *At the Mind's Limits: Contemplations by a Survivor on Auschwitz and Its Realities,* trans. Sidney Rosenfeld and Stella P. Rosenfeld (Bloomington and Indianapolis: Indiana University Press, 1980), 7.

9 Concentration camp prisoners existed on approximately 1,800 calories daily. Conditions were much worse in the extermination camps, where the *Häftlinge* received morning coffee, soup at noon, as well as two hundred grams of dry bread and seven grams of margarine in the evening.

10 Giorgio Agamben, *Remnants of Auschwitz: The Witness and the Archive,* trans. Daniel Heller-Roazen (New York: Zone Books, 1999), 42.

11 Ibid., 168.

12 Robert S. Wistrich, *Hitler and the Holocaust* (New York: Random House, 2001), 233.

13 Bettelheim, *Surviving and Other Essays,* 64.

14 Primo Levi, *Survival in Auschwitz: The Nazi Assault on Humanity,* trans. Stuart Woolf (New York: Macmillan, 1993), 61.

15 Terrence Des Pres, *The Survivor: An Anatomy of Life in the Death Camps* (New York: Oxford University Press, 1976), 57.

16 Ibid., 66.

17 Améry, *At the Mind's Limits,* 33.

18 Levi, *Survival in Auschwitz,* 171.

19 Delbo, *Auschwitz and After,* 168.

20 Des Pres, *The Survivor,* vii.

21 Ibid., 202.

22 For a study of problems associated with memory and language in conveying Delbo's Auschwitz experience, see Renée A. Kingcaid, "Charlotte Delbo's *Auschwitz et après*: The Struggle for Signification," *French Forum* 9, no. 1 (1984): 98–109.

23 For more information about Delbo's life prior to her liberation from incarceration at Ravensbrück, and her subsequent need to "carry the word" by honoring the dead through her plays and prose, see Rosette C. Lamont, "The Triple Courage of Charlotte Delbo," *Massachusetts Review* 4, no. 4 (2000–01): 483–97.

24 Robert Skloot, "Introduction," in *The Theatre of the Holocaust,* vol. 1, ed. Robert Skloot (Madison: University of Wisconsin Press, 1982), 34.

25 Claude Schumacher, who first met Delbo in 1974, asserts that Françoise, a character present in all of Delbo's Holocaust dramas, "is clearly the writer's double and speaks on Charlotte Delbo's behalf." See Schumacher, "Charlotte Delbo: Theatre as a Means of Survival," in *Staging the Holocaust: The Shoah in Drama and Performance,* ed. Claude Schumacher (Cambridge: Cambridge University Press, 1998), 218–19. Moreover, Françoise, intelligent, creative, and rational, like Delbo, seems to function as the narrator of the play.

26 Karein K. Goertz, "Body, Trauma, and the Rituals of Memory: Charlotte Delbo and Ruth Klüger," in *Shaping Losses: Cultural Memory and the Holocaust,* eds. Julia Epstein and Lori Hope Lefkovitz (Urbana and Chicago: University of Illinois Press, 2001), 177.

27 Charlotte Delbo, *Who Will Carry the Word?,* trans. Cynthia Haft, in *The Theatre of the Holocaust,* vol. 1, ed. Robert Skloot (Madison: University of Wisconsin Press, 1982), 276. All subsequent citations are from this edition and will be included within parentheses in the text.

28 Lawrence L. Langer, *The Age of Atrocity: Death in Modern Literature* (Boston: Beacon, 1978), 206.

29 Jennifer L. Geddes, "Banal Evil and Useless Knowledge: Hannah Arendt and Charlotte Delbo on Evil After the Holocaust," *Hypatia: A Journal of Feminist Philosophy* 18, no. 1 (2003): 110.

30 Delbo, *Auschwitz and After,* 25.

31 Vivian M. Patraka, *Spectacular Suffering: Theatre, Fascism, and the Holocaust* (Bloomington and Indianapolis: Indiana University Press, 1999), 104.

32 Delbo, *Auschwitz and After,* 142.

33 Nicole Thatcher, *A Literary Analysis of Charlotte Delbo's Concentration Camp Re-Presentation* (Lewiston: Edwin Mellen, 2000), 156.

34 Nicole Thatcher, "Charlotte Delbo's Voice: The Conscious and Unconscious Determinants of a Woman Writer," *L'Esprit Créatur* 40, no. 2 (2000): 44.

35 Des Pres, *The Survivor*, vii.

36 Vivian M. Patraka, "Contemporary Drama, Fascism, and the Holocaust," *Theatre Journal* 39, no. 1 (1987): 70.

37 Rosette C. Lamont, "Charlotte Delbo's Frozen Friezes," *L' Esprit Créatur* 19, no. 2 (1979): 73.

38 Vinaver has since prepared a more abbreviated (*super-brève*) edition that was published in volume 1 of his *Théâtre complet* (1986).

39 Michel Vinaver, *Écrits sur le théâtre* (Lausanne: Éditions de l'Aire, 1982), 315.

40 Michel Vinaver, *Les Travaux et les jours* (Paris: L'Arche, 1979), 74.

41 David Bradby, "A Theatre of the Everyday: The Plays of Michel Vinaver," *New Theatre Quarterly* 7, no. 27 (1991): 281–82.

42 Vinaver, *Les Travaux et les jours*, 74.

43 Vinaver, *Écrits sur le théâtre*, 123.

44 David Bradby, *The Theater of Michel Vinaver* (Ann Arbor: University of Michigan Press, 1993), 2.

45 Michel Vinaver, "A Reflection on My Works," trans. Christopher de Haan, *Theater* 28, no. 1 (1997): 77.

46 Gideon Lester, "Industrial Art: The Theater of Michel Vinaver," *Theater* 28, no. 1 (1997): 69.

47 Passemar has much in common with Vinaver. Both are playwrights existing within the confines of a corporate world and are penning scripts about big business. In 1967, when Vinaver wrote *Par-dessus bord*, he broke a seven-year playwriting block, not having written a play since *Iphigénie Hôtel* in 1960; Passemar suffers from a ten-year writer's block. Both men received their jobs by putting a notice in the classified section of the newspaper, were hired as energetic young executives, continued to write plays while ascending the corporate hierarchy, got married, and had children. Meanwhile, Passemar, like Vinaver, has reservations about serving the corporate deities and would much rather gravitate toward the arts. Vinaver essentially views this situation as comic, a clownish self-portrait at the time of writing;

as a buffoon, Passemar's comments are also constantly being undercut and interrupted by other characters. See Vinaver, "A Reflection on My Works," 75. Moreover, Passemar seems to get his inspiration from Professor Onde's scholarly history of the Ases and the Vanes, much like Vinaver himself, who was heavily influenced by an academic: his uncle Eugène Vinaver, professor of Romance Languages at Manchester University. Finally, Yvonne Y. Hsieh shrewdly reveals that Passemar is forty-two years old, the same age as Vinaver when he finished the play in 1969. See Hsieh, "Un 'Théâtre total': *Par-dessus bord* de Michel Vinaver," *French Review* 75, no. 3 (2002): 497.

48 Anne Ubersfeld, *Vinaver dramaturge* (Paris: Librairie Théâtrale, 1989), 125.

49 Rosette C. Lamont, "'Des Petits Ebranlements Capillaires ...': The Art of Michel Vinaver," *Modern Drama* 31, no. 3 (1988): 391.

50 Michael David Fox, "Anus Mundi: Jews, the Holocaust, and Excremental Assault in Michel Vinaver's *Overboard* (*Par-dessus bord*)," *Modern Drama* 45, no. 1 (2002): 35.

51 Ibid., 43.

52 Michel Vinaver, *Overboard*, trans. Gideon Lester, in *Plays: 1* (London: Methuen, 1997), 48. All subsequent citations are from this edition and will be included within parentheses in the text.

53 Kevin Elstob, *The Plays of Michel Vinaver: Political Theatre in France* (New York: Peter Lang, 1992), 104.

54 Oldenburg's "happenings" stressed music and sound rather than words. Each "happening" was performed as a unique experience that depended on the audience and the feeling of the moment for the artist. Although the "happenings" were partly scripted, they were largely spontaneous events based upon unrelated fragments of action presented sequentially or simultaneously.

55 In the Fifth Movement of the play, Jiji is performing one such "happening" when the stage directions make the connection between the "happening" and *Aktion* clearly evident. As Jiji directs the performers at The Clinic, where the musical instruments have been replaced by assorted objects, the stage directions indicate, "*Still on the ground, they perform various actions using the objects*" (125).

56 Fox, "Anus Mundi," 49.

57 David Bradby, "'Entre le mythique et le quotidien': Myth in the Theatre of Michel Vinaver," in *Myth and Its Making in the French Theatre*, eds. E. Freeman, H. Mason, M. O'Regan, and S. W. Taylor (Cambridge: Cambridge University Press, 1988), 212. Bradby's quotation is also reproduced in his book on Vinaver. See *The Theater of Michel Vinaver*, 49.

58 Vinaver credits Rabelais as one of the many sources of inspiration for *Par-dessus bord*. See Vinaver, *Écrits sur le théâtre*, 242. Other critics have noted the Rabelaisian aspects of anality prevalent in the play. For example, see David Bradby, *Modern French Drama, 1940–1990*, 2nd ed. (Cambridge: Cambridge University Press, 1991), 249.

59 John Burgess, "Paris," *Plays and Players* 22, no. 2 (1974): 38.

60 Fox, "Anus Mundi," 56.

5 Transcending the Holocaust

1 See Uwe Naumann, "Ein Stück der Versöhnung Zur Uraufführung des Mysterienspiels *Eli* von Nelly Sachs (1962)," *Exilforschung: Ein Internationales Jahrbuch* 4 (1986): 98–114.

2 One year earlier, in 1965, Sachs received the Peace Prize of the German Booksellers. Thus, although Sachs was a Swedish citizen, Germans cultivated her poetry in the spirit of healing German-Jewish relations.

3 Sidra DeKoven Ezrahi, *By Words Alone: The Holocaust in Literature* (Chicago and London: University of Chicago Press, 1980), 139.

4 David Bronsen, "The Dead Among the Living: Nelly Sachs' *Eli*," *Judaism* 16, no. 2 (1976): 127.

5 Hamida Bosmajian, "'Landschaft aus Schreien': The Shackled Leaps of Nelly Sachs," *Bucknell Review* 21, no. 1 (1973): 47.

6 For more information on Hasidism, see Martin Buber, *The Legend of the Baal-Shem* (New York: Harper and Row, 1955).

7 Ruth Dinesen, "The Search for Identity: Nelly Sachs's Jewishness," in *The Uneasy Examples of Nelly Sachs and Walter*

Benjamin, eds. Timothy Bahti and Marilyn Sibley Fries (Ann Arbor: University of Michigan Press, 1995), 33.

8 Gershom G. Scholem, *Major Trends in Jewish Mysticism*, rev. ed. (New York: Schocken Books, 1946), 4.

9 Ibid., 35–36.

10 Nelly Sachs, "Postscript to *Eli*," trans. Christopher Holme, in *Plays of the Holocaust: An International Anthology*, ed. Elinor Fuchs (New York: Theatre Communications Group, 1987), 52. All subsequent citations are from this edition and are included within parentheses in the text. This reference to the quiver and the arrow is a quotation attributed to the prophet Isaiah, who stated that God puts the arrow back in the quiver "so that it may remain in darkness."

11 Sidra DeKoven Ezrahi, "The Holocaust Writer and the Lamentation Tradition: Responses to Catastrophe in Jewish Literature," in *Confronting the Holocaust: The Impact of Elie Wiesel*, ed. Alvin H. Rosenfeld and Irving Greenberg (Bloomington and London: Indiana University Press, 1978), 146.

12 Dinah Dodds, "The Process of Renewal in Nelly Sachs' *Eli*," *German Quarterly* 49, no. 1 (1976): 50.

13 Vivian M. Patraka, *Spectacular Suffering: Theatre, Fascism, and the Holocaust* (Bloomington: Indiana University Press, 1999), 60. Also see Patraka, "Feminism and the Jewish Subject in the Plays of Sachs, Atlan, and Schenkar," in *Performing Feminisms: Feminist Critical Theory and Theatre*, ed. Sue-Ellen Case (Baltimore and London: Johns Hopkins University Press, 1990), 167.

14 Susan E. Cernyak-Spatz, *German Holocaust Literature* 1: Germanic Languages and Literature, vol. 29 (New York: Peter Lang, 1985), 107.

15 Ezrahi, *By Words Alone*, 140.

16 Dodds, "Process of Renewal," 53.

17 Ehrhard Bahr, "Shoemaking as a Mystic Symbol in Nelly Sachs' Mystery Play *Eli*," *German Quarterly* 45, no. 3 (1972): 480.

18 Ibid., 481.

19 Dodds, "Process of Renewal," 57.

20 Elinor Fuchs, "Introduction," in *Plays of the Holocaust: An International Anthology* (New York: Theatre Communications Group, 1987), xiv.

21 Bahr, "Shoemaking as Mystic Symbol," 482.

22 Anders Österling, "Presentation Address," in *Nelly Sachs, Jean-Paul Sartre, Bernard Shaw, Eemil Sillanpää, René Sully-Prudhomme* (New York: Helvetica Press, 1971), 4.

23 Crawford first sought out Maxwell Anderson to adapt the diary, and when he bowed out of the project, Carson McCullers was approached. By 1953, Doubleday had withdrawn as Otto's agent, largely due to hostile wranglings with Levin. Crawford had persuaded Levin that if he could not get his adapted theatrical version of the diary staged by any of fourteen producers that she had on her prescribed list, he would withdraw from the project. Levin, of course, failed to interest any of Crawford's cronies in producing the play but persisted nonetheless. Crawford withdrew her services as producer on 22 April 1953, so obviously McCullers, without a viable ally, was no longer to be considered by Otto.

24 Ralph Melnick, *The Stolen Legacy of Anne Frank: Meyer Levin, Lillian Hellman, and the Staging of the "Diary"* (New Haven and London: Yale University Press, 1997), 37.

25 For more details on the role of the HUAC hearings in the genesis of *The Diary of Anne Frank*, see Judith E. Doneson, "The American History of Anne Frank's Diary," in *Anne Frank: Reflections on Her Life and Legacy*, eds. Hyman Aaron Enzer and Sandra Solotaroff-Enzer (Urbana: University of Illinois Press, 2000), 123–38.

26 Melnick, *Stolen Legacy of Anne Frank*, 43.

27 Otto Frank was a formal, well-educated Old World Jew who graduated from Lessing Gymnasium and was briefly enrolled in the prestigious University of Heidelberg in 1908. His lineage was a cultivated Frankfurt banking family with established business connections. Like Hellman, Otto was a nominal Jew: he did not attend Hebrew school, was not bar mitzvahed, maintained a secular orientation, and was anti-Zionist. Consequently, his daughters never received any formal religious training. Thus,

when Levin constantly exhorted Otto in his letters to allow him to adapt the diary for the stage because he was a Jewish writer who understood Anne's feelings toward anti-Semitism, Otto reluctantly acknowledged Levin's arguments but was only tangentially interested. Otto was making considerable money on the translations of Anne's diary and envisioned a bigger pay day once the play was produced on Broadway. He argued that the readers of the diary were mainly gentiles anyway. Levin, with no Broadway experience and with his insistence on emphasizing the Holocaust as a Jewish experience, which producers told Otto would be box-office disaster, became a liability.

28 For more biographical information about Goodrich and Hackett, see Mark Rowland, "Frances Goodrich and Albert Hackett: Perfectionists," *Backstory: Interviews With Screenwriters of Hollywood's Golden Age,* ed. Pat McGilligan (Berkeley: University of California Press, 1986), 196–211.

29 There were several iterations of the script, so there is some doubt that the version prepared by Goodrich and Hackett was the one that was ultimately filmed.

30 Melnick, *Stolen Legacy of Anne Frank,* 92.

31 Cynthia Ozick, "Who Owns Anne Frank?" *New Yorker,* 6 October 1997, 85.

32 Melnick, *Stolen Legacy of Anne Frank,* 128.

33 On 14 October, slightly more than a week after the play opened on Broadway, Levin sued Otto and Bloomgarden, claiming that Goodrich and Hackett fraudulently represented and plagiarized his play. On 9 January 1958, a jury awarded Levin $50,000 in damages; the judge later set aside the monetary amount, so Meyer filed for a new trial. The case was adjudicated outside court in October 1959 when Otto agreed to pay Levin $15,000 (barely enough to cover his legal expenses) if he would abdicate his rights to the play. Levin's own dramatized version of the diary eventually was produced on 26 November 1966 at the Israeli Soldiers Theatre in Tel Aviv. A group of students at Brandeis University also staged Levin's version in April 1972. The first American professional production of Levin's adaptation was performed in 1983

at Boston's Lyric Stage, where the play was later revived in 1991. Throughout Levin's ordeal to get his play professionally produced, he consistently argued to journalists, theater professionals, and Jewish clergymen that his play was ignored in favor of the version adapted by Goodrich and Hackett because his adaptation was too Jewish, and communists such as Hellman preferred focusing on the anti-fascist elements of the diary. Levin's battle to vindicate himself and validate his own version of the play over the one written by Goodrich and Hackett became a lifelong obsession, ultimately contributing to his wife Tereska's suicide attempt. Levin tried to exorcise his demons by publishing *The Fanatic* in 1964, a supposedly fictitious novel with parallels to his frustrating experiences with his battle over the diary. His twenty-year fixation over the diary is explicated in his memoir, *The Obsession*, published by Simon and Schuster in 1973. For more information on Levin and his battle to get his version of the diary staged, see Melnick, *Stolen Legacy of Anne Frank* and Lawrence Graver, *An Obsession With Anne Frank* (Berkeley: University of California Press, 1995).

34 For more information on the German reception of the play and the diary, see Alex Sagon, "An Optimistic Icon: Anne Frank's Canonization in Postwar Culture," *German Politics and Society* 13 (Fall 1995): 95–107.

35 Alvin H. Rosenfeld, "Popularization and Memory: The Case of Anne Frank," in *Lessons and Legacies: The Meaning of the Holocaust in a Changing World*, ed. Peter Hayes (Evanston: Northwestern University Press, 1991), 261.

36 Martha Ravitz, "To Work in the World: Anne Frank and American Literary History," *Women's Studies: An Interdisciplinary Journal* 27, no. 4 (1998): 13.

37 Molly Magid Hoagland, "Anne Frank, On and Off Broadway," *Commentary* 105, no. 3 (1998): 60.

38 Anne Frank, *The Diary of a Young Girl: The Definitive Edition*, trans. Susan Massotty and eds. Otto H. Frank and Mirjam Pressler (New York: Doubleday, 1995), 54. All subsequent citations are from this edition and are included within parentheses in the text.

39 Ozick, "Who Owns Anne Frank?" 78.

40 Hannah Elisabeth Pick-Goslar, "Her Last Days," trans. Alison Meersschaert, in *Anne Frank: Reflections on Her Life and Legacy*, eds. Hyman Aaron Enzer and Sandra Solotaroff-Enzer (Urbana: University of Illinois Press, 2000), 50.

41 Ernst Schnabel, *Anne Frank: A Portrait in Courage*, trans. Richard and Clara Winston (New York: Harcourt, Brace & World, 1958), 177.

42 Lawrence L. Langer, "The Americanization of the Holocaust on Stage and Screen," in *From Hester Street to Hollywood: The Jewish-American Stage and Screen*, ed. Sarah Blacher Cohen (Bloomington: Indiana University Press, 1983), 215.

43 Rosenfeld, "Popularization and Memory," 250.

44 Frances Goodrich and Albert Hackett, *The Diary of Anne Frank* (New York: Random House, 1956), 22. All subsequent citations are from this edition and are included within parentheses in the text.

45 Edward R. Isser, *Stages of Annihilation: Theatrical Representations of the Holocaust* (Madison: Fairleigh Dickinson University Press, 1997), 74.

46 Bernard Kalb, "Diary Footnotes," *New York Times*, 2 October 1955, sec. 2, 3.

47 David Jortner, "Martyrs and Victims: *The Diary of Anne Frank* and *The Island*," *Text and Presentation: The Journal of the Comparative Drama Conference* 23 (April 2002): 49.

48 Perhaps one reason why the play has been so successful in West and East Germany is because of its reassurance to the Germans that people are truly good at heart, and any responsibility for the Holocaust must fall on the political ideology of the Nazis rather than on themselves.

49 Bruno Bettelheim, *Surviving and Other Essays* (New York: Alfred A. Knopf, 1979), 251.

50 Melnick, *Stolen Legacy of Anne Frank*, 112.

51 Albert Wertheim, *Staging the War: American Drama After World War II* (Bloomington and Indianapolis: Indiana University Press, 2004), 282.

52 Doneson, "The American History of Anne Frank's Diary," 135.

53 Melnick, *Stolen Legacy of Anne Frank*, 146.

54 Gary Saul Morson, "How Did Dostoevsky Know?" *New Criterion* 17, no. 9 (1999): 23.

55 Ozick, "Who Owns Anne Frank?" 80.

56 Wertheim, *Staging the War*, 282.

57 Norbert Muhlen, "The Return of Anne Frank," *ADL Bulletin*, June 1957, 2.

58 Alan Mintz, *Popular Culture and the Shaping of Holocaust Memory in America* (Seattle and London: University of Washington Press, 2001), 18.

59 Isser, *Stages of Annihilation*, 74.

60 Lawrence L. Langer, *Using and Abusing the Holocaust* (Bloomington and Indianapolis: Indiana University Press, 2006), 19.

6 Marxism and the Holocaust

1 Oliver Clausen, "Weiss/Propagandist and Weiss/Playwright," *New York Times Magazine*, 2 October 1966, 128.

2 Robert Cohen, *Understanding Peter Weiss* (Columbia: University of South Carolina Press, 1993), 14.

3 See Peter Weiss, *Notizbücher, 1960–1971* (Frankfurt am Main: Suhrkamp, 1982), 306.

4 Jürgen E. Schlunk, "Auschwitz and Its Function in Peter Weiss' Search for Identity," *German Studies Review* 10, no. 1 (1987): 27.

5 Peter Weiss, "My Place," trans. Christopher Middleton, in *German Writing Today*, ed. Christopher Middleton (Baltimore: Penguin, 1967), 20.

6 Robert Holub, "1965: The Premiere of Peter Weiss's *The Investigation: Oratorio in Eleven Songs*, a Drama Written From the Documentation of the Frankfurt Auschwitz Trial, Is Staged," in *Yale Companion to Jewish Writing and Thought in German Culture, 1096–1996*, eds. Sander L. Gilman and Jack Zipes (New Haven and London: Yale University Press, 1997), 730.

7 For information about the German productions in 1965, see Joel Carmichael, "German Reactions to a New Play About

Auschwitz," *American–German Review* 32, no. 3 (1966): 30–31, and Roland H. Wiegenstein, "Peter Weiss: *Die Ermittlung*, The Auschwitz Trial on Stage," *American–German Review* 32 (December 1965): 33–35.

8 For more information on Piscator's production, see Christopher Innes, *Modern German Drama: A Study in Form* (Cambridge: Cambridge University Press, 1979), 172–73.

9 See Hatja Garloff, *Words From Abroad: Trauma and Displacement in Postwar German Jewish Writers* (Detroit: Wayne State University Press, 2005), 86.

10 Many scholars and theater critics are confused by Weiss's intentions to model *The Investigation* on the structure of Dante's *Commedia*. For the most accurate analyses of how Weiss structured the play as the antithesis to Dante's model, see Otto F. Best, *Peter Weiss*, trans. Ursule Molinaro (New York: Frederick Ungar, 1976), 93–94, and Erika Salloch, "The *Divina Commedia* as Model and Anti-Model for *The Investigation* by Peter Weiss," *Modern Drama* 14, no. 1 (1971): 1–12. Weiss himself explains Inferno, Paradiso, and Purgatorio in an interview he gave to the *New York Times* shortly after *Die Ermittlung* premiered in Germany. See A. Alvarez, "Peter Weiss: The Truths That Are Uttered in a Madhouse," *New York Times*, 26 December 1965, sec. 2, 3, 14.

11 A. V. Subiotto argues that the dialectic revolves around the structure of entrance, descent, and ascent, derived from the topography of Auschwitz. Weiss, however, does not use these terms. See Subiotto, "Dante and the Holocaust: The Cases of Primo Levi and Peter Weiss," *New Comparison* 11 (Spring 1991): 74.

12 Actually, the *Divine Comedy* contains thirty-four cantos in the *Inferno*. Weiss eliminated one canto to create balance in the text.

13 Christopher Innes also notes that the Third Witness "is the key figure who spells out the political significance of the facts." See Innes, *Modern German Drama*, 176.

14 See Peter Weiss, "Gespräch über Dante," in *Rapporte* (Frankfurt am Main: Suhrkamp, 1968), 144.

15 Salloch, "*Divina Commedia* as Model and Anti-Model," 2.

16 Peter Weiss, *The Investigation*, trans. Jon Swan and Ulu Grosbard (New York: Pocket Books, 1967), ix. All subsequent citations from the play are from this edition and are included within parentheses in the text.

17 Peter Weiss, "Notes on the Contemporary Theater," trans. Joel Agee, in *Essays on German Theater*, ed. Margaret Herzfeld-Sander (New York: Continuum, 1985), 298.

18 Clausen, "Weiss/Propagandist and Weiss/Playwright," 28.

19 Hedy Ehrlich, "*The Investigation*," *Jewish Frontier* 30, no. 2 (1966): 20.

20 Walter Wager, ed., *The Playwrights Speak* (New York: Delacorte Press, 1967), 197.

21 Roger Ellis, *Peter Weiss in Exile: A Critical Study of His Works* (Ann Arbor: UMI Research Press, 1987), 150.

22 Paul Gray, "A Living World: An Interview With Peter Weiss," *Tulane Drama Review* 11, no. 1 (1966): 112.

23 A. Alvarez, "Peter Weiss in Conversation," *Encore* 12, no. 4 (1965): 18.

24 Clausen, "Weiss/Propagandist and Weiss/Playwright," 128.

25 Alvarez, "Peter Weiss in Conversation," 18.

26 Gray, "Living World," 108.

27 Wager, *Playwrights Speak*, 205.

28 Weiss's reliance on the statistics and raw data derived from courtroom testimony is fundamentally different to the approach taken by his mentor, Brecht, who preferred to shape the overall play's dialectic (and dialectics within the various *stationen*) as parables.

29 Salloch, "*Divina Commedia* as Model and Anti-Model," 8.

30 In his book on Weiss, Olaf Berwald remarks, "Throughout his life, Weiss maintained an ambivalent relationship to his Jewish heritage. Not only did he refuse to see himself as a victim, but he rejected the importance of any national or ethnic categories for his personal identity." See Berwald, *An Introduction to the Works of Peter Weiss* (Rochester, NY: Camden House, 2003), 6.

31 Robert Skloot, *The Darkness We Carry: The Drama of the Holocaust* (Madison: University of Wisconsin Press, 1988), 105.

357

Susan E. Cernyak-Spatz disagrees with Skloot, arguing that Weiss's exclusion of the word "Jew" from the play "can be seen as an extreme attempt at emotional objectivity, since Weiss himself is a German Jew." See Cernyak-Spatz, *German Holocaust Literature*, American University Studies 1, vol. 29 (New York: Peter Lang, 1985), 84.

32 Sidra DeKoven Ezrahi, *By Words Alone: The Holocaust in Literature* (Chicago and London: University of Chicago Press, 1980), 39.

33 Gray, "Living World," 110.

34 Brecht's plays did not always match his theoretical concepts. In principle, Brecht preferred a narrator to create emotional distance. For example, in *The Caucasian Chalk Circle*, the setting is a kolchos of a village in the Caucasus mountains during the time of the Nazi invasion. The singer, Arkadi Cheidze, narrates the tale of The Chalk Circle, which occurs centuries earlier in Grusinia (Transcaucasia). Although the events seen on stage take place in Grusinia, the audience is constantly aware that the setting is during World War II because Russian peasants are performing the play, thus using makeshift props to represent the setting, and the acting by the peasants is obviously amateurish. As Brecht noted, amateur acting precludes emotional identification, thus leading the audience to think about the parable. The narrator's function is essentially show and tell. However, in many of Brecht's plays, no narrator is present.

35 Robert Cohen, "On March 13, in the Middle of Rehearsals for the Premiere of *Marat/Sade*, Peter Weiss Attends the Frankfurt Auschwitz Trial," in *Yale Companion to Jewish Writing and Thought in German Culture, 1096–1996*, eds. Sander L. Gilman and Jack Zipes (New Haven and London: Yale University Press, 1997), 724.

36 Garloff, *Words From Abroad*, 90.

37 Clausen, "Weiss/Propagandist and Weiss/Playwright," 128.

38 Berwald, *Introduction to the Works of Peter Weiss*, 24.

39 Richard F. Shepard, "Peter Weiss, Visiting Here, Talks About His Auschwitz Trial Play," *New York Times*, 22 April 1966, A30.

40 Clausen, "Weiss/Propagandist and Weiss/Playwright," 132.

41 Cohen, *Understanding Peter Weiss*, 92.

42 Ian Hilton, *Peter Weiss: A Search for Affinities*, Modern German Authors: Texts and Contexts, vol. 3 (London: Oswald Wolff, 1970), 47.

43 Best, *Peter Weiss*, 90.

44 Clausen, "Weiss/Propagandist and Weiss/Playwright," 134.

45 During the initial staging of the play throughout West Germany in 1965, representatives from Krupp, Siemens, and I-G Farben protested being associated with a system that exterminated labor for profit. When the play was performed in Cologne, which is close to Krupp headquarters in Essen, all references to Krupp were excised from the script.

46 Here, Weiss's conflation of victim and executioner becomes apropos. Audiences may subliminally associate Jews with capitalists and industrialists–the same values of acquisition shared by the fascists. Thus, the implication is that if Jews had outnumbered Nazis instead of being in the minority, they could easily have been the exploiters. Racial ideology entirely disappears from the Marxist view of the Holocaust.

47 Catharine Hughes, *Plays, Politics, and Polemics* (New York: Drama Book Specialists, 1973), 142.

48 Primo Levi, "The Memory of Offense," in *Bitburg in Moral and Political Perspective*, ed. Geoffrey H. Hartman (Bloomington: Indiana University Press, 1986), 131.

49 Alvin H. Rosenfeld, *A Double Dying: Reflections on Holocaust Literature* (Bloomington and London: Indiana University Press, 1980), 157.

50 Daniel Jonah Goldhagen, *Hitler's Willing Executioners: Ordinary Germans and the Holocaust* (New York: Alfred A. Knopf, 1996), 427.

51 Clausen, "Weiss/Propagandist and Weiss/Playwright," 130.

52 Ellis, *Peter Weiss in Exile*, 53.

53 Kushner originally worked with 3P (poetry, politics, and popcorn) Productions as a playwright and director. When the theater company folded, several of its members formed the Heat & Light

Company, which was modeled on British alternative theater groups 7:84 and Monstrous Regiment, as well as their American counterparts, Mabou Mines and the Wooster Group.

54 David Savran, "Tony Kushner," in *Speaking on Stage: Interviews With Contemporary American Playwrights*, eds. Philip C. Kolin and Colby H. Kullman (Tuscaloosa and London: University of Alabama Press, 1996), 294.

55 Carl Weber, "I Always Go Back to Brecht: A Conversation With the Playwright Tony Kushner," *Brecht Yearbook* 20 (1995): 74–75.

56 Savran, "Tony Kushner," 309.

57 Wendy Arons, "'Preaching to the Converted?'–'You Couldn't Possibly Do Any Better!'–An Interview With Tony Kushner on September 19, 1994," *Communications From the International Brecht Society* 23, no. 2 (1994): 53. During this interview, Kushner also noted, "I think theatre is inherently political. Everything that Brecht said about theatre is absolutely true" (54).

58 Tony Kushner, "Afterword," in *A Bright Room Called Day* (New York: Theatre Communications Group, 1994), 179. All subsequent citations from the play are from this edition and are included within parentheses in the text.

59 In the Afterword, Kushner wrote, "For my friend Kimberly I wrote the part of Rosa Malek; in her clarity, intelligence, courage and commitment, Rosa resembles Kim, and Rosa escapes from Berlin" (174).

60 Christopher Bigsby, *Contemporary American Playwrights* (Cambridge: Cambridge University Press, 1999), 96.

61 James Fisher, *The Theater of Tony Kushner: Living Past Hope* (New York and London: Routledge, 2001), 25.

62 Bigsby, *Contemporary American Playwrights*, 96.

63 Kushner's rejection of Agnes's retreat into isolation and fear seems understandable, but his opposition to exile should be dubious for him. His mentor, Brecht, was in exile from 1933 to 1948. Had Brecht remained in Germany during the Third Reich when the Nazis were burning his plays and placing him on the list of banned writers, he surely would have been executed. Brecht's reputation largely rests on the plays he wrote in exile, including

Mother Courage and Her Children (1939), *Galileo* (1939), *The Good Woman of Setzuan* (1940), *The Resistible Rise of Arturo Ui* (1941), and *The Caucasian Chalk Circle* (1944–45), rather than on his early and middle plays. If Brecht had not gone into exile and had been murdered by the Nazis before he had a chance to write his mature plays, his international reputation and influence would be vastly different from what it has been since 1933.

64 Tony Kushner, *Plays by Tony Kushner* (New York: Broadway Play Publishing, 1992), 12.

65 Bigsby, *Contemporary American Playwrights*, 94.

66 See Kenneth Seeskin, "Coming to Terms With Failure: A Philosophical Dilemma," in *Writing and the Holocaust*, ed. Berel Lang (New York and London: Holmes & Meier, 1988), 110–21.

67 Ibid., 113.

68 Patrick R. Pachero, "AIDS, Angels, Activism and Sex in the Nineties," in *Tony Kushner in Conversation*, ed. Robert Vorlicky (Ann Arbor: University of Michigan Press, 1998), 54.

69 Ibid.

70 Bruce McLeod, "The Oddest Phenomena in Modern History," in *Tony Kushner in Conversation*, ed. Robert Vorlicky (Ann Arbor: University of Michigan Press, 1998), 78.

71 Ibid., 78.

7 Aryan Responsibility During the Holocaust, I

1 Primo, Levi, "The Memory of Offense," in *Bitburg in Moral and Political Perspective*, ed. Geoffrey H. Hartman (Bloomington: Indiana University Press, 1986), 134.

2 Daniel Jonah Goldhagen, *Hitler's Willing Executioners: Ordinary Germans and the Holocaust* (New York: Alfred A. Knopf, 1996), 221.

3 Ibid., 253.

4 Raul Hilberg, *The Destruction of the European Jews*, rev. ed., vol. 3 (New York and London: Holmes & Meier, 1985), 1024–25.

5 Goldhagen, *Hitler's Willing Executioners*, 379.

6 One notable protest was from the Catholic priest Bernard Lichtenberg of St. Hedwig's Cathedral in Berlin, who defied Nazi policy and prayed publicly for the Jews. Lichtenberg's major

mistake was to declare himself an opponent of the tenets of Nazism. For this transgression, he was denounced and then placed into custody, where he announced that he wanted to share the fate of the deported Jews in the East. After serving a two-year prison sentence, he was released and then, too sick to travel, died on the way to being transported to Dachau. As a result of such a public protest, the Nazis obviously did not shoot or torture Lichtenberg, proving that notable individuals had the ability to question Nazi policies of genocide without life-threatening retribution.

7 Bruno Bettelheim, *Surviving and Other Essays* (New York: Alfred A. Knopf, 1979), 270.

8 For a philosophical discussion of morality and ethics during the Holocaust, see Herbert Hirsch, "Reflections on 'Ethics,' 'Morality,' and 'Responsibility' After the Holocaust," in *Remembering for the Future: The Holocaust in an Age of Genocide*, vol. 2: Ethics and Religion, ed. Margot Levy (Basingstoke and New York: Palgrave, 2001), 123–32.

9 Hilberg, *Destruction of the European Jews*, 1011.

10 Giorgio Agamben, *Remnants of Auschwitz: The Witness and the Archive* (New York: Zone Books, 1999), 24.

11 Victoria Stewart argues that Norton-Taylor chose these four defendants because they best engage the audience in the theatricality of the trial proceedings. We have seen earlier, especially with regard to Weiss's *The Investigation*, how documentary theater can bog down the playwright in minutiae when attempting to reproduce courtroom testimony verbatim for the purpose of maintaining historical veracity. In paring down the multitude of pages of testimony, Norton-Taylor focused on passages that proved to be entertaining to audiences, whereas Weiss was more interested in using Brechtian alienation effects to distance the audience emotionally in order to engage them scientifically as objective observers. See Stewart, "Dramatic Justice? The Aftermath of the Holocaust in Ronald Harwood's *Taking Sides* and *The Handyman*," *Modern Drama*, 43, no. 1 (2000): 4–5.

12 Richard Norton-Taylor, "On the Trail of the Trial," *Guardian*, 1 May 1996, sec. 2, 13.

13 Richard Norton-Taylor, *Nuremberg: The War Crimes Trial* (London: Nick Hern, 1997), 4. All subsequent citations from the play are from this edition and are included within parentheses in the text.

14 The role of Little Slam is demanding, for an actor must be adept at mime to play the part effectively. Apparently, Ségal, a connoisseur of mime through his apprenticeship with Marceau and Barrault, envisioned this to be a great role for himself.

15 Gilles Ségal, *All the Tricks but One*, trans. Sara O'Connor (New York: Samuel French, 1993), 35. All subsequent citations from the play are from this edition and are included within parentheses in the text.

16 Edward R. Isser, *Stages of Annihilation: Theatrical Representations of the Holocaust* (Madison: Fairleigh Dickinson University Press, 1997), 121.

17 Ibid., 122.

18 Arthur Miller, "Hitler's Quarry," *ANQ: A Quarterly Journal of Short Articles, Notes, and Reviews* 13, no. 1 (2000): 36–37.

19 George W. Crandell, "Arthur Miller's Unheard Plea for Jewish Refugees: 'Hitler's Quarry,'" *ANQ: A Quarterly Journal of Short Articles, Notes, and Reviews* 13, no. 1 (2000): 34.

20 Arthur Miller, "The Nazi Trials and the German Heart," in *Echoes Down the Corridor: Arthur Miller, Collected Essays, 1944–2000*, ed. Steven R. Centola (New York: Penguin Putnam, 2000), 67–68. This essay was originally published as "Arthur Miller: How the Nazi Trials Search the Hearts of All Germans" in the *New York Herald Tribune* on 15 March 1964 and was soon reprinted in other newspapers around the world. For another reprint besides the one in Centola's collection of essays, see Robert Lee Feldman, "Arthur Miller's Neglected Article on the Nazi War Criminals' Trials: A Vision of Evil," *Resources for American Literary Study* 15, no. 2 (1985): 191–96.

21 Arthur Miller, *Timebends: A Life* (New York: Grove Press, 1987), 538.

22 Ingeborg Morath's fate was similar to that of Prince von Schwarzenberg. As a native of Austria, she refused to cooperate

with the Nazis and was relegated to slave labor, assembling airplane parts in a German war factory.

23 Barbara Gelb, "Question: 'Am I My Brother's Keeper?'" *New York Times*, 29 November 1964, sec. 2, 1.

24 The idea of characters waiting for an unknown destiny in what Miller depicts as an absurd universe gave critics the opportunity to compare *Incident at Vichy* to Beckett's *Waiting for Godot*. Of course, the tone, diction, language (circular, stichomythic, and rhythmic for Beckett, direct and poignant for Miller), time (a timeless universe in Beckett's play, whereas Miller's drama takes place in 1942), and setting (Beckett's is nebulous while Miller's occurs in the distinctly realistic world of Vichy, France) of the two plays indicate a sharp contrast. More significantly, Miller's existential vision of faith in individual responsibility is quite different from Beckett's absurd universe where neither divine intervention nor human action can assuage the deeply rooted *angoisse* of able-bodied, disabled, or, in his later plays, disembodied voices.

25 Martin Gottfried, *Arthur Miller: His Life and Work* (Cambridge: Da Capo Press, 2003), 380.

26 Arthur Miller, "Our Guilt for the World's Evil," *New York Times*, 3 January 1965, sec. 6, 11.

27 Christopher Bigsby, *Arthur Miller: A Critical Study* (Cambridge: Cambridge University Press, 2005), 259.

28 Miller, "Our Guilt for the World's Evil," sec. 6, 11.

29 Bigsby, *Arthur Miller*, 251.

30 Eric Sterling, "Fear of Being 'The Other': Racial Purity and Social Responsibility in Arthur Miller's *Incident at Vichy*," *Publications of the Arkansas Philological Association* 20, no. 2 (1994): 67.

31 Edward I. Isser, questioning the historical accuracy of the play by claiming that Vichy Jews with French citizenship were protected from deportation through April 1944, wonders how Lebeau should have known of the German invasion of France in 1939. Moreover, in 1939, no one knew the extent of the Nazi policy of genocide or how it would affect Jewish citizens of foreign countries. See Isser, *Stages of Annihilation*, 68.

32 Arthur Miller, *Incident at Vichy* (New York: Penguin, 1985), 6. All subsequent citations from the play are from this edition and are included within parentheses in the text.

33 Sheila Huftel, *Arthur Miller: The Burning Glass* (New York: Citadel Press, 1965), 222.

34 Lawrence D. Lowenthal, "Arthur Miller's *Incident at Vichy*: A Sartrean Interpretation," in *Arthur Miller: New Perspectives*, ed. Robert A. Martin (Englewood Cliffs, NJ: Prentice-Hall, 1982), 174.

35 Ibid., 182.

36 Janet N. Balakian, "The Holocaust, the Depression and McCarthyism: Miller in the Sixties," in *The Cambridge Companion to Arthur Miller*, ed. Christopher Bigsby (Cambridge: Cambridge University Press, 1997), 128.

37 June Schlueter and James K. Flanagan, *Arthur Miller* (New York: Ungar, 1987), 103.

38 Steven R. Centola, "'The Will to Live': An Interview With Arthur Miller," in *Conversations With Arthur Miller*, ed. Matthew C. Roudané (Jackson and London: University Press of Mississippi, 1987), 358.

39 Harold Clurman, "Arthur Miller's Later Plays," in *Arthur Miller: A Collection of Critical Essays*, ed. Robert W. Corrigan (Englewood Cliffs, NJ: Prentice-Hall, 1969), 161.

40 Lowenthal, "Arthur Miller's *Incident at Vichy*," 180.

41 Edward Murray, *Arthur Miller, Dramatist* (New York: Frederick Ungar, 1967), 169.

42 Dennis Welland, *Miller: The Playwright* (London and New York: Methuen, 1983), 110.

43 Lowenthal, "Arthur Miller's *Incident at Vichy*," 181.

44 Terry Otten, *The Temptation of Innocence in the Dramas of Arthur Miller* (Columbia and London: University of Missouri Press, 2002), 140–41.

45 Robert Feldman, "Arthur Miller on the Theme of Evil: An Interview," *Resources for American Literary Study* 17, no. 1 (1990): 93.

46 Leonard Moss, *Arthur Miller*, rev. ed. (Boston: G. K. Hall, 1980), 75.

47 Benjamin Nelson, *Arthur Miller: Portrait of a Playwright* (New York: David McKay, 1970), 286.

48 Richard I. Evans, *Psychology and Arthur Miller* (New York: E. P. Dutton, 1969), 75.

49 Kinereth Meyer, "'A Jew Can Have a Jewish Face': Arthur Miller, Autobiography, and the Holocaust," *Prooftexts: A Journal of Jewish Literary History* 18, no. 3 (1998): 251.

50 Lawrence L. Langer, "The Americanization of the Holocaust on Stage and Screen," in *From Hester Street to Hollywood: The Jewish–American Stage and Screen*, ed. Sarah Blacher Cohen (Bloomington: Indiana University Press, 1983), 223.

51 Ibid., 224.

52 Bigsby, *Arthur Miller*, 250.

8 Aryan Responsibility During the Holocaust, II

1 Egon Schwarz, "Rolf Hochhuth's *The Representative*," *Germanic Review* 39, no. 3 (1964): 211.

2 Eric Bentley, ed., "Foreword," in *The Storm Over The Deputy*, (New York: Grove Press, 1964), 8.

3 Alfred G. Aronowitz, "The Play That Rocked Europe," *Saturday Evening Post*, 29 February 1964, 42.

4 Hochhuth also received inspiration from Albert Camus, who, in 1944, had already questioned the pope's silence. French novelist François Mauriac and Austrian philosopher Friedrich Heer had also earlier searched for answers to the pope's noncommittal response to the plight of the Jews.

5 Hochhuth moved to Basel in May 1963, choosing to live in exile from his native Germany, a country he no longer respected.

6 For example, in his essay on Hochhuth, Arthur Olsen calls him "young" twice within the first two sentences and then states that he lived thirty-one years in "the still backwaters of provincial West Germany." See Olsen, "An Interview With Rolf Hochhuth," *New York Times Book Review*, 1 March 1964, 31.

7 Alfred Gong, "Rolf Hochhuth's *The Deputy*," *American–Germanic Review* 30, no. 3 (1964): 40.

8 Francis Cardinal Spellman, "A Statement by Francis Cardinal Spellman," in *The Storm Over The Deputy*, ed. Eric Bentley (New York: Grove Press, 1964), 38.

9 G. B. Cardinal Montini, "Pius XII and the Jews," in *The Storm Over the Deputy*, ed. Eric Bentley (New York: Grove Press, 1964), 67–68.

10 Of course, critics of these theologians counter that the fate of the Jews could not have been worse than being deported to their deaths in Auschwitz. Moreover, at the time of the Italian deportations in October 1943, most religious and political leaders knew exactly what deportation meant.

11 Jack D. Zipes loosely defines documentary drama as theater that reports the results of the author's historical research and provokes audience thinking, rather than the way most scholars view it, which is a staged version of condensed or adapted trial transcription. Thus, according to this definition, Zipes classifies *The Deputy* as documentary drama. See Zipes, "Documentary Drama in Germany: Mending the Circuit," *Germanic Review* 42, no. 1 (1967): 49–62.

12 Walter Kaufmann, *Tragedy and Philosophy* (Princeton: Princeton University Press, 1968), 387.

13 Rainer Taëni, *Rolf Hochhuth*, trans. R. W. Last, Modern German Authors, New Series, vol. 5 (London: Oswald Wolff, 1977), 63.

14 Patricia Marx, "Interview With Rolf Hochhuth," in *The Storm Over The Deputy*, ed. Eric Bentley (New York: Grove Press, 1964), 53.

15 R. C. Perry, "Historical Authenticity and Dramatic Form: Hochhuth's *Der Stellvertreter* and Weiss's *Die Ermittlung*," *Modern Language Review* 64, no. 4 (1969): 833.

16 Robert Skloot, *The Darkness We Carry: The Drama of the Holocaust* (Madison: University of Wisconsin Press, 1988), 100.

17 Susan E. Cernyak-Spatz, *German Holocaust Literature*, American University Studies 1, vol. 29 (New York: Peter Lang, 1985), 80.

18 Hamida Bosmajian, *Metaphors of Evil: Contemporary German Literature and the Shadow of Nazism* (Iowa City: University of Iowa Press, 1979), 162.

19 Rolf Hochhuth, *The Deputy*, trans. Richard and Clara Winston (New York: Grove Press, 1964), 77. All subsequent citations from the play are from this edition and are included within parentheses in the text.

20 Emanuela Barasch-Rubinstein, *The Devil, the Saints, and the Church: Reading Hochhuth's "The Deputy"* (New York: Peter Lang, 2004), 68–69.

21 Friedrich Heer, "The Need for Confession," in *The Deputy Reader: Studies in Moral Responsibility*, eds. Dolores Barracano Schmidt and Earl Robert Schmidt (Glenview, Il: Scott, Foresman, 1965), 192.

22 Robert Lieber, "On Hochhuth's Historical Sources," in *The Deputy Reader: Studies in Moral Responsibility*, eds. Dolores Barracano Schmidt and Earl Robert Schmidt (Glenview, Il: Scott, Foresman, 1965), 163.

23 Hochhuth's point about the effectiveness of Bishop Galen's protest against the Nazi policy of euthanasia is open to debate. Michael Burleigh and Wolfgang Wippermann argue that the protests that ensued among Galen's colleagues may not have affected the official euthanasia program; instead, the Nazis halted the program because they reached their initial target figure. See Burleigh and Wipperman, *The Racial State: Germany, 1933–1945* (Cambridge: Cambridge University Press, 1991), 153.

24 "Should the Pope Have Remained Silent?" in *The Deputy Reader*, eds. Dolores Barracano Schmidt and Earl Robert Schmidt (Glenview, Il: Scott, Foresman, 1965), 186–87.

25 Rolf Hochhuth, "The Playwright Answers," in *The Storm Over the Deputy*, ed. Eric Bentley (New York: Grove Press, 1964), 77.

26 However, the situation was much different in Holland. After the Dutch bishops protested against the seizure of Jews, the Nazis accelerated their anti-Jewish activities and deported any priest or monk that had any trace of Jewish blood; Edith Stein, the well-known Carmelite nun, was among those exterminated. Thus, the

Nazis were not always consistent with regard to their treatment of clergymen who protested against genocide.

27 For example, Heinrich Himmler was raised in a respected Catholic family in Bavaria; his uncle was Suffragen Bishop of Bamberg. Hans Frank, the governor-general of the *Generalgouvernment* in German-occupied Poland from 1939 to 1945, had become reconciled to the Catholic Church and even attacked Hitler as a war criminal. Joseph Goebbels grew up in a pious working-class Catholic family and was educated in Catholic schools. Rudolf Höss, the first commandant of Auschwitz, was raised in a strict Catholic household in Baden-Baden. Several high-ranking Nazis, such as Himmler, even rebelled against their strict Catholic upbringing yet were nevertheless hesitant about antagonizing the Vatican.

28 Critics may argue that Pacelli always had strong ties with Germany and thus could never be neutral. He was the nuncio in Bavaria from 1917 to 1925 and to the Reich from 1920 to 1929. As cardinal-state secretary (1930–39), he maintained correspondence with the German ambassador, testifying to his strong interest in German affairs. He was also active in drawing up the Bavarian, Prussian, and Baden concordats.

29 Barasch-Rubinstein, *The Devil, the Saints, and the Church*, 82.

30 Albrecht von Kessel, "The Pope and the Jews," in *The Storm Over The Deputy*, ed. Eric Bentley (New York: Grove Press, 1964), 75.

31 E. Elaine Murdaugh, "The Apostate Ethic: The Alternative to Faith in Hochhuth's *Der Stellvertreter*," *Seminar* 15 (1979): 277.

32 Ibid.

33 Alvin H. Rosenfeld, *A Double Dying: Reflections on Holocaust Literature* (Bloomington and London: Indiana University Press, 1980), 148.

34 See Catharine Hughes, *Plays, Politics, and Polemics* (New York: Drama Book Specialists, 1973), 136, and Taëni, *Rolf Hochhuth*, 65.

35 James Trainer, "Hochhuth's Play *Der Stellvertreter*," *Forum for Modern Language Studies* 1 (1965): 21.

36 Rosenfeld, *Double Dying*, 149.

37 Marx, "Interview With Rolf Hochhuth," 58.

38 Christopher Bigsby, *Remembering and Imagining the Holocaust: The Chain of Memory* (Cambridge: Cambridge University Press, 2006), 129.

39 In virtually all of the productions, directors have had to make decisions about which scenes to cut. Theater reviewers typically have not made an issue about the length of the play because they are writing about productions that are three to four hours long in which half of the text has been eliminated. In most productions, act five is usually discarded.

40 At the beginning of the *Jägerkeller* scene, Hochhuth notes in the stage directions that Mengele was never apprehended for his crimes. The implication is that the devil is never caught but instead remains a spirit that is ubiquitous.

41 Rosenfeld, *Double Dying*, 144.

42 Bosmajian, *Metaphors of Evil*, 165.

43 Leonidas E. Hill, "History and Rolf Hochhuth's *The Deputy*," *Mosaic: A Journal for the Comparative Study of Literature* 1, no. 1 (1967): 128.

44 Rosenfeld, *Double Dying*, 150.

45 Peter Demetz, *Postwar German Literature: A Critical Introduction* (New York: Pegasus, 1970), 141.

46 Christopher Innes, *Modern German Drama: A Study in Form* (Cambridge: Cambridge University Press, 1979), 203.

9 Heroism and Moral Responsibility in the Ghettoes

1 Lucy S. Davidowicz, *The War Against the Jews*, 1933–1945 (New York: Bantam, 1975), 415.

2 Ibid., 473.

3 Lerner's only other Holocaust drama besides *Kastner* is *The Witness*, performed in 1986 in Tel Aviv by the National Theatre for Youth. The play, based on a novella by Shulamit Har'even, is about a young Jew from Poland who flees to Palestine in 1942, where his reports about Nazi atrocities are disbelieved.

4 For more information on this award, see S. Avigal, Ada Ben Nahum, and Dan Orian, "*Kastner* Was Awarded the 'Aharon

Meskin Prize' of the Israel Centre of the I.T.I." *Modern International Drama* 27, no. 1 (1993): 37–38.

5 Raul Hilberg, *The Destruction of the European Jews*, vol. 2 (New York and London: Holmes & Meier, 1985), 797.

6 See "Motti Lerner," *Modern International Drama* 27, no. 1 (1993): 35.

7 Dan Laor, "Theatrical Interpretation of the Shoah: Image and Counter-image," in *Staging the Holocaust: The Shoah in Drama and Performance*, ed. Claude Schumacher (Cambridge: Cambridge University Press, 1998), 104.

8 Motti Lerner, *Kastner*, trans. Imre Goldstein, in *Israeli Holocaust Drama*, ed. Michael Taub (Syracuse: Syracuse University Press, 1996), 188. All subsequent citations are from this edition and are included within parentheses in the text.

9 Glenda Abramson, "The Cultural Uses of the Holocaust," in *The Conscience of Humankind: Literature and Traumatic Experiences*, ed. Elrud Ibsch (Amsterdam: Rodopi, 2000), 15.

10 Although Lerner's research on the Holocaust in Hungary is represented in the play as factually accurate, certain character traits were embellished within those historical parameters. For example, in scene forty, Eichmann tells Jewish jokes to Hungarian collaborators Endre and Baky, an amusing touch to Eichmann's notorious demeanor but fiction nonetheless.

11 Michael Taub, "Israeli Theater and the Holocaust," in *Israeli Holocaust Drama*, ed. Michael Taub (Syracuse: Syracuse University Press, 1996), 14.

12 Abramson, "The Cultural Uses of the Holocaust," 16.

13 For Israeli audiences there were other implicit subtexts to the play. First, *Kastner* implied to Israeli audiences of the 1980s that negotiation, rather than physical force, could be a viable means of contending with their Arab neighbors. Second, the play reflects a movement away from Israeli Holocaust dramas of decades earlier that depicted Diaspora Jews as acquiescing or merely going to the slaughter like sheep.

14 In the play, Adam's last name is spelled two different ways: Rolenik and Rolenick.

15 See Yitzhak Arad, "Vilna," in *Encyclopedia of the Holocaust*, vol. 4, ed. Israel Gutman (New York: Macmillan, 1990), 1573.

16 Joshua Sobol, *Adam*, trans. Ron Jenkins, in *Israeli Holocaust Drama*, ed. Michael Taub (Syracuse: Syracuse University Press, 1996), 275. All subsequent citations are from this edition and are included within parentheses in the text.

17 In *Ghetto*, Gens maintained that the most viable means of saving the ghetto was to create a large labor force that would be economically useful to the Nazis. However, Sobol omits this point from consideration in *Adam*.

18 Taub, "Israeli Theater and the Holocaust," 10.

19 Reuben Ainsztein, *Jewish Resistance in Nazi-Occupied Eastern Europe* (New York: Harper & Row, 1974), 512.

20 Israel Gutman, "Wittenberg, Yitzhak," in *Encyclopedia of the Holocaust*, vol. 4, ed. Israel Gutman (New York: Macmillan, 1990), 1658.

21 Eric Sterling, "The Ultimate Sacrifice: The Death of Resistance Hero Yitzhak Wittenberg and the Decline of the United Partisan Organization," in *Resisting the Holocaust*, ed. Ruby Rohrlich (Oxford: Berg, 1998), 62.

22 Ibid., 70.

23 Yitzhak Arad, "Gens, Jacob," in *Encyclopedia of the Holocaust*, vol. 2, ed. Israel Gutman (New York: Macmillan, 1990), 556.

24 Freddie Rokem, "Jehoshua Sobol's Theatre of the Ghetto," in *Small Is Beautiful: Small Countries Theatre Conference*, eds. Claude Schumacher and Derek Fogg (Glasgow: Theatre Studies Publications, 1991), 145.

25 Taub, "Israeli Theater and the Holocaust," 10.

26 Harold Lieberman and Edith Lieberman, "Production Notes," to *Throne of Straw*, in *The Theatre of the Holocaust: Four Plays*, ed. Robert Skloot (Madison: University of Wisconsin Press, 1982), 118.

27 See Robert Skloot, "Directing the Holocaust Play," *Theatre Journal* 31, no. 4 (1979): 534–37.

28 Shmuel Krakowski, "Lódz," in *Encyclopedia of the Holocaust*, vol. 3, ed. Israel Gutman (New York: Macmillan, 1990), 904.

29 Ibid., 908.

30 Harold and Edith Lieberman, *Throne of Straw*, 134. All subsequent citations are from this edition and are included within parentheses in the text.

31 Ellen Schiff, *From Stereotype to Metaphor: The Jew in Contemporary Drama* (Albany: State University of New York Press, 1982), 189.

32 Ellen Schiff, "American Authors and Ghetto Kings: Challenges and Perplexities," in *Holocaust Studies Annual*, vol. 1: *America and the Holocaust*, eds. Sanford Pinsker and Jack Fischel (Greenwood, Fl: Penkevill Publishing, 1984), 21.

33 Robert Skloot, *The Darkness We Carry: The Drama of the Holocaust* (Madison: University of Wisconsin Press, 1988), 14.

34 Schiff, "American Authors and Ghetto Kings," 19–20.

35 Shimon Wincelberg, *Resort 76*, in *The Theatre of the Holocaust: Four Plays*, vol. 1, ed. Robert Skloot (Madison: University of Wisconsin Press, 1982), 48–49. All subsequent citations are from this edition and are included within parentheses in the text.

36 Robert Skloot, ed., "Introduction," in *The Theatre of the Holocaust: Four Plays* (Madison: University of Wisconsin Press, 1982), 23.

37 Eric Sterling, "Loss and Growth of Identity in Shimon Wincelberg's *Resort 76*," in *Literature and Ethnic Discrimination*, ed. Michael J. Meyer (Amsterdam: Rodopi, 1997), 76.

38 The ironically cruel message here is that Jews remained prisoners in the ghetto, yet a cat is allowed freedom thanks to the Jews, who are considered to be immoral criminals by the Nazis.

39 Skloot, "Introduction," 24.

40 Sterling, "Loss and Growth of Identity," 78.

41 Ibid., 75.

42 For more information about the Levinson Archives, see "Editor's Prologue," in John Hersey, *The Wall* (New York: Alfred A. Knopf, 1950), 3–11.

43 For a historical account of the Broadway production and the reasons for its failure, see Robert Franciosi, "Bringing *The Wall* to Broadway," *Journal of American Drama and Theatre* 16, no. 2 (2004): 88–97.

44 Ibid., 97.

45 For more information about the Warsaw ghetto uprising, see Ainsztein, *Jewish Resistance in Nazi-Occupied Eastern Europe*, 551–671, and Israel Gutman, "Warsaw," in *Encyclopedia of the Holocaust*, vol. 4, ed. Israel Gutman (New York: Macmillan, 1990), 1598–1625.

46 See Hilberg, *Destruction of the European Jews*, vol. 2, 515, and Gutman, "Warsaw," 1624.

47 Millard Lampell, "Introduction," in *The Wall* (New York: Alfred A. Knopf, 1961), xiv.

48 Dawidowicz, *The War Against the Jews, 1933–1945*, 472.

49 Lampell, "Introduction," xvii.

50 Dawidowicz, *The War Against the Jews, 1933–1945*, 294.

51 Lampell, "Introduction," xvii.

52 For an extended discussion of the comic elements in the play, see Skloot, *The Darkness We Carry*, 48–50.

53 Millard Lampell, *The Wall*, 12. All subsequent citations are from this edition and are included within parentheses in the text.

54 The Kogan family was not included in Hersey's novel, yet Lampell obviously believed that they would be visible representations of the increasing atrocities in Warsaw as time passed. Director Da Costa obviously thought they were extraneous, so he eliminated them soon after opening night of the Broadway production, perhaps in an attempt to reduce the lengthy running time of the play.

55 Several women took the lead as members of the underground movement in Poland. The most noteworthy was Zivia Lubetkin, who was married to Yitzhak Zukerman, whom Lampell interviewed as one of the Warsaw ghetto uprising survivors. Lubetkin founded the Antifascist Bloc, the first organization in Warsaw to offer armed resistance during the Nazi occupation. Like Rachel Apt, Lubetkin spent her final days of the uprising in the bunker before passing through the sewers to the "Aryan" section of Warsaw.

56 Lawrence L. Langer objects to Lampell's theme of finding dignity in the overwhelmingly despairing story of the Holocaust. Langer argues that the affirmation of the heroic fate of the few

Warsaw survivors mutes the doom of the majority who suffered greatly and eventually died for nothing. Langer implies that in writing the play, Lampell catered to what he hoped would be a Broadway audience. In particular, Langer criticizes the denouement in which Rutka tries to silence her baby, whose crying will reveal the bunker's location to the advancing Germans: "We have ample evidence of parents smothering their infants to protect themselves and often larger groups from detection, but Lampell flinches before this ultimate rejection of the family bond: it, too, would have been too dark–too dark altogether;" Hersey actually depicts the suffocation of a baby in his novel. Indeed, in the revised version presented at Arena Stage, the baby is smothered by Rutka. In addition, Langer complains that verisimilitude would indicate that the Jews should have been captured by the Nazis. Instead, Berson surrenders himself to the soldiers by playing "Dort'n, Dort'n," a death-defying song, on his concertina after Rachel had delivered her famous line about countering death with more life. Berson thus heroically sacrifices himself in order for the baby to survive along with the other partisans. See Langer, "The Americanization of the Holocaust on Stage and Screen," in *From Hester Street to Hollywood: The Jewish-American Stage and Screen*, ed. Sarah Blacher Cohen (Bloomington: Indiana University Press, 1983), 217–20.

57 Lampell, "Introduction," xxiv.

58 See Anat Feinberg, "Erwin Sylvanus and the Theatre of the Holocaust," *Amsterdamer Beiträge zur Neueren Germanistik* 16 (1983): 168 n13.

59 Hilberg, *The Destruction of the European Jews*, vol. 2, 504.

60 Erwin Sylvanus, *Dr. Korczak and the Children*, trans. George E. Wellwarth, in *Postwar German Theatre: An Anthology of Plays*, eds. Michael Benedikt and George E. Wellwarth (London: Macmillan, 1968), 116. All subsequent citations are from this edition and are included within parentheses in the text.

61 Edward R. Isser, *Stages of Annihilation: Theatrical Representations of the Holocaust* (Madison: Fairleigh Dickinson University Press, 1997), 94.

62 Sidra DeKoven Ezrahi, *By Words Alone: The Holocaust in Literature* (Chicago and London: University of Chicago Press, 1980), 40.

63 George E. Wellwarth, "Introduction," in *Postwar German Theatre: An Anthology of Plays*, eds. Michael Benedikt and George E. Wellwarth (London: Macmillan, 1968), xvii.

64 Isser, *Stages of Annihilation*, 93.

65 Skloot, *The Darkness We Carry*, 98.

10 Dignity in the Concentration Camps

1 Jean Améry, *At the Mind's Limits: Contemplations by a Survivor on Auschwitz and Its Realities*, trans. Sidney Rosenfeld and Stella P. Rosenfeld (Bloomington and Indianapolis: Indiana University Press, 1980), 47.

2 Bruno Bettelheim, *Surviving and Other Essays* (New York: Alfred A. Knopf, 1979), 48.

3 Charlotte Delbo, *Auschwitz and After*, trans. Rosette C. Lamont (New Haven and London: Yale University Press, 1995), 117.

4 Améry, *At the Mind's Limits*, 70.

5 Bettelheim, *Surviving and Other Essays*, 102.

6 Giorgio Agamben, *Remnants of Auschwitz: The Witness and the Archive*, trans. Daniel Heller-Roazen (New York: Zone Books, 1999), 75.

7 Primo Levi, *Survival in Auschwitz*, trans. Stuart Woolf (New York: Macmillan, 1993), 41.

8 Terrence Des Pres, *The Survivor: An Anatomy of Life in the Death Camps* (New York: Oxford University Press, 1976), 131.

9 In particular, Griffiths urged Sherman to seek a larger venue for his plays. See Alan Sinfield, *Out on Stage: Lesbian and Gay Theatre in the Twentieth Century* (New Haven and London: Yale University Press, 1999), 307.

10 For a detailed account of the history of the play from script to production at the Royal Court, see Nicholas de Jongh, *Homosexuality on Stage* (London and New York: Routledge, 1992), 147–50.

11 John M. Clum, *Still Acting Gay: Male Homosexuality in Modern Drama* (New York: St. Martin's, 2000), 321 n15.

12 Frank Rector, *The Nazi Extermination of Homosexuals* (New York: Stein and Day, 1981), 31.

13 Much of the media attempt to denigrate the Nazis introduces the idea that high-ranking Nazi officials were themselves homosexual. See, for example, Luchino Visconti's 1969 film, *The Damned*, Bernardo Bertolucci's *The Conformist*, and the 1936 Soviet film, Gustav von Wangenheim's *The Fighters*–all of which depict the Nazis as homosexual perverts. However, after the Night of the Long Knives, no high-ranking Nazi official was homosexual.

14 Richard Plant, *The Pink Triangle: The Nazi War Against Homosexuals* (New York: Henry Holt, 1986), 89.

15 Hans Peter Bleuel, *Sex and Society in Nazi Germany*, trans. J. Maxwell Brownjohn (Philadelphia and New York: J. B. Lippincott, 1973), 212.

16 Ibid., 149.

17 Kai Hammermeister, "Inventing History: Toward a Gay Holocaust Literature," *German Quarterly* 70, no. 1 (1997): 19.

18 The major studies in English about homosexual people during the Holocaust are those by Rector and Plant, both of which were written after 1979. Several critics state that *Bent* even spurred the research conducted by both Rector and Plant; Plant indeed mentions the play in his book (14). Sherman probably read Heinz Hegel's 1972 treatise, *The Men With the Pink Triangle*, the only major study written in English before 1979. If he knew German, Sherman could have consulted Rüdiger Lautmann's *Seminar: Gesellschaft und Homosexualität*, published by Suhrkamp in 1977.

19 Sherman's depiction of homosexual people worshiping Nazi iconography was controversial since it was insulting to homosexuals. Sherman could have implied that Max likes rough sex without evoking the image of storm troopers.

20 Martin Sherman, *Bent* (New York: Applause, 1979), 12–13. All subsequent citations are from this edition and are included within parentheses in the text.

21 Eric Sterling, "Bent Straight: The Destruction of Self in Martin Sherman's *Bent*," *Journal of European Studies*, 32, no. 4 (2002): 374.

22 de Jongh, *Homosexuality on Stage*, 151.

23 The argument over whether trading the yellow star for the pink triangle was justifiable formed the major critical commentary about the play and became more than just a debate (arguably inconclusive) over whether Jews or homosexuals suffered the most. For example, Robert Skloot writes, "The real problem with Max's situation concerns the premise that sees his survival in terms of its relationship to another set of Holocaust victims, the Jews." See Skloot, *The Darkness We Carry: The Drama of the Holocaust* (Madison: University of Wisconsin Press, 1988), 120. Vivian M. Patraka concurs with Skloot: "If the play itself represents a necessary foregrounding of oppression on the basis of sexuality in the Holocaust, it should not have to diminish the suffering of ethnic groups in order to achieve its aim." See Patraka, *Spectacular Suffering: Theatre, Fascism, and the Holocaust* (Bloomington and Indianapolis: Indiana University Press, 1999), 46. Nevertheless, the trading of the pink triangle for the yellow star is factually accurate. Frank Rector asserts, "Inasmuch as gays were considered the lowest strata of KZ prisoners, and were generally singled out for the 'worst' treatment, there were cases in which homosexuals attempted to 'upgrade' their status by secretly trading a pink triangle for a Jewish yellow star or some other insignia in the hope of improving the chance of surviving concentration camp internment." See Rector, *The Nazi Extermination of Homosexuals*, 127. Rüdiger Lautmann argues that gay people were at the bottom of the hierarchy and were therefore treated more brutally than other prisoners in the concentration camps of the 1930s. See Lautmann, "The Pink Triangle: The Persecution of Homosexual Males in Concentration Camps in Nazi Germany," *Journal of Homosexuality* 6, no. 12 (1980–81): 153. Lautmann has also estimated that 60% of homosexuals died in the concentration camps, compared to 41% of political prisoners and 35% of Jehovah's Witnesses, yet he provides no figures for deaths of Jewish inmates. See Lautmann, *Seminar*, 351. Homosexuals may have been persecuted more severely than any of the ethnic groups in the 1930s (e.g., marriage to an Aryan protected German Jews

from being sent to a concentration camp, but marriage provided no such protection for homosexuals), and since *Bent* is set in Dachau in 1936, the play is factually accurate; however, when the campaign against the Jews escalated after Kristallnacht in late November 1938, the sheer number of Jews murdered far exceeded the number of homosexual deaths. Estimates of Jews murdered during the Shoah range from a low of 5.1 million to approximately 6 million. Richard Plant claims that between five thousand and fifteen thousand homosexuals perished in the concentration camps. See Plant, *Pink Triangle*, 154. Although he understands that the estimates of homosexuals who were exterminated by the Nazis is inconclusive, Frank Rector decides that, based on research conducted by the Protestant Church of Austria, at least 220,000 homosexuals died in the camps, and perhaps as many as 500,000 were executed during the Nazi genocide. See Rector, *The Nazi Extermination of Homosexuals*, 113, 116. Jewish genocide spread throughout the occupied territories, but that was not true of homosexual genocide. Since the Nazis considered homosexuals to be a direct threat to the Volk but were merely a degenerate form of subspecies outside Germany, persecution of homosexuals was virtually nonexistent in countries such as Poland and Russia, where Jews were indiscriminately murdered. On the other hand, since many homosexuals were serving prison time in the occupied territories of Poland and Russia, they became victims when the Nazis emptied the prisons of "criminals." There is also no doubt that homosexuals were treated brutally in the concentration camps within Germany, which were not extermination camps, such as the ones in Poland where Jewish genocide flourished. There are several reasons why homosexuals were afforded advantages over Jews. First, Jews born into the religion having at least one Jewish grandparent were defined as Jews, whereas homosexuality was more difficult to determine. Homosexuals often had to be interrogated by the Gestapo before they admitted their sexual behavior; Jews were deported without any need for such an investigation. The result was that many homosexuals could go undetected in the Reich while Jews could not. Second,

Himmler believed that homosexuals could be cured of their deviant behavior through hard labor. See Bleuel, *Sex and Society*, 220. Homosexuals in the camps were at times shown the body of a dead woman, and if they had an erection, they were believed to be salvageable. At various concentration camps (Flossenburg, for example), Himmler set up bordellos with the goal that frequent visits to the brothels would lead homosexuals to heterosexuality. Indeed, in *Bent*, Max proves he is straight, not "bent," by having sex on the train with a dead thirteen-year-old girl while the Nazis watched in derision. Jews, however, always remained Jews and could not convert to another religion even if they sought to do so. Finally, young homosexuals were often seen as *Piepel* (little dolls) or *Puppenjungen* (dolly boys) who secured favors in the camps as concubines for the kapos and select SS guards, the most important privilege being exclusion from death or torture. Sex with Jews, however, was risky for the kapos and strictly forbidden for the SS.

24 Sterling, "Bent Straight," 378.

25 Clum, *Still Acting Gay*, 184.

26 Hammermeister, "Inventing History," 25.

27 Skloot, *The Darkness We Carry*, 120.

28 See Anat Feinberg, *Embodied Memory: The Theatre of George Tabori* (Iowa City: University of Iowa Press, 1999), 198.

29 See Peter von Becker, "Die grosse Lebensreise: George Tabori, Zeuge des Jahrhunderts, im Gespräch mit Peter von Becker," *Theater Heute* 5 (1994): 14.

30 Tabori's encounters with Brecht spurred his interest in theater and helped him craft his experimental plays. Tabori admitted that Brecht had no influence on his political development. See Martin Kagel, "George Tabori in Conversation With Martin Kagel (and Nikolaus Merck)," *Brecht Yearbook* 23 (1997): 71. While attending rehearsals for *Galileo*, which was directed by Joseph Losey in Hollywood in 1947, Tabori met Brecht through Losey. Tabori then assisted Charles Laughton and Brecht in translating *Galileo* into English. As mentioned earlier, Tabori put together a collection of Brecht's songs, poems, and excerpts from his plays into a performance piece, *Brecht on Brecht*, which was staged by the

American National Theater and Academy (ANTA) in 1961. *Brecht on Brecht* was later performed in London at the Royal Court Theatre. Tabori's goal initially was to translate Brecht's plays to make them more accessible to English-speaking audiences, much like Eric Bentley was trying to do. Tabori's translation of *Der Aufhaltsame Aufstieg des Arturo Ui* was staged in New York by Tony Richardson in 1963. Tabori then translated *Die Gewehre der Frau Carrar* and *Mutter Courage,* directing the latter play at Castleton State College in Vermont in 1967. In 1968, Tabori and his wife Viveca Lindfors participated with various writers, directors, and actors in the Brecht-Dialog in East Berlin, to honor Brecht's seventieth birthday. After a lapse of several years, Tabori was again associated with Brecht when he directed *Der Jasager und der Neinsager,* which premiered at the Staatstheater in Kassel on 9 May 1981. Tabori also wrote the screenplay for *The Brecht File,* a documentary account of the FBI dossier on Brecht, including his testimony before the House Un-American Activities Committee in 1947.

31 George Tabori, *The Cannibals,* in *The Theatre of the Holocaust: Four Plays,* vol. 1, ed. Robert Skloot (Madison: University of Wisconsin Press, 1982), 201. All subsequent citations are from this edition and are included within parentheses in the text.

32 Edward R. Isser, *Stages of Annihilation: Theatrical Representations of the Holocaust* (Madison: Fairleigh Dickinson University Press, 1997), 127.

33 Jack Zipes, "George Tabori and the Jewish Question," *Theater* 29, no. 2 (1999): 103.

34 Feinberg, *Embodied Memory,* 305 n3.

35 Ibid., 202.

36 For a discussion of Genet's theater as black mass, see Gene A. Plunka, *The Rites of Passage of Jean Genet: The Art and Aesthetics of Risk Taking* (Cranbury, NJ: Fairleigh Dickinson University Press, 1992), 131–32.

37 The play becomes an exorcism for Tabori's own ghosts as well. The actors are the sons of the victims, much like Tabori himself, whose father perished in Auschwitz. As the sons seem to improvise

what they perceive to be the conditions of the *lager*, they engage in a type of catharsis in an attempt to recreate an encounter with which they obviously feel guilt and shame. Typically, the children of Holocaust victims try to forget or suppress the horrors their parents went through, but this play becomes a type of psychodrama that exorcises these pent-up demons. Simultaneously, the sons who enact the tale confront their fathers in an attempt to understand their motives toward the cannibalism. Uncle is believed to be modeled on Tabori's father, and in a Freudian slip, Professor Glatz conflates the two of them when he says, "They arrested Uncle Tabori this morning" (244). In this context, *The Cannibals* represents Tabori's attempt to come to grips with the rumor that his father maintained his sense of dignity to the very end.

38 Robert Skloot, ed., "Introduction," in *The Theatre of the Holocaust: Four Plays* (Madison: University of Wisconsin Press, 1982), 28.

39 Feinberg, *Embodied Memory*, 204.

40 Ibid., 200.

11 Holocaust Survivors in the United States and Israel

1 Michael Brenner, "Displaced Persons," in *The Holocaust Encyclopedia*, ed. Walter Laqueur (New Haven and London: Yale University Press, 2001), 157.

2 Aaron Hass, *The Aftermath: Living With the Holocaust* (Cambridge: Cambridge University Press, 1995), 16–17.

3 Eva Fogelman, "Therapeutic Alternatives for Holocaust Survivors and Second Generation," in *The Psychological Perspectives of the Holocaust and of Its Aftermath*, ed. Randolph L. Braham (New York: Columbia University Press, 1988), 98.

4 Hass, *Aftermath*, 90.

5 Fogelman, "Therapeutic Alternatives," 86.

6 Geoffrey H. Hartman, "Introduction: Darkness Visible," in *Holocaust Remembrance: The Shapes of Memory*, ed. Geoffrey H. Hartman (Oxford: Blackwell, 1994), 8.

7 Yael Danieli, "The Heterogeneity of Postwar Adaptation in Families of Holocaust Survivors," in *The Psychological*

Perspectives of the Holocaust and of Its Aftermath, ed. Randolph L. Braham (New York: Columbia University Press, 1988), 111.

8 Barbara Lebow, *A Shayna Maidel* (New York: Dramatists Play Service, 1988), 32–33. All subsequent citations are from this edition and are included within parentheses in the text.

9 Hass, *Aftermath*, 43.

10 Alvin Goldfarb, "Inadequate Memories: The Survivor in Plays by Mann, Kesselman, Lebow and Baitz," in *Staging the Holocaust: The Shoah in Drama and Performance*, ed. Claude Schumacher (Cambridge: Cambridge University Press, 1998), 118.

11 William G. Niederland, "The Clinical Aftereffects of the Holocaust in Survivors and Their Offspring," in *The Psychological Perspectives of the Holocaust and of Its Aftermath*, ed. Randolph L. Braham (New York: Columbia University Press, 1988), 45.

12 Rather than focusing on *A Shayna Maidel* as a tale of insurmountable odds facing Holocaust survivors who tried to assimilate into postwar American society, scholars have instead criticized Lebow for turning the play into a sentimental domestic melodrama. *A Shayna Maidel* thus becomes linked with other such American dramas that ostensibly sugar-coat the Shoah. Critics often cite the last scene of the play in which Lusia, in a fantasy sequence, is reunited with Duvid, Hanna, and her mother. Edward R. Isser asserts, "The playwright retreats to a safe sentimental conclusion that pushes the terror of the death camps far into the background." See Isser, "Toward a Feminist Perspective in American Holocaust Drama," *Studies in the Humanities* 17, no. 2 (1990): 147, reprinted in Isser, *Stages of Annihilation: Theatrical Representations of the Holocaust* (Madison: Fairleigh Dickinson University Press, 1997), 84. Alvin Goldfarb echoes Isser's comment, describing the play as romanticized and Americanized: "In the last fantasy scene, there is a well-made resolution which transcends the death camps; even those who perished in the Holocaust are reunited with those who did not." See Goldfarb, "Inadequate Memories," 124. Isser and Goldfarb conclude that Lebow's use of the family as a redemptive tool precludes audiences from considering the true extent of Jewish dehumanization by the Nazis. I prefer to consider

the fantasy scenes as representations of the once-comfortable Old World Jewish domestic life that the Nazis obliterated–a world forever lost to survivors. Lusia's inability to assimilate is Lebow's way of indicating that these survivors are constantly in exile and have lost their sense of identity.

13 Bette Mandl, "'Alive Still, in You:' Memory and Silence in *A Shayna Maidel*," in *Staging Difference: Cultural Pluralism in American Theatre and Drama*, ed. Marc Maufort (New York: Peter Lang, 1995), 260.

14 For a counterargument to the comparison of *Lady of the Castle* to Ibsen's plays, see Glenda Abramson, *Modern Hebrew Drama* (New York: St. Martin's Press), 1979, 124–25. Abramson's main point is that Ibsen's characters are "beings with explicit biographies" (124), while Goldberg depicts merely typed personae. Moreover, although Ibsen and Goldberg seek the truth while destroying the ghosts of the past, the levels of exposition vary widely between the two playwrights.

15 Robert Skloot, *The Darkness We Carry: The Drama of the Holocaust* (Madison: University of Wisconsin Press, 1988), 58.

16 Leah Goldberg, *Lady of the Castle*, trans. T. Carmi, in *Israeli Holocaust Drama*, ed. Michael Taub (Syracuse: Syracuse University Press, 1996), 22. All subsequent citations are from this edition and are included within parentheses in the text.

17 Abramson, *Modern Hebrew Drama*, 117.

18 Ibid., 119.

19 Michael Taub, "Israeli Theater and the Holocaust," in *Israeli Holocaust Drama*, ed. Michael Taub (Syracuse: Syracuse University Press, 1996), 17.

20 Hass, *Aftermath*, 31.

21 Matti Megged, "Introduction," in *Lea Goldberg: Selected Poetry and Drama*, ed. Rachel Tzvia Back (New Milford, CT: Toby Press, 2005), 240

22 Strangely enough, although Zabrodsky is evidently a connoisseur of Europe's great cultural tradition and surrounds himself with art treasures and masterpieces of literature, the only acknowledgments in the play of any specific connection to that tradition are

his references to Voltaire and Lena's comment about the count's wonderful ability to play Chopin.

23 Abramson, *Modern Hebrew Drama*, 121.

24 Aaron Hass noted that the predominant attitude in the kibbutz was that the Old World Jews were considered to be abused and humiliated victims. He writes, "No one wanted to hear what the survivors had seen and endured. At that time, they were not referred to with the heroically and sympathetically implied appellation 'survivor.' They were simply refugees." See Hass, *Aftermath*, 20.

25 Skloot, *The Darkness We Carry*, 59.

26 Rachel Feldhay Brenner, "Discourses of Mourning and Rebirth in Post-Holocaust Israeli Literature: Leah Goldberg's *Lady of the Castle* and Shulamith Hareven's 'The Witness,'" *Hebrew Studies* 31 (1990): 74–75.

27 Niederland, "Clinical Aftereffects of the Holocaust," 46.

28 Danieli, "The Heterogeneity of Postwar Adaptation," 122.

29 Fogelman, "Therapeutic Alternatives," 87.

30 Ben-Zion Tomer, *Children of the Shadows*, trans. Hillel Halkin, in *Israeli Holocaust Drama*, ed. Michael Taub (Syracuse: Syracuse University Press, 1996), 140. All subsequent citations are from this edition and are included within parentheses in the text.

31 Haim Shoham, "*Here* and *There*: The Israeli Playwright and His Jewish Shadow," *Modern Hebrew Literature* 10, nos. 1–2 (1984): 33.

32 Abramson, *Modern Hebrew Drama*, 126.

33 Michael Taub, "Ben Zion Tomer," in *Holocaust Literature: An Encyclopedia of Writers and Their Work*, vol. 2, ed. S. Lillian Kremer (New York and London: Routledge, 2003), 1268.

12 The Survivor Syndrome and the Effects of the Holocaust on Survivor Families

1 Terrence Des Pres, *The Survivor: An Anatomy of Life in the Death Camps* (New York: Oxford University Press, 1976), 31.

2 Annette Wieviorka, "On Testimony," in *Holocaust Remembrance: The Shapes of Memory*, ed. Geoffrey Hartman (Oxford: Blackwell, 1994), 29.

3 Charlotte Delbo, *Auschwitz and After*, trans. Rosette C. Lamont (New Haven and London: Yale University Press, 1995), 236, 255.

4 Ibid., 238.

5 Jean Améry, *At the Mind's Limits: Contemplations by a Survivor on Auschwitz and Its Realities*, trans. Sidney Rosenfeld and Stella P. Rosenfeld (Bloomington and Indianapolis: Indiana University Press, 1980), 20.

6 Bruno Bettelheim, *Surviving and Other Essays* (New York: Alfred A. Knopf, 1979), 100–101.

7 Des Pres, *The Survivor*, 155.

8 Leslie Berger, "The Long-Term Psychological Consequences of the Holocaust on the Survivors and Their Offspring," in *The Psychological Perspectives of the Holocaust and of Its Aftermath*, ed. Randolph L. Braham (New York: Columbia University Press, 1988), 177.

9 William G. Niederland, "The Clinical Aftereffects of the Holocaust in Survivors and Their Offspring," in *The Psychological Perspectives of the Holocaust and of Its Aftermath*, ed. Randolph L. Braham (New York: Columbia University Press, 1988), 46.

10 Aaron Hass, *The Aftermath: Living With the Holocaust* (Cambridge: Cambridge University Press, 1995), 2–3.

11 Eva Fogelman, "Therapeutic Alternatives for Holocaust Survivors and Second Generation," in *The Psychological Perspectives of the Holocaust and of Its Aftermath*, ed. Randolph L. Braham (New York: Columbia University Press, 1988), 79.

12 Charlotte Delbo provides examples of incidents in which Holocaust survivors were so terrified of the various nightmares that they invented all types of excuses to avoid going to sleep. Jeanne, one of Delbo's surviving comrades, confessed that the insomnia was so acute that no sleeping pill could put her to sleep. See Delbo, *Auschwitz and After*, 344–45.

13 Paul Marcus and Alan Rosenberg, "A Philosophical Critique of the 'Survivor Syndrome' and Some Implications for Treatment," in *The Psychological Perspectives of the Holocaust and of Its Aftermath*, ed. Randolph L. Braham (New York: Columbia University Press, 1988), 58.

14 Yael Danieli, "The Heterogeneity of Postwar Adaptation in Families of Holocaust Survivors," in *The Psychological Perspectives of the Holocaust and of its Aftermath*, ed. Randolph L. Braham (New York: Columbia University Press, 1988), 122.

15 Aharon Appelfeld, "The Awakening," trans. Jeffrey M. Green, in *Holocaust Remembrance: The Shapes of Memory*, ed. Geoffrey H. Hartman (Oxford: Blackwell, 1994), 150.

16 Delbo, *Auschwitz and After*, 267.

17 See Hass, *Aftermath*, 92 and passim.

18 Gilles Ségal, *The Puppetmaster of Lodz*, trans. Sara O'Connor (New York: Samuel French, 1989), 50. All subsequent citations are from this edition and are included within parentheses in the text.

19 Maria Rosenbloom, "Lessons of the Holocaust for Mental Health Practice," in *The Psychological Perspectives of the Holocaust and of Its Aftermath*, ed. Randolph L. Braham (New York: Columbia University Press, 1988), 152.

20 Hass, *Aftermath*, 59.

21 Ibid., 99.

22 Edward R. Isser, *Stages of Annihilation: Theatrical Representations of the Holocaust* (Madison: Fairleigh Dickinson University Press, 1997), 118.

23 Giorgio Agambem, *Remnants of Auschwitz: The Witness and the Archive*, trans. Daniel Heller-Roazen (New York: Zone Books, 1999), 89.

24 Fogelman, "Therapeutic Alternatives," 82.

25 Peter Flannery, *Singer* (London: Nick Hern, 1992), 4. All subsequent citations are from this edition and are included within parentheses in the text.

26 Vivian M. Patraka compares Zinger's brutal striking of Manik with Max's beating of Rudy in *Bent*. Both Zinger and Max are forced to deny any relationship with their friend, the beaten man. Rudy dies at Max's hands while Manik's beating retards his mental capacities. See Patraka, *Spectacular Suffering: Theatre, Fascism, and the Holocaust* (Bloomington and Indianapolis: Indiana University Press, 1999), 100.

27 Améry, *At the Mind's Limits*, 69.

28 Hass, *Aftermath*, 191.

29 Theodor W. Adorno, *Negative Dialectics*, trans. E. B. Ashton (New York: Seabury Press, 1973), 363.

30 British audiences would have recognized Peter Singer as being modeled on Peter Rachman, the notorious slumlord of the 1950s, whose rapacious tactics became known as Rachmanism. Flannery's inspiration for *Singer* was provided by Shirley Green's biography of Rachman, who was himself a Holocaust survivor.

31 Hass, *Aftermath*, 75.

32 The attack on the politics of the Thatcher administration and the business practices embraced by the Conservative Party was Flannery's indirect means of equating contemporary (1989) Britain with Hitler's Germany. Comparing Thatcher to Hitler is similar to Kushner's conflation of Reaganism with Nazism in *A Bright Room Called Day*. In making these comparisons, Flannery, like Kushner, left himself open to criticism that he had trivialized the Holocaust.

33 Hass, *Aftermath*, 6.

34 For example, see Brian Pocknell, "Jean-Claude Grumberg's Holocaust Plays: Presenting the Jewish Experience," *Modern Drama* 41, no. 3 (1998): 399–400.

35 Leo Shua Eitinger, "Survivors, Psychology of," in *Encyclopedia of the Holocaust*, vol. 4, ed. Israel Gutman (New York: Macmillan, 1990), 1429.

36 Jean-Claude Grumberg, *The Workroom*, trans. Catherine Temerson, in *The Free Zone and The Workroom* (New York: Ubu Repertory Theater Publications, 1993), 181–82. All subsequent citations are from this edition and are included within parentheses in the text.

37 Robert L. King, "Psychic Numbing and Grumberg's *L'Atelier*," *Massachusetts Review* 26, no. 4 (1985): 582.

38 David Bradby, *Modern French Drama*, 1940–1990, 2nd ed. (Cambridge: Cambridge University Press, 1991), 235.

39 Janice F. Bistritz, "Transgenerational Pathology in Families of Holocaust Survivors," in *The Psychological Perspectives of the*

Holocaust and of Its Aftermath, ed. Randolph L. Braham (New York: Columbia University Press, 1988), 135.

40 Stanley L. Rustin, "A Psychological Examination of the Survivors of the Holocaust and the Generation After," in *The Psychological Perspectives of the Holocaust and of Its Aftermath*, ed. Randolph L. Braham (New York: Columbia University Press, 1988), 162.

41 Leslie Berger, "The Long-term Psychological Consequences of the Holocaust on the Survivors and Their Offspring," in *The Psychological Perspectives of the Holocaust and of Its Aftermath*, ed. Randolph L. Braham (New York: Columbia University Press, 1988), 204.

13 Holocaust Survivor Memory

1 Geoffrey H. Hartman, "Introduction: Darkness Visible," in *Holocaust Remembrance: The Shapes of Memory*, ed. Geoffrey H. Hartman (Oxford: Blackwell, 1994), 10.

2 Aharon Appelfeld, "The Awakening," trans. Jeffrey M. Green, in *Holocaust Remembrance: The Shapes of Memory*, ed. Geoffrey H. Hartman (Oxford: Blackwell, 1994), 150.

3 Sidra DeKoven Ezrahi, *By Words Alone: The Holocaust in Literature* (Chicago and London: University of Chicago Press, 1980), 21.

4 Lawrence L. Langer, "Introduction," in Charlotte Delbo, *Auschwitz and After*, trans. Rosette C. Lamont (New Haven and London: Yale University Press, 1995), xviii.

5 Annette Wieviorka, "On Testimony," trans. Kathy Aschheim, in *Holocaust Remembrance: The Shapes of Memory*, ed. Geoffrey H. Hartman (Oxford: Blackwell, 1994), 30.

6 Lawrence L. Langer, "Interpreting Survivor Testimony," in *Writing and the Holocaust*, ed. Berel Lang (New York and London: Holmes & Meier, 1988), 32.

7 Charlotte Delbo, *Auschwitz and After*, trans. Rosette C. Lamont (New Haven and London: Yale University Press, 1995), 255.

8 Primo Levi, *The Drowned and the Saved*, trans. Raymond Rosenthal (New York: Simon & Schuster, 1988), 31.

9 Karein K. Goertz, "Body, Trauma, and the Rituals of Memory: Charlotte Delbo and Ruth Klüger," in *Shaping Losses: Cultural Memory and the Holocaust*, eds. Julia Epstein and Lori Hope Lefkovitz (Urbana and Chicago: University of Illinois Press, 2001), 169.

10 Lawrence L. Langer, "Remembering Survival," in *Holocaust Remembrance: The Shapes of Memory*, ed. Geoffrey H. Hartman (Oxford: Blackwell, 1994), 77.

11 Ellen S. Fine, "The Absent Memory: The Act of Writing in Post-Holocaust French Literature," in *Writing and the Holocaust*, ed. Berel Lang (New York and London: Holmes & Meier, 1988), 42.

12 More than twenty years after writing *Annulla*, Mann, still very much committed to the literature of the Holocaust, adapted Isaac Bashevis Singer's 1981 novel, *Meshugah*, for the stage. The play focuses on the choices survivors had to make in the death camps in order to remain alive. *Meshugah* premiered at Princeton University's McCarter Theater on 20 October 1998 and was subsequently staged in New York City at the Kirk Theater during May 2003.

13 Emily Mann, "In Conversation," *Theatre Topics* 10, no. 1 (2000): 3.

14 See Kathleen Betsko and Rachel Koenig, eds., "Emily Mann," in *Interviews With Contemporary Women Playwrights* (New York: William Morrow, 1987), 281.

15 Emily Mann, "Playwright's Note," in *Annulla, An Autobiography* (New York: Theatre Communications Group, 1985), unpaginated. All subsequent citations are from this edition and are included within parentheses in the text. This version of the play, in a slightly revised edition, was reprinted in 1997. See Emily Mann, *Annulla (An Autobiography)*, in *Testimonies: Four Plays* (New York: Theatre Communications Group, 1997).

16 Christopher Bigsby, *Contemporary American Playwrights* (Cambridge: Cambridge University Press, 1999), 134.

17 Alexis Greene, ed., *Women Who Write Plays: Interviews With American Dramatists* (Hanover, NH: Smith and Kraus, 2001), 306.

18 Melissa Salz Bernstein, "Emily Mann: Having Her Say," *American Drama* 6, no. 2 (1997): 94.

19 Greene, *Women Who Write Plays*, 299. Mann repeated to Melissa Salz Bernstein the notion that *Annulla*, like her other plays, particularly *Still Life*, is mainly concerned with memories of a traumatic event. See Bernstein, "Emily Mann," 88–89.

20 Christopher Bigsby, *Modern American Drama, 1945–2000* (Cambridge: Cambridge University Press, 2000), 340.

21 Alvin Goldfarb, "Inadequate Memories: The Survivor in Plays by Mann, Kesselman, Lebow and Baitz," in *Staging the Holocaust: The Shoah in Drama and Performance*, ed. Claude Schumacher (Cambridge: Cambridge University Press, 1998), 127.

22 David Savran, ed., *In Their Own Words: Contemporary American Playwrights* (New York: Theatre Communications Group, 1988), 149.

23 Claudia Koonz, *Mothers in the Fatherland: Women, the Family and Nazi Politics* (New York: St. Martin's Press, 1987), xxxiv.

24 Ibid., 4.

25 Michael Burleigh and Wolfgang Wippermann, *The Racial State: Germany, 1933–1945* (Cambridge: Cambridge University Press, 1991), 266.

26 In an interview that Bettina Knapp conducted with Gatti, he admitted that it took him three years to write *La Deuxième existence du camp de Tatenberg*. See Knapp, "Document: Armand Gatti–A Theatre of Action," *Kentucky Romance Quarterly* 14, no. 4 (1967): 409.

27 Dorothy Knowles, *Armand Gatti in the Theatre: Wild Duck Against the Wind* (London: Athlone Press, 1989), 13.

28 Knapp, "Document: Armand Gatti," 410.

29 John Ireland: "Armand Gatti, Subject to History: The Problem of Representation," *Modern Drama* 25, no. 3 (1982): 376.

30 Bettina L. Knapp, "Armand Gatti: Multiplicity of Vision in Action Theatre," *Modern Drama* 12, no. 1 (1969): 59.

31 Richard N. Coe, "The Theatre of the Last Chance: Catastrophe-Theory in the Plays of Armand Gatti," *Australian Journal of French Studies* 20, no. 2 (1983): 80.

32 Agnieszka Tworek, "Monstre-victime: *La Deuxième existence du camp de Tatenberg*," in *Victims and Victimization in French and Francophone Literature*, ed. Buford Norman (Amsterdam and New York: Rodopi, 2005), 40.

33 Armand Gatti, *Armand Gatti: Three Plays*, ed. and trans. Joseph Long (Sheffield, UK: Sheffield Academic Press, 2000), 20. All subsequent citations are from this edition and are included within parentheses in the text.

34 Ireland, "Armand Gatti, Subject to History," 379.

35 Armand Gatti, "Seventeen Ideograms and the Search for the Wandering Word," trans. Wesley Hutchinson, *New Theatre Quarterly* 10, no. 38 (1994): 109.

36 John Ireland, "History, Utopia and the Concentration Camp in Gatti's Early Plays," in *Staging the Holocaust: The Shoah in Drama and Performance*, ed. Claude Schumacher (Cambridge: Cambridge University Press, 1998), 192.

37 Richard N. Coe, "Armand Gatti's Carnival of Compassion: *La Deuxième Existence du camp de Tatenberg*," *Yale French Studies* 46 (1971): 64–65.

38 Ellen Schiff, *From Stereotype to Metaphor: The Jew in Contemporary Drama* (Albany: State University of New York Press, 1982), 197.

39 Knowles, *Armand Gatti in the Theatre*, 76.

40 Schiff, *Stereotype to Metaphor*, 201–2.

14 The Holocaust and Collective Memory

1 Geoffrey H. Hartman, "Introduction: Darkness Visible," in *Holocaust Remembrance: The Shapes of Memory*, ed. Geoffrey H. Hartman (Oxford: Blackwell, 1994), 6.

2 Marc Silverstein, "'Talking About Some Kind of Atrocity': *Ashes to Ashes* in Barcelona," in *The Pinter Review: Collected Essays, 1997 and 1998*, eds. Francis Gillen and Steven H. Gale (Tampa: University of Tampa Press, 1999), 84.

3 Michael Billington, *The Life and Work of Harold Pinter* (London: Faber and Faber, 1996), 374.

4 Ibid., 375.

5 D. Keith Peacock, *Harold Pinter and the New British Theatre*, Contributions in Drama and Theatre Studies 77 (Westport, CT: Greenwood, 1997), 159.

6 Harold Pinter, *Ashes to Ashes* (New York: Grove Press, 1996), 1. All subsequent citations are from this edition and are included within parentheses in the text.

7 Susan Hollis Merritt, "Harold Pinter's *Ashes to Ashes*: Political/ Personal Echoes of the Holocaust," in *The Pinter Review: Collected Essays, 1999 and 2000*, eds. Francis Gillen and Steven H. Gale (Tampa: University of Tampa Press, 2000), 77.

8 Silverstein, "'Talking About Some Kind of Atrocity,'" 75.

9 Mireia Aragay, "Writing, Politics, and *Ashes to Ashes*: An Interview With Harold Pinter," in *The Pinter Review: Annual Essays, 1995 and 1996*, eds. Francis Gillen and Steven H. Gale (Tampa: University of Tampa Press, 1997), 10.

10 Ibid.

11 Manuela M. Reiter, "Old Times Revisited: Harold Pinter's *Ashes to Ashes*," *Arbeiten aus Anglistik und Amerikanistik* 22, no. 2 (1997): 187.

12 Billington, *The Life and Work of Harold Pinter*, 377.

13 Martin S. Regal, "'You Can Only End Once': Time in *Ashes to Ashes*," *Cycnos* 14, no. 1 (1997): 102.

14 Charles Grimes, *Harold Pinter's Politics: A Silence Beyond Echo* (Madison, NJ: Fairleigh Dickinson University Press, 2005), 203.

15 Interestingly, Susan Hollis Merritt, who examined Pinter's first draft of *Ashes to Ashes* in the archives of the British Library, discovered that Pinter referred to Rebecca's former lover as "monster" throughout the text but later changed it to read "lover." See Merritt, "*Ashes to Ashes* in New York," in *The Pinter Review: Collected Essays, 1997 and 1998*, eds. Francis Gillen and Steven H. Gale (Tampa: University of Tampa Press, 1999), 156.

16 Craig N. Owens, "The *Unheimlich* Maneuver: *Ashes to Ashes* and the Structure of Repression," in *The Pinter Review: Collected Essays, 2001 and 2002*, eds. Francis Gillen and Steven H. Gale (Tampa: University of Tampa Press, 2002), 79, 90.

17 Anyone familiar with Pinter's theater will recognize that the barrage of questions posed to an almost silent, reluctant victim has been a trademark of his plays from the beginning of his career. One may recall Goldberg and McCann questioning Stanley in *The Birthday Party*, Gus's harassment of Ben in *The Dumb Waiter*, Lenny's philosophical probing of Ruth and Teddy in *The Homecoming*, and the interrogative style of revue sketches, "Applicant" and "Interview"–all of which led to the fascistic interrogations permeating the political plays, especially *One for the Road, Mountain Language,* and *New World Order*.

18 Geoffrey H. Hartman, "Memory.com: Tele-Suffering and Testimony in the Dot Com Era," *Raritan* 19, no. 3 (2000): 14.

19 Ann C. Hall, "'You're Speaking to Someone and You Suddenly Become Another Person': Storytelling in Pinter's *Moonlight* and *Ashes to Ashes*," in *Pinter at 70: A Casebook*, ed. Lois Gordon (New York and London: Routledge, 2001), 273.

20 Hanna Scolnicov, "*Ashes to Ashes*: Pinter's Holocaust Play," *Cycnos* 18, no. 1 (2001): 19.

21 Katherine H. Burkman, "Harold Pinter's *Ashes to Ashes*: Rebecca and Devlin as Albert Speer," in *The Pinter Review: Collected Essays, 1997 and 1998*, eds. Francis Gillen and Steven H. Gale (Tampa: University of Tampa Press, 1999), 89.

22 Varun Begley, *Harold Pinter and the Twilight of Modernism* (Toronto: University of Toronto Press, 2005), 179.

23 Grimes, *Harold Pinter's Politics*, 209.

24 Geoffrey H. Hartman argues that Pinter reproduces the very words of Holocaust survivor Bessie K., chronicled in the Fortunoff Video Archive for Holocaust Testimonies at Yale University. Hartman, realizing that Pinter probably did not peruse the archives at Yale, surmises that the British playwright saw those words in Lawrence L. Langer's *Holocaust Testimonies: The Ruins of Memory*. See Hartman, "Memory.com," 15. Susan Hollis Merritt mentions that Pinter may have viewed the documentary, *Witness: Voices From the Holocaust*, in which Bessie K., who lived in Kovno before being sent to Estonian and Stutthof concentration camps, was interviewed

about her experiences during the Shoah. See Merritt, "Harold Pinter's *Ashes to Ashes*," 81.

25 Owens, "The *Unheimlich* Maneuver," 94.

26 Francis Gillen, "History as a Single Act: Pinter's *Ashes to Ashes*," *Cycnos* 14, no. 1 (1997): 97.

27 *Ashes to Ashes* is thus open to charges that by equating the Authoritarian Personality with the Holocaust, Pinter is trivializing or simplifying the Shoah. Of course, there were many cultural, social, socioeconomic, and historical factors in Germany, which, coupled with a history of anti-Semitism, led to the Holocaust. Certainly, a rigid German educational system that indoctrinated students with the need to obey figures of authority helped to nurture the mind-set of the perpetrators, but this adherence to authoritarianism must be factored in with the other variables mentioned as well. There simply is no direct correlation between the Authoritarian Personality and anti-Semitism.

28 Katherine H. Burkman, "Harold Pinter and the Case of the Guilty Pen," in *The Pinter Review: Collected Essays, 1999 and 2000*, eds. Francis Gillen and Steven H. Gale (Tampa: University of Tampa Press, 2000), 19.

29 Billington, *The Life and Work of Harold Pinter*, 382.

Bibliography

Abbotson, Susan C. W. "Re-Visiting the Holocaust for 1980s Television: Arthur Miller's *Playing for Time.*" *American Drama* 8, no. 2 (1999): 61–78.

Abramson, Glenda. "The Cultural Uses of the Holocaust." In *The Conscience of Humankind: Literature and Traumatic Experiences*, edited by Elrud Ibsch, 11–23. Amsterdam: Rodopi, 2000.

———. *Modern Hebrew Drama.* New York: St. Martin's Press, 1979.

Adorno, Theodor W. "Engagement." In *Noten zur Literatur III*, 409–30. Frankfurt: Suhrkamp Verlag, 1974.

———. "Kulturkritik und Gesellschaft." In *Prismen*, 7–26. Frankfurt: Suhrkamp Verlag, 1955.

———. *Negative Dialectics.* Translated by E. B. Ashton. New York: Seabury Press, 1973.

———. "What Does Coming to Terms With the Past Mean?" In *Bitburg in Moral and Political Perspective*, edited by Geoffrey H. Hartman, 114–29. Bloomington: Indiana University Press, 1986.

Agamben, Giorgio. *Remnants of Auschwitz: The Witness and the Archive.* Translated by Daniel Heller-Roazen. New York: Zone Books, 1999.

"Aharon Megged." *Modern International Drama* 27, no. 1 (1993): 97–99.

Ainsztein, Reuben. *Jewish Resistance in Nazi-Occupied Eastern Europe.* New York: Harper & Row, 1974.

Alvarez, A. "Peter Weiss in Conversation With A. Alvarez." *Encore* 12, no. 4 (1965): 16–22.

———. "Peter Weiss: The Truths That Are Uttered in a Madhouse." *New York Times*, 26 December 1965, sec. 2, 3, 14.

Améry, Jean. *At the Mind's Limits: Contemplations by a Survivor on Auschwitz and Its Realities*. Translated by Sidney Rosenfeld and Stella P. Rosenfeld. Bloomington and Indianapolis: Indiana University Press, 1980.

Antler, Joyce. "The Americanization of the Holocaust." *American Theatre* 12, no. 2 (1995): 16–20.

Appelfeld, Aharon. "The Awakening." Translated by Jeffrey M. Green. In *Holocaust Remembrance: The Shapes of Memory*, 149–52. Oxford: Blackwell, 1994.

Arad, Yitzhak. "Gens, Jacob." In *Encyclopedia of the Holocaust*. Vol. 2, edited by Israel Gutman, 555–56. New York: Macmillan, 1990.

———. "Vilna." In *Encyclopedia of the Holocaust*. Vol. 4, edited by Israel Gutman, 1571–75. New York: Macmillan, 1990.

Aragay, Mireia. "Writing, Politics, and *Ashes to Ashes*: An Interview With Harold Pinter." In *The Pinter Review: Annual Essays, 1995 and 1996*, edited by Francis Gillen and Steven H. Gale, 4–15. Tampa: University of Tampa Press, 1997.

Arendt, Hannah. *Eichmann in Jerusalem*. New York: Viking Press, 1964.

Aronowitz, Alfred G. "The Play That Rocked Europe." *Saturday Evening Post*, 29 February 1964, 36, 39, 42–43.

Arons, Wendy. "'Preaching to the Converted?'–'You Couldn't Possibly Do Any Better!': An Interview With Tony Kushner on September 19, 1994." *Communications From the International Brecht Society* 23, no. 2 (1994): 51–59.

Atlan, Liliane. *Mister Fugue or Earth Sick*. Translated by Marguerite Feitlowitz. In *Plays of the Holocaust: An International Anthology*, edited by Elinor Fuchs, 53–104. New York: Theatre Communications Group, 1987.

Avigal, S., Ada Ben Nahum, and Dan Orian. "*Kastner* Was Awarded the 'Aharon Meskin Prize' of the Israel Centre of the I.T.I." *Modern International Drama* 27, no. 1 (1993): 37–38.

Back, Rachel Tzvia, ed. *Lea Goldberg: Selected Poetry and Drama*. New Milford, CT: Toby Press, 2005.

Bahr, Ehrhard. "Shoemaking as a Mystic Symbol in Nelly Sachs' Mystery Play *Eli*." *German Quarterly* 45, no. 3 (1972): 480–83.

Balakian, Janet N. "The Holocaust, the Depression and McCarthyism: Miller in the Sixties." In *The Cambridge Companion to Arthur Miller*, edited by Christopher Bigsby, 115–38. Cambridge: Cambridge University Press, 1997.

Barasch-Rubinstein, Emanuela. *The Devil, the Saints, and the Church: Reading Hochhuth's "The Deputy"*. New York: Peter Lang, 2004.

Barnes, Peter. *Auschwitz*. In *Plays of the Holocaust: An International Anthology*, edited by Elinor Fuchs, 105–45. New York: Theatre Communications Group, 1987.

———. "*Laughter!*" In *Collected Plays*, by Peter Barnes, 339–67. London: Heinemann, 1981.

———. "On Class, Christianity, and Questions of Comedy." *New Theatre Quarterly* 6, no. 21 (1990): 5–24.

Bauer, Yehuda. *A History of the Holocaust*. New York: Franklin Watts, 1982.

Becker, Peter von. "Die grosse Lebensreise: George Tabori, Zeuge des Jahrhunderts, im Gespräch mit Peter von Becker." *Theater Heute* 5 (1994): 14.

Begley, Varun. *Harold Pinter and the Twilight of Modernism*. Toronto: University of Toronto Press, 2005.

Bentley, Eric. "Foreword." In *The Storm Over The Deputy*, edited by Eric Bentley, 8–10. New York: Grove Press, 1964.

———., ed. *The Storm Over The Deputy*. New York: Grove Press, 1964.

Berger, Leslie. "The Long-Term Psychological Consequences of the Holocaust on the Survivors and Their Offspring." In *The Psychological Perspectives of the Holocaust and of Its Aftermath*, edited by Randolph L. Braham, 175–221. New York: Columbia University Press, 1988.

Bernhard, Thomas. "Ich Könnte auf dem Papier Jemand Umbringen." *Spiegel*, 23 June 1980, 172, 174, 176, 178–80, 182.

————. *The President and Eve of Retirement*. Translated by Gitta Honegger, 115–207. New York: Performing Arts Journal Publications, 1982.

Bernstein, Melissa Salz. "Emily Mann: Having Her Say." *American Drama* 6, no. 2 (1997): 81–99.

Berwald, Olaf. *An Introduction to the Works of Peter Weiss*. Rochester: Camden House, 2003.

Best, Otto F. *Peter Weiss*. Translated by Ursule Molinaro. New York: Frederick Ungar, 1976.

Betsko, Kathleen and Rachel Koenig, eds. *Interviews With Contemporary Women Playwrights*. New York: William Morrow, 1987.

Bettelheim, Bruno. *Surviving and Other Essays*. New York: Alfred A. Knopf, 1979.

Bienen, Leigh Buchanan. "Emily Mann." In *Speaking on Stage: Interviews With Contemporary American Playwrights*, edited by Philip C. Kolin and Colby H. Kullman, 205–15. Tuscaloosa and London: University of Alabama Press, 1996.

Biggs, Murray. "The American Jewishness of Arthur Miller." In *A Companion to Twentieth-Century American Drama*, edited by David Krasner, 209–28. Oxford: Blackwell, 2005.

Bigsby, Christopher. *Arthur Miller: A Critical Study*. Cambridge: Cambridge University Press, 2005.

————., ed. *The Cambridge Companion to Arthur Miller*. Cambridge: Cambridge University Press, 1997.

————. *Contemporary American Playwrights*. Cambridge: Cambridge University Press, 1999.

————. *Modern American Drama, 1945–2000*. Cambridge: Cambridge University Press, 2000.

————. *Remembering and Imagining the Holocaust: The Chain of Memory*. Cambridge: Cambridge University Press, 2006.

Billington, Michael. *The Life and Work of Harold Pinter*. London: Faber & Faber, 1996.

Bistritz, Janice F. "Transgenerational Pathology in Families of Holocaust Survivors." In *The Psychological Perspectives of the*

Holocaust and of Its Aftermath, edited by Randolph L. Braham, 129–44. New York: Columbia University Press, 1988.

Bleuel, Hans Peter. *Sex and Society in Nazi Germany*. Translated by J. Maxwell Brownjohn. Philadelphia and New York: J. B. Lippincott, 1973.

Bloom, Harold, ed. *Bloom's Biocritiques: Arthur Miller*. Philadelphia: Chelsea House, 2003.

Bly, Mark and Doug Wager. "Theater of the Extreme: An Interview With Peter Barnes." *Theater* 12, no. 2 (1981): 43–48.

Böhme, Erich and Hellmuth Karasek. "'Ich Könnte auf dem Papier Jemand Umbringen': Der Schriffsteller Thomas Bernhard Über Wirkung und Öffentlichkeit Seiner Texte." *Der Spiegel*, 23 June 1980, 178.

Boles, William C. "Martin Sherman." In *Twentieth-Century American Dramatists*, Second Series, edited by Christopher J. Wheatley, 230–40. Detroit: Gale Group, 2000.

Bosmajian, Hamida. "'Landschaft aus Schreien': The Shackled Leaps of Nelly Sachs." *Bucknell Review* 21, no. 1 (1973): 43–62.

———. *Metaphors of Evil: Contemporary German Literature and the Shadow of Nazism*. Iowa City: University of Iowa Press, 1979.

Bower, Kathrin M. *Ethics and Remembrance in the Poetry of Nelly Sachs and Rose Ausländer*. Rochester: Camden House, 2000.

Bradby, David. "'Entre le mythique et le quotidien': Myth in the Theatre of Michel Vinaver." In *Myth and Its Making in the French Theatre*, edited by E. Freeman, H. Mason, M. O'Regan, and S. W. Taylor, 205–14. Cambridge: Cambridge University Press, 1988.

———. *Modern French Drama, 1940–1990*. 2nd ed. Cambridge: Cambridge University Press, 1991.

———. *The Theater of Michel Vinaver*. Ann Arbor: University of Michigan Press, 1993.

———. "A Theater of the Everyday: The Plays of Michel Vinaver." *New Theatre Quarterly* 7, no. 27 (1991): 261–83.

Braham, Randolph L., ed. *The Psychological Perspectives of the Holocaust and of its Aftermath*. New York: Columbia University Press, 1988.

Brater, Enoch. *Arthur Miller: A Playwright's Life and Works*. New York and London: Thames & Hudson, 2005.

———. "Ethics and Ethnicity in the Plays of Arthur Miller." In *From Hester Street to Hollywood: The Jewish–American Stage and Screen*, edited by Sarah Blacher Cohen, 123–36. Bloomington: Indiana University Press, 1983.

Brenner, Michael. "Displaced Persons." In *The Holocaust Encyclopedia*, edited by Walter Laqueur. New Haven and London: Yale University Press, 2001.

Brenner, Rachel Feldhay. "Discourses of Mourning and Rebirth in Post-Holocaust Israeli Literature: Leah Goldberg's *Lady of the Castle* and Shulamith Harevan's 'The Witness'." *Hebrew Studies* 31 (1990): 71–85.

Breslauer, Jan and Susan Mason. "Emily Mann." *Theater* 15, no. 2 (1984): 27–32.

Bronsen, David. "The Dead Among the Living: Nelly Sachs's *Eli*." *Judaism* 16, no. 2 (1976): 120–28.

Buber, Martin. *The Legend of the Baal-Shem*. New York: Harper & Row, 1955.

Burgess, John. "Paris." *Plays and Players* 22, no. 2 (1974): 37, 39.

Burkman, Katherine H. "Harold Pinter and the Case of the Guilty Pen." In *The Pinter Review: Collected Essays, 1999 and 2000*, edited by Francis Gillen and Steven H. Gale, 11–22. Tampa: University of Tampa Press, 2000.

———. "Harold Pinter's *Ashes to Ashes*: Rebecca and Devlin as Albert Speer." In *The Pinter Review: Collected Essays, 1997 and 1998*, edited by Francis Gillen and Steven H. Gale, 86–96. Tampa: University of Tampa Press, 1999.

Burleigh, Michael and Wolfgang Wippermann. *The Racial State: Germany, 1933–1945*. Cambridge: Cambridge University Press, 1991.

Calandra, Dennis. *New German Dramatists: A Study of Peter Handke, Franz Xaver Kroetz, Rainer Werner Fassbinder, Heiner*

Müller, Thomas Brasch, Thomas Bernhard, and Botho Strauss. New York: Grove Press, 1983.

Calder, Robert R., and Silvia Mergenthal. "Hitler on the Ballachulish Beat: The Plays of C. P. Taylor." *Revista Canaria de Estudios Ingleses* 41 (November 2000): 43–54.

Carlsen, James W. "Images of the Gay Male in Contemporary Drama." In *Gayspeak: Gay Male and Lesbian Communication,* edited by James W. Cheseboro, 165–74. New York: Pilgrim Press, 1981.

Carmichael, Joel. "German Reactions to a New Play About Auschwitz." *American-German Review* 32, no. 3 (1966): 30–31.

Cave, Richard Allen. *New British Drama in Performance on the London Stage: 1970 to 1985.* New York: St. Martin's Press, 1988.

Centola, Steven R., ed. *Echoes Down the Corridor: Arthur Miller, Collected Essays, 1944–2000.* New York: Penguin Putnam, 2000.

———. "'The Will to Live': An Interview With Arthur Miller." In *Conversations With Arthur Miller,* edited by Matthew C. Roudané, 343–59. Jackson and London: University Press of Mississippi, 1987.

Cernyak-Spatz, Susan E. *German Holocaust Literature.* American University Studies 1: Germanic Languages and Literature, vol. 29. New York: Peter Lang, 1985.

Champagne, Lenora. *French Theatre Experiment Since 1968.* Ann Arbor: UMI Research Press, 1984.

Chapman, John. "*Man in Glass Booth* Not Very Transparent." In *New York Theatre Critics' Reviews,* 7 October 1968, 236.

Cismaru, Alfred. "*Ghetto*: A Recollection of Vilna." *Cimarron Review* 87 (April 1989): 29–35.

Clausen, Oliver. "Weiss/Propagandist and Weiss/Playwright." *New York Times Magazine,* 2 October 1966, 28–29, 124, 126, 128, 130–34.

Clum, John M. *Still Acting Gay: Male Homosexuality in Modern Drama.* New York: St. Martin's Press, 2000.

Clurman, Harold. "Arthur Miller's Later Plays." In *Arthur Miller: A Collection of Critical Essays,* edited by Robert W. Corrigan, 143–68. Englewood Cliffs, NJ: Prentice-Hall, 1969.

Coe, Richard N. "Armand Gatti's Carnival of Compassion: *La Deuxième Existence du camp de Tatenberg.*" *Yale French Studies* 46 (1971): 60–74.

———. "The Theatre of the Last Chance: Catastrophe-Theory in the Plays of Armand Gatti." *Australian Journal of French Studies* 20, no. 1 (1983): 71–92.

Cohen, Robert. "On March 13, in the Middle of Rehearsals for the Premiere of *Marat/Sade*, Peter Weiss Attends the Frankfurt Auschwitz Trial." In *Yale Companion to Jewish Writing and Thought in German Culture, 1096–1996*, edited by Sander L. Gilman and Jack Zipes, 722–28. New Haven and London: Yale University Press, 1997.

———. "The Political Aesthetics of Holocaust Literature." *History and Memory* 10, no. 2 (1998): 43–67.

———. *Understanding Peter Weiss.* Columbia: University of South Carolina Press, 1993.

Conklin, Robert. "Political and Personal Worlds of Play: Women at Play Perform Pinter's *Ashes to Ashes.*" In *The Pinter Review: Collected Essays, 1999 and 2000*, edited by Francis Gillen and Steven H. Gale, 131–39. Tampa: University of Tampa Press, 2000.

Cook, Kimberly K. "Self-Preservation in Arthur Miller's Holocaust Dramas." *Journal of Evolutionary Psychology* 14, nos. 1–2 (1993): 99–108.

Corrigan, Robert, ed. *Arthur Miller: A Collection of Critical Essays.* Englewood Cliffs, NJ: Prentice-Hall, 1969.

Cox, J. Robert. "Performing Memory/Speech: Aesthetic Boundaries and 'the Other' in *Ghetto* and *The Normal Heart.*" *Text and Performance Quarterly* 12, no. 4 (1992): 385–90.

Crandell, George W. "Arthur Miller's Unheard Plea for Jewish Refugees: 'Hitler's Quarry'." *ANQ: A Quarterly Journal of Short Articles, Notes, and Reviews* 13, no. 1 (2000): 33–38.

Curtis, Nick. "Barnes Stormer." *Plays and Players* 440 (July 1990): 11–13.

Danieli, Yael. "The Heterogeneity of Postwar Adaptation in Families of Holocaust Survivors." In *The Psychological Perspectives of the Holocaust and of Its Aftermath*, edited by Randolph

L. Braham, 109–27. New York: Columbia University Press, 1988.

Dawidowicz, Lucy. *The War Against the Jews, 1933–1945.* New York: Bantam, 1975.

de Jongh, Nicholas. *Homosexuality on Stage.* London and New York: Routledge, 1992.

Delbo, Charlotte, *Auschwitz and After.* Translated by Rosette C. Lamont. New Haven and London: Yale University Press, 1995.

———. *Who Will Carry the Word?* Translated by Cynthia Haft. In *The Theatre of the Holocaust.* Vol. 1: Four plays, edited by Robert Skloot, 267–325. Madison: University of Wisconsin Press, 1982.

Demeritt, Linda C., and Margarete Lamb-Faffelberger, eds. *Postwar Austrian Theater: Text and Performance.* Riverside: Ariadne Press, 2002.

DeMetz, Peter. *After the Fires: Recent Writing in the Germanies, Austria and Switzerland.* New York and San Diego: Harcourt Brace Jovanovich, 1986.

———. *Postwar German Literature: A Critical Introduction.* New York: Pegasus, 1970.

Des Pres, Terrence. "Holocaust *Laughter?*" in *Writing and the Holocaust,* edited by Berel Lang, 216–33. New York and London: Holmes & Meier, 1988.

———. *The Survivor: An Anatomy of Life in the Death Camps.* New York: Oxford University Press, 1976.

Dinesen, Ruth. "Nelly Sachs." In *Women Writers in German-Speaking Countries: A Bio-Bibliographical Sourcebook,* edited by Elke P. Frederiksen and Elizabeth G. Ametsbichler, 407–17. Westport, CT: Greenwood Press, 1998.

———. "The Search for Identity: Nelly Sachs's Jewishness." In *Jewish Writers, German Literature: The Uneasy Examples of Nelly Sachs and Walter Benjamin,* edited by Timothy Bahti and Marilyn Sibley Fries, 23–42. Ann Arbor: University of Michigan Press, 1995.

Dittmar, Jens. "Documentary Drama." *Times Literary Supplement,* 10 February 1966, 103.

————., ed. *Thomas Bernhard Werkgeschichte*. Frankfurt: Suhrkamp Verlag, 1981.

Dodds, Dinah. "The Process of Renewal in Nelly Sachs' *Eli*." *German Quarterly* 49, no. 1 (1976): 50–58.

Doneson, Judith E. "The American History of Anne Frank's Diary." In *Anne Frank: Reflections on Her Life and Legacy*, edited by Hyman Aaron Enzer and Sandra Solotaroff-Enzer, 123–38. Urbana: University of Illinois Press, 2000.

Dowden, Stephen D. *Understanding Thomas Bernhard*. Columbia: University of South Carolina Press, 1991.

Dukore, Bernard F. *Barnestorm: The Plays of Peter Barnes*. New York and London: Garland, 1995.

————. "Newer Peter Barnes, With Links to the Past." *Essays in Theatre* 5, no. 1 (1986): 47–59.

————. "People Like You and Me: The Auschwitz Plays of Peter Barnes and C. P. Taylor." *Essays in Theatre* 3, no. 2 (1985): 108–24.

————. "Peter Barnes." In *Essays on Contemporary British Drama*, edited by Hedwig Bock and Albert Wertheim, 97–115. Munich: Max Hueber Verlag, 1981.

————. "Peter Barnes and the Problem of Goodness." In *Around the Absurd: Essays on Modern and Postmodern Drama*, edited by Enoch Brater and Ruby Cohn, 155–74. Ann Arbor: University of Michigan Press, 1990.

Ehrlich, Hedy. "*The Investigation*." *Jewish Frontier* 30, no. 2 (1966): 20–26

Eisner, Nicholas. "*Theatertheater/Theaterspiele*: The Plays of Thomas Bernhard." *Modern Drama* 30, no. 1 (1987): 104–14.

Eitinger, Leo Shua. "Survivors, Psychology of." In *Encyclopedia of the Holocaust*. Vol. 4, edited by Israel Gutman, 1426–31. New York: Macmillan, 1990.

Ellis, Roger. *Peter Weiss in Exile: A Critical Study of His Work*. Ann Arbor: UMI Research Press, 1987.

Elstob, Kevin. *The Plays of Michel Vinaver: Political Theatre in France*. American University Studies 2: Romance Languages and Literature, vol. 178. New York: Peter Lang, 1992.

Enzer, Hyman Aaron and Sandra Solotaroff-Enzer, eds. *Anne Frank: Reflections on Her Life and Legacy.* Urbana: University of Illinois Press, 2000.

Esslin, Martin. "Beckett and Bernhard: A Comparison." *Modern Austrian Literature* 18, no. 2 (1985): 67–78.

———. "A Drama of Disease and Derision: The Plays of Thomas Bernhard." *Modern Drama* 23, no. 4 (1981): 367–84.

Evans, Richard I. *Psychology and Arthur Miller.* New York: E. P. Dutton, 1969.

Ezrahi, Sidra DeKoven. *By Words Alone: The Holocaust in Literature.* Chicago and London: University of Chicago Press, 1980.

———. "The Holocaust Writer and the Lamentation Tradition: Responses to Catastrophe in Jewish Literature." In *Confronting the Holocaust: The Impact of Elie Wiesel,* edited by Alvin H. Rosenfeld and Irving Greenberg, 133–49. Bloomington and London: Indiana University Press, 1978.

Federico, Joseph A. "Millenarianism, Legitimation, and the National Socialist Universe in Thomas Bernhard's *Vor dem Ruhestand.*" *Germanic Review* 59, no. 4 (1984): 142–48.

Feinberg, Anat. "Anat Feinberg Interviews: Aharon Megged." *Modern Hebrew Literature,* Fall–Winter 1988, 47–49.

———. "The Appeal of the Executive: Adolf Eichmann on the Stage." *Monatshefte* 78, no. 2 (1986): 203–14.

———. *Embodied Memory: The Theatre of George Tabori.* Iowa City: University of Iowa Press, 1999.

———. "Erwin Sylvanus and the Theatre of the Holocaust." *Amsterdamer Beiträge zur Neueren Germanistik* 16 (1983): 163–75.

Feldman, Robert Lee. "Arthur Miller on the Theme of Evil: An Interview." *Resources for American Literary Study* 17, no. 1 (1990): 87–93.

———. "Arthur Miller's Neglected Article on the Nazi War Criminals' Trials: A Vision of Evil." *Resources for American Literary Study* 15, no. 2 (1985): 187–96.

Feldman, Yael S. "'Identification-With-the-Aggressor' or the 'Victim Complex'? Holocaust and Ideology in Israeli Theater:

Ghetto by Joshua Sobol." *Modern Judaism* 9, no. 2 (1989): 165–78.

———. "Zionism: Neurosis or Cure? The 'Historical' Drama of Yehoshua Sobol." *Prooftexts: A Journal of Jewish Literary History* 7, no. 2 (1987): 145–62.

Fine, Ellen S. "The Absent Memory: The Act of Writing in Post-Holocaust French Literature." In *Writing and the Holocaust*, edited by Berel Lang, 41–57. New York and London: Holmes & Meier, 1988.

Fisher, James. *The Theater of Tony Kushner: Living Past Hope.* New York and London: Routledge, 2001.

———., ed. *Tony Kushner: New Essays on the Art and Politics of the Plays.* Jefferson, NC: McFarland & Company, 2006.

Flannery, Peter. *Singer.* London: Nick Hern, 1992.

Fogelman, Eva. "Therapeutic Alternatives for Holocaust Survivors and Second Generation." In *The Psychological Perspectives of the Holocaust and of Its Aftermath*, edited by Randolph L. Braham, 79–108. New York: Columbia University Press, 1988.

Forsyth, Alison. "Beyond Representation: The Drama of Traumatic Realism in Arthur Miller's *Broken Glass*." *Hungarian Journal of English and American Studies* 11, no. 2 (2005): 89–107.

Fox, Michael David. "Anus Mundi: Jews, the Holocaust, and Excremental Assault in Michel Vinaver's *Overboard (Par-dessus bord)*." *Modern Drama* 45, no. 1 (2002): 35–60.

Franciosi, Robert. "Bringing *The Wall* to Broadway." *Journal of American Drama and Theatre* 16, no. 2 (2004): 88–97.

Frank, Anne. *The Diary of a Young Girl: The Definitive Edition.* Translated by Susan Massotty. New York: Doubleday, 1995.

Freed, Donald. *The White Crow: Eichmann in Jerusalem.* Imperial Beach, CA: VRI Theatre Library, 1985.

Friesner, Susan. "The Plays of C. P. Taylor." *Contemporary Review* 255, no. 1487 (1989): 309–11.

————. "Travails of a Naked Typist: The Plays of C. P. Taylor." *New Theatre Quarterly* 9, no. 33 (1993): 44–58.

Fuchs, Elinor, ed. *Plays of the Holocaust: An International Anthology.* New York: Theatre Communications Group, 1987.

Fulbrook, Mary. *German National Identity After the Holocaust.* Cambridge: Polity Press, 1999.

Garber, Zev and Bruce Zuckerman. "Why Do We Call the Holocaust 'The Holocaust?' An Inquiry Into the Psychology of Labels." *Modern Judaism* 9, no. 3 (1989): 197–211.

Garloff, Hatja. *Words From Abroad: Trauma and Displacement in Postwar German Jewish Writers.* Detroit: Wayne State University Press, 2005.

Gartland, Patricia A. "Three Holocaust Writers: Speaking the Unspeakable." *Critique: Studies in Modern Fiction* 25, no. 1 (1983): 45–56.

Gatti, Armand. *Armand Gatti: Three Plays.* Edited and translated by Joseph Long. Sheffield, UK: Sheffield Academic Press, 2000.

————. "Seventeen Ideograms and the Search for the Wandering Word." Translated by Wesley Hutchinson. *New Theatre Quarterly* 10, no. 38 (1994): 107–16.

Geddes, Jennifer L. "Banal Evil and Useless Knowledge: Hannah Arendt and Charlotte Delbo on Evil After the Holocaust." *Hypatia: A Journal of Feminist Philosophy* 18, no. 1 (2003): 104–15.

Gelb, Barbara. "Question: 'Am I My Brother's Keeper?'" *New York Times,* 29 November 1964, sec. 2, 1, 3.

Gill, Brendan. "The Theatre: Make-Believe." *New Yorker,* 5 October 1968, 95–98.

Gillen, Francis. "History as a Single Act: Pinter's *Ashes to Ashes.*" *Cycnos* 14, no. 1 (1997): 91–97.

Glenn, Lane A. "Harwood, Ronald." In *Contemporary Authors, New Revision Series.* Vol. 2, edited by Jeff Chapman and John D. Jorgenson, 216–20. Detroit: Gale, 1997.

Goertz, Karein K. "Body, Trauma, and the Rituals of Memory: Charlotte Delbo and Ruth Klüger." In *Shaping Losses: Cultural Memory and the Holocaust,* edited by Julia Epstein and Lori Hope Lefkovitz, 161–85. Urbana and Chicago: University of Illinois Press, 2001.

Goldberg, Leah. *Lady of the Castle*. Translated by T. Carmi. In *Israeli Holocaust Drama*, edited by Michael Taub, 21–78. Syracuse: Syracuse University Press, 1996.

Goldfarb, Alvin. "Inadequate Memories: The Survivor in Plays by Mann, Kesselman, Lebow and Baitz." In *Staging the Holocaust: The Shoah in Drama and Performance*, edited by Claude Schumacher, 111–29. Cambridge: Cambridge University Press, 1998.

———. "Select Bibliography of Holocaust Plays, 1933–1997." In *Staging the Holocaust: The Shoah in Drama and Performance*, edited by Claude Schumacher, 298–334. Cambridge: Cambridge University Press, 1998.

Goldhagen, Daniel Jonah. *Hitler's Willing Executioners: Ordinary Germans and the Holocaust*. New York: Alfred A. Knopf, 1996.

Gong, Alfred. "Rolf Hochhuth's *The Deputy*." *American-Germanic Review* 30, no. 3 (1964): 38–40.

Goodrich, Frances and Albert Hackett. *The Diary of Anne Frank*. New York: Random House, 1956.

Gordon, Lois, ed. *Pinter at 70: A Casebook*. New York and London: Routledge, 2001.

Görner, Rüdiger. "The Excitement of Boredom–Thomas Bernhard." In *A Radical Stage: Theatre in Germany in the 1970s and 1980s*, edited by W. G. Sebald, 161–73. Oxford and New York: Berg, 1988.

Gottfried, Martin. *Arthur Miller: His Life and Work*. Cambridge: Da Capo Press, 2003.

———. "*The Man in the Glass Booth*." In *New York Theatre Critics' Reviews*, 7 October 1968, 236.

Graver, Lawrence. *An Obsession With Anne Frank*. Berkeley: University of California Press, 1995.

Gray, Paul. "Living World: An Interview With Peter Weiss." *Tulane Drama Review* 11, no. 1 (1966): 106–14.

Greene, Alexis, ed. *Women Who Write Plays: Interviews With American Dramatists*. Hanover, NH: Smith & Kraus, 2001.

―――. *Women Writing Plays: Three Decades of the Susan Smith Blackburn Prize.* Austin: University of Texas Press, 2006.

Griffin, Alice. *Understanding Arthur Miller.* Columbia: University of South Carolina Press, 1996.

Grimes, Charles. *Harold Pinter's Politics: A Silence Beyond Echo.* Madison, NJ: Fairleigh Dickinson University Press, 2005.

Gruber, William E. *Missing Persons: Character and Characterization in Modern Drama.* Athens and London: University of Georgia Press, 1994.

Grumberg, Jean-Claude. *The Free Zone and The Workroom.* Translated by Catherine Temerson. New York: Ubu Repertory Theater Publications, 1993.

Gutman, Israel. "Warsaw." In *Encyclopedia of the Holocaust.* Vol. 4, edited by Israel Gutman, 1598–1625. New York: Macmillan, 1990.

―――. "Wittenberg, Yitzhak." In *Encyclopedia of the Holocaust.* Vol. 4, edited by Israel Gutman, 1657–1658. New York: Macmillan, 1990.

Gutman, Israel., ed. *Encyclopedia of the Holocaust.* 4 vols. New York: Macmillan, 1990.

Hadomi, Leah. "The Historical and Mythical in Tabori's Plays." *Forum Modernes Theater* 9, no. 1 (1993): 3–6.

Halio, Jay L. "Arthur Miller's Broken Jews." In *American Literary Dimensions: Poems and Essays in Honor of Melvin J. Friedman,* edited by Ben Siegel and Jay L. Halio, 128–35. Newark: University of Delaware Press, 1999.

Hall, Ann C. "'You're Speaking to Someone and You Suddenly Become Another Person': Storytelling in Pinter's *Moonlight* and *Ashes to Ashes.*" In *Pinter at 70: A Casebook,* edited by Lois Gordon, 263–78. New York and London: Routledge, 2001.

Hamaoui, Lee Fridman. "Art and Testimony: The Representation of Historical Horror in Literary Works by Piotr Rawicz and Charlotte Delbo." *Cardozo Studies in Law and Literature* 3, no. 2 (1991): 243–59.

Hammermeister, Kai. "Inventing History: Toward a Gay Male Holocaust Literature." *German Quarterly* 70, no. 1 (1997): 18–26.

Handelsaltz, Michael. "The Levin-Sobol Syndrome: Two Faces of Modern Israeli Drama." *Modern Hebrew Literature* 1 (Fall/Winter 1998): 21–24.

Harford, Margaret. "*Hannah Senesh,* Drama of Wartime Heroine." *Los Angeles Times,* 8 May 1964, sec. 4, 12.

Hartman, Geoffrey H., ed. *Holocaust Remembrance: The Shapes of Memory.* Oxford: Blackwell, 1994.

———. "Introduction: Darkness Visible." In *Holocaust Remembrance: The Shapes of Memory,* edited by Geoffrey H. Hartman, 1–22. Oxford: Blackwell, 1994.

———. "Memory.com: Tele-Suffering and Testimony in the Dot Com Era." *Raritan* 19, no. 3 (2000): 1–18.

Hass, Aaron. *The Aftermath: Living With the Holocaust.* Cambridge: Cambridge University Press, 1995.

Heer, Friedrich. "The Need for Confession." In *The Deputy Reader: Studies in Moral Responsibility,* edited by Dolores Barracano Schmidt and Earl Robert Schmidt, 188–93. Glenview, Il: Scott, Foresman, 1965.

Hersey, John. *The Wall.* New York: Alfred A. Knopf, 1950.

Hersh, Amy. "A Survivor's Voice." *American Theatre* 5, no. 8 (1988): 8–9.

Hicks, Sander. "Martin Sherman." *Bomb* 62 (Winter 1998): 74–80.

Hilberg, Raul. *The Destruction of the European Jews.* Rev. ed. 3 vols. New York: Holmes & Meier, 1985.

Hiley, Jim. "Liberating Laughter." *Plays and Players* 25, no. 5 (1978): 14–17.

Hill, Leonidas E. "History and Rolf Hochhuth's *The Deputy.*" *Mosaic* 1, no. 1 (1967): 118–31.

Hilton, Ian. *Peter Weiss: A Search for Affinities.* Modern German Authors: Texts and Contexts, vol. 3. London: Oswald Wolff, 1970.

Hirsch, Herbert. "Reflections on 'Ethics,' 'Morality,' and 'Responsibility' After the Holocaust." In *Remembering for the Future: The Holocaust in the Age of Genocide.* Vol. 2, *Ethics and*

Religion, edited by Margot Levy, 123–32. Basingstoke and New York: Palgrave, 2001.

Hoagland, Molly Magid. "Anne Frank, On and Off Broadway." *Commentary* 105, no. 3 (1998): 58–63.

Hochhuth, Rolf. *The Deputy*. Translated by Richard and Clara Winston. New York: Grove Press, 1964.

———. "The Playwright Answers." In *The Storm Over The Deputy*, edited by Eric Bentley, 76–80. New York: Grove Press, 1964.

Hoffmeister, Donna L. "Post-Modern Theater: A Contradiction in Terms? Handke, Strauss, Bernhard and the Contemporary Scene." *Monatshefte* 79, no. 4 (1987): 424–38.

Holub, Robert. "The Premiere of Peter Weiss's *The Investigation: Oratorio in Eleven Songs*, a Drama Written from the Documentation of the Frankfurt Auschwitz Trial, Is Staged." In *Yale Companion to Jewish Writing and Thought in German Culture, 1096–1996*, edited by Sander L. Gilman and Jack Zipes, 729–35. New Haven and London: Yale University Press, 1997.

Honegger, Gitta. "Acoustic Masks: Strategies of Language in the Theater of Canetti, Bernhard, and Handke." *Modern Austrian Literature* 18, no. 2 (1985): 57–66.

———. "The Stranger Inside the Word: From Thomas Bernhard's Plays to the Anatomical Theater of Elfriede Jelinek." In *A Companion to the Works of Thomas Bernhard*, edited by Matthias Konzett, 137–48. Rochester: Camden House, 2002.

———. "The Theatre of Thomas Bernhard." In *The President and Eve of Retirement*, by Thomas Bernhard. Translated by Gitta Honegger, 9–16. New York: Performing Arts Journal Publications, 1982.

———. *Thomas Bernhard: The Making of an Austrian*. New Haven and London: Yale University Press, 2001.

———. "Wittgenstein's Children: The Writings of Thomas Bernhard." *Theater* 15, no. 1 (1983): 58–62.

Howe, Irving. "Writing and the Holocaust." *New Republic,* 27 October 1986, 27–36, 38–39.

Hsieh, Yvonne Y. "Un 'Théâtre total': *Par-dessus bord* de Michel Vinaver." *French Review* 75, no. 3 (2002): 489–99.

Huftel, Sheila. *Arthur Miller: The Burning Glass.* New York: Citadel Press, 1965.

Hughes, Catharine. *Plays, Politics, and Polemics.* New York: Drama Book Specialists, 1973.

Innes, Christopher. *Holy Theatre: Ritual and the Avant Garde.* Cambridge: Cambridge University Press, 1981.

———. *Modern British Drama, 1890–1990.* Cambridge: Cambridge University Press, 1992.

———. *Modern German Drama: A Study in Form.* Cambridge: Cambridge University Press, 1979.

Inverso, Marybeth. "*Der Straf-block*: Performance and Execution in Barnes, Griffith, and Wertenbaker." *Modern Drama* 36, no. 3 (1993): 420–30.

———. *The Gothic Impulse in Contemporary Drama.* Ann Arbor: UMI Research Press, 1990.

Ireland, John. "Armand Gatti, Subject to History: The Problem of Representation." *Modern Drama* 25, no. 3 (1982): 374–86.

———. "History, Utopia and the Concentration Camp in Gatti's Early Plays." In *Staging the Holocaust: The Shoah in Drama and Performance,* edited by Claude Schumacher, 184–202. Cambridge: Cambridge University Press, 1998.

Isser, Edward R. *Stages of Annihilation: Theatrical Representations of the Holocaust.* Madison, NJ: Fairleigh Dickinson University Press, 1997.

———. "Toward a Feminist Perspective in American Holocaust Drama." *Studies in the Humanities* 17, no. 2 (1990): 139–48.

Jeutter, Ralf. "Polarity and Breathing–Aspects of Thomas Bernhard's Plays." In *Centre Stage: Contemporary Drama in Austria,* edited by Frank Finlay and Ralf Jeutter, 181–92. Amsterdam: Rodopi, 1999.

Jortner, David. "Martyrs and Victims: *The Diary of Anne Frank* and *The Island.*" *Text and Presentation: The Journal of the Comparative Drama Conference* 23 (April 2002): 45–55.

Kaes, Anton. "The American Television Series *Holocaust* Is Shown in West Germany." In *Yale Companion to Jewish Writing and Thought in German Culture, 1096–1996,* edited by Sander L. Gilman and Jack Zipes, 783–89. New Haven and London: Yale University Press, 1997.

Kagel, Martin. "George Tabori in Conversation With Martin Kagel (and Nikolaus Merck)." *Brecht Yearbook* 23 (1997): 70–75.

Kalb, Bernard. "Diary Footnotes." *New York Times,* 2 October 1955, sec. 2, 1, 3.

Karasek, Hellmuth. "*Vor dem Ruhestand.*" In *Thomas Bernhard Werkgeschicte,* edited by Jens Dittmar, Frankfurt: Suhrkamp Verlag, 1981.

Kaufmann, Walter. *Tragedy and Philosophy.* Princeton: Princeton University Press, 1968.

Kessel, Albrecht von. "The Pope and the Jews." In *The Storm Over The Deputy,* edited by Eric Bentley, 71–76. New York: Grove Press, 1964.

King, Robert L. "Psychic Numbing in Grumberg's *L'Atelier.*" *Massachusetts Review* 26, no. 4 (1985): 580–94.

Kingcaid, Renée A. "Charlotte Delbo's *Auschwitz et Après*: The Struggle for Signification." *French Forum* 9, no. 1 (1984): 98–109.

Knapp, Bettina L. "Armand Gatti: Multiplicity of Vision in Action Theatre." *Modern Drama* 12, no. 1 (1969): 57–63.

———. "Collective Creation From Paris to Jerusalem: An Interview With Liliane Atlan." *Theater* 13, no. 1 (1981–82): 43–50.

———. "Document: Armand Gatti–A Theatre of Action." *Kentucky Romance Quarterly* 14, no. 4 (1967): 405–20.

———. *French Theater Since 1968.* New York: Twayne, 1995.

———. "Introduction." In *Theatre Pieces: An Anthology,* by Liliane Atlan. Translated by Marguerite Feitlowitz, 1–17. Greenwood, Fl: Penkevill Publishing, 1985.

———. *Liliane Atlan.* Amsterdam: Rodopi, 1988.

————., ed. *Off-Stage Voices. Interviews With Modern French Dramatists.* Troy, NY: Whitston, 1975.

Knowles, Dorothy. *Armand Gatti in the Theatre: Wild Duck Against the Wind.* London: Athlone Press, 1989.

Kolin, Philip C., and LaNelle Daniel. "Emily Mann: A Classified Bibliography." *Studies in American Drama, 1945–Present* 4 (1989): 222–66.

Koonz, Claudia. *Mothers in the Fatherland: Women, the Family and Nazi Politics.* New York: St. Martin's Press, 1987.

Krakowski, Shmuel. "Lódz." In *Encyclopedia of the Holocaust.* Vol. 3, edited by Israel Gutman, 900–909. New York: Macmillan, 1990.

Kramer, Richard E. "Review of *Annulla, An Autobiography.*" *Studies in American Drama, 1945–Present* 4 (1989): 286–89.

Kremer, S. Lillian, ed. *Holocaust Literature: An Encyclopedia of Writers and Their Work.* 2 vols. New York and London: Routledge, 2003.

Kröll, Jack. "Through a Glass Darkly." *Newsweek,* 16 October 1968, 116.

Kushner, Tony. *A Bright Room Called Day.* New York: Theatre Communications Group, 1994.

————. *Plays by Tony Kushner.* New York: Broadway Play Publishing, 1992.

Lahr, John. "*Laughter!*" *Plays and Players* 25, no. 6 (1978): 26–27.

Lamont, Rosette C. "Charlotte Delbo, a Woman/Book." In *Faith of a (Woman) Writer,* edited by Alice Kessler-Harris and William McBrien, 247–52. Contributions in Women's Studies, 86. Westport, CT: Greenwood Press, 1988.

————. "Charlotte Delbo's Frozen Friezes." *L'Esprit créatur* 19, no. 2 (1979): 65–74.

————. "'Des Petits Ebranlements Capillaires ... ': The Art of Michel Vinaver." *Modern Drama* 31, no. 3 (1988): 380–94.

————. "Interviews With Alain Françon and Michel Vinaver." *Western European Stages* 11, no. 3 (1999): 49–56.

————. "Literature, the Exile's Agent of Survival: Alexander Solzhenitsyn and Charlotte Delbo." *Mosaic* 9, no. 1 (1975): 1–17.

———. "The Triple Courage of Charlotte Delbo." *Massachusetts Review* 4, no. 4 (2000–2001): 483–97.

Lampell, Millard. "Fragments From a Munich Diary." *American Judaism* 11 (Spring 1962): 12–13.

———. *The Wall*. New York: Alfred A. Knopf, 1961.

———. "*The Wall*: Its Message Is Life." *ADL Bulletin* 18 (June 1961): 4–6.

Lang, Berel. "The Concept of Genocide." *Philosophical Forum* 16, nos. 1–2 (1984–85): 1–18.

Lang, Berel., ed. *Writing and the Holocaust*. New York and London: Holmes & Meier, 1988.

Langer, Lawrence L. *The Age of Atrocity: Death in Modern Literature*. Boston: Beacon, 1978.

———. "The Americanization of the Holocaust on Stage and Screen." In *From Hester Street to Hollywood: The Jewish–American Stage and Screen*, edited by Sarah Blacher Cohen, 213–30. Bloomington: Indiana University Press, 1983.

———. *The Holocaust and the Literary Imagination*. New Haven and London: Yale University Press, 1975.

———. "Interpreting Survivor Testimony." In *Writing and the Holocaust*, edited by Berel Lang, 26–40. New York and London: Holmes & Meier, 1988.

———. "Introduction." In *Auschwitz and After*, by Charlotte Delbo. Translated by Rosette C. Lamont, ix–xviii. New Haven and London: Yale University Press, 1995.

———. "Remembering Survival." In *Holocaust Remembrance: The Shapes of Memory*, edited by Geoffrey H. Hartman, 70–148. Oxford: Blackwell, 1994.

———. *Using and Abusing the Holocaust*. Bloomington and Indianapolis: Indiana University Press, 2006.

Langworthy, Douglas. "When Choosing Good Is Not an Option: An Interview With Joshua Sobol." *Theater* 22, no. 3 (1991): 10–17.

Laor, Dan. "Theatrical Interpretation of the Shoah: Image and Counter-image." In *Staging the Holocaust: The Shoah in Drama and Performance*, edited by Claude Schumacher. Cambridge: Cambridge University Press, 1998.

Laqueur, Walter, ed. *The Holocaust Encyclopedia*. New Haven and London: Yale University Press, 2001.

Lautmann, Rüdiger. "The Pink Triangle: The Persecution of Homosexual Males in Concentration Camps in Nazi Germany." *Journal of Homosexuality* 6, no. 12 (1980/1981): 141–60.

———. *Seminar: Gesellschaft und Homosexualität*. Frankfurt: Suhrkamp, 1977.

Lebow, Barbara. *A Shayna Maidel*. New York: Dramatists Play Service, 1988.

Leiber, Robert. "On Hochhuth's Historical Sources." In *The Deputy Reader: Studies in Moral Responsibility*, edited by Dolores Barracano Schmidt and Earl Robert Schmidt, 161–64. Glenview, Il: Scott, Foresman, 1965.

Lerner, Motti. *Kastner*. Translated by Imre Goldstein. In *Israeli Holocaust Drama*, edited by Michael Taub, 186–267. Syracuse: Syracuse University Press, 1996.

Lester, Gideon. "Industrial Art: The Theater of Michel Vinaver." *Theater* 28, no. 1 (1997): 69–73.

Lev-Aladgem, Shulamith. "Ritualising the Holocaust: Creating a Universal Metaphor of Evil." *Assaph: Studies in the Theatre* 12 (1997): 149–65.

Levi, Primo. *The Drowned and the Saved*. Translated by Raymond Rosenthal. New York: Simon & Schuster, 1988.

———. "The Memory of Offense." In *Bitburg in Moral and Political Perspective*, edited by Geoffrey H. Hartman, 130–37. Bloomington: Indiana University Press, 1986.

———. *Survival in Auschwitz: The Nazi Assault on Humanity*. Translated by Stuart Woolf. New York: Macmillan, 1993.

Lewis, Theophilus. "*The Man in the Glass Booth*." *America*, 12 October 1968, 336.

Lieberman, Harold and Edith Lieberman. *Throne of Straw*. In *Theatre of the Holocaust*. Vol. 1: Four plays, edited by Robert Skloot, 113–96. Madison: University of Wisconsin Press, 1982.

Llewellyn-Jones, Margaret. "Peter Flannery." In *British and Irish Dramatists Since World War II*, edited by John Bull, 120–27. Detroit: Gale Group, 2001.

Lowenthal, Lawrence D. "Arthur Miller's *Incident at Vichy*: A Sartrean Interpretation." In *Arthur Miller: New Perspectives*, edited by Robert A. Martin, 173–87. Englewood Cliffs, NJ: Prentice-Hall, 1982.

Lyotard, Jean-François. "Ticket to a New Decor." Translated by Brian Massumi and W. G. J. Niesluchowski. *Copyright* 1 (1987): 14–16.

Malkin, Jeanette R. *Memory-Theater and Postmodern Drama*. Ann Arbor: University of Michigan Press, 1999.

———. "Pulling the Pants Off History: Politics and Postmodernism in Thomas Bernhard's *Eve of Retirement*." *Theatre Journal* 47, no. 1 (1995): 105–19.

Mandl, Bette. "'Alive Still, in You': Memory and Silence in *A Shayna Maidel*." In *Staging Difference: Cultural Pluralism in American Theatre and Drama*, edited by Marc Maufort, 259–65. New York: Peter Lang, 1995.

Mann, Emily. *Annulla, An Autobiography. Plays in Process.* Vol. 6, no. 7. New York: Theatre Communications Group, 1985.

———. *Annulla (An Autobiography)*. In *Testimonies: Four Plays*, by Emily Mann, 1–30. New York: Theatre Communications Group, 1997.

———. "In Conversation." *Theatre Topics* 10, no. 1 (2000): 1–16.

Mann, Judy. "Art Is Long, but Life, Politics Are Short." *Washington Post*, 26 September 1980, B1, B6.

Marcus, Paul and Alan Rosenberg. "A Philosophical Critique of the 'Survivor Syndrome' and Some Implications for Treatment." In *The Psychological Perspectives of the Holocaust and of Its Aftermath*, edited by Randolph L. Braham, 53–78. New York: Columbia University Press, 1988.

Margolis, Harriet. "'Nur Schauspieler': Spectacular Politics, *Mephisto*, and *Good*." In *Film and Literature: A Comparative Approach to Adaptation*, edited by Wendell Aycock and Michael Schoenecke, 81–95. Studies in Comparative Literature 19. Lubbock: Texas Tech University Press, 1988.

Mason, Jeffrey. "Arthur Miller's Staging of the Threshold of Violence." *Arthur Miller Journal* 1, no. 1 (2006): 31–48.

Martin, Robert A., ed. *Arthur Miller: New Perspectives*. Englewood Cliffs, NJ: Prentice-Hall, 1982.

"Martin Sherman." In *The Bedford Introduction to Drama*, edited by Lee A. Jacobus, 905–7. New York: St. Martin's Press, 1989.

Marx, Patricia. "Interview With Rolf Hochhuth." In *The Storm Over The Deputy*, edited by Eric Bentley, 52–65. New York: Grove Press, 1964.

McGowan, Christina S. "Emily Mann." In *Twentieth-Century American Dramatists*, Fourth Series, edited by Christopher J. Wheatley, 178–84. Farmington Hills, MI: Gale, 2003.

McLeod, Bruce. "The Oddest Phenomenon in Modern History." In *Tony Kushner in Conversation*, edited by Robert Vorlicky, 77–84. Ann Arbor: University of Michigan Press, 1998.

Megged, Matti. "Introduction." In *Lea Goldberg: Selected Poetry and Drama*, edited by Rachel Tzvia Back, 239–42. New Milford, CT: Toby Press, 2005.

Melnick, Ralph. *The Stolen Legacy of Anne Frank: Meyer Levin, Lillian Hellman and the Staging of the "Diary."* New Haven and London: Yale University Press, 1997.

Merritt, Susan Hollis. "Harold Pinter's *Ashes to Ashes*: Political/ Personal Echoes of the Holocaust." In *The Pinter Review: Collected Essays, 1999 and 2000*, edited by Francis Gillen and Steven H. Gale, 73–84. Tampa: University of Tampa Press, 2000.

Meyer, Kinereth. "'A Jew Can Have a Jewish Face': Arthur Miller, Autobiography, and the Holocaust." *Prooftexts: A Journal of Jewish Literary History* 18, no. 3 (1998): 239–58.

Miller, Arthur. "Hitler's Quarry." *ANQ: A Quarterly Journal of Short Articles, Notes, and Reviews* 13, no. 1 (2000): 36–37.

———. *Incident at Vichy*. New York: Penguin, 1985.

———. "The Nazi Trials and the German Heart." In *Echoes Down the Corridor: Arthur Miller, Collected Essays, 1944–2000*, edited by Steven R. Centola. New York: Penguin Putnam, 2000.

———. "Our Guilt for the World's Evil." *New York Times*, 3 January 1965, sec. 6, 10–11, 48.

———. *Playing for Time.* Woodstock, Il: Dramatic Publishing, 1985.

———. *Timebends: A Life.* New York: Grove Press, 1987.

Mintz, Alan. *Popular Culture and the Shaping of Holocaust Memory in America.* Seattle and London: University of Washington Press, 2001.

Montini, G. B. Cardinal. "Pius XII and the Jews." In *The Storm Over The Deputy*, edited by Eric Bentley, 66–69. New York: Grove Press, 1964.

Morson, Gary Saul. "How Did Dostoevsky Know?" *New Criterion* 17, no. 9 (1999): 21–30.

Moss, Leonard. *Arthur Miller.* Rev. ed. Boston: G. K. Hall, 1980.

"Motti Lerner." *Modern International Drama* 27, no. 1 (1993): 35–38.

Muhlen, Norbert. "The Return of Anne Frank." *ADL Bulletin*, June 1957, 1–2, 8.

Murdaugh, E. Elaine. "The Apostate Ethic: The Alternative to Faith in Hochhuth's *Der Stellvertreter*." *Seminar* 15 (1979): 275–89.

Murray, Edward. *Arthur Miller, Dramatist.* New York: Frederick Ungar, 1967.

Nakatani, Tomokazu. "A Theater in a Graveyard." *Look Japan* 41, no. 477 (1995): 30–32.

Nathan, David. "*The Jewish Chronicle Interview*." *Jewish Chronicle*, 26 March 1982, 26, 36.

Naumann, Uwe. "Ein Stück der Versöhnung: Zur Uraufführung des Mysterienspiels *Eli* von Nelly Sachs (1962)." *Exilforschung: Ein Internationales Jahrbuch* 4 (1986): 98–114.

Nelson, Benjamin. *Arthur Miller: Portrait of a Playwright.* New York: David McKay Company, 1970.

Niederland, William G. "The Clinical Aftereffects of the Holocaust in Survivors and Their Offspring." In *The Psychological Perspectives of the Holocaust and of Its Aftermath*, edited by Randolph L. Braham, 45–52. New York: Columbia University Press, 1988.

Nightingale, Benedict. "C. P. Taylor." *Stand* 23 (1982): 32–33.

Norton-Taylor, Richard. *Nuremberg: The War Crimes Trial*. London: Nick Hern, 1997.

———. "On the Trail of the Trial." *Guardian*, 1 May 1996, sec. 2, 13.

Olsen, Arthur. "An Interview With Rolf Hochhuth." *New York Times Book Review*, 1 March 1964, 31.

Österling, Anders. "Presentation Address." In *Nelly Sachs, Jean-Paul Sartre, George Bernard Shaw, Eemil Sillanpää, René Sully-Prudhomme*, 3–4. New York: Helvetica Press, 1971.

Otten, Terry. *The Temptation of Innocence in the Dramas of Arthur Miller*. Columbia and London: University of Missouri Press, 2002.

Owens, Craig N. "The *Unheimlich* Maneuver: *Ashes to Ashes* and the Structure of Repression." In *The Pinter Review: Collected Essays, 2001 and 2002*, edited by Francis Gillen and Steven H. Gale, 78–96. Tampa: University of Tampa Press, 2002.

Ozick, Cynthia. "Who Owns Anne Frank?" *New Yorker*, 6 October 1997, 76–87.

Pachero, Patrick R. "AIDS, Angels, Activism and Sex in the Nineties." In *Tony Kushner in Conversation*, edited by Robert Vorlicky, 51–61. Ann Arbor: University of Michigan Press, 1998.

Pakendorf, Gunther. "'I Have Arrived Twenty Years Too Late ... ': The Intertext of Peter Weiss' Investigation Into Auschwitz." *Acta Germanica* 23 (1995): 69–78.

Panikkar, N. Bhaskara. *Individual Morality and Social Happiness in Arthur Miller*. New Delhi: Milind Publications, 1982.

Patraka, Vivian M. "Contemporary Drama, Fascism, and the Holocaust." *Theatre Journal* 39, no. 1 (1987): 65–77.

———. "Fascist Ideology and Theatricalization." In *Critical Theory and Performance*, edited by Janelle G. Reinelt and Joseph R. Roach, 336–49. Ann Arbor: University of Michigan Press, 1992.

———. "Feminism and the Jewish Subject in the Plays of Sachs, Atlan, and Schenkar." In *Performing Feminisms: Feminist Critical Theory and Theatre*, edited by Sue-Ellen Case,

160–74. Baltimore and London: Johns Hopkins University Press, 1990.

———. *Spectacular Suffering: Theatre, Fascism, and the Holocaust.* Bloomington and Indianapolis: Indiana University Press, 1999.

Peacock, D. Keith. *Harold Pinter and the New British Theatre.* Contributions in Drama and Theatre Studies, 77. Westport, CT: Greenwood Press, 1997.

Perry, R. C. "Historical Authenticity and Dramatic Form: Hochhuth's *Der Stellvertreter* and Weiss's *Die Ermittlung.*" *Modern Language Review* 64, no. 4 (1969): 828–39.

———. "Peter Weiss." In *The Playwrights Speak*, edited by Walter Wager, 189–212. New York: Delacorte Press, 1967.

Pick-Goslar, Hannah Elisabeth. "Her Last Days." Translated by Alison Meersschaert. In *Anne Frank: Reflections on Her Life and Legacy*, edited by Hyman Aaron Enzer and Sandra Solotaroff-Enzer, 46–51. Urbana: University of Illinois Press, 2000.

Pinter, Harold. *Ashes to Ashes.* New York: Grove Press, 1996.

Plant, Richard. *The Pink Triangle: The Nazi War Against Homosexuals.* New York: Henry Holt, 1986.

Plunka, Gene A. *The Black Comedy of John Guare.* Newark: University of Delaware Press, 2002.

———. *The Rites of Passage of Jean Genet: The Art and Aesthetics of Risk Taking.* Cranbury, NJ: Fairleigh Dickinson University Press, 1992.

Pocknell, Brian. "Jean-Claude Grumberg's Holocaust Plays: Presenting the Jewish Experience." *Modern Drama* 41, no. 3 (1998): 399–410.

Polster, Joshua E. "The Revolt of Responsibility: A Symbolic Reading of Miller's *Incident at Vichy.*" *Arthur Miller Journal* 2, no. 1 (2007): 25–47.

Prinz, Jessica. "'You Brought It Upon Yourself': Subjectivity and Culpability in *Ashes to Ashes.*" In *The Pinter Review: Collected Essays, 2001 and 2002*, edited by Francis Gillen and Steven H. Gale, 97–105. Tampa: University of Tampa Press, 2002.

Rabey, David Ian. *British and Irish Political Drama in the Twentieth Century: Implicating the Audience.* New York: St. Martin's Press, 1986.

Ravitz, Martha. "To Work in the World: Anne Frank and American Literary History." *Women's Studies: An Interdisciplinary Journal* 27, no. 4 (1998): 1–30.

Rector, Frank. *The Nazi Extermination of Homosexuals.* New York: Stein and Day, 1981.

Regal, Martin S. "'You Can Only End Once': Time in *Ashes to Ashes.*" *Cycnos* 14, no. 1 (1997): 99–104.

Reinelt, Janelle. "Performing Justice for the Future of our Time." *European Studies: A Journal of European Culture, History and Politics* 17 (2001): 37–51.

Reiter, Manuela M. "Old Times Revisited: Harold Pinter's *Ashes to Ashes.*" *Arbeiten aus Anglistik und Amerikanistik* 22, no. 2 (1997): 173–94.

Richardson, Jack. "History as Drama." *Commentary*, February 1969, 22, 24–26.

Rokem, Freddie. "Jehoshua Sobel's Theatre of the Ghetto." In *Small Is Beautiful: Small Countries Theatre Conference*, edited by Claude Schumacher and Derek Fogg, 140–46. Glasgow: Theatre Studies Publications, 1991.

———. "On the Fantastic in Holocaust Performances." In *Staging the Holocaust: The Shoah in Drama and Performance*, edited by Claude Schumacher, 40–52. Cambridge: Cambridge University Press, 1998.

Rosenbloom, Maria. "Lessons of the Holocaust for Mental Health Practice." In *The Psychological Perspectives of the Holocaust and of Its Aftermath*, edited by Randolph L. Braham, 145–59. New York: Columbia University Press, 1988.

Rosenfeld, Alvin H. *A Double Dying: Reflections on Holocaust Literature.* Bloomington and London: Indiana University Press, 1980.

———. "Popularization and Memory: The Case of Anne Frank." In *Lessons and Legacies: The Meaning of the Holocaust in a Changing World*, edited by Peter Hayes, 243–78. Evanston: Northwestern University Press, 1991.

———. "Steiner's Hitler." *Salmagundi: A Quarterly of the Humanities and Social Sciences*, Spring–Summer 1981, 160–74.

Roth, Martin. "Sept-d'un-Coup." *Chicago Review* 19, no. 1 (1966): 108–111.

Rothstein, Mervyn. "When Art Becomes a Matter of Life and Death." *New York Times*, 30 April 1989, sec. 2, 1, 8.

Roubiczek, Hjördis. "*Der Stellvertreter* and Its Critics." *German Life and Letters* 17 (1963–64): 193–99.

Roudané, Matthew C., ed. *Conversations With Arthur Miller*. Jackson and London: University Press of Mississippi, 1987.

Rousset, David. *The Other Kingdom*. Translated by Ramon Guthrie. New York: Reynal & Hitchcock, 1947.

Rowland, Mark. "Frances Goodrich and Albert Hackett: Perfectionists." In *Backstory: Interviews With Screenwriters of Hollywood's Golden Age*, edited by Pat McGilligan, 196–211. Berkeley: University of California Press, 1986.

Rustin, Stanley L. "A Psychological Examination of the Survivors of the Holocaust and the Generation After." In *The Psychological Perspectives of the Holocaust and of Its Aftermath*, edited by Randolph L. Braham, 161–73. New York: Columbia University Press, 1988.

Sachs, Nelly. *Eli: A Mystery Play of the Sufferings of Israel*. Translated by Christopher Holme. In *Plays of the Holocaust: An International Anthology*, edited by Elinor Fuchs, 1–52. New York: Theatre Communications Group, 1987.

Sagan, Alex. "An Optimistic Icon: Anne Frank's Canonization in Postwar Culture." *German Politics and Society* 13, no. 3 (1995): 95–107.

Salloch, Erica. "The *Divina Commedia* as Model and Anti-Model for *The Investigation* by Peter Weiss." *Modern Drama* 14, no. 1 (1971): 1–12.

Savran, David, ed. *In Their Own Words: Contemporary American Playwrights*. New York: Theatre Communications Group, 1988.

———. "Tony Kushner." In *Speaking on Stage: Interviews With Contemporary American Playwrights*, edited by Philip C. Kolin and Colby H. Kullman, 291–313. Tuscaloosa and London: University of Alabama Press, 1996.

Schafer, Yvonne. "An Interview With Peter Barnes." *Journal of Dramatic Theory and Criticism* 2, no. 1 (1987): 87–94.

Schiff, Ellen. "American Authors and Ghetto Kings: Challenges and Perplexities." In *Holocaust Studies Annual. Vol. 1, America and the Holocaust*, edited by Sanford Pinsker and Jack Fischel, 7–34. Greenwood, Fl: Penkevill Publishing, 1984.

———. *From Stereotype to Metaphor: The Jew in Contemporary Drama*. Albany: State University of New York Press, 1982.

Schlueter, June and James K. Flanagan. *Arthur Miller*. New York: Ungar, 1987.

Schlunk, Jürgen E. "Auschwitz and Its Function in Peter Weiss' Search for Identity." *German Studies Review* 10, no. 1 (1987): 11–30.

Schmidt, Dolores Barracano and Earl Robert Schmidt, eds. *The Deputy Reader: Studies in Moral Responsibility*. Glenview, Il: Scott, Foresman, 1965.

Schnabel, Ernst. *Anne Frank: A Portrait in Courage*. Translated by Richard and Clara Winston. New York: Harcourt, Brace & World, 1958.

Schneider, Judith Morganroth. "Liliane Atlan: Jewish Difference in Postmodern French Writing." *Symposium: A Quarterly Journal in Modern Foreign Literatures* 43, no. 1 (1989): 274–83.

Scholem, Gershom G. *Major Trends in Jewish Mysticism*. Rev. ed. New York: Schocken Books, 1946.

Schumacher, Claude. "Charlotte Delbo: Theatre as a Means of Survival." In *Staging the Holocaust: The Shoah in Drama and Performance*, edited by Claude Schumacher, 216–28. Cambridge: Cambridge University Press, 1998.

———., ed. *Staging the Holocaust: The Shoah in Drama and Performance.* Cambridge: Cambridge University Press, 1998.

Schwarz, Egon. "Rolf Hochhuth's *The Representative.*" *Germanic Review* 39, no. 3 (1964): 211–30.

Scolnicov, Hanna. "*Ashes to Ashes*: Pinter's Holocaust Play." *Cycnos* 18, no. 1 (2001): 15–24.

Seeskin, Kenneth. "Coming to Terms With Failure: A Philosophical Dilemma." In *Writing and the Holocaust,* edited by Berel Lang, 110–21. New York and London: Holmes & Meier, 1988.

Ségal, Gilles. *All The Tricks but One.* Translated by Sara O'Connor. New York: Samuel French, 1993.

———. *Le Marionnettiste de Lodz; suivi de Le Temps des muets.* Paris: Actes Sud, 1992.

———. *The Puppetmaster of Lodz.* Translated by Sara O'Connor. New York: Samuel French, 1989.

Seltser, Barry Jay. "Realists, Idealists, and Political Heroes." *Soundings: An Interdisciplinary Journal* 68, no. 1 (1985): 21–41.

Shepard, Richard F. "Peter Weiss, Visiting Here, Talks About His Auschwitz Trial Play." *New York Times,* 22 April 1966, A30.

Sherman, Martin. *Bent.* New York and London: Applause Books, 1998.

Shlaes, Amity. "Thomas Bernhard and the German Literary Scene." *New Criterion* 5, no. 5 (1987): 26–32.

Shoham, Haim. "*Here and There*: The Israeli Playwright and His Jewish Shadow." *Modern Hebrew Literature* 10, nos. 1/2 (1984): 31–34.

"Should the Pope Have Remained Silent?" In *The Deputy Reader: Studies in Moral Responsibility,* edited by Dolores Barracano Schmidt and Earl Robert Schmidt, 186–88. Glenview, Il: Scott, Foresman, 1965.

Shteir, Rachel. "In Search of Sobol." *Theater* 21, no. 3 (1990): 39–42.

Silverstein, Marc. "Talking About Some Kind of Atrocity': *Ashes to Ashes* in Barcelona." In *The Pinter Review: Collected Essays, 1997 and 1998,* edited by Francis Gillen and Steven H. Gale, 74–85. Tampa: University of Tampa Press, 1999.

426

Sinclair, Clive. "Joshua Sobol: Interview." *Index on Censorship* 14, no. 1 (1985): 24–25, 54.

Sinfield, Alan. *Out on Stage: Lesbian and Gay Theatre in the Twentieth Century*. New Haven and London: Yale University Press, 1999.

Skloot, Robert. *The Darkness We Carry: The Drama of the Holocaust*. Madison: University of Wisconsin Press, 1988.

———. "Directing the Holocaust Play." *Theatre Journal* 31, no. 4 (1979): 526–40.

———. "Stage Nazis: The Politics and Aesthetics of Memory." *History and Memory* 6, no. 2 (1994): 57–87.

———. "Teaching the Holocaust Through Theatre." In *What Have We Learned? Telling the Story and Teaching the Lessons of the Holocaust*, edited by Franklin H. Littell, Alan L. Berger, and Hurbert G. Locke, 311–22. Lewiston, NY: Edwin Mellen Press, 1993.

———. "'Where Does it Hurt?': Genocide, the Theatre and the Human Body." *Theatre Research International* 23, no. 1 (1998): 51–58.

Skloot, Robert., ed. *The Theatre of the Holocaust*. Vol. 1: Four plays. Madison: University of Wisconsin Press, 1982.

———., ed. *The Theatre of the Holocaust*. Vol. 2: Six plays. Madison: University of Wisconsin Press, 1999.

Sobol, Joshua. *Adam*. Translated by Ron Jenkins. In *Israeli Holocaust Drama*, edited by Michael Taub, 268–330. Syracuse: Syracuse University Press, 1996.

———. *Ghetto*. Translated by Kathleen Komar and Jack Viertal. In *Plays of the Holocaust: An International Anthology*, edited by Elinor Fuchs, 153–224. New York: Theatre Communications Group, 1987.

———. "Interview." *Index on Censorship* 14, no. 1 (1985): 25.

———. "Postscript: A Theatre in the Wilna Ghetto." In *Plays of the Holocaust: An International Anthology*, edited by Elinor Fuchs, 228. New York: Theatre Communications Group, 1987.

427

————. "Theatricality of Political Theater." *Maske und Kothurn* 33, nos. 3–4 (1987): 107–12.

Spellman, Francis Cardinal. "A Statement by Francis Cardinal Spellman." In *The Storm Over The Deputy*, edited by Eric Bentley, 37–38. New York: Grove Press, 1964.

Stanlake, Christy. "Shaping Ambiguity: The Chemistry Between Silence, Ghosting, and Framing Devices Within a Production of Harold Pinter's *Ashes to Ashes*." In *The Pinter Review: Collected Essays, 1999 and 2000*, edited by Francis Gillen and Steven H. Gale, 141–51. Tampa: University of Tampa Press, 2000.

Steiner, George. *Bluebeard's Castle: Some Notes Towards the Redefinition of Culture*. New Haven: Yale University Press, 1975.

————. *Language and Silence: Essays on Language, Literature, and the Inhuman*. New York: Atheneum, 1967.

Sterling, Eric. "Bent Straight: The Destruction of Self in Martin Sherman's *Bent*." *Journal of European Studies* 32, no. 4 (2002): 369–88.

————. "Fear of Being 'The Other': Racial Purity and Social Responsibility in Arthur Miller's *Incident at Vichy*." *Publications of the Arkansas Philological Association* 20, no. 2 (1994): 67–75.

————. "Loss and Growth of Identity in Shimon Wincelberg's *Resort 76*." In *Literature and Ethnic Discrimination*, edited by Michael J. Meyer, 71–81. Amsterdam: Rodopi, 1997.

————. "Peter Barnes's *Auschwitz* and the Comedic Dilemma." *European Studies Journal* 17–18, nos. 1–2 (2000–2001): 197–211.

————. "The Ultimate Sacrifice: The Death of Resistance Hero Yitzhak Wittenberg and the Decline of the United Partisan Organization." In *Resisting the Holocaust*, edited by Ruby Rohrlich, 59–76. Oxford: Berg, 1998.

Stewart, Victoria. "Dramatic Justice? The Aftermath of the Holocaust in Ronald Harwood's *Taking Sides* and *The Handyman*." *Modern Drama* 43, no. 1 (2000): 1–12.

Stodder, Joseph H. *"The White Crow." Theatre Journal* 37, no. 2 (1985): 233–35.

Strenger, Elisabeth. "Nelly Sachs and the Dance of Language." In *Brücken über dem Abgrund: Auseinandersetzungen Antisemitismus und Exil,* edited by Amy Cohen and Elisabeth Strenger, 225–36. Munich: Wilhelm Fink, 1994.

Subiotto, A. V. "Dante and the Holocaust: The Cases of Primo Levi and Peter Weiss." *New Comparison* 11 (Spring 1991): 70–89.

Sylvanus, Erwin. *Dr. Korczak and the Children.* Translated by George E. Wellwarth. In *Postwar German Theatre: An Anthology of Plays,* edited by Michael Benedikt and George E. Wellwarth, 115–57. London: Macmillan, 1968.

Tabori, George. *The Cannibals.* In *The Theatre of the Holocaust.* Vol. 1: Four plays, edited by Robert Skloot, 197–265. Madison: University of Wisconsin Press, 1982.

———. "Diese Grosse Lebensreise." *Theater Heute* 5 (1994): 8–18.

Taëni, Rainer. *Rolf Hochhuth.* Translated by R. W. Last. Modern German Authors, n.s., vol. 5. London: Oswald Wolff, 1977.

Taub, Michael. "Ben-Zion Tomer." In *Holocaust Literature: An Encyclopedia of Writers and Their Work.* Vol. 2, edited by S. Lillian Kremer, 1266–68. New York and London: Routledge, 2003.

———., ed. *Israeli Holocaust Drama.* Syracuse: Syracuse University Press, 1996.

———. "Israeli Theater and the Holocaust." In *Israeli Holocaust Drama,* edited by Michael Taub, 8–18. Syracuse: Syracuse University Press, 1996.

Taylor, C. P. *Good.* London: Methuen, 1983.

Thatcher, Nicole. "Charlotte Delbo's Voice: The Conscious and Unconscious Determinants of a Woman Writer." *L'Esprit Créatur* 40, no. 2 (2000): 41–51.

———. *A Literary Analysis of Charlotte Delbo's Concentration Camp Re-Presentation.* Lewiston, NY: Edwin Mellen Press, 2000.

Tolansky, Ethel and Nicole Thatcher. "Testimony and Vision: Poetic Responses to Concentration Camp Experience." *Romance Studies* 30 (Autumn 1997): 59–72.

Tomer, Ben-Zion. *Children of the Shadows.* Translated by Hillel Halkin. In *Israeli Holocaust Drama*, edited by Michael Taub, 127–85. Syracuse: Syracuse University Press, 1996.

Trainer, James. "Hochhuth's Play *Der Stellvertreter.*" *Forum for Modern Language Studies* 1 (1965): 17–25.

Tworek, Agnieszka. "Monstre-victime: *La Deuxième existence du camp de Tatenberg.*" In *Victims and Victimization in French and Francophone Literature*, edited by Buford Norman, 35–43. Amsterdam and New York: Rodopi, 2005.

Ubersfeld, Anne. *Vinaver dramaturge.* Paris: Librairie Théâtrale, 1989.

Vinaver, Michel. *Écrits sur le théâtre.* Lausanne: Éditions de L'Aire, 1982.

———. *Overboard.* Translated by Gideon Lester. In *Plays: I*, edited by David Bradby, 1–147. London: Methuen, 1997.

———. "A Reflection on My Works." *Theater* 28, no. 1 (1997): 74–78.

———. *Les Travaux et les jours.* Paris: L'Arche, 1979.

Wager, Walter, ed. *The Playwrights Speak.* New York: Delacorte Press, 1967.

Ward, Margaret E. *Rolf Hochhuth.* Boston: G. K. Hall, 1977.

Weber, Carl. "I Always Go Back to Brecht: A Conversation With the Playwright Tony Kushner." *Brecht Yearbook* 20 (1995): 67–88.

Weintraub, Stanley, ed. *Dictionary of Literary Biography.* Vol. 13: *British Dramatists Since World War II.* Detroit: Gale Research, 1982.

Weiss, Peter. "Gespräch über Dante." In *Rapporte.* Frankfurt am Main: Suhrkamp, 1968.

———. *The Investigation.* Translated by Jon Swan and Ulu Grosbard. New York: Pocket Books, 1967.

———. "My Place." In *German Writing Today*, edited by Christopher Middleton, 20–28. Baltimore: Penguin, 1967.

———. "Notes on the Contemporary Theater." Translated by Joel Agee. In *Essays on German Theater*, edited by Margaret Herzfeld-Sander, 294–301. New York: Continuum, 1985.

———. *Notizbücher, 1960–1971.* Frankfurt am Main: Suhrkamp, 1982.

Welland, Dennis. *Miller: The Playwright*. London and New York: Methuen, 1983.

Wellwarth, George E. "Introduction." In *Postwar German Theatre: An Anthology of Plays*, edited by Michael Benedikt and George E. Wellwarth. London: Macmillan, 1968.

Wertheim, Albert. *Staging the War: American Drama After World War II*. Bloomington and Indianapolis: Indiana University Press, 2004.

Wiegenstein, Roland H. "Peter Weiss: *Die Ermittlung*, the Auschwitz Trial on Stage." *American-German Review* 32 (December 1965–January 1966): 33–35.

Wiesel, Elie. "Art and the Holocaust: Trivializing Memory." *New York Times*, 11 June 1989, sec. 2, 1, 38.

———. *Legends of Our Time*. Translated by Steven Donadio. New York: Holt, Rinehart & Winston, 1968.

———. *One Generation After*. Translated by Lily Edelman. New York: Random House, 1970.

Wieviorka, Annette. "On Testimony." Translated by Kathy Aschheim. In *Holocaust Remembrance: The Shapes of Memory*, edited by Geoffrey H. Hartman, 23–32. Oxford: Blackwell, 1994.

Wincelberg, Shimon. *Resort 76*. In *The Theatre of the Holocaust*. Vol. 1: Four plays, edited by Robert Skloot, 39–112. Madison: University of Wisconsin Press, 1982.

Winkler, Elizabeth Hale. *The Function of Song in Contemporary British Drama*. Newark: University of Delaware Press, 1990.

Winston, Clara. "The Matter of *The Deputy*." *Massachusetts Review* 5, no. 3 (1964): 423–36.

Wistrich, Robert S. *Hitler and the Holocaust*. New York: Random House, 2001.

Wixson, Christopher. "'I'm Compelled to Ask You Questions': Interrogative Comedy and Harold Pinter's *Ashes to Ashes*." In *The Pinter Review: Collected Essays, 2003 and 2004*, edited by Francis Gillen and Steven H. Gale, 7–28. Tampa: University of Tampa Press, 2004.

Woolland, Brian. *Dark Attractions: The Theatre of Peter Barnes.* London: Methuen, 2004.

———. "His Very Own Ben: Peter Barnes and Ben Jonson." In *Jonsonians: Living Traditions,* edited by Brian Woolland, 153–66. Hampshire, UK: Ashgate, 2003.

———. "Peter Barnes." In *British and Irish Dramatists Since World War II,* 2nd ser., edited by John Bull, 22–34. Detroit: Gale, 2001.

———. "'A Whole New World Still to Make': A Valedictory for Peter Barnes." *New Theatre Quarterly* 21, no. 81 (2005): 23–27.

Worthen, W. B. *Modern Drama and the Rhetoric of Theater.* Berkeley: University of California Press, 1992.

Wyschogrod, Michael. "Some Theological Reflections on the Holocaust." *Response: A Contemporary Jewish Review* 25 (Spring 1975): 65–68.

Yahil, Leni. *The Holocaust: The Fate of European Jewry, 1932–1945.* Translated by Ina Friedman and Haya Galai. New York and Oxford: Oxford University Press, 1990.

Yordon, Judy E. "More Than a Sense of the Other: An Account of the Events Surrounding a Production of Joshua Sobol's *Ghetto.*" *Text and Performance Quarterly* 12, no. 4 (1992): 372–76.

Zarhy-Levo, Yael. "The Riddling Map of Harold Pinter's *Ashes to Ashes.*" *Journal of Theatre and Drama* 4 (1998): 133–46.

Zipes, Jack D. "Documentary Drama in Germany: Mending the Circuit." *Germanic Review* 42, no. 1 (1967): 49–62.

———. "George Tabori and the Jewish Question." *Theater* 29, no. 2 (1999): 98–107.

Zohn, Harry. "The Life and Works of Nelly Sachs." In *Nelly Sachs, Jean-Paul Sartre, George Bernard Shaw, Eemil Sillanpää, René Sully-Prudhomme,* 63–68. New York: Helvetica Press, 1971.

Index